From
Edward Brooke
to
Barack Obama

University of Missouri Press   Columbia and London

From
Edward Brooke
to
Barack Obama

African American

Political Success

1966–2008

Dennis S. Nordin

Cataloging-in-Publication data available from the Library of Congress.
ISBN 978-0-8262-1977-0

∞™ This paper meets the requirements of the
American National Standard for Permanence of Paper
for Printed Library Materials, Z39.48, 1984.

Design and composition: Jennifer Cropp
Printing and binding: Thomson-Shore, Inc.
Typefaces: Minion and Myriad

Contents

Preface

African American officeholders dependent upon either white leadership or votes face a threshold of how much tolerance Caucasians would have regarding race. When minority politicians cross the imaginary line by showing too much interest in what whites will tend to interpret as pandering to African American causes and interests, a loss of white support results in most cases. In other words, a threshold for minority matters exists, and crossing it has consequences. A parameter of this in action occurred in Chicago after the election to and during the four terms in the House of Representatives of Arthur Wergs Mitchell. For him in this particular case, a nomination to run in 1934 had come from Pat Nash and Ed Kelly's Democratic Machine, and the black congressman's four consecutive election victories had resulted from pliancy by the minority candidate. In his first victory, it was overwhelming white support and just enough African American votes that resulted in the unseating of a three-term Republican incumbent and civil rights activist, Oscar DePriest. Mitchell then held onto the House seat by once again, defeating the former congressman in 1936, and by winning in 1938 and 1940 over two other black foes. Opportunities had come to Mitchell because of Chicago's Democratic bosses' anger and frustrations with the way DePriest had conducted himself in Congress. To their judgment and to the First District's white working-class electorate generally, the Republican incumbent had fussed altogether too much about racial discrimination and in the process had upset Franklin D. Roosevelt by agitating and voting against New Deal legislation. While in Congress, in contrast to the record of the black Republican, Mitchell managed for the better part of his tenure to retain favor with white voters and Windy City power brokers; he retained their support by proclaiming often and demonstrating that his only interests were service to his constituents and to the president. In fulfilling these commitments to his immediate base of constituents as the only African American in Congress, Mitchell disavowed any role as "the Negro representative" on Capitol Hill. He continued to serve with conspicuous and pliant dependence and allegiance to the Machine for his first three terms in the House; in his fourth term, however, he defiantly dared to cross the threshold of willing cooperation with demonstrated degrees of freedom and some tempered interest in civil rights. For the four-term lawmaker, a sudden movement from the course set out for him resulted in the Machine removing the incumbent from the Democratic ticket in 1942—an action that now mattered little to Mitchell because he had already laid down retirement plans and had set a personal goal of becoming an elder black statesman. William L. Dawson, a man with an established record of obedience, silence, pliancy, and unassertiveness on racial issues, replaced Mitchell on the ballot. A succession of Chicago bosses remained solidly behind Dawson for some thirty years until his death; he retained their support because of a clear understanding on his part to stand behind the threshold of defiance.

Meanwhile, in Harlem, a totally different kind of African American elected official emerged. The Reverend Adam Clayton Powell Jr. won and held firmly onto his Gotham congressional seat because of two factors. His protests and attacks against racism earned him passionate loyalty and made him a most admired public figure in an overwhelmingly black district. Unlike Chicago, New York City's decentralized municipal setup meant neither individuals nor political parties were ever strong enough to exercise control over or undermine a popular political maverick like Powell, who consistently demonstrated a strong determination to adhere to a personal agenda that included the black lawmaker's unwavering disparagement for racists and all programs with discriminatory features. And his constituents never rescinded their loyalty to him; no matter the outlandishness of Powell's behavior and actions, Harlem voters gave their beloved congressman committed support and encouragement, and they provided him with huge reelection pluralities. In complete contrast to the pair of Chicago lawmakers, the Harlem politician moved freely without fear of constituent consequences for showing unbridled outspokenness about or criticisms of American injustices.

Herein rests the focus of this study. From the 1966 election of Edward Brooke to the United States Senate by the electorate of Massachusetts, to the popularity of Colin Powell and Barack Obama many decades later, African American public figures have enjoyed either more acceptability to white majorities or less favor. For black leaders like Jesse Jackson and Al Sharpton, white voters have tended to show fear and apprehension. When wins have come to blacks in mixed-race jurisdictions, these successes have occurred because of the existence of enough "salt-and-pepper" support to ensure victories. In almost every case, successful pursuits for office had occurred because African American office seekers were careful to develop and follow a formula of downplaying racial issues to such degree as not to threaten or take exception to the status quo of privilege and endowment historically enjoyed by America's white majority. In referring to these efforts at avoidance, one school of political scientists has named the practice of skirting race "deracialization." Some of these political thinkers have even suggested that adopting a strategy of evading racial issues altogether has great potential for becoming a winning recipe for convincing enough white voters to insure electoral victories. Embedded in this study are examinations of ten randomly selected examples of black politicians who, through their obvious adoptions of what amounted to reassuring strategies for whites, successfully won enough white votes to obtain various elective offices. The focused selectees include a pair of United States senators, two minority members of the House of Representatives, five mayors, and a governor. Three of the victors were elected to office as Republican candidates, while the other seven enjoyed successful candidacies as Democrats. The introductory chapter is a breakdown of candidates who primarily directed their appeals at African American voters and a group of minority politicians who tailored color-neutral campaigns. The first chapter also emphasizes and shows the many shifts and nuances involved in politics and race.

The decision for Barack Obama's inclusion as a concluding separate chapter was obvious once it became abundantly clear that a classic example of possible success by an African American candidate for the nation's highest office was unfolding with white support and votes. If anything, with the presidency at stake, Obama's racial identity became a more integral part of discussions about his bid for office than this factor had ever been for ten predecessors' pursuits of less-important positions. Yet, the U.S. Senator from Illinois, like the others, pandered as little as possible to black voters. Obama spoke in generalized terms of a need for change with positive effects for all Americans, and was most skillfully adroit at galvanizing solidarity behind issues of mutual interest and immediate urgency to the general electorate. The concerns that he emphasized in speeches included his intentions to end a very unpopular war in Iraq; a restoration of America's sagging global prestige; a planned provision of sustainable and equitable healthcare; a removal of educational deficiencies; and clearly most importantly of all, a resuscitation of a suffering national economy with its mounting unemployment, soaring home foreclosures, declining property values, and falling stock prices. In other words, Obama as a candidate for president in 2008 ran in the tradition of liberal Democrats, and not specifically as an African American. By adhering as much as possible to this race-free strategy, he ably capitalized upon the unpopularity of President George W. Bush and other Republicans. In essence, therefore, Obama's great victory mirrored to some extent the earlier victories by ten other victorious African Americans had also won over enough white voters to gain elective offices. Thus, in what the author initially conceived as a study to determine how a group of randomly selected minority candidates had won with the help of whites, the focus surprisingly turned to the most-watched presidential election of all time in order to ascertain if it adhered to what had worked so well in the past for a mixed group of ten other African American politicians in need of appealing to those outside their race for support.

Acknowledgments

For fear of overlooking valuable contributors, the task of thanking helpful persons is always a risky undertaking because one might unintentionally forget people who have offered important assistance. Chair Steve Turner, members, and staff of the Department of Agricultural Economics at Mississippi State University have been most generous, offering office space, supplies, and Internet access. John Johnsey, the department's computer guru, has intervened on several occasions to show the way to overcoming technical problems beyond the comprehension of this author. Mitchell Memorial Library at Mississippi State University deserves mention because of its excellent online database that provided connections to numerous articles, and also because of the staff's willingness to secure rolls of microfilmed newspapers on interlibrary loans. Friend and scholar Tom Cockrell sacrificed time and energy to examine a preliminary draft of the manuscript to offer useful inputs for its improvement. Although unnamed, two "blind" readers of the manuscript during two rounds of evaluations offered a variety of thorough and critical suggestions which improved the manuscript's content and style, and also directed the author's explorations into previously uncovered and neglected areas of research. In addition to finding scholars willing to judge and advise, four people at the University of Missouri Press are deserving of special praise and gratitude. Clair Wilcox displayed candor and patience, Sara Davis coordinated a team on the author's behalf to assemble the varied pieces of a manuscript into a published book, and Jessica LeTourneur did a painstaking word-by-word combing to improve the style and to advise of deficiencies for correction. Although not an official member of the staff but a person recommended by the Press's editorial team, Pippa Letsky used her freelance editing skills to patiently help the manuscript to read better. Finally, as has been the case for five other books, wife Gun again encouraged her author husband to escape to an island of research and composition away from her to fulfill another ambition for writing another monograph.

From
Edward Brooke
to
Barack Obama

Chapter 1

Deracializing or Racializing Campaigns

From many angles and perspectives, race as a factor in American life has received considerable attention. Some assessments emphasize its persistence and others emphasize a gradual demise. In determining the role of race in elective politics, revisionists assert that a path to electoral victories opened for African American office seekers in the late 1980s when victories had become possible even where black voters were a decisively outnumbered minority. What is suggested as the winning formula is, in effect, more like sealing a pact with the devil. It might substantially increase odds for white approval, but the actual requirement for gaining white acceptance, appearance suggests, is something akin to Joe Hardy's desperate deal in *Damn Yankees*. As with the baseball player in this musical comedy, the compromising strategists recommend that the requisite for the success of any black candidate's campaign—in those cases where white votes are needed in order to win—is some "soul" bartering by the minority office seeker in order to garner white votes. The key factor in such tradeoffs is to resist all temptations to discuss or demonstrate any substantial interests in basic African American issues such as affirmative action. The "smart" African American candidate will never insist or even imply that more tax revenues should go to poor people.

Stephan and Abigail Thernstrom are among the advisors who have urged blacks to sell out on the race issue in order to garner white votes, citing several examples of how non-engagement has worked. In their book, *America in Black and White*, they showcase and admire—as evidence of how generously white electorates can be at rewarding pliancy with votes—several victories by African Americans whose campaigns and actions have generally ignored race. In contrast were the "old-school civil rights warriors [with their] little concern for white sensibilities." These were the militant, offensive Congressional Black Caucus (CBC) members,[1] the Thernstroms chide. For particular criticism, the scholarly couple single out William Clay, a Democratic congressman from Missouri and a CBC leader, for a vituperative letter he wrote to Republican Representative Gary Franks after the latter's 1996 reelection loss in Connecticut. In the letter Clay described the GOP loser as "a Negro Dr. Kevorkian [whose Capitol Hill ambition had been] to maim and kill other blacks for the gratification and entertainment of . . . ultraconservative white racists."[2]

The implication from the Thernstroms—and from other scholars who agree with them on how African American politicians can achieve political success in the white world—is that they must intuitively discover a "new black politic"; the formula, in other words, that is based on pleasing whites by ignoring race. Had the Thernstroms scrutinized the career paths and activities of Chicago Machine—supported Mitchell and Dawson, or to some extent even those of Senator Edward Brooke III of Massachusetts, they might have learned something about how these three had mastered the art of steering clear of white voter concerns and worries about electing African Americans. White support bestowed upon Mitchell, Dawson, and Brooke demonstrates how these politicians understood the thresholds of unacceptable behavior and their knowledge of the perils entailed in crossing the invisible racial line. Decades earlier, these three had just as much awareness of the dangers to their political careers as the several practitioners singled out for adulation and praise by the Thernstroms. The pioneering Chicago pair and several others who followed them into elected offices with Machine backing did not engage in offering racially charged, provocative solutions to the many unique problems faced by African Americans, nor did they tend to raise serious objections to racism.

Although the Thernstroms have probably provoked more reactions to their advice than other analysts with similar counsel, suggestions from other scholars also deserve mention. As early as 1971, Matthew Holden Jr., in an article titled "Black Politicians in the Time of the 'New' Urban Politics," counseled African American politicians to "ready themselves to explore the potentialities of a détente with the 'white ethnics.'"[3] Sensing a change of attitudes and the possibilities of white voters shedding the race issue as the final determiner of whom to elect for political offices, the Democratic National Committee in 1976 asked political scientist Charles V. Hamilton of Columbia University to find a smart course of strategic action and to report back to party leaders. The result was simple advice: direct African American candidates seeking white votes to refrain from alienating those voters—in other words, downplay race by ignoring it. As Hamilton explained, "de-racialization does not presume the absurd—that racism is no longer a critical factor in American life. . . . Instead, it is precisely because racism is still . . . a most prevalent, oppressive force in this society that Blacks—as Blacks— must be ever mindful of our collective interests, our collective resources, and our collective capacities. The burden, if we are as a group to be capacious, is to be as collectively calculating as we are frequently cacophonous."[4]

A noteworthy discussion on race and politics by a twenty-one-member panel emerged as a published manual containing instructions on how African American candidates running for office might succeed with electorates consisting of white voters to such extent that African American office seekers, to be successful, must obtain a significant percentage of the Caucasian vote. The result of a one-day symposium during 1983, held under the auspices of the Joint Center for Political Studies (JCPS), the publication featured a diversity of opinions by several contributors on the subject of how to elect African Americans with white support. Andrew J. Young, in the preface, put the proposition succinctly by suggesting a "black candidate running to win must perform a balancing act: holding and strengthening a black base while reaching out to the rest of the population for support." In order to counter race as the issue against white opponents, the general consensus was that taking the initiative on race would constitute the best strategy—doing what one panelist called advocating "incremental blackness," or the act of being first out in public with one's racial background. Republican pollster V. Lance Tarrance, a key advisor who in 1982 assisted George Deukmejian's defeat of African American Tom Bradley's bid for California's governorship, suggested that, for publicity purposes, specially arranged ethnic groups should always surround an African American candidate in need of Caucasian support to win elections. Always showing an African American office seeker among evenly split racial groups, Torrance contended, provides a subtle message that the African American running for office could succeed at "pulling the races together."[5]

More suggestions followed between 1989 and the early 1990s, after several touted landmark African American wins with varying degrees of white support. Three assessments followed, describing how these victories were achieved: Paul Sniderman and Thomas Piazza's *The Scar of Race*, Carol Swain's *Black Faces, Black Interests*, and Katherine Tate's *From Protest to Politics*. Reviewer Linda Williams discovered similarities among these three works—that is, the argument "that the politics of race has changed." Candidates' color no longer seemed to determine per se how the white vote might go. What seemed to prevail as the most important factor in the minds of many white voters now was the sharing of views. Swain even went so far as to claim African Americans could achieve meaningful representation without benefit of gerrymandered African American districts.[6]

In 1990 and 1993 respectively, William Julius Wilson in "Race—Neutral Programs and the Democratic Coalition" looked at successes by African American political aspirants, and Georgia A. Persons collected a number of essays entitled *Dilemmas of Black Politics*. They found more or less the same bases for victories: stridency was the attribute to avoid. As much as "overt racial appeals" worked well among minority-majority electorates, "insurgency . . . provoked white resistance" everywhere else. Persons added that, as much as "the black presence in American politics has traditionally been associated with the threat of system-changing action, the *new crossover politics* [author's emphasis] significantly disassociates the black presence from system challenge and instead emphasizes the 'positive symbolism' of race."[7]

Studies to ascertain under which circumstances whites have opted to elect minority candidates reveal several trends. Questioning if there is any importance in "being one of us," Jane J. Mansbridge answers with a "contingent 'yes.'" Unlike normative theorists or empirical political scientists, she appreciates the value of "descriptive" representatives who are "typical of the larger class of persons whom they represent."[8] Mansbridge's critics respond that this is an incorrect assessment, however. Citing degrees of diversity among the racial minority, they find interracial common ground based upon social position and, thus, a shared purpose permeating the middle class. When given opportunities to prove this, African American elected officials can, according to Zoltan L. Hajnal, put to rest white fears of losing influence. However, situations where blacks have obtained power because of a plurality work against goodwill and assurance. Hajnal summarizes, "A higher percentage of blacks in the city means greater antiblack affect [sic], increased racial resentment, and a greater sense of racial group conflict as well as less willingness to support school integration or special assistance to blacks."[9]

A quartet of scholars produced an article entitled "Black Candidates, White Voters," to demonstrate their understanding of racial bias. Scholars Carol K. Sigelman, Lee Sigelman, Barbara J. Walkosz, and Michael Nitz categorize African American candidates into three groupings: "the Jesse Jackson-style activist," "the Kurt Schmoke-style pragmatist," and "the Clarence Thomas-style conservative." With these classifications in mind, the authors explore African American electability in places where whites hold the balance between victories and defeats. They caution that, "even though conservative and middle-of-the-road minority candidates face formidable obstacles, their ability to project competent leadership, 'mainstream' values, and special understanding of so-called compassion issues make them viable competitors for white votes traditionally withheld from minority candidates."[10]

Ronald Walters understood there to be "a veritable conspiracy by some media analysts to create" what he quotes Congresswoman Maxine Waters' characterization of "a neutered black official that's been 'mainstreamed' not [to] be an advocate for the poor and disenfranchised."[11] Yet there have been other elements also in the equation of success. One factor is skin color. Nayda Terkildsen has studied skin color as a component in the decision-making process, and her research has led to a most interesting preliminary conclusion that "the dark-skinned black candidate was evaluated much more harshly [by white voters] than his lighter skinned peer." Party affiliation is another key variable. Given Republican positions on many social and economic questions, some whites perceive an African American GOP candidate, due to party affiliation, as being safer than an African American Democrat. Pamela Johnston Conover and Stanley Feldman conclude "party cues figured prominently in the voters' assessments of . . . candidates' positions." Although Conover and Feldman's reference was not in regards to African American candidates seeking white votes, it makes sense to infer as much about its applicability.[12]

A most decisive bifurcation of attitudes and reactions in how a white majority views the African American minority occurred during the sixty years after World War II. For roughly the first thirty years or so, according to Andrew Hacker, "white Americans found themselves embarrassed by blatant cases of discrimination." Then a shift in attitude took place—from being "willing to support measures aimed at assisting blacks" to reacting negatively to aid programs. The change, notes Hacker, has had partisan implications. "One of the two major parties—the Republicans—has all but explicitly stated that it is willing to have itself regarded as a white party, prepared to represent white Americans and defend their interests." Reconstructing district boundaries to make them more racially homogeneous has resulted in more African American elected officials in both state legislatures and Congress. In the process, Hacker and other analysts observe, a corresponding loss of minority influence has occurred. Often in order to win in mixed-race jurisdictions, candidates needed to rely somewhat on African American support, a reality that tended to liberalize representation. Department of Justice attorneys under Ronald Reagan and George H. W. Bush clearly understood the link and its consequences for fostering a conservative agenda, and this comprehension by the attorneys from the two administrations led to litigation for the creation of predominantly racial minority districts. The motive behind these efforts of the Reagan and Bush administrations to affect more predominantly black congressional districts was transparent as something more than interest in giving African Americans a greater voice in government. By gerrymandering districts in order to render a few of them essentially all-black enclaves instead of biracial ones, the Republicans realized, with the subsequent increase in the number of racially polarized districts, the office seekers running in the increased number of white jurisdictions would no longer need to appeal to the minority's special interests in order to win elections.[13]

The pro-race agenda of African American officeholders from majority-minority enclaves has tended to deepen the interracial division separating white and African American voters. Social psychologists Myron Rothbard and Oliver P. John, in their provocative article "Intergroup Relations and Stereotype Change," express pessimism about the change to more single-race districts, seeing it occurring "glacially." There is logic behind their negative conclusion; statements and demands from African Americans concerning their expectations of their elected officials have done little to ease white fears. At work is a process of interracial competition that is both easily explained and difficult to overcome. M. E. Olsen's thesis, paraphrased by Michael W. Giles and Arthur Evans in the *Journal of Conflict Resolution*, follows this reasoning: "As racial and ethnic groups develop, they seek to maximize their power, privilege, and prestige by restricting membership to a limited circle of eligible persons. . . . Hence closure among the advantaged serves to maintain the stratification order, while the solidarity promoted by less advantaged groups represents a challenge to that order." As African American Congressman Bennie Thompson of Mississippi once noted about the likelihood of an African American voter backing his GOP opponent, Hayes Dent, "A vote for Dent is like a chicken voting for Colonel Sanders. There's no way you'll vote for your [own] execution."[14]

Moderating on race can only occur when white candidates need African American votes to win, but the likelihood of either of these scenarios occurring is not great. Theoretically, the Fair Housing Act of 1968 should have desegregated residential patterns, but only rarely have substantially integrated neighborhoods resulted.[15] Separation of the races has brought stereotyping. When pollsters have asked Caucasians for an evaluation or an assessment of African Americans, attitudinal surveys reveal much negativity concerning the minority. A 1991 polling of 1,841 whites showed to what extent they were blaming racial minority members for poverty and other social problems such as high rates of illegitimate births. Some 33–50 percent of respondents evaluated African Americans as "lazy" and "violent," while 59.7 percent considered the minority to be lacking in self-discipline.[16]

These stereotyped perceptions of African Americans by whites entail many political consequences. In Mark Peffley and Jon Hurwitz's interpretation, the marketing of Clarence Thomas to socially conservative whites involved portraying George H.W. Bush's African American Supreme Court nominee as a man who had worked hard to raise himself by his own bootstraps. A self-serving autobiography entitled *Confronting the Future* testifies to alleged achievements—Thomas the author interpreting them as resulting from his Thomas's personal preferences for individual initiative and hard work rather than from liberal government spending—in contrast to the formula pushed by CBC members and their liberal Democratic allies as the way to facilitate minority gains. Offering these testimonials of success as the result of personal diligence and determination, the Republicans ably satisfied whites who were unwilling to pay more taxes in order to support programs that were beneficial to African Americans. The keys to understanding why so few African Americans have won at-large elections are the stereotyped images and perceptions of what African Americans expect and demand from the government. Scholar Linda Williams puts it succinctly when she observes that "the number of blacks holding office occurs disproportionately in areas having a black majority." All evidence, she concludes, points to the fact that negative stereotypes and white-bloc voting continue to handicap minority political candidates, but an occasional success can occur if these candidates adopt and emphasize what she calls a "PIES" strategy of "pragmatism, independence, experience, and skills."[17]

Other factors have also contributed to the failures of African American candidates to win white approval and votes. Prior even to their attempts at gaining elective offices, white and African American candidates possess major differences in their backgrounds. In many cases, prior to seeking public careers, African Americans were involved in civil rights activities, in religious vocations, or both, whereas their white counterparts' occupational beginnings were in government service. Operational bases have also differed. African Americans have generally emerged from poor, urban districts, while whites have tended to have either rural or middle-class suburban origins. Global causes and interests have also divided candidates from the two races. During the last quarter of the twentieth century, African Americans made repeated calls for increasing American assistance to African and Caribbean nations, for giving refugee status and sanctuary to the Haitian boat people, and for tightening sanctions against South Africa's apartheid regime. Non-whites have also experienced difficulties with fundraising. Their base constituencies, so often much poorer than those of white candidates, typically have less money with which to bolster favorite candidates. As two investigators discovered in Charlotte, North Carolina, and across Mecklenburg County, "race helps to align contributor and candidate." Although a limited review of only one locale and possibly unrepresentative of others elsewhere, the study, "Race and Campaign Finance in Charlotte, N.C.," concludes that there is an apparent problem for blacks candidates to raise funds for campaigns—especially for the minority candidates who are vying against white opponents for political offices.[18]

At times, to ensure victories by whites over African Americans, officials of election boards have altered boundaries to ensure adjustments favorable to Caucasians. Another popular means of helping whites to remain in control involved establishing a metropolitan government. In most cases, this has worked well when the population of an outlying area is overwhelmingly white and outnumbered city residents are predominately African American. Another trick was to eliminate districts, so that elections then turn into contests that transcend an entire county or state. The result makes white-bloc voting most effective at eliminating minority office holding.[19]

White politicians who are dependent upon African American support in order to hold onto public offices have demonstrated various degrees of subterfuge. President Bill Clinton, for example, owed a close victory over an incumbent in 1992 to his gaining an overwhelming majority of the minority vote. His payback was appointing more African Americans to federal posts than any previous chief executive. Yet this "political visibility at the national level," as Hanes Walton Jr. put it, provided little towards meeting minority needs in "unemployment and jobs training, housing, civil rights enforcement, political empowerment, health care, urban renewal, education, legal rights, and economic progress." Walton calls these appointments "a substitute for social justice." Even more damaging to Clinton's position, in one critic's opinion, was how Clinton quickly abandoned African American appointees Lani Guinier and Henry Foster after conservative Republicans began protesting against the nominees' civil rights activism and liberal positions.[20]

The president's withdrawals of the Guinier and Foster nominations show the limited tolerance displayed by whites for African American demands and the ongoing consequences of majority uneasiness. All of this underscores many basic realities about African American officeholders' effectiveness and demonstrates how holding elective office tends to separate elected officials from the demands for increased action and protests that are presented by leaders of African American nationalism. A major counterpoint to the value of African Americans' winning elections is their demonstrated inability to influence structure and policy.

Various forces have worked towards mitigating inputs that might have been helpful in ending the equality gaps within American society. The modern-day Republican Southern Strategy surfaced in Richard Nixon's 1968 presidential campaign, coinciding with an end to the civil rights era. Designers of this GOP-developed policy sought to gain the allegiance of frustrated southern white Democrats, but in the end the policy had equally strong effects in the North among disenchanted whites who felt themselves threatened by African American power. But, beginning with Jimmy Carter's presidency and ending with Clinton's two terms in the White House, two Democratic administrations and party strategists have also subtly shown considerable similarities to their Republican counterparts. Leaders of both political parties by and large ignored the agenda and concerns of the Congressional Black Caucus. As both candidate and president, Clinton made conscious efforts to separate himself from Jesse Jackson's demands and overtly rejected the activist's campaign support.[21]

African Americans faced not only the dilemma of having nowhere to turn for support but also the subsequent disarray among efforts by minority officials and activists to unify and stand behind programs and people. Robert C. Smith aptly captured the problem in the title of his book, *We Have No Leaders: African Americans in the Post-Civil Rights Era.* The origins of this unraveling of unity, Smith believes, were in an ineffective boycott—undertaken by Martin Luther King Jr., Whitney Young, Roy Wilkins, and Bayard Rustin—and in a poorly attended and publicized conference promoted and hosted by Adam C. Powell Jr., held in 1967 in Newark. In both instances, evidence of the spirit demonstrated earlier during the Civil Rights era was missing, and the collapse of leadership was showing. As a result, the boycott never materialized, and the meetings in Newark produced no tangible effects.

The Congressional Black Caucus was founded in 1969 and gained early solidarity in March 1971 with its Sixty Recommendations to President Richard M. Nixon, but a degree of disintegration of unity came with the CBC's mixed reactions to the bid by caucus member Shirley Chisholm in 1972 to become the Democratic presidential nominee. Convinced that the New York congresswoman's effort represented a futile distraction that would only jeopardize the possibilities of a Nixon reelection defeat by other Democratic Party presidential candidates with more favorable credentials than Chisholm, several African American lawmakers were critical of her declaration to run. The divided response among African American congressional leaders to Chisholm's insistence on seeking the nomination was only one driving wedge in solidarity. Irritation spread as well from a rift involving African American elected officials such as Georgia state legislator Julian Bond—who gained national attention as a young, defiant critic of segregation as the first black elected to his state's general assembly—and outspoken minority radicals such as Newark resident Amiri Baraka whose nationalistic poetry was critical of compromise with the white establishment. Militants like Bond and Baraka looked unfavorably upon many African American officeholders, suggesting that they were too ready to compromise and capitulate. These officials, in response, offered a standard defense for why they had acted so deliberately and reconcilably. In their justifications, they claimed incremental steps were better than no progress. African American elected politicians also liked to claim that less forceful responses had resulted from the difference between having and not having more inclusive constituencies. As victors in most every instance from minority-majority districts, black officeholders asserted that their abilities for effective alliances with white lawmakers from majority-majority jurisdictions were not easily made because few white legislators wanted to face their constituents with records showing a pro-black agenda.

Polls of African American opinion of nationalistic ideology, taken in 1984 and 1993–94, tended to support Bond and Baraka on most issues. As much as the minority respondents were generally negative and pessimistic about their chances of being treated with fairness and of ever achieving full equality, they also sensed that their common experiences had forged a racial bonding. Yet to questions about whether their minority's candidates should always have African American support, results in both polls were decisively negative. As chair of the National Association for the Advancement of Colored People (NAACP), Bond explained when it would be appropriate to deprioritize race. Likening conservative African Americans to "ventriloquists' dummies," he considered party and ideology to be the paramount factors in any decision process for blacks.[22]

Election results confirm Bond's assessment. Nothing unified African Americans more than minority members who supported GOP policies and leadership. Seen as traitors Benedict Arnolds, these backers of the Reagan and Bush administrations and of Newt Gingrich's Contract with America garnered neither admiration nor respect for their roles and opinions. Color generally crossed class lines as African Americans sensed how race was affecting their identities considerably more than social position. Asked about this during a television interview on February 11, 2007 (the day after announcing his bid for the 2008 Democratic presidential nomination), pioneering African American Senator Barack Obama noted how his frustrations in trying to flag down taxis would always remind him of his racial identity.

Discussing the solidarity between the CBC and a majority of African Americans, Paul Frymer separates issues into which ones have caused breakdowns and which ones have welded African Americans together. What brings consensus within the race is a common goal for "increased [governmental] spending on domestic services such as education, welfare, health care, and employment opportunities." Yet, according to *Washington Post* reporter, National Public Radio analyst, and Fox television commentator Juan Williams, it is just such demands as these for "more special programs for minorities . . . [that have] pushed black America out of the mainstream of the national political dialogue."[23]

This goes to the core of the reason white voters have hesitated to support many African American candidates. Responsiveness to race increases in a direct relationship to the percentage of African Americans in the overall population of a particular constituency. Where there is a significant concentration of a minority population, there is a greater likelihood for the enactment of policies and programs that are favorable to that majority minority. As Guinier correctly assesses this phenomenon, race becomes "a proxy for interests."[24] In order to push their agenda at all levels of government, African Americans formed representative bodies. In addition to the CBC, other nationally organized minority caucuses include those formed for aldermen and town councilors, mayors, school board members, judges, county officeholders, and state lawmakers. Since influencing politics on behalf of African Americans has clearly been the goal of each of these minority groups, a clear message has reached the majority: African Americans have a race-centered agenda, so remain vigilant, and remain reluctant to entrust any governing level to the minority. Simply put, slating African Americans before white voters has the immediate effect of racializing political contests.[25]

Chapter 2

The DuBois-Washington Debates
in Congressional Politics since 1928

W. E. B. DuBois reacted harshly to Booker T. Washington's compromising advice to African Americans at the 1895 Cotton States and International Exposition. Accepting inequality from whites was not something DuBois was willing to accept. Decades later, a national and a congressional debate continues about which course—one of accommodation or one of direct confrontation toward America's white majority—would prove the most beneficial to African Americans. Arthur Wergs Mitchell, a passionate defender of Washington , spent much of his adulthood and certainly his two electoral contests against Oscar DePriest defending the Wizard of Tuskegee's position and tactics. Mitchell's Republican rival preferred the NAACP's more direct approach of challenging and confronting injustice. A careful check of the two men's records in Congress shows how much they disagreed about a drive for federal anti-lynching legislation and about obtaining service in the Capitol restaurant. During DePriest's congressional tenure, from 1929 to 1935, as an ex-officio insider surrogate of the civil rights organization, he favored a meaningful bill and pushed to integrate the lawmakers' eating facility. Mitchell, his Democratic rival and successor, opposed the NAACP-backed bill and quietly acquiesced to the cafeteria's whites-only policy.[1]

Angry exchanges between Mitchell and the civil rights organization continued until 1942 and the end of his four-term congressional tenure. Mitchell's successor, William Levi Dawson, began his Capitol Hill career with the same restraints as his predecessor, and during his long House tenure, he rarely spoke out against the discriminatory and racist practices defended by fellow Democrats from southern districts. For remaining generally still about societal injustices or, if he did act, for contributing largely unnoticed inputs to bills behind the closed doors of committee sessions, Chicago's South Side African American representative failed to gain recognition or a reputation as a civil rights activist. A good example of Dawson acting as the unwilling warrior came with his steadfast refusal in 1955 to endorse a bill mandating integration in schools. Then, as he had done so numerously in the past, his nonsupport disappointed and greatly frustrated civil rights forces. His "avowed support for gradual change of racial policy and his desire to prove his loyalty to the party," claims political scientist James L. Cooper, "made it difficult for him to address distinctly black problems in a meaningful way." A writer for the African American-owned *Chicago Defender* agreed. The South Side district's passive congressman was "noncommittal [and] evasive and seldom takes an outspoken stand on anything. Bill Dawson is, by all odds, ultraconservative."[2]

Dawson's demeanor sharply contrasted to that of an African American who, after the 1944 off-year elections, was preparing for a conspicuous entrance into the House of Representatives. It is no exaggeration to assert that the Reverend Adam Clayton Powell Jr. arrived in the District of Columbia from his Harlem-based district literally yelling and screaming about the unfair treatment African Americans had received both as defenders of democracy and as private citizen contributors to the nation's wartime economy. So here were two House members, Dawson and Powell, who apparently had very little in common. That both men sat on the Democratic side of the aisle was the most conspicuous thing uniting them. Unlike his contemporary from Chicago, whose quiet presence on Capitol Hill rarely annoyed or challenged his racist colleagues, Dawson's New York counterpart was a boisterous, flamboyant lawmaker who apparently thoroughly enjoyed making headlines with his sensational criticisms, outbursts, and bizarre behavior. Beyond the clear-cut differences of style and method between the two, there were many subtle reminders as to why, decades before, so many whites had rallied to Washington, and not to DuBois. For at least one generation, Powell came to symbolize why seemingly most whites were hesitant about entrusting political power to African Americans. Promoting and elevating questions and issues of race to pinnacle status became the Harlem representative's major interest, and his all-absorbing focus on minority rights would transfer opposition most directly onto other black politicians whose critics accused them of being overly fixated on civil rights.

Powell biographer Charles V. Hamilton, in a sentence, captures the true essence of his subject's intentions. In Hamilton's view, Powell had an overriding desire to get whites so irritated and so annoyed that they would squirm. Powell's "aim in race relations was *not* to be polite, but rather deliberately to raise the discomfort level as high as possible on this subject." Whites were the main recipients of the politician's venom, but they were not always alone. To the more conservative African Americans who either expressed embarrassment with or disavowed the Harlem pastor's vituperative rhetoric and uncompromising methods, Powell applied the dismissive label of "Uncle Tom." When these critics, along with New

York's white political establishment, tried to defeat him in 1958, their effort failed completely. Powell, the controversial and extroverted official, affixed all his focus on one overarching issue—"America's treatment of the downtrodden, especially black people."[3]

Eventually four other African Americans joined Dawson and Powell in Congress. None of the newcomers were as nonassertive about pushing civil rights and exposing racism as their Chicago colleague, nor were they ever as demonstrative and passionate about these matters as Harlem's number-one public servant. Bidding for Congress in 1954 with "a something-for-all platform designed to appeal to a constituency 55 percent white," Charles C. Diggs Jr. outpolled a Republican adversary two to one in a largely blue-collar Detroit district. To his supporters, he interpreted electoral success as a "victory for all the people." He continued to employ a theme of inclusiveness on Capitol Hill but reminded everyone of the importance of his victory for African Americans while at the same time cautioning that "we must none of us forget for one moment that I am here to represent all of the people of my district." By and large, as long as his Michigan district remained racially mixed, Diggs's pledge to evenhandedness continued. During his first congressional year, he traveled to Mississippi as an observer of the jury trial of two white men accused of torturing and murdering the Chicago teenager Emmett Till; after an all-white jury's verdict of not guilty, the lawmaker appealed to President Dwight D. Eisenhower's conscience to intervene in order to initiate federal charges against the pair of alleged murderers. Such race-neutral issues as federal money for school construction, support for the United Nations, and work on behalf of increasing Social Security pensions were also important to Diggs.[4]

Of the other three men who served with both Dawson and Powell, two remained more or less anonymous in Congress, doing and saying very little so long as their constituencies were racially mixed. Greater Philadelphia sent Robert N. C. Nix Sr. to Capitol Hill in 1958, and Los Angeles sent Augustus Hawkins five years later. Although roll-call ratings by Americans for Democratic Action (ADA) showed consistent votes by these two minority congressmen with the House of Representatives' liberal bloc, not much distinguished their first years in Congress until after their districts' majority was African American. On the other hand, there is no way John Conyers Jr. of Michigan could be described as having a laid-back approach. He was always working to secure power and equality for his race, and he became a key CBC organizer in 1969. In 1972 there was even some speculation about Conyers seeking the presidency. Rather than denying the rumors, the lawmaker from Detroit responded that going for the nation's highest office might just "stimulate registration, . . . encourage many Black citizens to run for delegate seats, . . . and exert maximum leverage in the decision making." If there remained a question for the energetic and outspoken legislator to answer it was "How do we maximize the power of twenty-four million Black

Americans?" One possible reason that Diggs and Nix in the beginning of their congressional careers did not espouse as much on specific African American issues as Conyers is that their representations had begun with them more or less significantly beholden to white-majority electorates.[5]

In 1969, the incoming class of African American representatives included one female and two male newcomers to Washington. That year, Powell also returned to Congress after he had been expelled from the House in 1967 by congressional colleagues, for what a majority of representatives alleged were improprieties and indiscretions unbefitting a representative on Capitol Hill. Altogether, the number of African American members in the House had now reached nine, but more important than the quantitative increase were the circumstances behind their electoral victories and the incoming president's philosophies and priorities. Brooklyn's Shirley A. Chisholm (the first African American woman elected to Congress), St. Louis native William L. Clay Sr., and Cleveland's Louis Stokes all indicated from the outset of their first terms that racial issues would absorb their interests. Helping to direct a focus in this direction was newly inaugurated President Richard M. Nixon, a Republican, and the elected beneficiary of his party's Southern Strategy. He had deliberately aimed part of his campaign at Dixie's malcontented Democrats. Here were disgruntled citizens who considered themselves ignored and abandoned by their old political party. The new chief executive wasted no time in beginning a series of attacks against predecessor Lyndon B. Johnson's Great Society mix of domestic programs. As intended, the Nixon assault plan pleased conservatives and frustrated liberals. Since elevating an impoverished African American population to higher social statuses constituted a primary goal of much of the previous administration's War on Poverty initiatives, Nixon, through a dismantling of LBJ's efforts aimed at involving and assisting downtrodden citizens, immediately incurred negative reactions from liberals.

The nine African Americans in the House of Representatives saw Nixon's intentions to undo these civil rights gains as justifying their participation in an organized push to stop the onslaught. Diggs spearheaded a movement among his African American House counterparts to galvanize efforts against the president's plans to abolish programs that were helpful to African Americans. The result, in January 1969, was the formal establishment of the Congressional Democratic Select Committee (CDSC)—a misnamed body because it only included the nine African American representatives. During its infancy, the organization represented and championed several matters seriously important and relevant to African Americans.

Beside its role as protector against presidential initiatives to sidetrack civil rights achievements and roll back progressive programs, the African American congressional forum assumed an interested and vital third-party role in the investigative hearings held to probe the Hampton-Clark murders in Chicago. (In an early morning raid orchestrated by police under the direction of the Cook

County sheriff, Richard Elrod, two Black Panthers were fatally shot.) Held in the Windy City, the investigative sessions attracted the entire nine-member African American congressional delegation; they came at the special invitation of Illinois state lawmakers Charles Chew, Richard Newhouse, and Harold Washington. The presence of nine lawmakers from Congress no doubt was a decisive factor behind a critical report, the "Investigation of Panther Slayings," that pinned blame directly upon law enforcement officials for the two activists' violent deaths.

Unity again surfaced in the African American lawmakers' vehement opposition to President Nixon's choice of judge Clement F. Haynsworth Jr. of South Carolina as Justice Abraham Fortas's replacement on the Supreme Court. Almost at once, after the president's announced appointment on August 21, 1969, criticisms of Haynsworth's rulings and statements surfaced. The CDSC could do no more than voice strong feelings opposing to Nixon's selection, but its input represented every concern expressed by the NAACP and by Senate liberals from both parties against confirming an apparent unreformed racist. On November 2, 1969, the nine African American House members could rejoice; by a vote of 55-45 the Senate rejected Nixon's embattled nominee. Celebration proved premature, however. Nixon was determined to appoint a southern white man to the bench, and on January 19, 1970, he offered the vacancy on the Court to George Harrold Carswell of Florida. A check into Carswell's judicial background showed that he was an equally objectionable choice. For CDSC members and their astute civil rights supporters, Nixon's nomination of Carswell was almost déjà vu. Once again, a nonpartisan vote of 51-45 in the Senate on April 8, 1970, resulted in the disapproval of another Nixon selection, which again gave nine African American House members reasons for jubilation for their role in the defeat.[6]

Supported by some successful efforts and worried by many concerns, Charles B. Rangel (Powell's replacement in Congress from Harlem) offered African American House colleagues a motion to bond under the Congressional Black Caucus. In February 1971, a coalition of twelve regular members of Congress and the District of Columbia's non-voting delegate, Walter Fauntroy, formally founded a structured organization. In Marguerite R. Barnett's judgment, the emergence of CBC occurred just "when the civil rights movement was in a period of decline." The result was the formation of a lobbying organization that considered itself "Congressmen at large for 20 million black people." In this role, members projected "group consciousness that translates into a definition of their constituency in terms that [would] transcend their electoral district boundaries."[7]

Two early incidents placed the coalition of minority representatives on a precedent-setting course of action. Both involved Republican Edward W. Brooke, the African American senator from Massachusetts. The first followed a deadly assault upon African American students by police on the campus of Jackson State College in Mississippi during May 1970. A delegation of CBC members with plans to conduct an on-site investigation invited Brooke to accompany them to the southern state, but he chose to travel by himself one day ahead of the House representatives in order to conduct personal investigating at the historically African American institution. During Brooke's visit to Mississippi, he met privately with John Bell Williams, the segregationist governor of Mississippi, and during their meeting the senator apparently offered no challenge to the governor's blaming the police assault entirely on the demonstrators. This alleged failure to speak up, Brooke found, caused critics to doubt his loyalty to the African American cause. As one CBC House member assessed the Republican's silence: "Brooke's skin is nearly black, but his mind isn't black." Skepticism about Brooke's loyalty resurfaced during President Nixon's 1971 State of the Union address. African American representatives boycotted the president's speech because of Nixon's earlier refusal to schedule a meeting with them for proposed discussions on policy concerns. By attending the annual presidential presentation, Brooke again acted independently, while the remaining African American members of Congress made a strong statement with their absence. Hawkins showed a degree of empathy and understanding for the senator's peculiar situation; he concluded that Brooke's "problems are somewhat different from ours. We represent ghettos. Our problems are the problems of ghettos. He represents a state . . . with a small black population." Lessons were twofold. The CBC eventually became an African American-only coalition, with membership available only to an African American legislator possessing full commitment to the race's special problems. The requirement virtually eliminated all Republican participation, and it validated what Black Power advocates earlier had demanded as a vital qualification for any person representing African Americans—something more substantial than "merely putting black faces in office."[8]

Commanding leverage and influence as the highest-ranking African American officeholder, Brooke managed to somewhat redeem his standing with CBC members. He did it by convincing Nixon to consider the political benefits of conferring with the House's African Americans. At a meeting arranged on March 25, 1971, caucus chair Diggs presented President Nixon with a comprehensive list of Sixty Recommendations. In many ways more ceremonial than constructive, the session with the president did not change any minds. Nixon did not waver in his commitment to a silent majority that allegedly found the ongoing demands of African Americans more disgusting than ever. And CBC opposition remained equally steadfast in fighting the president and his contrary agenda. Nixon's agreeing to a session provided one benefit to the CBC, however. The publicity surrounding the president's reversal of attitude, and his newfound willingness to meet with minority members, elevated their organization to greater prominence as an important liberal force on Capitol Hill and gave its agenda more media attention.[9]

With origins during Nixon's inaugural year in the White House, its constant attacks of his presidency, expressions of doubt concerning Brooke's loyalty to

African Americans, and its partisan membership, the CBC early in its history represented to Republican critics a faction of House Democrats in lockstep opposition to the GOP. Partisanship charges continued after August 9, 1974, when Gerald Ford replaced a then-disgraced ex-president. By meeting CBC chair Rangel at the Oval Office only twelve days after Nixon's departure, the unelected president signaled his intention to improve presidential relations with African American lawmakers. Ford promised to appoint more African Americans to key posts in the executive branch. Important as this gesture seemed to the White House guest, the future appointees' race was not as important as their sympathies, in Rangel's judgment. As Powell's successor, he thought what mattered most were "the needs of the poor and minorities." In Rangel's opinion, the latest presidential appointees' "ideological and philosophical commitment[s] and . . . who they are" would hold greater significance. For proposing on his third day in office to have an exploratory session with Rangel, Ford at least seemed willing to listen to CBC concerns. The New York City representative and Harlem-based lawmaker appreciated this from the president, but Rangel still had reservations: "optimism cannot be sustained unless it is fed by concrete accomplishment, and although we stand ready to work with the President if he proves his good will, we stand equally ready to oppose him if he does not." With Ford's pardon of Nixon and his strong presidential disapproval of federal-court ordered "forced busing," expressed in a news conference in October 1974, cordial relations all but ended; the initial signs of possibilities for a productive relationship between Ford and CBC members vanished seemingly beyond recovery.[10]

As the Republican president departed office on January 20, 1977, and a Democrat, Jimmy Carter, replaced him, charges from conservative critics that the CBC was primarily a partisan organization were to some degree disproved. Missouri representative William Clay Sr., describing the coalition's alleged ties to Democrats, stated, "Democrat or Republican. We will challenge anybody who seeks to undermine the basic interests of our people." Most every policy and action coming from Jimmy Carter brought careful scrutiny and, more often than not, attack from the African American body of lawmakers. Carter's appointing Patricia Harris and CBC member Andrew Young to cabinet-level positions received CBC praise, but a general consensus emerged that Carter had broken his campaign promises to the more than 90 percent of African Americans who had voted for him. To the dissatisfaction and disappointment of many CBC members, the Carter administration demonstrated neither enough interest in, nor commitment to, dealing with unemployment and a lack of jobs, to providing adequate housing, or to eliminating poverty. The CBC's more liberal legislative agenda often clashed with issues that were apparently more important to moderate, fiscally conservative Carter. Carter lacked the resolve and willingness to push as vigorously as African American lawmakers on social issues. Especially disappointing to them was Carter's tepid support of the Humphrey-Hawkins full employment bill. Authored and jointly boosted by Hubert Humphrey and August Hawkins, the bill's goal was to end unemployment by guaranteeing all Americans a job. Liberals supported the measure, and conservatives opposed it. The president's decision in August 1979 to remove Andrew Young as America's UN ambassador after disclosure of a secret meeting between Young and representatives of the Palestine Liberation Organization also caused considerable irritation and animosity with the president. A close associate of Martin Luther King Jr. in the civil rights movement and an ex-congressman from Georgia with CBC membership, Young had support for his action from the black members of Congress. The angry departure of Detroit congressman John Conyers from a White House conference with Carter and Vice President Walter Mondale illustrates how much tension and disappointment existed among minority lawmakers with the Democratic president. After failing to make headway with Carter and Mondale on matters of concern to CBC members, the Michigan lawmaker stormed out of the meeting. During the 1980 election and Carter's face off against Ronald W. Reagan, representative Cardiss Collins from Chicago's West Side found good reason for having what she called a "sense of despair" as she, like so many other CBC members, was given a choice of deciding between a "lessor [sic] of two evils."[11]

The CBC's criticisms of Carter looked mild and sporadic compared to their responses to the next administration. From the very outset, African American members of Congress were doubtful about a former film actor being in charge of the United States. The conservative Hollywood personality seldom minced his words. Reagan unequivocally intended to change the nation's values and direction in order to align them with rugged individualism, narrowly defined morality, and personal responsibility. Decoded, this agenda left few ambiguities for CBC members. The Californian launched his 1980 presidential campaign in Mississippi, with an address to a receptive white audience at the Neshoba County Fair—not far from the site where Ku Klux Klansmen had buried three slain civil rights workers in 1964. It was clear Reagan would give little support to programs aimed at alleviating poverty and promoting justice and equality. Nothing along those lines—he pledged to rousing cheers from his white audience—would ever result from a Reagan presidency. The Republican presidential candidate told listeners at the Mississippi fairgrounds of plans to "restore to states and local governments the power that properly belongs to them." On August 11, 1980, Andrew Young expressed serious misgivings about the implications of Reagan's speech in a *Washington Post* editorial titled "Chilling Words in Neshoba County." Young wrote, "code words like 'states' rights' and symbolic places like Philadelphia, Miss. leaves [sic] me cold."[12]

From Reagan's November victory until halfway through his first presidential term, he and his closest advisors demonstrated various degrees of ambivalence concerning their intended dealings with African Americans. One month after the 1980 election, longtime Reagan backer and future attorney general

Edwin Meese hosted the Fairmont Conference. Those assembled by invitation for planning sessions with the Reagan official were right-wing African Americans; behind the well-publicized unity forum was a calculated attempt to provide attendees with opportunities "to embrace and espouse conservative philosophy and programs as the solution to problems in the African American ghetto, under class, and middle class." Then, seemingly in contradiction to all prior indicators as to which people in or out of government Reagan would agree to consult, in December 1982 the president invited CBC chair George T. Leland of Texas to the Oval Office for a discussion of African famine relief. Afterward, the African American lawmaker reported feeling "really happy—for the first time proud—that President Reagan was our President. He was far more concerned than I had seen him on any issue dealing with human beings." What pleased Leland (momentarily) so much from the meeting with Reagan was the president's spontaneous decision to divert an American ship carrying a cargo of food from India to drought-stricken Ethiopia.

Leland's joy was short-lived, however. Reagan never again conferred with another CBC member—a decision that changed Leland's estimation of the president forever. Relations with the very conservative president became, he complained, "non-existent." The Texas lawmaker considered Reagan's unwillingness to meet as "being just insensitive"; a good example of the president's essentially "evil character." On more than twenty major issues and policies, Reagan and the CBC were completely polarized. Reagan's steadfast insistence on maintaining positive relations with racist South Africa, on prioritizing cuts in inflation over creating jobs, and on opposing civil rights legislation represented only a few of several sharp disagreements. In a handful of notable instances, Congress overrode presidential vetoes. The Anti-Apartheid Act of 1986 and the Civil Rights Restoration Act of 1988 are two key examples of when at least two-thirds of the House and Senate membership countered Reagan's objections. Despite an occasional victory, however, CBC members assessed the Reagan era as a time of significant setback for African Americans. Nobody in the coalition demonstrated more hostility and pessimism than Parren J. Mitchell of Maryland. In the midst of Reagan's bid for reelection in 1984, this former lawmaker found the national mood very discouraging. As he imagined America's future then, "Even if Reagan gets kicked out, what you have in this country is a whole new mindset. There is an anti-black mood and an economic problem that we must address. The question for us is who will best cushion blacks."[13]

Although omnipresent (especially within Nixon and Ford's administrations), conservative African American politicians at the federal level of government did not receive much media attention. Reagan's presidency changed this. Decades after a decisive switch by African Americans from Abraham Lincoln's Republican party to Franklin Roosevelt's Democrats in the 1930s, a minority of African Americans remained loyal to the GOP. There has always existed a less politically loyal African American Democratic bloc, which advocated less racial-bloc voting as the most productive way to effect stronger commitments to African Americans. And in fairness to many Republicans in Congress before the Reagan revolution, there were a substantial number of committed devotees to civil rights and liberal reforms permeating the GOP.

Emboldened by the philosophical changes among the higher echelon of the Republican Party leadership there emerged a contemporary hard corps of African American heirs of Booker T. Washington, the founder of Tuskegee University. These individuals became loudly outspoken critics of affirmative action, welfare, urban renewal, and any special treatment or assistance for their race. African American neoconservatives generally went along with Reagan's push to extend the 1965 Voting Rights Act for only ten years, to confer tax-exempt status to southern segregated academies, to oppose the establishment of a national holiday to honor Dr. Martin Luther King Jr., and to weaken (to the point of destroying altogether through restructuring) the Civil Rights Commission (CRC). African American commissioner Clarence Pendleton referred to African American civil rightists as "the new racists." Other black conservatives adamantly denied that Reagan's policies were unfriendly to African American interests. In their opinion, the policies were in fact neutral on racial matters. Defending the right-wing GOP president and eschewing civil rights programs, according to Hanes Walton Jr., became key ways for African American Republicans to advance within the party ranks and for them to obtain influential administration appointments as saboteurs of past benefits to African Americans.[14]

Like his GOP predecessor, George H. W. Bush utilized "social issues with veiled racial messages" to his own advantage. GOP campaign strategist Lee Atwater was brilliant at finding and exploiting these issues. During Vice President Bush's 1988 presidential campaign against governor Michael Dukakis of Massachusetts, Atwater subtly encoded race into a most effective Bush political campaign advertisement that alleged the Democratic nominee's softness on crime. A murder committed by a Dukakis-furloughed African American inmate, Willie Horton, was Atwater's evidence. As Keith Reeves clearly shows in his book title, *Voting Hopes or Fear?*, a majority of voters allowed their negative emotions to sway a tight contest in the GOP candidate's favor. Once in office, Bush scheduled regular meetings with CBC members, and instructed administration officials to follow his example. Better for publicity than for actual results, these sessions often ended in stalemates with Bush being on one side of an issue and his CBC guests taking an opposite position. On such key matters as reducing defense expenditures, increasing aid to inner cities, supporting the Civil Rights Act of 1991, and offering Haitian boat people asylum, the two sides failed to find grounds for agreement. The CBC's vehement criticism of and unflinching opposition to presidential Supreme Court nominee Clarence Thomas not only demonstrated how the coalition's judicial and political philosophy differed from Bush's; the case against Thomas also showed how race loyalty mattered less to most CBC law-makers than this appointee's record on minority rights. Most disturbing to CBC members about Thomas's record occurred while he was directing and setting policy at the Equal Employment Opportunity Commission. Thomas had shown a strong past tendency to align himself with Bush and against set-aside con-tracts and Affirmative Action, which gave good cause to fear how he might rule as a justice.[15]

After Bill Clinton's inauguration in 1993, CBC members once more showed a capacity for non-partisanship. Popular as the Democratic president was with black voters, he could not always count on unwavering support from his party's African Americans in Congress. The president's proclivity to move toward the center of the political spectrum lost him their backing; taking centrist positions brought Clinton the most trouble with many African American lawmakers and caused their greatest disenchantment with him. While bidding for the presiden-cy in 1992, Clinton had deliberately cast himself as a moderate "New Democrat," and in general he kept his campaign commitment to maintaining a middle-of-the-road agenda. CBC members in most cases, however, were left-of-center lib-erals with goals either to keep proactive programs alive or to generate support behind new ones such as universal health care for all Americans. Clinton's call for reduced federal spending on entitlement programs and on job creation gen-erated degrees of frustration among many prominent African Americans in the House; at times his positions even generated some sharply worded rebuttals. With a political crisis in Haiti deepening, and its poverty increasing, increasing numbers of boat people began arriving in Florida after journeying on danger-ous voyages across the Caribbean. As a presidential candidate in 1992, Clinton had offered his commitment to reverse the Bush administration's policy of re-turning most of these West Indians to their homeland. But, once in office as a Democratic president, Clinton followed his Republican predecessor's example on this issue. Changing course and breaking his promise of humanitarian ref-uge for all Haitians caused considerable concern—and even generated outspo-ken disapproval—from civil rights activists such as Jesse Jackson and from most CBC members.

Anger over Clinton's failure to show true compassion to people of color flee-ing dangerous, poverty-stricken Haiti was only one of several instances of emo-tional differences. When he succumbed to conservative critics' pressure over the nomination of Lani Guinier as first choice to direct the Civil Rights Division of the Department of Justice, Clinton was seen to be meekly surrendering to viru-lent reactionaries who objected to Guinier because of her outspoken opinions on democracy and voting. The president's withdrawal of her appointment preceded a Senate confirmation hearing. Shortly after capitulating on June 9, 1993, Clinton met for three hours with African American congressional leaders. The tone was "decidedly angry," not only due to his sacrificing Guinier to expediency but also because of his recommended budget, which included entitlement cuts. Speaking to reporters after the confrontational session with Clinton, CBC chair Kweisi Mfume announced that he and thirty-six other CBC members had no intention of giving the president "blind loyalty" in order that they might "be seen and not heard." Mfume issued a warning that the membership's expectation was for a "first-class partnership" with Clinton or none at all.[16]

This first-class relationship never materialized, because the president knew his harshest critics in the CBC had nowhere to go with their anger and discontentment. Congress was now controlled by Newt Gingrich, a Republican right-wing ideologue hailing from Georgia, who was intent on pushing a conservative program he called the "Contract with America." After the 1994 congressional elections, with Democrats the minority party in both the Senate and House of Representatives, political realities forced Clinton to rely upon and placate Republicans, not the African American liberals. The effects of the GOP takeover were nowhere more evident than in welfare reform. Back in the 1992 presidential campaign, Clinton had expressed his intention to "end welfare as we know it," but the plan did not become an important agenda item until after Republican chairs had gained control of all House and Senate committees in the 104th Congress. As a direct result of this conservative takeover of Capitol Hill and against a general backdrop of CBC negativity and protests, Congress enacted the Personal Responsibility and Work Opportunity Act of 1996. It did not seem to matter that in the final version, the enacted bill embodied harsher and clearly more punitive features than Clinton had advocated earlier in his presidential campaign; he signed it into law, nevertheless. Presidential candidate Clinton had desired incentives to make work more attractive than welfare; he had not wanted to punish aid recipients and their dependents.[17]

From Nixon's through Clinton's presidencies, CBC memberships generally demonstrated a consistent pattern of supporting what representative Bobby Rush of Chicago has called "race" politics. Ultimately, in terms of criticisms and negative responses, it mattered only slightly if administrations were Republican or Democratic. Tests of a policy and a legislative proposal's acceptability or rejection always followed similar parameters. CBC members judged programs, bills, and policies as positive if a particular action would bring about beneficial effects to African Americans and negative if it would have harmful results. Here was the crux; no other factor—not even Democratic partisanship—determined how any final verdict would go as much as the perceived impact on African Americans. And there was an excellent reason that CBC members could assume this responsibility. Only rarely did these lawmakers ever need to answer to white constituents; their districts seldom possessed majority-majority status. An exception was Ronald Dellums. At the beginning of a congressional career, his House district in Northern California contained more whites than blacks, but this situation was unique; at its hub was liberal Berkeley.

As much as CBC members shared a common resolve to serve and protect minority and African American interests, differences did develop among them. Representatives who came to Congress from the South often tended to represent constituents with greater interests in matters such as national defense and military bases, space programs, and gun-owners' rights than their northern and western compatriots who often looked at these issues differently. For example, Mississippi's Mike Espy represented the cotton-growing Delta; thus he looked after and spoke for the agricultural interests of his white and African American constituents more than urban black lawmakers who probably had no reason to be interested in farming. In some cases, CBC members concluded that their colleagues' positions were too extreme. Chicago's Gus Savage, for example, gained almost no support for claiming that whites were "irrelevant," and for proclaiming they should be "under siege." Most CBC members disagreed with the Chicagoan on these wild conclusions because they understood that greater gains were possible from a "collegial" style with "coalition-building" than from Savage's combative statements and constant confrontations. In reality, it was only when CBC members judged as damaging the effects of specific legislation or governmental actions that their responses became almost unanimous. Diversity of opinion could and often did occur on almost everything else. Two examples were over how to evaluate Louis Farrakhan of the Nation of Islam and how to react to African American entries in presidential primaries. A strong House resolution denouncing the Black Muslim's anti-Semitic rhetoric easily passed (361–34), but voting among CBC members was considerably closer (21–11). Divisions also occurred over the wisdom of backing blacks against highly favored whites in Democratic presidential primaries. First it was Shirley Chisholm who sought votes and support in her 1972 bid for the party's nomination. Then, later, in 1984 and 1988, it was Jesse Jackson who was splitting CBC members with his appeals for their support during his two quests to gain delegates pledged to him at national party conventions. In both cases, the majority of African Americans in Congress considered the Chisholm and Jackson requests to be divisive, and their attempts at securing nominations to be fruitless, futile, and even frivolous efforts.[18]

Splintered as CBC members were over backing African Americans in primary elections for presidential nominations and over supporting some nonracial issues, unanimous opinion developed against Republican conservatism as well as in opposition to the agendas of two African Americans with right-wing ideologies who were elected to the House of Representatives. House victories in 1990 by Connecticut right-winger Gary Franks and four years later by equally conservative and reactionary Julius Caesar Watts in Oklahoma occurred within overwhelmingly white congressional districts. As candidates, both winners had loudly and clearly proclaimed their intentions to oppose affirmative action and most other federal assistance programs for minorities. As their alternatives to governmental intervention, they advised more or less the century-old Tuskegee

University formula of individual self-improvement and personal responsibility. For assuming independence from their fellow congressional African Americans about the course of action that would be most beneficial to the minority, these two black maverick representatives and scores of equally reactionary African Americans with similar ideas and orientations received applause from some sympathetic social scientists, who began to imagine conservative African Americans as the harbingers of something new and unique for the minority to consider and embrace politically. They interpreted this as evidence, allegedly, of an emergent colorblindness or deracialization among white voters.[19]

Whether by conviction or pragmatism, African American politicians who had chosen to follow the national conservative trend provoked both skepticism and anguish among those blacks more committed to civil rights. In the late 1920s, upon coming to Chicago for better political opportunities, Arthur Wergs Mitchell saw that chances for success in the GOP were minimal, and this led him to make what would prove to be a shrewd decision. He joined the Democratic Party and became an active member. Changing affiliations brought the ambitious newcomer into a political party without many African American competitors. Within five years, Mitchell, both across the South Side and among Cook County Democrats, gained attention and eventually the political machine's backing for the congressional seat held by Republican Oscar DePriest. After 1960, the thought of switching political parties to invert what Mitchell had done must have occurred to some ambitious African Americans who viewed as extremely frustrating any opportunities to advance to prominence within the Democratic Party. Of course, it is pure speculation and perhaps unfair to the individual minority conservatives simply to apply selfish, pragmatic explanations for their moves to the GOP, but the truth is that among young African Americans more of them have risen to prominent positions at both appointive and elective levels of government as Republicans than their Democratic counterparts. A cynic might consider these greater possibilities for appointments and nominations as GOP-style "affirmative action." As point of fact, some of the harshest critics of affirmative action within the minority are the individuals who experienced rapid advancements in the GOP's ranks. In addition to Thomas, who gained an appointment on the Supreme Court with minimal judicial experience, African American recipients of Republican largess who also possessed only marginal qualifications to advance were also apparent beneficiaries because of their outspoken conservatism. The long list of right-wing ideologues who served the Republican Party well enough for eventual rewards includes Kenneth Blackwell, Melvin Bradley, Jerry Burley, Maurice Dawkins, Thelma Duggin, Arthur Fletcher, Thaddeus Garret, Alan Keyes, Clarence Pendleton, Joseph Rogers, Thomas Sowell, Roy West, and Michael L. Williams. In their capacity both as candidates and as executive department appointees, these individuals, by their very placement and empowerment, defused to some degree the harshest critics' charges that taking conservative positions was somehow anti-African American. To such claims, Reagan and Bush together with the presidents' most ardent white backers countered that not all African Americans agreed with CBC members and other civil rights activists that the nation and Congress needed to provide special treatment to or to pass federal programs primarily for minorities. Then, in order to deny any unified opinion among all African Americans, that all wanted or embraced government assistance, conservative whites pointed to the berating of all liberals by syndicated talk radio's Armstrong Williams, an African American right-winger who liked to claim that too many of "his" folks used racism as a crutch and an excuse.[20]

The African American conservatives who were the recipients of generous Republican largesse often obtained harsh attacks for their views and actions. No critic of Justice Thomas was more severe than film director Spike Lee, who characterized the black judge as a "handkerchief head, a chicken and biscuit-eating Uncle Tom." In 1996, some five years after the judge's elevation to the Court, *Emerge* magazine captioned its scurrilous caricature of Thomas with "Uncle Thomas, lawn jockey for the far right." In several other cases, a majority of African American assaulters of minority conservatives preferred blanket criticisms to individualized character assassinations. National public television's (PBS) African American commentator and author Tavis Smiley subtly asked readers of his book, *Hard Left,* to contemplate "the last time you have heard Black conservatives say anything even remotely positive about Black people?" Then Smiley turned more emphatic: "They [minority defenders of GOP reactionaries] do nothing more than provide cover and justification for White conservatives who cannot get away with uttering such racist and discriminating comments." By and large, academician Adolph Reed limits himself to noting a general lack of "intellectual sophistication" among African American conservatives; he argues that none of their "output rises above banality and fatuity."[21]

Entering Congress in the 1990s amid swirling insinuations and vilifications hurled at and absorbed by these conservatives was a proud pair of African American Republicans. Both in their public appearances and in their congressional votes from the House floor, Gary Franks and Julius Caesar Watts Jr. generally supported the Reagan-Bush agenda against providing minorities with special treatment. Although Franks and Watts shared similar ideologies, their personal backgrounds and constituencies were most dissimilar. Raised in a labor-class family with southern roots, Franks progressed from a Roman Catholic parochial education in hometown Waterbury, Connecticut, to studies at Yale University. It is ironic that a scholarship program created to diversify enrollment enabled Franks to attend a prestigious and expensive Ivy League school. He played collegiate basketball for the Bulldogs, although Watts clearly was the more gifted athlete. High school quarterbacking skills in Eufaula, Oklahoma, earned Watts a full athletic scholarship to play football at the University of Oklahoma. While there, he led the Sooners to consecutive Big Eight Conference titles and Orange Bowl championships. After stardom at Oklahoma, Watts's playing career continued in the Canadian Football League with the Ottawa Rough Riders. During his first professional season, Watts guided his team to playing for the Grey Cup. Although Ottawa lost the title game and the Canadian championship to the Edmonton Eskimos, a panel of sportswriters named the rookie signal caller from Oklahoma the contest's Most Valuable Player.

Unlike Watts, who had a postcollegiate athletic career, Franks followed his Yale graduation by working in corporate lower management as a human-relations officer. Watts concluded a football career and answered a "calling" to take a Southern Baptist Convention associate pastorate in Del City, Oklahoma. Meanwhile, Franks returned to Waterbury to become a rental property investor. Prior to running for the House of Representatives, neither man had accumulated much of a political résumé. From 1986 to 1990, the Yale graduate served Waterbury residents as an alderman, and in 1990, the year Franks won his first congressional race, Oklahoma voters elected their ex-football hero to a seat on the State Corporation Commission. Four years later, Watts won a congressional election.

Although almost fourteen hundred miles separated Franks's and Watts's districts, they had various characteristics in common. Most important, the two congressional jurisdictions possessed populations with an overwhelming majority-majority. The two men's electorates tended toward political and social conservatism in ideology. At 96 percent white, the Connecticut district blended various European ethnic groups with New England Yankees. There existed among the population strong opposition to both legalized abortion and the feminist movement. Accounting for these inflexible positions was the fact that so many residents were faithful Roman Catholics. In the Southwest, where Watts lived and sought a House seat, the bailiwick was 94 percent white with a relatively homogeneous population. Religious polls showed a majority of Watts's Oklahoma constituency believing in and accepting the Bible literally, as true revelation, and most residents preferred fundamentalist Protestant denominations over the more liberal churches. A closer examination of Franks and Watts will bring into clear focus two individuals who mirrored their constituents more than would have African American Democrats in the House.

Gary Franks

Preceding Watts to Congress by four years, Franks established a conservative path that the Oklahoman could easily follow. As a campaigner for a House seat, the African American New Englander clearly indicated to audiences how he would vote as a representative on several types of issues. Democrat Tony Moffett, his opponent, tried hard to evidence these positions as too extreme and to place his GOP foe ideologically with Senator Jesse Helms, the infamous North Carolinian so well-known for his opposition to civil rights and progressive legislation. One African American critic of Franks went further, claiming that when listening to him, "I hear . . . Helms and David Dukes." (Dukes boasted that he was a Ku Klux Klan leader; in 1990 he lost a close election as the Republican challenger for the U.S. Senate from Louisiana.)[22]

Regarding specific campaign pledges in 1990, Franks stated his opposition to tax increases, national health insurance, more mandates by government for employers, and additional federal regulations. He supported military action against Iraq, and he favored a trimming down of the federal deficit. On energy production, his preferences were for generating more electricity with nuclear energy, natural gas, and coal. Moffett claimed to have found the motivation behind Franks's choices, and to audiences across the district the Democrat disclosed the major sources of his rival's campaign funds. Electing Franks would bring "a tool of the oil companies and utility companies" into the House of Representatives. Real estate interests, medical organizations, and business associations were among other key contributors to Franks's campaign. Rather than deny the source of his revenue, the conservative African American candidate went on the offense, characterizing his Democratic rival as a "limousine liberal" who "is trying to buy this race with outside money." Franks's countercharge contained an element of truth; a significant portion of the challenger's campaign funds had, in fact, come from organized labor, pro-choice groups, and environmental organizations not based in the district.[23]

To bolster campaigns, both Moffett and Franks used prominent members of their political parties as spokespersons. Appearing for the African American Republican in Connecticut to endorse his run for a congressional seat there were a myriad of GOP notables, including the Drug Enforcement Agency czar William Bennett, First Lady Barbara Bush, and President George H. W. Bush. The presidential appearance in Connecticut was a fundraiser for Franks, and it came immediately after Bush's veto of the Civil Rights Bill of 1990. His action resulted in picketing by local NAACP chapter members outside the Sheraton Hotel, where Bush was to appear. Commenting on the demonstration and its relation to Franks, protest spokesperson Dennis King "held [the GOP's African American candidate] accountable for turning his back on the Afro-American community. We feel he's forgotten his roots and turned his back on the civil rights struggle."[24] Several famous supporters of the Democratic nominee also came to help him. Rock musician Steven Stills, along with senators Edward Kennedy and Albert Gore, highlighted an impressive list of celebrities who spoke or performed on behalf of Moffett's candidacy. As for any conceivable effects from editorial endorsements, only one major newspaper spanned the entire district with some degree of influence, and this was the *Waterbury Republican-American*. Without comment as to why Franks and not Moffett should go to Congress, the partisan editor of this daily publication chose the

African American candidate, but then again he preferred every GOP politician over his or her Democratic opponent.[25]

Franks defeated Moffett by a comfortable margin of 7,721 votes. The difference came from Franks's overwhelming Republican pluralities accumulated in suburban and rural precincts. An analysis of the Fifth Congressional District in 1990 reveals some pertinent facts that bear on his strong showing. In the district, registered independents outnumbered Democrats and Republicans by 106,973 to 94,670 and 81,366, respectively. This imbalance created a strong likelihood for success coming from the relatively unknown African American political neophyte's strategy of repeatedly labeling his opponent a "professional politician." This simple message against Moffett resonated well with many unaffiliated voters. To validate his charge and to solidify it in the minds of residents, the Republican Franks frequently referred to his opponent's "carpetbagger" status, constantly reminding voters of Moffett's move to the district the previous January with the express purpose of qualifying to run for a vacant House seat. These factors had probably more influence on the election's outcome than the two contenders' tit-for-tat attacks. For example, Moffett's attempt to embarrass his Republican rival with an exposé of building code violations at Franks's rental properties went nowhere; it actually backfired because there followed counterstatements by several tenants who volunteered defenses of their politician landlord's maintenance record of his apartments. Moffett's failure to arouse concern over Franks's alleged slumlording preceded labeling him "Phantom Franks" because, it was alleged, the Waterbury alderman missed every meeting of the city's Civil Service Commission.[26]

Entering Congress at the midterm of Bush's presidency, Franks received questions about his choice of political parties; many reporters were curious about why the new congressman had become a Republican and not a Democrat. In the preface of his autobiography, the Waterbury native repeated his often-stated explanation; he attributed his political affiliation as much to the Carter years of "high interest rates, high unemployment, and high inflation" as to what he alleged to be the failures of a "tax-and-spend, big-government of the Democratic Party." Franks, by clearly placing himself in lockstep with a GOP majority, arrived on Capitol Hill advocating the death penalty, tax reductions, balanced budgets, open school enrollment, welfare reform, and silent reflection periods at the start to each school day. Combined with his gaining an election victory as the first African American Republican to take a House seat since Oscar DePriest's election in 1928, these views brought Franks considerable attention. Before casting his first vote as a GOP representative, the new legislator with such unusual partisan credentials for an African American congressman made a guest appearance on ABC Television's program, *Nightline,* and *USA Today*'s Sunday magazine featured the congressman elect's picture on its cover. Even months before his win in the November election, the *Wall Street Journal* carried an article anticipating what it saw as a new trend in political alignments; the story about an alleged shift in partisanship came with a celebratory headline proclaiming "New Generation: Black Moderates Win at Polls by Targeting Once-Elusive Whites." There was a degree of curiosity and some speculation about the possible reactions of CBC members to the presence of an outspoken African American conservative Republican among them with such a very different political outlook, and questions arose about his presence and about its effects upon his eligibility to belong to an African American legislative coalition consisting entirely of progressive activists. Asked for a reaction to all this, CBC executive director Amelia Parker indicated an open willingness to consider the African American dissident's inclusion in the organization.[27]

Matters changed quickly, however. The divisive issue was the advisability of confirming Clarence Thomas. By a lopsided vote of 25–1, the CBC opposed having a highly controversial African American conservative attorney on the Supreme Court; Franks was a lone supporter of Bush's embattled appointee. Representative Harold Ford Sr. of Memphis became the first of many CBC members to speak out negatively about the freshman lawmaker from Connecticut. In the Tennessean's opinion, Franks actually did not qualify as an African American member of Congress; rather, he was "a congressman who happens to be black and [who] is representing white people."[28]

If having a roll-call record like all other CBC members indicates inclusion in the minority body, then Ford's judgment was correct about the Republican. An examination of Franks's votes on important legislative bills during his first three congressional years reveals a definite disconnection in comparison with those of a cross-section of other African American lawmakers (see Table 1). Franks established an undisputable pattern of voting most matters according to an ideologically conservative philosophy, whereas the votes of all of the other African American congressmen more or less adhered to liberalism.

Table 1. CBC scorecard contrasting Franks with five colleagues

Congressman, State	ADA	ACU	AFL-CIO	C of C, USA
Gary Franks, CT	20%	88%	25%	100%
William Clay, MO	95%	0%	91%	20%
Cardiss Collins, IL	85%	0%	92%	20%
John Lewis, GA	95%	0%	92%	0%
Kweisi Mfume, MD	95%	0%	92%	20%
Charles Rangel, NY	95%	0%	92%	20%

Source: *Black Enterprise,* January 24, 1994.

To ascertain patterns and to comprehend how Franks operated differently from the other African Americans in Congress, it becomes necessary to more closely scrutinize not only these votes, but those registered for the remaining years of the Connecticut African American Republican's tenure as well. A review of *Congressional Record* roll calls and statements for the 102nd through the 104th congresses confirm the existence of a threshold that set Franks clearly apart from CBC Democrats. When Franks was speaking about and voting on legislative proposals that were especially related to minorities but that had only symbolic value, then the representative from Waterbury had no problem. He happily supported bills of low magnitude because enacting them in effect would not result with any apparent economic implications or social costs. So on several occasions, the Republican memorialized and recognized outstanding individual African Americans and their institutions because involvement in these efforts was philosophically neutral and the actions taken entailed no significant consequences. Whether it was Franks's cosponsorships of a bill extending the Black Revolutionary War Patriots Foundation for two more years or of another resolution that designated April 1993 as "National African-American Health Awareness Month," Franks feared no ramifications from a conservative white base back in Connecticut or from GOP House leaders. Nor could party bosses find fault in his expressing appreciation for retiring African American representative William H. Gray III after serving many years of dedicated service in the House, or for suggesting that a federal building in Chicago be named after the recently deceased African American Olympian and ex-House member Ralph Metcalf. Franks certainly did not stir up controversies for the praise and encouragement he offered to the nation's historically African American colleges and universities. In foreign affairs, his voicing support for Haiti's quick return to democracy in 1991, and for a cosponsored affirmation of American approval of South Africa's transition to interracial government in 1993, are two more examples of Franks's ability to claim personal involvement in matters of interest to his race—while at the same time doing nothing to upset fellow Republican conservatives by taking opposing views to them on the more volatile minority issues.[29]

For a GOP majority in Congress, a representative's opposition to affirmative action was the touchstone as to whether a Republican truly accepted the conservative agenda on civil rights. Franks knew that offering a politically harmless resolution in praise of legendary jazz performer John B. "Dizzy" Gillespie, or another condemning arson attacks on African American churches in the South would not upset anyone in his party. He also understood that a sudden bolting to the left as either an avid backer of employment quotas for minorities or an open advocate of federal contract set-aside programs would cause concern. Thus during Franks's three terms on Capitol Hill, as personal affirmations of his strong negativity toward these issues had not changed or wavered, the carefully watched Republican periodically asked for time to address the House about his solidly based opposition to all forms of special treatment. On March 8, 1996, Franks's commentary on affirmative action was representative of what he had uttered all along as to why he strongly objected to it. Like every loving parent, Franks noted how he was seeking for his three children equal opportunities for success, but he followed this desire with a careful, qualifying condition. His offspring, he said, should "know that, when selected, they are not just the best black person for the job, but that they are the best person for the job."[30]

Franks showed consistency as a self-proclaimed Republican conservative. Through three terms on Capitol Hill, he carefully followed his party's leadership on a range of subjects that came before the House of Representatives. GOP congressional head Newt Gingrich could count on a reliable partisan follower, who eagerly and consistently confirmed to the Republican right-wing agenda when both speaking about and voting on bills. And Franks carefully avoided doing or saying anything that might disappoint his party. Clearly this African American lawmaker was the complete antithesis of a GOP maverick; he more or less completely opposed the CBC's agenda in favor of his political affiliation.

Primary devotion to the party occurred with so many issues that Franks's positions consistently put him in conflict with African American Democrats in the House. On no matter was the disagreement more obvious than on welfare reform, as all the debating on the issue would show on May 4, 1994, when a conservative-liberal split occurred. Franks emerged as a main proponent of overhauling the entire system. Labeling relief dependency as "slavery" and categorizing "the plantation [as] being very similar to a [public housing] project," the Republican Party's leading African American spokesperson on Capitol Hill gave solid support to the position held by Representative Tom DeLay of Texas, the captain of a GOP team that included Clay Shaw and Susan Molinari. In a prolonged verbal battle over the continuing status of public assistance programs, Lynn Woolsey and Eleanor Holmes Norton led the Democratic House opposition. Although representing the CBC, Norton's role was as a non-voting congressional delegate from the District of Columbia. Among the points emphasized by Franks was an unsubstantiated claim that welfare dollars were going to drug dealers. He wanted to replace direct payments to aid recipients with debit cards, which would mean that recipients could cover only payments of rents, utilities, and other assorted legitimate expenditures. According to Franks's argument, debit cards would also provide an accurate accounting of all disbursements. Referring to the matter of eligibility for these, Norton questioned Franks if he would make any distinction between unwed mothers and divorcees with children. His emphatic answer was "No." Then coming up in the floor debate was a discussion of the matter of providing birth-prevention counseling and devices to young girls without the means to support babies. To these possibilities the African American Republican gave a clear answer: by continuing to offer young mothers welfare eligibility, the government not only encouraged but perpetuated teenage irresponsibility and reckless choices. As for the fathers of babies, Franks insisted, obligations must follow paternity. In his judgment, there were only three choices available to anyone siring a baby: "find a job and support your children, go to jail, or . . . have . . . a . . . community service type job." To deal with instances where paternal responsibility was concerned, Franks had in the previous session of Congress introduced HR 892, a legislative proposal that would have required fathers to support their children.[31]

In comparison to all other matters before Congress, Franks elaborated more extensively and passionately on behalf of what he perceived to be the major legislative priority—the elimination of welfare dependence. In general, he swayed very little from conventional social and political conservatism. On only very few of the issues he faced as a congressman did he show any degree of independence. Franks was reliable on the matter of education initiatives; he consistently backed the giving of vouchers, because in his opinion they would provide all parents with similar opportunities to choose between private and public schools, and they would result in competition for students, which ultimately would force every underperforming school either to improve or to close. He also offered bills to permit voluntary prayer or moments of silence in both schools and federal buildings. Regarding legal jurisdiction over and penalties for criminal activities, Franks wanted an expanded list of federal crimes and for more of these to be eligible for the death penalty. In his judgment, the register of serious offenses should include car hijackings and drive-by shootings; and judges should be empowered to condemn to death every person guilty of these crimes and of all acts of terrorism. In order to reduce wasteful governmental expenditures and federal deficits, and to eliminate "pork" from appropriation bills, Franks favored giving the president line-item veto authority. Like most Republicans he opposed Clinton's request to raise taxes, but he saw nothing odd about favoring a repeal of taxes on luxury items such as yachts.

Harking back to Nixon's advocacy of enterprise zones, Franks also believed the solution to most inner-city joblessness would come from enticing Fortune 500 companies into pockets of poverty and high unemployment. As he imagined a key consequence of his cosponsored Urban Entrepreneurs Opportunity Act, "the marriage between potential entrepreneurs and experienced corporate giants can only yield one end result: success."[32] Along with most other Republican legislators, Franks was an outspoken foe of Democrat-sponsored legislation for family medical leave. On the volatile issue of whether gays might serve openly in the armed forces, by his cosponsorship of a legislative directive against their inclusion, Franks again demonstrated conservative consistency. Another key example of how fully he agreed with fellow conservatives was his and their agreement on the desirable effects of privatizing public housing projects. Secretary of Housing Jack Kemp proposed a plan for this known as Project HOPE (Housing Opportunities for People Everywhere). During the early 1990s Project HOPE split CBC members as much as any issue. Together with Franks, African American Democratic House members Mike Espy, Harold Ford, and William J. Jefferson were all avid HOPE supporters.[33]

It was more common, however, that CBC members united against Franks than with him on issues coming before Congress. A key exception followed one of his rare displays of political independence. Franks's endorsement of a plan offering access to family-planning assistance for low-income women was unusual. Unlike so many religious fundamentalists in the conservative movement, Franks believed that public funds for birth-control clinics were necessary in the fight against teenage pregnancy and sexually transmitted diseases such as AIDS. As he laid out his arguments in support of Planned Parenthood, he stated "This program must be authorized and legitimized to insure these services remain available, accessible, and affordable to women."[34] He opposed any "gag rule" that "will impede them [the providers of professional health care] from giving the care and information women have a right and need to know."[35] In order to not irritate fellow conservatives too much by this support, Franks mollified his stance by cosponsoring bills against federally funded abortions.[36]

One year after his election to Congress, Franks spoke favorably of HR 2707, an omnibus funding bill. The targets for appropriations from it were the Low-Income Housing Energy Assistance Program (LIHEAP); Head Start; maternal and child health; substance abuse; and AIDS research, prevention, and treatment. His willingness to show this kind of open support for a generally liberal legislative package demonstrated a rare instance of political independence from the Connecticut Republican. But, since this deviation occurred so early in his legislative career, one might speculate that the party whips had not yet instructed him on what in fact did constitute for a conservative appropriate positions on specific issues.[37]

If an occasional moment of maverick bolting raised the ire of Republican colleagues, Franks never disappointed them on civil rights issues. On this subject, he was always the ubiquitous opponent of every program on the CBC's agenda. His few liberal moments did little to reduce the importance he gave his party. Franks's general opposition legitimated GOP hostility towards minority programs. The stands he made on these issues helped dispel any claims or charges that racism in any way motivated Republican actions. Franks had been in Congress only a few months when his usefulness as an African American foe of the CBC emerged. Two major civil rights bills reached the floor for attention. President Bush and the conservatives were backing one of these bills, and the liberals and the entire CBC membership, except Franks, supported the other proposal. The GOP-backed bill called for the removal of all traces of quotas, and it put a cap on damages from lawsuits involving discrimination. As a proponent noted about the bill, its enactment would have eliminated "a plaintiffs' lawyer paradise." Speaking for the other side, Congressman Clay chided presidential "antics" and

Bush's "rantings" on behalf of a "dismal message." At this point, Franks entered the fray to defend his party colleagues Robert Michel and Henry Hyde, the co-sponsors of amendments to HR 1. What they were advising, argued the freshman lawmaker, "will not institutionalize or reverse discrimination, promote costly and endless litigation, inhibit American businesses from hiring the best qualified and promoting the most productive workers." The changes proposed by Michel and Hyde failed to gain approval by an overwhelming margin of 266–162. Franks was the only CBC member who had supported the Michel-Hyde amendments.[38]

The CBC majority may have been irritated by its GOP member's differing opinions concerning affirmative action, but Franks's opposition to what he maintained was "racial gerrymandering of congressional districts" caused even more anger.[39] As the Connecticut Republican argued, in an opinion about the court-ordered creation of several new minority districts, "If black political aspirants do not believe that they can get elected unless the district is a majority-minority district, that is too bad."[40] To this end, five weeks after concluding this on reapportionment from the House floor, Franks submitted a bill "prohibiting the intentional creation of legislative districts based on the race, color, or language minority status of voters within such districts."[41] Although this attempt to override the courts garnered considerable support among Republicans and some Southern Democrats, it almost brought an end to Franks's membership in the CBC. Cleo Fields of Louisiana and Alcee L. Hastings of Florida reacted more angrily than most other African American lawmakers. Judicial intervention had developed special meaning for them, because a court order had resulted in two redrawn districts, which in the final analysis had improved their opportunities to win House seats. Franks's critics minced no matters in stating why the dissident member deserved to be expelled from the caucus. It was because of Franks's "historically blasphemous and racially traitorous views on civil rights." Despite hearing strong demands for his ouster, however, Chair Mfume finally persuaded fellow members to allow the conservative to remain in the coalition.[42]

Whether it was Franks's doubts about the existence of redlining practices by the nation's insurance companies to deny policy protection to residents of prominently black neighborhoods or the lawmaker's boycott of Louis Farrakhan's attempt to push paternal responsibility through the Million Man March on Washington, DC in 1994 because of Franks's disapproval of the Muslim leader's "warped beliefs," the Republican's actions and statements stirred up considerable media sensation and also generated strong animosity towards him among African Americans. A candid assertion that the Nation of Islam resembled the Ku Klux Klan attracted so much attention that Franks ended up receiving invitations to appear on several television news and interview shows. He appeared on *Larry King Live* and *Meet the Press*, where he explained his controversial judgment. Right-wing radio talk show hosts Pat Buchanan and Rush Limbaugh also welcomed the outspoken minority congressman on their programs. Seemingly as a result of his willingness to publicize such an unusual perspective for an African American politician, as a television and radio guest Franks enjoyed the notoriety of his unique role as African American conservatism's most famous spokesperson. The personal negative consequences did not seem to disturb him. He was not affected by the fact that other African Americans—such as Congressman Billy McKinley of Georgia—increasingly referred to him as "an Uncle Tom, a black Judas [guilty of] selling the brothers out." Franks knew that only he could answer what the Georgian wanted to know about an undesirable GOP colleague: "what did they [likely a reference to Republican leaders] give you, you nigger?"[43]

In 1992, when nationally voters rejected Bush for Clinton, Franks did not experience any similar reelection difficulties. The lawmaker's message apparently still resonated with his electorate, and pitted in a three-person contest for one congressional seat, the African American incumbent was reelected with only 44 percent of the vote because of a split among the Democrats in his district. Democrat Jim Lawlor secured 31 percent and Connecticut Party candidate Lynn Taborsake received 18 percent, which seems to indicate some apparent district dissatisfaction with Franks, but the Lawlor-Taborsake infighting gave the incumbent his second term. Charges made against Franks during the election obviously did not matter enough to prevent his return to Capitol Hill for the 103rd Congress. For example, during the campaign, the onetime maverick Republican-turned-independent Lowell Weicker categorized Congressman Franks as "an embarrassment to his race," and several Democrats labeled the GOP incumbent "the legislative equivalent of Clarence Thomas."[44]

During the 1994 off-year elections, while Republicans were doing well enough nationally to wrest control of Congress, Franks won his second reelection. This was a two-man race in which the incumbent garnered approximately 54 percent of his district's vote. His Democratic foe, James H. Maloney, attracted only 46 percent. By the 1994 November elections, Franks was a national celebrity because of his critical remarks and negative assessments of fellow African Americans, and he Franks was already beginning to show evidence of overconfidence. In the view of many district residents, the black Republican congressman had started to ignore constituent concerns.

Certainly by the 1996 election, Franks's attitude and arrogance had finally begun to put the incumbent at a disadvantage. His challenger was once again Maloney. In press releases as well as speeches, the Democrat reiterated a theme that was coming to reflect the conclusion of many district residents: "Mr. Franks always has something better to do than be in the 5th District." Despite having a third consecutive editorial endorsement from the *Republican-American* and more than double the amount of campaign funds to spend as Maloney, Franks lost this election (98,990–85,332). Responding to a jubilant audience's shouting chorus of "Union! Union!," the victor replied with personal greetings of appreciation to his enthusiastic supporters. Meanwhile a bitter loser blamed defeat on what he called Democratic "lies." "They're [*sic*] attacks have all been lies." Others interpreted Franks's defeat differently. As an independent voter explained his vote for Maloney, "I [had] always voted for Franks. But not this time. He took the people for granted." Agreeing in large part with this, a retired manufacturer's representative claimed to have lost respect for the conservative lawmaker. As he summarized the Republican incumbent's overbearing demeanor, "His sense of arrogance is overwhelming. Franks gives you the impression that as long as he goes along with Newt Gingrich, he can ignore the little people of his district." The Waterbury newspaper that had always supported the African American lawmaker's campaigns offered an altogether different explanation for Franks's loss to Maloney. It called Franks "his own worst enemy." Elaborating, the editor wrote how Franks had definitely shown a "penchant for poor decision-making—from his staff choices, putting his wife on the payroll, dodging debates—that played smack into the hands of James Maloney." Upon learning of Franks's defeat, Congressman Clay reacted by rejoicing and celebrating; within only a few days after the Republican's loss, the African American lawmaker from St. Louis made his often-quoted remark about Franks being the "Negro Dr. Kevorkian," a man on a mission to destroy his race.[45]

As much as Clay's assessment seems like hyperbole in order to solidify a judgment, evidence backs the contention that, through his words and deeds, Franks harmed more than he helped African Americans in Congress. Often without many personal contacts with another race, whites (who often imagined only the worst conceivable things about the minority) now heard this African American conservative affirm on radio and television talk shows everything they had long suspected. Claiming—as Franks often did—that 25 percent of welfare recipients were drug users and maintaining that sex, illegal drugs, music, and dance ranked as the favorite pleasures of all poor African Americans, of course, did much to enhance the exaggerated images of the minority in the minds of whites. The polls showed that many whites shared with Franks such recklessly construed myths as these, and that they, like him, opposed most all legislative efforts directed at improving the quality of life for impoverished people. The congressman's positions on these and other issues clearly were not contributors to his defeat in 1996, but his holding so securely to the negative right-wing agenda probably validated in some ways Clay's critical assessment of Franks's public impact.[46]

Julius Caesar Watts Jr.

To white Oklahomans in 1994, J. C. Watts—delivering to his electorate more or less the same message that Franks had delivered earlier in Connecticut—gained enough voter confidence to defeat a Democratic opponent for the right to represent District Four in Congress. Soon after his arrival on Capitol Hill, the Sooner-hero-turned-conservative-politician announced that he had no plans to join the Congressional Black Caucus. Days before the November election, an *Oklahoma Eagle* editorial endorsement described Watts as "a rare politician, who while conservative, understands the plight of people of color." The son of the first African American policeman in his hometown, Eufaula, reasoned that belonging to the CBC would make no sense for him, because Democrats in the coalition would outvote him and Franks on every issue 40–2. Elaborating, Watts observed how membership "plays right into the hands of the Beltway press that wants to 'cynicize' [sic] every issue. They [Washington reporters] don't give us [Watts and Franks] the flexibility to say what we want, how we want to. Instead, joining puts us in a very difficult situation where it looks like it's the black Republicans versus the black Democrats."[47]

Watts came to Congress with other preconceptions. One regarded welfare. From early in his life of growing up impoverished in rural Oklahoma, he remembered how circumstances had forced his father to work several jobs in order to support his family. This, for Watts's father, meant assuming personal responsibility—a duty and an obligation that his recently elected congressman son proclaimed a source of personal pride infinitely preferable to accepting "galling" welfare. As Watts put it, "Even a minimum wage job can grow into bigger and better things." His uncompromising solution to poverty reflected the Reagan belief that the private sector could eliminate hardship better than government programs could. In order to allow a private sector cure to begin, Watts reasoned, businesses needed tax credits as well as a complete elimination of capital gains taxes.[48]

Generally, like most freshman lawmakers on Capitol Hill, Watts during his first year was more an observer than a participant. His first input of any significance came on September 29, 1995, when the congressman gave a "pledge of allegiance to the right to life." On this day, House members were considering a Department of Defense appropriations bill for the following fiscal year, and the Oklahoma lawmaker voiced his view for the *Record* of his opposition to using military-controlled health facilities for abortions. Watts's only other speech to Congress in 1995 came on December 12, and it was more commemorative than substantive. He rose then to mention that on this particular day, 125 years ago, Hiram R. Revels of Mississippi entered the Senate as its first African American member. As with Franks, honoring the major deeds and achievements of African Americans became a way to celebrate their race without giving offense. Thus, on a regular basis, Watts involved the minority in this way. During Watts's eight-year tenure in the House, his honor roll of celebrities included African American Revolutionary War heroes, opera's Marian Anderson, Major League Baseball integrator Jackie Robinson, home-run slugger Henry Aaron, and heroine Rosa Parks of the Montgomery bus boycott. Like Franks, Watts knew he would make no waves and incur no repercussions by recognizing "the importance and the significance of . . . historically Black colleges and universities," Carter G. Woodson's establishment of Black History Month, the Supreme Court's *Brown vs. the Board of Education*, plans for the establishment of a National Museum of African American History and Culture, or the anniversary of Abraham Lincoln issuing the Emancipation Proclamation. Watts also knew his conservative constituents well enough to be aware that his condemning arsonists for torching African American churches and abhorring the racist hate groups behind such heinous crimes as the sadistic dragging death of James Byrd Jr. outside Jasper, Texas, would not link him to African American militants or separatists.[49]

Some definite limitations existed, however. As much as the Oklahoma conservative liked to denounce prejudice and hatred in the most generous terms, he was not willing to target any specific groups, at least not in any legislation. Watts's House Resolution 121 of 1999, for example, was no more than a blanket, toothless condemnation of hatred. It did not condemn the Council of Conservative Citizens (CCC), one organization that Watts's critics maintained should absolutely be identified as a hate group, but taking this stand was something the Oklahoman refused to do, for this extremist group allegedly had too many links with too many prominent Republicans. As a result of Watts's failure of include the CCC in his resolution, critics refused to pass what they viewed as a "sham and a joke."[50]

As tentative as Watts was about naming offensive racist groups, he adamantly opposed any more federal governmental involvement in civil rights. Whenever asked to clarify his reasoning, he was ready with the explanation about what his constituents appeared to appreciate most about him—an ability to reply in simple "down-home" syntax that connected him to them. His favorites were "I've always felt that if somebody was bothered by the color of my skin, that was their problem" and "My papa always said that the only helping hand you can rely on is at the end of your sleeve." As much as he liked to connect personal values to family, his hometown, and experiences at the University of Oklahoma, clearly not all Watts family members agreed with his position on race and conservatism. The Reverend Wade Watts, the ex-football player's paternal uncle and a lifelong Democrat, maintained a completely different outlook. In 1948, while the state chair of the NAACP, the older Watts had worked diligently to obtain Ada Lois Sipuel's court-ordered admission into the University of Oklahoma. Speaking of this fight and the younger man's hostility to tougher civil rights laws, the minister reminded his brother's son of all the many past struggles of African Americans to obtain equal opportunities: "If we hadn't gotten [her] in, he [the lawmaker] never would have had a chance to show how good he was at football. . . . He couldn't have stuck his head in the door [at the Norman institution]."[51] Reverend Wade Watts also had no appreciation for the representative's GOP membership because his political party has had so little commitment to "poor people, working people, common people."[52]

Derisively called a "poster boy" for conservative causes, Watts often seemed to enjoy all the opportunities to live up to what his critics considered an insult.

As his uncle, the senior preacher and civil rights leader in the family, acclaimed about his nephew: "They're [Republican leaders] showboating him."[53] One example was J. C.'s consent to having a cameo appearance in a National Rifle Association (NRA) promotional advertisement to defend the gun lobby's position that all citizens have a constitutional right to own weapons. In this promotion, it showed the minority legislator with a rifle raised, and directly above a caption read, "as American as mom, baseball, and apple pie." From campaigning first for a congressional seat in 1994 through eight years on Capitol Hill, the Oklahoman never tired of jabbing welfare and its recipients.

As Watts was catapulting into national prominence, the cynicism was growing among several eyewitnesses of his meteoric rise within Republican Party ranks. Earlier when he had given his first thoughts to running for political office as a Democrat, party leaders allegedly advised the former Sooner athlete to "get in line." Reflecting upon this advice, Uncle Watts was frank about his nephew's chances in the other party: "I don't think he would have gotten off the ground as a Democrat." As for the possibilities of J. C. Watts running a successful campaign in Oklahoma with a liberal message, Democratic representative from Philadelphia and CBC member Chaka Fattah was certain there was none: "If he felt as I do on many issues, he would not have been elected to Congress from Oklahoma."[54]

Not only had the Republicans slated the politically inexperienced Watts for Congress, but they quickly showcased the photogenic, articulate African American conservative nationally on several occasions before diverse audiences, for he was considered "a hot property" and a perfect symbol of the biracial inclusiveness within the GOP ranks. Party strategists viewed Watts as having great potential as an ideal promoter of their party. Thus the former collegiate and professional football star went before network cameras, appearing first on national television at the 1996 Republican National Convention in San Diego as a prime-time featured speaker for his party. Essentially what Watts addressed on this occasion to delegates and television viewers across America reflected more or less what he had uttered throughout his brief political career: "We [he and others in the GOP] don't define compassion by how many people are on welfare, or AFDC [Aid to Families with Dependent Children], or living in public housing—but how few."[55]

Obviously pleased by Watts's performance, GOP congressional leaders chose him to offer the official Republican response to Bill Clinton's 1997 State of the Union address. Prior to assuming this major responsibility, the Eufaula native had stirred up considerable controversy by referring to unnamed civil rights leaders as "race-hustling poverty pimps" and for accusing liberal Democrats of "hook[ing] blacks on government checks." Watts later expressed regrets for these remarks, but his apology never gained as much footing as his characterizations. As for his rebuttal to the president, three action points emerged. The first of these was nothing more than the standard Watts diatribe about how, during the past thirty years, the nation budgeted "5 trillion dollars trying to erase poverty, . . . [only to] spread it [while all these programs] destroyed the self-esteem of millions of people, grinding them down in a welfare system." Then he argued for "get[ting] our government's financial affairs in order" by taking the "biggest step"—enacting a constitutional amendment to mandate balanced federal budgets. As his final point, Watts offered what only an African American person could do for the GOP conservatives without garnering charges of racism: he asserted that the federal government could never heal America's racial divide by enacting more civil rights legislation.[56]

For loyalty and service as a dependable Republican, Watts gained his reward in 1998. By a vote of 121–93, his peers elected their African American spokesperson as chair of the party conference over the longer tenured and more experienced John Boehner of Ohio. Now Watts had emerged as the fourth most powerful Republican, in terms of rank, among all GOP House members. In the aftermath of victory, he announced which party goals would receive priority attention. These included cutting taxes, strengthening national defense and social security, and improving America's inconsistent health care system.

In general, reactions to Watts's elevation to a leadership role varied from congratulatory wishes to caution and skepticism. Political analyst Ronald Walters from the University of Maryland placed the African American in a precarious position; knowing that "control of the party apparatus is in the hands of the conservatives . . ., he'll have to be very respectful of this. He's not a free agent by any stretch of the imagination." From close to the Capitol at Howard University, political scientist Alvin Thornton offered a more hopeful reaction—but one mixed with doubts. Given the Oklahoman's position, the professor expected now "to see Watts' imprint" on "what the [Republican] party is doing when it comes to black folks." But Thornton had doubts that there would be any significant opportunities for Watts to use his position as chair to influence GOP policies and decisions. According to Thornton's understanding of the GOP agenda development, to have an effect or cause any major changes would take more than Watts's "willing[ness] to raise the decibel level of . . . opposition." The reputable scholar of government institutions minimized Watts's role as leader in his party priorities: "You can't see him [Watts] telling Henry Hyde what to do or think, so that leads me to believe this [him being chair] is more of an image job."[57]

Despite Thornton's wish that the congressman would use his position as chair for some direct activism on behalf of African American people, Watts's statements and his Capitol Hill record did not change from what they had been prior to his appointment. His key message and political philosophy remained both constant and conservative, whether shared with district constituents or uttered inside the Washington Beltway. This consistency was the very reason he had received an editorial endorsement for reelection from the *Oklahoma City Black Chronicle* in 1998. As the editor put his support, "Mr. Watts has never forgotten his constituency either nor has he forgotten who he is." And the lawmaker's Capitol Hill activities reflected this truth. For example, following ex-housing secretary Jack Kemp's initiative and joining with Representative James Talent of Missouri, Watts announced on May 14, 1996, "a conservative blueprint for helping poor urban and rural communities." Nothing really innovative, the resubmission of Kemp's plan was nothing more than the repeat of an earlier Republican effort to entice private sector leaders with promises of reduced capital gains taxes in exchange for their relocating business and industrial activities to poverty-stricken areas. The black lawmaker's involvement in these efforts to rekindle support for an old GOP idea dating back to Richard Nixon's presidency—along with his support for other right-wing solutions such as providing federally funded school vouchers to private schools and offering "faith-based" remedies for social problems—continued through 2002 when Watts retired from Congress. Whether it was his opposition to partial-birth abortions and to public distributions of birth control pills to teenaged girls without any parental notification, the actions of this African American Republican did not contradict the values of his Oklahoma constituents, the people who had elected him three times as their representative in Washington.

Watts was unlike Gary Franks in one way, however. The ex-Sooner football star refrained from pushing for an end to affirmative action. As Brent Staples of the *New York Times* reported and the *Tulsa World* carried about Watts's position, "society has no choice but to open opportunities for the disadvantaged" until "a stronger commitment to education . . . level[s] the playing field, making affirmative action unnecessary." Also on a positive side, through Watts's introduction of a bill on May 15, 2001, he became a loyal champion of aid and relief for African American farmers from federal tax liabilities after their settlement of claims against the U.S. Department of Agriculture's discriminatory practice of unfairly distributing farm credit and benefit programs.[58]

From a reading of Watt's book, *What Color is a Conservative?: My Life and My Politics*, one cannot help but grasp an overriding understanding of the man. Eufaula was his yardstick and his basis for judgments and political philosophy. As a lawmaker and spokesperson, Watts never saw that the keys to solving national problems might require more than what he had observed as workable in his hometown. As he liked to stress for audiences, "the values of faith, family, personal responsibility, and hard work" are the ones that have importance. His father, J. C. "Buddy" Watts Sr., was the source of many of his son's simple homilies. The lawmaker's favorite quote from "Daddy" was "'Spending money ought to be as difficult as it was to earn it.'" Throughout Watts's years on Capitol Hill, a small town remained his most important frame of reference and his connection to a constituency, but at the same time his narrow outlook caused him to appear utterly out of touch to cosmopolitan critics with much broader horizons and more sophisticated solutions.[59]

In judging and summarizing the House careers of two conservative African American Republicans, Franks and Watts, it is a mistake to underestimate the one overriding factor that both men readily admitted was a major reason behind their successful campaigns in two largely white congressional districts. They ran for office as GOP candidates who happened to be members of a racial minority, and never as African American men who happened to belong to the Republican Party. A subtle but important distinction, this certainly bound the candidates philosophically to the views of the majorities in both districts. Constituents in both Connecticut and Oklahoma shared with Franks and Watts views on a wide range of issues from opposition to abortion to tax reduction. In a prologue to *African American Power and Politics*, Kenneth A. Jordan and Modibo M. Kadalie imply an agreement with "those white pundits who argue that whites will vote for African Americans if they hold mainstream values. By mainstream, they [constituents] mean right wing ultra conservatives such as African American congressmen Gerald [*sic*] Franks and J. C. Watts, whose political views are no different than whites who take positions that are inimical to African American progress and advancement." Keith Reeves in *Voting Hopes or Fears?* injected a "dispiriting reality" in the terms of both Republican winners: "black officeseekers who compete in majority-white settings in the main are unable to attract consistent widespread support because *race perniciously influences both the tenor of their electoral campaigns and their outcomes* [Reeves's emphasis]." This appears true, but for some analysts certain questions remain apparently unanswered concerning this pair of African American representatives' tenure in Washington. Did the Republican Party gain more from giving Franks and Watts public exposure? Or did these two officeholders obtain significantly more from exploiting their positions as black members of the GOP? These questions each deserve a decisive, affirmative answer. Since elevating and exposing Franks and Watts to the nation did not turn African Americans into Republican voters, the party clearly lost from its experiment with inclusiveness at the congressional level. Franks and Watts were clearly the ones who emerged victorious. In final analysis, the GOP's blatant actions of parading this odd pair of minority politicians as African American champions of conservatism won for these men not only congressional seats but notoriety, and it seems the Republican Party in the process likely gained nothing remotely tangible for its efforts.[60]

Chapter 3

Retaining White Power with Black Mayors

In several municipal elections between the late 1960s and the end of the century, African American mayoral candidates won three different types of contests. First successes came in Northern minority-majority cities such as Newark, Gary, Detroit, and East St. Louis. Several African American mayoral candidates followed the wins gained in these urban centers by succeeding in southern municipalities where African Americans outnumbered whites. A revolutionary shift of control, this demographic transitioning of political power from Caucasian to African American in Dixie followed the 1965 Voting Rights Act. The transparent results of this legislation elevated African American office seekers to take command of city halls in New Orleans and Birmingham—two municipalities where favorable population breakdowns had become most helpful to African Americans gaining power. Finally, in some notable exceptions, there was another smaller group of African American mayoral contenders with minority-minority status, who adroitly managed to convince enough whites in their electorates that they deserved leadership opportunities. Among the cases of this phenomenon occurring, Chicago's was the one most observed and discussed of all the examples. Perhaps compared to the win in the Windy City, the two victories by a pair of African American mayoral candidates in New Haven and Seattle are easier to explain because their outcomes were certainly more predicted to transpire. This chapter devotes attention to these three categories as its prelude to more intensive case studies of the African Americans mayors from Los Angeles, Atlanta, New York, Philadelphia, and St. Louis. It concludes with an overall assessment of how specific black municipal chief executives have fared both as minority and as urban leaders.

Elmo Bush's Failure in East St. Louis, Illinois

As the more racially partisan African American voters in East St. Louis, Illinois, found to their dismay from a 1967 mayoral contest involving white incumbent Alvin G. Fields and black challenger Elmo Bush, some essential factors other than the clearly more obvious advantage of favorable demography could affect a municipal election. In this city, where 59 percent of all voting came from overwhelmingly African American precincts, neither Fields nor Bush tried especially hard to court voters of the opposite race. The white candidate ignored an invitation from the NAACP to attend a Q&A session, while his African American opponent avoided door-to-door canvassing in white neighborhoods. An analysis of the election reveals the degree to which Bush failed to connect with voters of both races. Among whites, he gained only 12 percent support, whereas in African American-populated areas of East St. Louis, Fields outpolled his foe by 40 to 60 percent.

Many contributing factors accounted for Bush's defeat. One of the most significant reasons was African American dependence upon the winner's political machine. By exerting tight control of the St. Clair County Economic Opportunities Commission under the federal antipoverty program, the mayor, through political allies, had charge of public assistance to needy black residents. Moreover, many African American church leaders held appointments on public committees and depended upon municipal jobs, and the incumbent mayoral regime doled out both as patronage. Even after Bush had arranged to share a campaign platform two days before the election with Stokely Carmichael, chair of the Student Nonviolent Coordinating Committee, the city's militants preferred to recall 1963 when the candidate had abandoned a leadership role in civil rights demonstrations. Among conservative churchgoers, Bush's unsavory reputation as a heavy drinker, playboy, and womanizer hurt his chances, too. Hence the vote among African Americans reflected more or less the cynicism of one African American East St. Louis resident who had the following reaction to the two mayoral aspirants, "I don't trust the *man*, but I don't the *boy* either."[1]

Carl B. Stokes in Cleveland, Ohio

In several other Northern cities, as whites were fleeing in large numbers to suburbs and as African Americans were significantly growing in urban population percentages, a favorable shift to minority empowerment logically followed. While the rapidly deteriorating Illinois river town was rejecting an African American mayoral candidate in 1967, Cleveland and Gary residents elected Carl B. Stokes and Richard Hatcher, respectively. A division among white voters in the Democratic primary was the significant factor affecting the African American politician's victory in the preliminary round of the Ohio mayoral contest. After a losing effort in 1963 to become his city's top official, Stokes capitalized on financiers and industrialists' dissatisfaction with the municipality's declining economy and image to garner from key leaders not only some tepid support but also essential campaign contributions. Additional legitimation for Stokes occurred on September 3 when the WASP-owned and–edited Cleveland *Plain Dealer* boldly endorsed the African American candidate in a front-page editorial, but not incumbent Ralph Locher or Frank Celeste. Yet for average rank-and-file white voters in Cleveland, both fear and resistance confronted them as they considered the possible proposition of having their metropolis administered by an African American mayor. From the previous summer, the white population had not forgotten a week of burning, looting, vandalizing, and sniping from across the Cuyahoga River in Cleveland's East Side ghetto. Here was a case of blame by racial association, and racist reactionaries dubbed Stokes's white backers do-gooders who simply did not understand urban racial conflict. Their efforts to enlist support for Stokes in the predominantly white West Side wards often ended in the African American candidate's staffers being physically and verbally assaulted. Meanwhile, a number of racists fired guns, smashed windows, and hurled a Molotov cocktail at Stokes's downtown headquarters. When primary day came, 211,599 Clevelanders voted. Stokes won, having received 52.3 percent of the total vote. Broken down, victory resulted from the minority challenger impressively gaining 96.2 percent of the African American vote and a surprising 15.2 percent from the remainder of Cleveland's electorate.[2]

Expressions of personal optimism about expected future victories and Stokes's nuanced references to how he, as mayor, would deal with racial questions marked his candidacies both in the Democratic primary and in the general election. Underplaying his identity as an African American, he pledged to "serve all the people without favor or unfair special consideration." Yet, with an odd twist of inconsistency in his pledge to racial impartiality, Stokes claimed that nobody but he among three mayoral candidates could maintain racial harmony in the strife-torn city. After his successful run against two Democrats, the only remaining major obstacle ahead for Cleveland's pioneering African American politician was a Republican opponent in the general election. The GOP candidate was Seth Taft—a foe who created what a pundit called the public's choice between the "grandson of a slave and the grandson of a president." Despite a long-standing Cleveland voter precedent and tradition of city voters generally supporting only Democratic candidates in all local elections, many party loyalists now refused to support an African American's bid to become the city's next mayor. Although Taft had failed to obtain editorial support from two major newspapers and had run a mostly dispirited campaign, he still managed to dislodge enough votes from Stokes to make the 1967 race for mayor an interesting and extremely tight battle. The final tabulation of 257,113 ballots in the mayoral contest declared Stokes, the Democrat, a close winner with a slim plurality of 1,679 votes.[3]

For the victor, running for mayor actually turned out to be easier than managing a divided city. Early in what became an often frustrating administrative career, Stokes discovered pitfalls and dilemmas accompanying his efforts to be all things to all people. A case in point occurred as soon as he began to make appointments. Since the all-empowering factor behind his mayoral victory had been solid African American backing, many supporters expected to receive significant patronage rewards. Yet the mayor sensed that showing too much generosity by doling out a disproportionate number of important jobs to African Americans would result in charges of reverse discrimination and might possibly create an impasse with the white-controlled city council. Therefore, in what was an obvious effort at fairness, Stokes's appointments followed a balanced approach in the selection process. Although he had appointed more African Americans than previous mayors, militant critics responded angrily to their perceptions of tokenism.

Other criticisms followed Stokes's attempts to involve white business leaders in urban regeneration. In what he considered the best means of redirecting Cleveland's future, Stokes liked to gather together city entrepreneurs for planning sessions. There were no doubts that improvements were necessary; to cynics Cleveland had become "the Mistake on the Lake." The Cuyahoga River passing through the Ohio city was literally burning, many factory jobs in key heavy industries were disappearing, and the infrastructure was decaying. In order to deal with urban problems and to make Cleveland more attractive to investors, Stokes launched an ambitious ten-year, $1.5-billion plan he called "Cleveland: Now!." At first praising the mayor's announcement, many initial enthusiasts rescinded their support after Stokes asked the city council for a 1 percent increase in the city's income tax. Despite preliminary objections from some council members, Stokes prevailed. The verdict after less than eight months in office as Cleveland's first African American mayor was primarily positive, and most early skepticism about Stokes's ability to govern a complex city waned because of some undeniable accomplishments. He fought to restore federal urban renewal funds to the city, kept peace after Martin Luther King's assassination, established Cleveland: Now!, and won the revenue battle for a tax increase.

The honeymoon ended on July 23, 1968, however. Fred "Ahmed" Evans was the provocateur. Evans was a militant African American nationalistic leader who claimed not only American but also Libyan citizenship. He had felt serious doubts from the beginning about any possibility of real gains from Stokes's election. As Evans and members of his small band of followers stockpiled arms and ammunition in a rented apartment, the building's landlord complained to the police about the physical dangers of using his premises as an arsenal. A confrontation ensued when the separatists refused to allow city inspectors into the building. A firefight began between the Evans forces and heavily armed law officers, which led to many shots being exchanged. Of more importance, trouble and confrontation quickly spilled over into neighborhood streets. The violence escalated into an open rebellion on the East Side—local youths against all authority figures. By the morning of July 24, seven people were dead, including three policemen.

At the center of all the blame for the tragedy was Stokes, because of his initial response to the unrest—he had ordered a withdrawal of all white officers from the confrontation. As he justified this most controversial tactic, "The problem is in the black community, and the black community will handle it." Many criticisms of the mayor followed after order was restored in a now looted and charred ghetto neighborhood. For his initial deployment order to employ only African American officers at the scene of early rioting, Stokes's reputation as a crisis manager plummeted. Critics unfairly blamed Stokes for the three policemen's deaths. Harsher attacks followed revelations that Evans had received $10,000 from Cleveland: Now! and that the rebellion leader had used the money to purchase weapons. Absurd as it was to associate the mayor with everything that had gone awry, suspicions of complicity occurred, nevertheless. Stokes's mishandling of an East Side riot was more than enough to resurrect doubts among many white Clevelanders about the current mayor's capacity to manage a diverse city beset by racial unrest. The result was an end to Stokes's control of the mayoral office.[4]

Richard Hatcher in Gary, Indiana

Like Rust-Belt Cleveland in 1967, steel-producing Gary was also in decline when a feisty young African American attorney challenged the white Lake County political machine for control of the city. As a candidate in Gary, Richard Hatcher had one advantage that his counterpart in Ohio lacked. Preliminary census estimates indicated that the Hoosier's quest for mayorship might turn out better because, unlike still predominantly white Cleveland, the racial demography of Gary had evidently shifted in Hatcher's favor. For the first time, it appeared, blacks were a majority in the northern Indiana city. As William E. Nelson Jr. and Philip J. Meranto attest for Gary, though, numbers can deceive. A resourceful and powerfully corrupt political machine's iron-fisted control of the municipality and "over the black precinct organization completely negated [any serious attempt at orchestrating] the successful mobilization of the black community by a black candidate for independent political action." For support of designated candidates, bosses distributed patronage appointments to grateful African American precinct committeemen. As early as 1960, Hatcher had actively tried to reform Gary's political setup. Then, as a reform-motivated community organizer working in the city, he had felt equally comfortable among Gary's poverty-stricken blacks as he had with the middle-class Jews in the city's Miller neighborhood. Yet it was a challenge for Hatcher to run against the incumbent, A. Martin Katz, because of the established officeholder's clear advantages. The primary problem was the black precinct workers who were loyal to the mayor's organization. They spread fear among poor residents by threatening that their pending welfare would be cut off if they dared to vote for Hatcher, not Katz.

The challenger's other significant problem was funding. On the positive side for Hatcher, just as also occurred in Cleveland's Democratic primary, an African American candidate had the pleasure of watching two white rivals battling over their voters. Bitter after his brother's loss to Katz in 1963, Bernard Konrady sought revenge for what appeared as a stolen victory. True to the prediction found on cards distributed to white voters at polling sites, "Think, A vote for Konrady is a vote for Hatcher." The final primary tally recorded 20,272 votes for Hatcher, 13,133 for Konrady, and 17,910 for Katz.

In the general election, Hatcher faced Gary furniture dealer Joseph Radigan, a "dull and lifeless" Republican. But no matter the opponent's personality, he was white, and race represented the all-important difference in Gary. From the outset, Hatcher understood the importance of downplaying color. With a theme of "Let's Get Ourselves Together," he promised Gary residents a multiracial Hatcher administration with respect and influence for every major religion in the city. John Krupa, the powerful chair of the Lake County Democratic Organization, denied Hatcher manpower support and money because of his refusal to grant the chair dictatorial powers over future appointments and patronage. On a tension-filled election day marked by an unusually high turnout among registered voters both black and white, Hatcher received 39,812 votes to Radigan's 37,947. From white voters, the winner received a total of 5,322 votes or roughly 14 percent of their ballots.[5]

Obviously upbeat and positive after a declaration of victory, Hatcher on election night thanked supporters and pledged fairness to all constituents. As he put it to triumphant followers in downtown Gary, "We shall prove that diversity can be a source of enrichment, that at least the people of one city in the nation have decided, finally, to get themselves together." The fact that less than 15 percent of the white electorate had voted for Hatcher was certainly no resolution for a racially divided city's residents "to get themselves together." At Hatcher's January 1, 1968, inauguration, the newly installed mayor expressed optimism about a bright future for Gary, with all residents working "to change the face of our city and unite the hearts of our citizens; to tear down slums and build healthy bodies; to destroy crime and create beauty; to expand industry and restrict pollution." As long as Mayor Hatcher and Gary could rely upon President Johnson as a generous benefactor, federal funds were available for improving the city. African Americans became the chief beneficiaries as money and jobs overwhelmingly went to the race's underprivileged residents, patronage recipients, and contractors. Left out to grumble were whites and a minority of African Americans with better-than-average incomes. As for Hatcher's reactions to opponents, he referred to them as "Uncle Toms and Aunt Sallys." Meanwhile blight spread, mills closed, crime soared, drug addiction rose, vacant houses increasingly marred whole city neighborhoods, and abandoned stores characterized downtown Gary's once bustling business district. Hatcher, though, remained optimistic throughout the city's abysmal decline, and prior to 1987 he continually won reelections. Then in Hatcher's fifth bid to stay on as Gary's mayor, he lost to Thomas Barnes. For the first time since 1967, whites and blacks united in opposition to their incumbent mayor. As Purdue University's Jon C. Teaford concluded about Gary residents' ouster of their longtime leader, Hatcher in defeat "had perhaps created a racial togetherness that escaped him in victory."[6] Dismal as the Indiana lakeshore city had become, placing the blame for its demise solely upon Hatcher is unfair. He had tried many different solutions with which to revive Gary, but he was generally helpless without infusions of federal funds, and with the Great Society's dismemberment, Republican presidents either terminated or underfunded federal programs for cities.[7]

Kenneth Gibson in Newark, New Jersey

Mayoral politics in Newark in 1970—in a manner reminiscent of what had transpired three years earlier in Cleveland and Gary—also posed obstacles for an African American political outsider who had enough courage to vie against the New Jersey city's white political establishment for control of the city. In many ways like 1967 in Ohio and Indiana, for a man to have enough courage and determination to run for mayor of Newark, and then to accomplish this forbidding task with the intention of serving *all* residents, presented dangerous challenges. The harder job was to govern the city effectively, and this task quickly proved even more daunting—as Kenneth Gibson soon discovered. Democratic voters during Newark's May 12 primary had the choice of renominating Hugh J. Addonizio—a two-term white mayor faced with an almost certain indictment for extortion—or of selecting Gibson, the African American challenger. Acting without restraint throughout the election, the incumbent attempted to frighten white voters with a characterization of his African American opponent as a close associate and political ally of Imamu Baraka (LeRoi Jones), a militant pan-African nationalist, inflammatory poet playwright, and well-known Newark resident. Addonizio especially enjoyed warning his white audiences about Jones, who, according to the mayor, "preaches hate whitey, rape their women, and steal from them." In contrast, Gibson conducted a moderate and low-key campaign. For Gibson, the emphasis was on the need for honest government and reform. With roughly 16 percent of white voters and 95 percent of the African American electorate choosing Gibson, Newark's citizens clearly desired change. The final tally showed that Gibson had won a landslide victory over Addonizio—55,097 votes to 43,086. The victor's plurality, however, did not silent detractors. Speaking sarcastically of African American victories in Gary, Cleveland, and then Newark, comedian Bill Cosby shocked a Saturday morning audience attending the weekly Chicago meeting of Operation PUSH, Jesse Jackson's activist self-help organization. Rather than celebrate the fact that another major city had chosen an African American mayor, Cosby mocked its overall significance, noting that one more time the only thing that the minority race had gained was another opportunity to govern a city that whites had abandoned and discarded as a worthless place to live. Although delivered in Cosby's deliberately slow but matter-of-fact way and clearly meant as bittersweet humor, few listeners found anything amusing about a sarcastic explanation for mayoral victories by Hatcher, Stokes, and Gibson.[8]

Coleman A. Young in Detroit, Michigan

Following the patterns and examples set in Gary, Cleveland, and Newark, Detroit's Coleman A. Young viewed enough encouraging signs in 1973 to embark upon the journey to become his city's mayor. More than six years earlier, during July 1967, several discouraging factors had led to a week of fatal shootings, looting, and burning. Among the catalysts for African Americans' revolt were hopelessness from unemployment and their low-wage jobs. Many bad experiences with and rumored reports of police brutality also fostered African Americans' resentment against authority. The Detroit race riot had not only caused many deaths and massive property destruction, it also generated more lasting legacies. Among these were a racially bifurcated urban population and continuing white flight to the suburbs from the city's neighborhoods. On November 4, 1969, with whites barely holding onto an electoral majority, their law-enforcement candidate for mayor, Roman Grubbs, barely defeated African American challenger Richard Austin in the "closest political contest in the city's history"[9] (257,312–250,000). But later, if the residents who had supported Grubbs had somehow maintained hopes for a reversal of urban unrest and for dominance again by whites in Detroit, their expectations went unfulfilled. In January 1971, with Grubbs's formation of STRESS (Stop the Robberies, Enjoy Safe Streets), the strain between African Americans and the city police accelerated.

Having lost almost all possibility for compromise, Grubbs drew a figurative line in the sand to set in motion a racially bifurcated mayoral contest in 1973. Coleman A. Young was on one side—a boisterous critic of harsh police tactics and a veteran civil rights champion. Police commissioner John Nichols was on the other side, the advocate of the white positions on law and order and the key architect and enforcer of STRESS. With the obvious strain of racial tensions running high in Motown on voting day, city residents split along racial lines. On November 7, 1973, whites overwhelmingly backed Nichols, and African Americans supported Young with equal unanimity. After the count, results showed that Young had won the election—by 233,674 votes to Nichols's 216,933. As the *Detroit News* concluded, "the 1973 Detroit Mayor's race was decided almost exclusively on racial grounds."[10]

For the few remaining white residents left in Detroit, Young's election elevated their fear of black retribution and favoritism to a compelling factor in many of their lives. Now possessing minority status in a city where African Americans had control, whites with the "economic means to flee" often did so as quickly as possible, leaving in their wake a weakened urban tax base, as well as fewer human and financial resources to tackle Detroit's mounting problems. To make matters even worse, the beginning of Young's mayoral career coincided with federal decisions that either sharply cut expenditures to cities or completely eliminated government programs for urban renewal and revitalization. Bitter because he had not received a fair chance to improve Detroit due to the massive white exodus, a hostile media, and Washington's stingy GOP administrations, Coleman A. Young became a frustrated mayor who eventually began to frequently lash out at the negative depictions of Detroit in national news reports: "The racist manner in which the media portrayed me made it difficult for my administration to institute change or attract investment to the city."[11]

The Changing Urban Scene in the South

Across the South, a different set of circumstances was unfolding. In major cities such as Atlanta, Birmingham, and New Orleans during the 1970s, African Americans—who for decades had retained minority-majority status but without any political clout—were now finally in the position to influence elections and even control city halls. What made the difference for a onetime largely disenfranchised race was the suffrage protection offered through federal voting-rights legislation; federal laws now guaranteed black citizens full constitutional powers. Measured by the number of registered voters in Birmingham and New Orleans, African Americans during the 1980s edged out whites for the first time since the outset of massive disfranchisement that had come before 1900. In Alabama, turnaround occurred in 1983, while in New Orleans it transpired three years later. Changes might have occurred even without the result of African American voting majorities because many white politicians were adjusting their attitudes to the changing political realities. Before 1975 and liberal-minded David Vann's mayoral victory in Birmingham, no African American had ever held an important executive staff position in Alabama's largest city. But under Vann's administration, African Americans gained four of the city's nine most desirable jobs, and another person of color headed a key department. Even earlier, in Louisiana, Moon Landrieu had integrated New Orleans. Prior to his win in the 1969 election, African Americans had never run a single Crescent City department, but after this reformer's inauguration they were managing five out of thirteen municipal operations.[12]

New Orleans and Birmingham

Elevating blacks to important positions with supervisory authority served in both cities as preliminary but very important steps to African Americans winning mayoral elections. The fact that minority managers could serve their municipalities with competence and fairness impacted so positively on a large enough number of open-minded whites that, when they were voting for city mayoral elections, they acted with enough willingness to overlook race as a primary factor in their selection. Sufficient numbers cooperated with solid minority voting blocs to elect Ernest N. "Dutch" Morial in 1977 and two years later Richard Arrington Jr. as the first non-white mayors of New Orleans and Birmingham, respectively. When Morial won, whites comprised 57 percent of the total number of registrants on Crescent City voting rolls, and in 1979 when Arrington competed for mayor, his victory represented what political scientists have classified as more or less a "deracialized campaign." It was an amazing feat because less than fifteen years earlier, pundits had derisively labeled Birmingham the "Johannesburg of America."[13] Yet by the city's 1979 election, a minority of whites had undergone a sufficient attitudinal change about race, resulting in the African American candidate receiving approximately 10 percent of all his winning plurality from members of the opposite race; apparently, liberal whites realized that their city's choice of a qualified African American to become the next mayor would symbolize progress for a city desperately trying to change its bad reputation. Probably in their roles as mayors in the South, Morial and Arrington caused more disappointments among members of their own race than among whites, because many African Americans had entertained unrealistically high expectations for jobs and favors. Most white residents, on the other hand, had simply hoped for nothing disastrous to occur from the presence of African Americans leading city governments in Louisiana and Alabama.[14]

Miami, Louisville, and Baltimore

In a few notable cases, mayoral campaigns did not end in victory for African American candidates in the South. Reasons for these failures varied. Following a large influx of Cubans into Miami, Florida, during the 1960s, diverse segments of the city's Hispanic community began to compete with both white and African American residents for political and economic power. In the large tourist and retail sectors of Miami's economy, the municipality's African American population found itself at a disadvantage because many jobs now required Spanish-language proficiency. Also, many Cubans who had arrived in Florida with middle-class mind-sets and experiences adjusted easily to the necessary requirements of starting and operating profitable business enterprises, and entrepreneurial activities generally went smoother for them than for African Americans. There was periodic civil unrest in some racially ghettoized neighborhoods and this, combined with a liberal African American political agenda, became an additional reason why neither unity nor shared purpose would grow between African Americans and Cubans. Latinos tended to prefer Republican over Democratic candidates because, often, GOP leaders proclaimed the most vigor in their commitment to fighting communism and liberating the Cuban regime from Fidel Castro. Cubans generally believed strongly in the value of individual initiative, and they opposed welfare and government-assistance programs. By 1990 the ever-growing Hispanic presence in Miami meant that forming a partnership with another hyphenated population was rendered pretty much unnecessary. The establishment of SALAD (the Spanish American League Against Discrimination), with its limited mission of protecting only Latino rights, was indicative of the Hispanic self-interest in Miami.[15]

For hopeful African American mayoral candidates elsewhere, it seemed that more chances of coalition building existed in Louisville and Baltimore than in Miami. As likely as the securing of white votes might have appeared at one time in Louisville, it would not occur in 1985. Entered in a three-way contest, Darryl Owens gained solid but not very enthusiastic African American support, and he received few votes from Louisville's white majority. Voter turnout in minority precincts was very low, and racial crossover voting was almost non-existent.

In an article, Sharon D. Wright discusses the difficulties that African American candidates have encountered in winning Louisville elections. By trying to balance the concerns of all potential coalition partners, African American office seekers have tended to weaken by default a vital position they might have held with their strongest and most enthusiastic supporters—the non-Caucasian electorate. In Baltimore in 1983, the efforts made by Judge William H. Murphy Jr. to ally with white feminists illustrate just how an attempt at gaining advantage with an outside group had the effect of alienating African American voters. As the election results show, Murphy miserably failed at connecting significantly with the entire electorate. Eventually through selection and not election, Baltimore had a black leader in city hall; in 1987 after Mayor William D. Schaefer's gubernatorial election victory, Clarence "Du" Burns received a council appointment as the governor-elect's temporary replacement. He was the first African American in Baltimore to occupy the highest municipal office. Burns's tenure ended only eleven months after his installation when he lost in a specially held vote to fill the office with a permanent elected official. Kurt Schmoke, an Ivy League-educated African American attorney, was the victor.[16]

Harold Washington in Chicago, Illinois

In terms of surprise and short-lived gains achieved by an African American winning a mayoral race, nothing surpassed the political aberration of Harold Washington's triumph in Chicago in 1983. Prior to this stunning victory, most of the twentieth century had witnessed Windy City politics under Democratic machine control, and African American congressmen such as Mitchell and Dawson and most minority representatives at city hall had depended upon white political bosses for their positions. The machine empowered and controlled an elaborate system with such complete power that political bosses manipulated and managed welfare payments and job distributions. Their power to offer giveaways had always enabled organizational leaders to provide precinct captains with enough tangible rewards to push for and guarantee election-day victories in exchange. Disgusted and discouraged as African American reformers were by this compromising arrangement, paralysis had prevailed in West and South Side ghetto neighborhoods because the sharpest critics of the machine could do no more than offer residents intangible promises of better, more democratic government.

Writing of Chicago in 1972, Quintard Taylor showed serious doubts about the machine's long-term sustainability. In the midst of Richard J. Daley's fifth mayoral term as undoubtedly the most powerful local politician in the United States, Taylor wrote, "The important question in the future will be whether the organization will be able to accommodate whites and Blacks simultaneously. It has been successful to this point, but it is not clear that it can continue to work its will." Daley's sudden death from heart failure on December 20, 1976, did not immediately answer Taylor's query, but machine control did eventually deteriorate— without "his honor" dominating city hall. Daley's successor, Michael Bilandic, lacked his predecessor's instincts for maintaining obedience and for exercising ultimate political power. After the daylong dumping of two feet of drifting snow on the city, on January 2, 1979, Chicagoans observed a figuratively paralyzed mayor. On television Bilandic proclaimed that there were passable side streets, but the residents living on these arteries knew differently. The absurdity of Bilandic's totally inaccurate assertions of successful plowing came just as he was starting his campaign for citizen support in the February 27, 1979, Democratic primary. The mayor's opponent was Jane Byrne, a rough, tough-talking rival who in her bid to unseat the mayor emphasized his inept supervision of snow removal. Bilandic lost to her. After Bilandic's most stunning primary loss to Byrne, the gruff victor easily defeated Republican Wallace D. Johnson on April 3, 1979, becoming Chicago's first female mayor. Both in the February primary and the April general election, African American voters offered Byrne their solid electoral support.[17]

For whatever reasons or motivations, Byrne erred by quickly distancing her office from her Bronzeville backers, thereby causing her African American constituents to feel both betrayal and resentment. She was also losing popular favor among many white residents. Opinion polls showed that Byrne's crude demeanor and Chicago's decline were both factors behind a growing alienation. Making matters worse for her, early in the 1980s a severe national economic slump caused disproportionate suffering in Chicago because so much of its life and prosperity depended on heavy manufacturing. In a once-vibrant urban environment where residents proudly boasted Chicago's reputation as "the city that works," many citizens were longing for a return to Daley-style control. Richard M. Daley, the deceased mayor's son, sensed the city's mood and Byrne's possible vulnerability in a bid for reelection. He decided to challenge her candidacy in the 1983 Democratic primary.

Meanwhile, opportunities also seemed better than at any time in the past for a successful African American mayoral bid. Aware of serious divisions among Chicago's whites, of promises from Jesse Jackson, and of encouragement and commitments from other African American leaders, Harold Washington somewhat reluctantly decided to accept the responsibility of running as the racial minority's hope to move Chicago in a more equitable direction. Washington, as a lawyer with experiences both in the state legislature and in Congress, first learned about Chicago-style politics from his father, Roy, a veteran South Side machine insider and a patronage recipient. Having observed the rewards his parent received for servile obedience, the son was content at the beginning of his political career to represent Mayor Daley in Springfield. Then, after the police slayings of Black Panthers Mark Clark and Fred Hampton in 1969, and in his reaction, like numerous other African American politicians in Chicago, Washington distanced himself from the machine to become independent and reform conscious.[18]

Byrne and Daley were so busy competing against each other that they dismissed almost entirely the possibility of their common rival's victory. The incumbent deceived herself into thinking that a few cameo appearances on the South and West Sides and some key endorsements from African American political hacks would suffice to restore enough voter confidence in her among the minority to ensure a second term. On the other hand, Daley did almost nothing to woo African American citizens, preferring instead to concentrate all his campaign efforts on the white neighborhoods. Neither Daley nor Byrne grasped how much anger had accumulated among Chicago's Latinos and African Americans.

For different reasons, but with similar results, whites living near the University of Chicago's Hyde Park campus and others residing in large Gold Coast mansions on the North Side or in expensive lakefront high-rise apartments along Lake Shore Drive also felt considerable disgust with Byrne—and distrust for Daley. Their alternative to voting for either of the two white contenders was to deliver a definitive message of discontent and protest in the form of support for Washington and his commitment to reform. Thus, in a total surprise, the result from primary-day voting on February 22, 1983, was a most astounding triumph by an underdog challenger over the status quo and traditional Chicago-style politics. The final vote showed Washington with 419,266 votes (36.3 percent), with Byrnes coming in second with 386,456 (33.5 percent), and trailing in third place, State's Attorney Daley with 343,506 (28.8 percent).

With a primary victory now recorded, Washington's next task was a campaign to win the city's general election for mayor. Bernard Epton, a mostly unknown figure among Chicagoans, emerged as the Republican candidate. While the Democratic nominee tried to keep the election focused on issues that were important to Chicagoans, his opponent relied upon a fear-mongering racist message. Epton advisors aimed television commercials at whites with a series of subtle suggestions, warning "now, before it's too late." Flyers circulating in white neighborhoods predicted "white women would be raped" if "Mr. Baboon gets into power." On election day, an estimated 82 percent of Chicago's white voters chose the previously little known GOP candidate with the race-baiting campaign. But the final votes show that Epton's scare tactics had not overcome the African American Democrat's more diverse support base of liberal whites, African Americans, Latinos, and organized labor; Washington's plurality was 48,321 votes out of some 1.28 million cast.[19]

Resistance to the African American did not end with his mayoral election. Recalcitrant forces at city hall were led by an opportunistic councilman, Edward R. "Fast Eddie" Vrdolyak, a slick politician who represented residents from an Eastern European immigrant enclave on Chicago's southeast corner, and an ambitious alderman from the Southwest Side, Edward M. Burke. There immediately began what pundits soon called "Council Wars." Among the fifty aldermen, Vrdolyak and Burke continued as the mayor's most obstructive foes in city council. The two men spearheaded an alignment of twenty-seven other members into a solid obstructionist bloc, which ably and consistently thwarted Washington. On any substantive reform issues introduced and backed by the mayor, there were almost always the twenty-nine aldermanic votes aligned against Washington-supported initiatives and twenty-one votes for them. In defending the status quo, the Vrdolyak-Burke aldermanic faction gave voice to white constituents' expectations, which was guardianship against an imagined revenge by Chicago African Americans for years of neglect and discriminatory treatment from successive postwar mayoral regimes.

An African American faculty member at Northeastern Illinois University put matters this way: "There's a fear among the white people. I can understand it. They think we're going to treat them the way they've treated us." Community-based organizations were at the core of Washington's agenda. His intended goals were neighborhood revitalization and power diffusion—actions aimed at dismantling and jettisoning machine politics. The mayor's reelection in April 1987 did much to end hostilities within the city council, and Chicago was clearly poised to benefit from an "era of good feelings." Then Washington suddenly died, on November 25, 1987, from a massive heart attack. His death quickly inspired old friends and foes to resurrect their hostilities. Eugene Sawyer emerged from chaotic fighting as a temporary beneficiary, because Vrdolyak-led forces opted to elevate this pliant African American alderman to the post of interim mayor. The selection of such a lackey and machine loyalist as Washington's replacement set off a firestorm of protest from aldermanic reformers led by the deceased mayor's supporters Danny Davis and Tim Evans. Both men had rivaled Sawyer for an opportunity to lead Chicago, but they lost. In 1989, after a special election held to complete Washington's four-year mayoral term, the Windy City returned to white rule with a victory by Richard M. Daley.[20]

Seattle and New Haven

In the same year, as a white resurgence occurred in the Windy City, completely different election stories unfolded in New Haven and Seattle. On opposite coasts, two cities—whose African American electorates did not constitute significant percentages of these municipalities' total populations—elected African American mayors. In neither case was the minority in any position to substantially contribute to candidate victories. In the home city of Yale University, where non-whites accounted for only one third of residents in 1989, John Daniels easily won a mayoral race on November 7, 1989, with about 68 percent of all the votes cast. In the primary and in the general election, Daniels obtained more white votes than any of his Caucasian opponents. Analysis of these two color-blind triumphs in Connecticut shows that white liberals combined with key elements from the business sector to support Daniels, as their dissatisfaction with and distrust of Mayor Ben DiLeto grew. Although DiLeto was not on the ballot, foes were certainly aware of the mayor's connection to candidate John DeStefano, the mayor's longtime political ally and friend. Consenting to be the outgoing mayor's stand-in surrogate for the New Haven political establishment earned DeStefano the sitting boss's unqualified endorsement as the only worthy successor. Daniels exploited New Haven's rising crime rate and its social service problems, and he linked the city's decline to the outgoing mayor's four terms of inept leadership. The sharpest criticisms directed at Daniels came from African American militants, who in their complaints asserted that the minority office seeker "was not Jesse Jackson"—a critical reference to the African American candidate's reluctance to discuss race during his campaigns.[21]

In the beautiful coastal city of Seattle where African Americans, at less than 8 percent of the population, represented a significantly smaller minority, Norman Rice's 1989 mayoral campaign also ended successfully. His victory redeemed a failed mayoral bid in 1985 as well as a loss for Congress in 1988. These defeats almost convinced Rice to abandon politics forever, but King County councilman Ron Sims was persuasive enough to change his mind. During a second try for the city's top political post Rice championed four causes: affordable housing, improved public education, crime prevention, and job creation. His white opponent, Doug Jewett, was a coauthor of "Initiative 34," a divisive ballot referendum. In addition to choosing Seattle's next mayor, voters faced a decision to vote either for or against Jewett's emotionally charged initiative against using mandatory busing to achieve integration in the municipality's public schools. With all opinion polls indicating strong electoral support for Jewett's proposal, busing became the main focus of his campaign. Although the primary-day ballot showed thirteen men vying for votes in the mayoral contest, the election evolved into a two-person race between Rice and Jewett. At 20 percent and 24 percent respectively, neither top contender won the required majority; the indecisive result forced the two into a runoff election. Once again, Jewett concentrated his campaign on support for Initiative 34, while Rice asserted that other issues had greater importance for Seattle residents. Asked for a position on busing, Rice replied that he was in favor of eliminating its mandatory use but only conditionally; first, every Seattle public school must provide all pupils with first-class learning experiences. Clearly stimulated by the electorate's interest in Initiative 34, voter turnout in the general election was unusually high for a Seattle mayoral contest. Rice's total of 93,491 votes (58 percent) overpowered his opponent's 67,276 (42 percent). Assessing how well Rice had done with an overwhelming white electorate, political scientist Mylon Winn imagined hopeful possibilities coming from Seattle's example; in particular, Winn foresaw similar victories occurring in other municipalities with equally insignificant African American populations. But in order for these to occur, Winn advised, minority candidates must follow "a campaign strategy that appeals to the entire population. When race becomes an issue it must be merged with a larger issue."[22]

Valuable perhaps as this counsel might appear as a useful formula for successful African American candidacies in cities where the racial makeup was predominantly Caucasian, Tom Bradley had already more or less practiced the same strategy since 1969 and his first attempt at becoming the mayor of Los Angeles. In fact, due to overarching effects on African American mayoral contenders nationally, Bradley—as the only non-white candidate ever to become a mayor of California's largest city—and some influential counterparts from Philadelphia, St. Louis, New York, and Atlanta deserve extended coverage and investigation. Excepting what would transpire in Georgia's capital, the African American mayors' experiences in the other four municipalities did not result in minorities permanently holding onto urban political power. Reasons for the loss of this control—together with analyses of victories and accomplishments—offer valuable lessons about the unwillingness of whites to share long-term city authority with African Americans.

Tom Bradley in Los Angeles

Born outside Calvert, Texas, in 1917 to poor sharecropper parents, young Tom Bradley arrived in Los Angeles seven years later with his mother and father. During his teen years, he traveled across town to attend the nearly all-white Polytechnic High School. While there the minority student's excellence in football and track attracted collegiate coaches' attention. Superb skills and speed earned the young man an athletic scholarship to attend the University of California, Los Angeles. After starring as a quarter-miler, Bradley left UCLA in 1940 sans degree and became a police officer. At that time the Los Angeles Police Department (LAPD) had some four thousand members; only about one hundred were African American, and two assignments awaited them. After becoming mayor, Bradley told a reporter from the *Los Angeles Times* about the special "colored" details: "you either worked Newton Street Division. . ., a predominantly black community, or you worked traffic downtown. You could not work with a white officer, and that continued until 1964."[23] As the officer's preparation for retirement from the LAPD, he attended law school at night. In 1961, after a twenty-one year career on the force, the veteran cop left law enforcement with the rank of lieutenant—the highest position heretofore achieved by an African American officer in LAPD history.

In addition to practicing law after retiring from the force, Bradley became politically active in the Democratic Party. In 1963 he made a first try for elective office, and he won a seat on the Los Angeles City Council—a feat never before attained by an African American in Los Angeles. Whites were clearly in the majority among Bradley's Tenth District constituents, but during the election some skillful coalition building helped him to overcome the hurdle of race to win. As a city councilman, Bradley criticized segregation within the LAPD and its brutal handling of the 1965 Watts Riots. During the ghetto neighborhood's eruption, Bradley noted how policemen abused their authority to detain and abuse anyone suspected of involvement in the rioting and looting. Carefully phrased, his complaints did not appear to come from an African American perspective. As the ex-policeman noted first about being a council member and then reconfirmed later as L.A.'s mayor, "I'm not a black this or a black that. I'm just Tom Bradley."[24]

More than empty words, this self-description characterized his 1969 effort to unseat Sam Yorty, Los Angeles' combative and conservative incumbent mayor. Probably no more than 18 percent of the population in 1969, African Americans were too few in number for any viable candidate (African American or white) to count on them as the base for waging a successful campaign in a citywide contest. Bradley understood the demographic mathematics of his city; he knew the obvious consequences of a one-sided appeal to so insignificant a constituency as L.A.'s African American voters. The idea never really featured in Bradley's political philosophy to leverage guilt concerning racism for selfish purposes. The ex-policeman comprehended the value of coalition building as the key to winning elections. Reliance upon this strategy had seen him elected to the city council. Once more, as he began preparing to run in the 1969 Los Angeles mayoral primary, he labored purposefully and with the most determined effort to incorporate some all-embracing liberal elements into the Bradley-for-mayor alliance. Jews were the most logical candidates for inclusion, because the city's WASPs had largely excluded them from political power(as they had with African Americans). Their base was the California Democratic Club (CDC), an activist body whose members loathed Yorty. Bradley was president of one of its integrated neighborhood chapters. Thus his appeal was twofold; among African Americans it revolved around racial identification, while among reform-minded whites it was the candidate's promise to provide "good government." Moreover, as a most vitally important third element of the challenger's coalition, organized labor became an integral part of the non-white candidate's support base.

Resulting from Yorty's alienation of business, labor, Democrats, and other factions, the incumbent looked so vulnerable that the mayoral primary in 1969 attracted not only Bradley's candidacy but also twelve other contenders. As much as the crowded field might have seemed disadvantageous to the African American councilman, it actually turned out to work to his advantage. One analyst concludes that this much competition helped Bradley's chances of winning: "several of the opponents were like quantities, cancelling one another out." Having an unprofessional organization became a much greater problem than a field congested with so many competitors, but the African American's excellent connections to liberal whites—as well as his successful penetration of the Hispanic community through his establishment of a cordial relationship with a powerful Mexican-American politician, Ed Roybal—compensated for what Bradley either lacked in political experience or lost from having an occasionally inept political operation. Part of the challenger's campaign strategy was to deliberately ignore African Americans; he meaningfully shunned them to give whites convincing proof that Bradley was not "the black candidate." All along during the primary, of course, nobody really had any doubts about the racial minority's support for Bradley. After obtaining 42 percent of the primary vote (but not the needed clear majority to prevent a runoff election), Bradley easily eclipsed incumbent Yorty's paltry 26 percent.

In the contest between an African American challenger and an incumbent mayor, Bradley seemed the one headed for victory. The *Los Angeles Times* endorsed the council member. So did California's two U.S. senators, Democrat Alan Cranston and Republican George Murphy. Jesse Unruh, a controversial figure but also a most powerful Californian because of commanding roles in Golden State Democratic politics and in the state general assembly as speaker, actively campaigned for Yorty's defeat. From both major political parties, assistance came to Bradley from nationally prominent leaders such as Republican Charles Percy and Democrats Eugene McCarthy, Hubert Humphrey, Adlai Stevenson, and Edward Kennedy. Hollywood movie stars made frequent appearances at Bradley rallies, speaking for the election of the African American city councilman. In response to a great outpouring of support for Bradley, the mayor relied on a major trump card—race. Yorty used it to frighten voters. Without any evidence he claimed his foe had a secret alliance with militant nationalists, and the mayor predicted the resignations of two thousand policemen should the election go to Bradley. Worse, Los Angeles' two-term incumbent placed a disturbing question before his audiences. He asked them, "Will your family be safe with this man?" With the civil unrest, looting, and arson of 1965 in Watts still very fresh in voters' memories, the mayor correctly calculated that utilizing a no-holds-barred strategy would have dramatic effects upon a large percentage of white Los Angelenos. The final count showed him winning the runoff with 53 percent to Bradley's 47 percent. The feisty incumbent registered significant victory margins among Chicano and white voters, while African Americans offered Bradley 89 percent of their vote total. In the analysis of John M. Allswang, the election results were easy to summarize: "Race and racism determined the outcome."[25]

With a proven legacy of relying upon strong determination to win athletic races while a student at UCLA and of overcoming racism in order to advance in rank as a LAPD officer, Tom Bradley demonstrated an unwillingness to allow his loss to Yorty thwart or undermine future plans to eventually become the mayor of L.A. This strong will to succeed resulted in some immediate preparations for the 1973 election. The first priority was to raise enough funds to hire a better, more professional election staff than the one available in 1969. Bradley was fearful that, without political talent onboard, his political message would never get to bombard Los Angeles airwaves in crucially influential commercials. By January 1, 1973, the second "Bradley for Mayor" effort had put together a campaign chest totaling more than a million dollars. With so much money on hand, the African American candidate had ample resources available to launch an important voter registration drive in African American neighborhoods. Bradley saw the need for taking this action after the board of elections had stripped numerous ghetto residents from the city voter rolls as a consequence of their nonparticipation in the 1972 elections. For the city sections of South Central Los Angeles and Watts, the systematic purges of the voting lists removed 30.35 percent and 26.56 percent, respectively, of all the previously registered voters. Bradley also supported a joint NAACP-United Auto Workers lawsuit that was on appeal to the California Supreme Court; its purpose was to enlist the justices by court order to restore some seven hundred thousand citizens to voter registries.[26]

Yorty had grown increasingly unpopular with Angelenos after the 1969 election, but his negative standing did not necessarily mean any decrease in obstacles ahead for Bradley. Stiff competition came from several other contenders. Months before Bradley's decision to run again for mayor, Unruh announced his candidacy for the municipal office, this only a short time after he had lost the governor's race to Ronald Reagan. Although Unruh enjoyed a great deal of support among African Americans because of his uncompromising liberalism on key social and economic issues, Yvonne Burke, a popular African American congresswoman from Los Angeles, admitted to feeling perplexed as to why anyone among the leaders of her race could ever support anyone but Bradley. In her opinion, he was "the only candidate for mayor all the people can rally around." Joel Wachs, a liberal council member, was another challenger with voter appeal; like Bradley, he had a loyal following among Jews in Los Angeles. As a strong law-and-order advocate, Tom Reddin, the ex-LAPD chief, was also in the running. He was a candidate with superb conservative credentials, but he appeared a threat to draw Democratic votes away more from Yorty than from the liberal trio of Bradley, Unruh, and Wachs.[27]

With primary day approaching, the candidates vied for endorsements. The Los Angeles County AFL-CIO Council announced its support for Unruh. In response, Yorty remarked that the union's leadership must "want someone in the mayor's office who is a stooge." An alliance of Protestant pastors favored the African American councilman. Expressing their preference in a full-page political advertisement that appeared in the *Los Angeles Sentinel* on March 22, 1973, the ministers who operated collectively as the "concerned clergy for Bradley for Mayor," elaborated on why they were backing the ex-policeman. Their case for Bradley revolved around his alleged better grasp of minority problems. Unruh also consistently relied upon this same weekly newspaper devoted to African American news. The state legislator incorporated a pair of major messages into his paid announcements: first, among African American elected officials, Bradley found himself without one endorsement from either a state legislator or a fellow council member; second, and even worse, was the former police officer's record in city government. Unruh was relentless in his criticisms of Bradley, emphasizing his foe's refusal to support a wage increase for sanitary workers. As shown by Bradley's positioning on this issue, the obvious conclusion, claimed Unruh, was that Bradley's overall record of providing help to African Americans was either detrimental or nonexistent. Editorially the *Sentinel* offered a considerably different and more upbeat assessment of the council member. It was the editor's opinion that the councilman possessed the integrity, experience, and background to become a superb mayor. According to the newspaper's endorsement, Bradley in fact "knows, understands, [and] loves Los Angeles." In a primary race that never emerged as a truly four-person race, winner Bradley outpolled everybody. He took 35.4 percent of the total vote; Yorty followed with 28.9 percent, Unruh gained 17.4 percent, Wachs and Redden combined to obtain 18.3 percent.[28]

Once more, because no mayoral primary contender actually achieved a majority, L.A. election law dictated another runoff to decide which of the two top vote recipients would emerge as the city's leader. Thus it was a repeat contest between Yorty and Bradley. According to several reports and polls, however, opinions as well as temperaments of Angelenos had changed considerably since 1969. The two mayoral candidates also demonstrated attitudinal shifts. Unlike in his bid for reelection four years earlier, the incumbent now referred less to Bradley's race; his preference in 1973 was to underscore Los Angeles' greatness. As a news magazine article explained, the Watergate scandal and the Nixon reelection team's dirty tricks had negatively affected the willingness and receptivity of white Angelenos to accept any ludicrous attempts by Yorty to link Bradley to any extreme positions by well-known African American revolutionaries. A white electorate—no longer as gullible for race-baiting tactics as it had been four years earlier—was generally more willing to accept, even embrace, Bradley's personal assurances about distancing himself from and not associating with African

American militants. In one of his statements that "exuded moderation," Bradley put race in this context: "This city is ready not for a black man, not for a red man, a yellow man, or a white man, but for the best man." As for their positions on actual issues, in fact, not much separated Bradley's views from Yorty's. Differences emerged over oil drilling in the Pacific Palisades and investing in public transportation. On the wisdom of tapping into the offshore petroleum deposits, Bradley opposed development, whereas the incumbent mayor favored opening up the area to drilling. Bradley championed Los Angeles' development of rapid public transportation, and Yorty completely ignored the subject. To downplay any perceptions of a weakness on crime, Bradley used a series of television commercials showing him dressed in his old police uniform. Always portraying himself in more or less the same way as "a politician who happens to be a black," the L.A. councilman apparently made Yorty's wild allegations and all his unfounded charges and insinuations look "silly" to a majority of the electorate. With each of Los Angeles' three main voting components, Bradley enjoyed successfully positive results. A preliminary city-voting analysis showed the challenger gaining 92 percent of the city's African American vote, more than 51 percent of the Hispanic electorate, and roughly 50 percent among white Angelenos. Yorty, bitterly disappointed after his trouncing 54 to 46 percent, blamed defeat on a lower than usual voter turnout among white working-class residents of San Fernando Valley. These citizens will be sorry, the embittered loser predicted, because "The change that will take place will be a very radical one. And there will be a lot of people who'll wish that they had gone out to vote."[29]

If four reelections and five terms are an indication of how a majority of white residents viewed their African American mayor, Yorty's dire prophesy that Angeleno whites would eventually regret their role in Bradley's mayoral victory never did come about. On July 5, 1973, only days after the winner's inauguration, the *Los Angeles Sentinel* cautioned African Americans against any overly high expectations. Essayist Emily F. Gibson wrote that, as minority residents of Los Angeles, "we are fooling ourselves if we expect life in Los Angeles to be appreciably different now that a black man sits in the highest seat." As a realist, she contemplated the city's future for members of her race: "black representation and black leadership cannot and will not solve our basic problems so long as the political-economic system of this country remains the same." Less pessimistic voices were also heard. A gospel singer who had performed at Bradley's July 1 swearing-in ceremony proclaimed how elevating an African American to mayor represented "a blessing from God." As perhaps the best verification of how wrong Yorty and the inaugural performer turned out to be—either in dismal predictions or in overly optimistic anticipations—note what white residents and the mayor asserted ten months after Bradley's elevation to the most important municipal office in Los Angeles. For residents suspicious and skeptical about the installation of an African American as their mayor, many whites now found enough relief in positive results to proclaim how "He's one of us." Bradley also expressed personal joy; as he put it, "these days I rarely hear the term 'black mayor.'"[30]

Then again the city he was overseeing was outwardly and racially different than Newark, Gary, Detroit, or Cleveland. As Shana Alexander, writing for *Newsweek*, distinguished the dynamic Southern California municipality: "Los Angeles is no decaying ghetto." It was a vibrant city with a growing economy. It was a mecca for both tourists and newcomers in search of job opportunities. Unlike the white flight taking place in other cities, African Americans had actually decreased as a percentage of Los Angeles' total population between 1960 and 1970. Here on the West Coast, a white majority never expressed as much fear of "them" taking over Los Angeles with Bradley at the helm as counterparts elsewhere surmised from similar political occurrences with minority leaders. Campaign donations to L.A.'s African American mayor for each of his four reelection efforts illustrate the point. His fund-raisers always netted large sums of money, which came primarily from affluent white donors. Bradley's mayoral efforts were well financed, never shoestring-budgeted affairs. After his first election in 1973, he was in the midst of hosting a reception for major contributors when his microphone stopped functioning. Aware of the problem Bradley was having, an electronics industry millionaire who had recently donated $200,000 to help bankroll the mayor's campaign volunteered to fix the malfunctioning device. In his response, Bradley, in his best imitation of the demeaning dialect from the *Amos 'n' Andy* radio show, brought laughter to a predominantly white audience of influential and affluent Angelenos with his rejection of the offer, saying "Ah iz de mayor now."[31]

His response illustrates much of the reason Bradley from 1973 to 1993 was able to retain office in a West Coast city where his race never hovered much above 18 percent of the total population. He cajoled whites instead of threatening them. Here was a resourceful man who understood survival in an otherwise hostile world for African American politicians. His talent, both he and Yorty agreed, was being evasive. Bradley considered himself "fiscally conservative and liberal on other issues; you cannot pin me down." Stating essentially the same thing, Bradley's former rival for office provided a simple but generally accurate assessment of the mayor's popularity in 1981: "He doesn't offend people because he doesn't take a stand on anything."[32]

For many African Americans living in Southern California, especially those from Watts and South Central Los Angeles, strong desires existed for their mayor to say and do more about the problems in the ghettos. Yet these blighted communities never became Bradley's priority. Six months after the inauguration, in answer to what the minority could expect from him, the mayor's reply was only a vague promise to maintain a strong resolution to act fairly and responsively on his personally comprehensive knowledge of African American difficulties. Yet Bradley's twenty-year tenure as mayor of Los Angeles accomplished little in measurable terms of altering the quality of life for ghetto residents. The city's racial minority remained, as always, mired in poverty, unemployment, grime, crime, and despair.[33]

If the African American mayor's five terms had not to any degree changed existences in blighted communities, one might question whether his empowerment left any positive legacies at all for African Americans—or if he actually contributed much of value for the remainder of Los Angeles. Within the municipal workforce, favorable gains for all minorities and women did in fact occur to some extent during the Bradley years. At the beginning of his mayoralty in 1973 (see Table 2), whites held almost two-thirds of all city jobs.

Table 2. L.A. Government Workers Identified by Ethnicity, Race, or Gender, 1973 and 1991

GROUP	1973 Percentage	1991 Percentage
Whites	64.1	46.0
Blacks	21.9	22.4
Latinos	9.3	19.9
Asians	4.0	7.5
Women of all backgrounds	16.0	25.5

Source: Sonenshein, Politics in Black and White, 152; the source denotes neither race nor ethnicity for women.

The percentage of white governmental employees dropped significantly, but in most instances their places did not pass to African Americans. It was Latinos, Asians, and women who gained the most jobs during the Bradley era.

African Americans fared better at obtaining the highest level placements. In terms of percentages for the same time span, it is possible to ascertain the degree to which supervisory-level positions passed from whites to the city's minorities(see Table 3).

Easily extrapolated from the figures for each minority group is the rise of better opportunities for municipal supervisory employment. For African Americans with experience and education, city jobs with greater responsibilities and higher salaries were finally opening up. Policies from Bradley thus promoted— for a relatively miniscule portion of L.A.'s entire African American community— some movement into middle-class status.[34]

During Yorty's twelve years as mayor, complaints of brutality by the LAPD were common from ghetto residents. Investigations into one neighborhood's violent explosion into days of rioting during 1965 declared that a major contributor

Table 3. Two Categories of Supervisory-Level Employment in Los Angeles, 1973–1991, Given in Percentages by Ethnicity, Race, and Gender.

	Officials/Administrators		Professionals	
GROUP	1973	1991	1973	1991
Whites	94.7	70.9	81.4	54.9
Blacks	1.3	10.5	5.0	12.0
Latinos	2.6	7.5	4.6	11.1
Asians	1.3	8.0	8.0	15.4
Women	3.0	14.9	11.9	29.9

Source: Sonenshein, Politics in Black and White, 153; the source denotes neither race nor ethnicity for these women.

to unrest was the unfair, harsh treatment of African Americans by white cops. Although Bradley introduced a degree of outside control over the police department and encouraged the recruitment of minority officers, William Parker remained in control as a more or less autonomous chief until his retirement and the passage of his commanding position to equally powerful Daryl Gates. The best evidence that changes from the Bradley-Gates administration had not resulted in significantly better treatment of residents from L.A.'s African American enclaves occurred on March 3, 1991.

Caught on video and shown around the world on the evening news two days later was a viciously brutal assault by Los Angeles uniformed policemen on detained African American motorist Rodney King. Within days, television viewers globally had become eyewitnesses to the beating. As a result of stiff pressure from Congresswoman Maxine Waters and several other African American leaders, Bradley publicly rebuked the police assailants and advised Gates to resign as the LAPD's chief of police. This suggestion ultimately split the mayor from ten of the thirteen city council members, and generated hostile disapproval among most white Angelenos. Finding so much support, Gates stubbornly refused to surrender his position as police chief. Meanwhile on April 29, 1992, after reviewing the prosecution's case against the policemen for their alleged use of unnecessary physical force against an unarmed civilian, a suburban jury found each of the involved officers innocent of all charges. At news of the verdict, Los Angeles erupted into days of rage; the rioting, according to Raphael Sonenshein, "seemed to endorse all the times that police officers [had] stopped, insulted, or injured African-Americans."

Moved seemingly by the inner city's violently destructive reaction, the mayor launched "Rebuild Los Angeles" (RLA), a nonprofit corporation that was chartered specifically to interest development of a private sector consortium to assist in bringing more jobs and prosperity to the worst of the city's blighted, strained neighborhoods. Much hoopla surrounded a one-billion-dollar pledge in investments in ghetto developments from a group of corporations, but later, for the community activists who observed almost no evidence of tangible results, the monetary commitment represented "ghost funds." As for Bradley, a consistent centrist, whatever still remained of his creditability and support among Los Angeles's ghetto residents vanished, seemingly now forever. In a move independent from the mayor, Congresswoman Waters became more active, developing in the process a stronger base of loyal, enthusiastic support among African American Angelenos than the mayor had going for him because of her demonstration of so much greater devotion to and interest in their issues.[35]

The example of Bradley—an African American mayor of a dynamic, growing city—held more intangible than practical value for most of the minority in Los Angeles. In one of the rare instances when the mayor did refer to race, he speculated about the role his political rise and empowerment might play for young people: "Uppermost in my mind was every black youngster who sees me as a role model and says, 'If Tom Bradley can make it, so can I.'" On behalf of the African American children of L.A., Bradley never gave their educational needs much attention by working to improve their deplorably inadequate public schools. During his first term, Bradley did express public concern about what he called "miseducation" and provided a brief outline of remedies, but nothing much in the nineteen years that followed gave any indication that he prioritized inner-city education. An observer, Eric Mann, was most critical in his assessment of the black mayor's twenty years at the head of the Los Angeles city government. In Mann's view, African Americans saw only a negative result from Bradley's two-decade tenure, and this critic reached the unflattering conclusion that the mayor's policies and actions actually contributed to furthering the "impoverishment, deindustrialization, and decline of L.A.'s black community."[36]

Mayor Bradley's will to politically survive in a majority white city explains why he, although an African American, was apparently so unmotivated to direct significant sums of money and attention to solving the problems in the Latino barrios and African American ghettos. Even if Bradley had not read Yorty's prediction in response to a defeat in 1973 that whites would quickly regret their lack of support for a white candidate, the mayor was acutely aware of the fragile nature of the enabling coalition behind his victory as an African American candidate in a predominantly majority-majority city. Significant financial support came for every Bradley campaign from powerful wealthy interests—the result of their selfish expectations, which had nothing to do with using municipal resources to improve conditions in the ghettos. The long-serving mayor was not naïve; from the outset, he knew that either downtown development would serve as the thrust of policies or his tenure would terminate after one term. Stephen Gayle offers insights into Bradley's predicament. The African American mayor became the Golden State's "own version of Dwight Eisenhower" because, as Gayle concludes, Bradley had close ties to big business, and he followed a middle-of-the-road approach in almost everything. As mayor, his city hall door, for example, remained always open to influential corporate representatives from Atlantic Richfield, Bank of America, Occidental Petroleum, and the Los Angeles Chamber of Commerce. A policy directed at downtown Los Angeles resulted in a new skyline, with massive glass and steel skyscrapers. Big tax incentives together with other inducements encouraged commercial real estate developers to buy and build on vacant or condemned land. Bradley gained a reputation as a builder and fiscal conservative who maintained tight control over public expenditures. Willie Brown, as speaker of the California state assembly, captured the reason for the mayor's political survival: "the secret of Bradley's success is that he is not perceived as a black by non-blacks, but he is perceived as a black by fellow blacks. He has never championed any black issue in a manner threatening or displeasing to non-blacks. Bradley has no enemies—people either like him or don't know him."[37]

Overall, in white voters' judgment, Bradley's successes exceeded setbacks. In addition to feeling pride for his important role in revitalizing and growing downtown Los Angeles, Bradley boasted of other accomplishments. His city hosted the 1984 Olympics without incurring any debt, which gave the mayor a great amount of personal satisfaction. His leadership in large part was responsible for the start to a rapid-transit system; his efforts were behind several factors allowing Los Angeles to boast that the city was the "capital of the Pacific Rim." *Businessweek* described Bradley as "one of Japan's favorite American politicians."[38]

On the other side of the ledger, however, throughout Bradley's twenty-year tenure one can find accusations of illegal activities and personal disappointments, too. The mayor had confidence in 1982 that across California he could benefit from assembling a coalition force similar to the one that had worked so well for his mayoral victories, enabling him to capture the state governorship. Republican opponent George Deukmejian focused a vituperative campaign on race against him, however, and the GOP candidate deliberately tried to connect the mayor of Los Angeles to unpopular governor Jerry Brown. Through election eve, opinion polls indicated that, by a landslide, California voters were about to elect an African American Democratic mayor as their next state governor. It failed to occur, however. In an extremely close contest, with a total registering of 7.7 million votes cast for the two gubernatorial candidates, the mayor's Republican foe won with a plurality of 93,000. So many white voters had told pollsters of their intention to vote for Bradley, the fact that they did not became known as the "Bradley effect"—an apparent reluctance of whites to admit their unwillingness to elect an African American candidate. Bradley—left stunned and saddened by this unexpected defeat in much the same way as he had been in 1969 after the Yorty victory—quickly recovered and succeeded in winning a fourth mayoral term in 1985. His confidence restored, Bradley decided that challenging the incumbent governor's reelection bid in 1986 might end this time in the Republican's defeat, but the second campaign effort against Deukmejian ended in an even more resounding defeat than his battle of four years earlier.[39]

Approximately two months later, and more than two years before the 1989 city elections, Bradley announced plans to go for a fifth mayoral term. Disclosures about conflicts of interest became public before a reelection campaign could begin, however. A series of damaging public revelations pointed to some awkward ties between Bradley and a pair of large banks doing business with Los Angeles. One of them he served as a paid director, and the other employed the mayor as a paid consultant. A paper trail reportedly showed an order issued by Bradley to the city treasurer to deposit two million dollars in one of these banks. Also emerging at this time to besmirch his reputation as an honorable public servant were some other unrelated allegations involving more conflicts of interest, insider investments, and several income-disclosure irregularities. As a consequence, final opinion polls taken before Bradley's retirement in 1993 showed a drop in his approval rating to their lowest level during the mayor's twenty-year tenure.[40]

Jesse Jackson, when mourning Bradley's death on September 29, 1998, offered a most positive eulogy, nevertheless. Considering the pioneering African American politician who had benefited from a Horatio Alger storybook rise to fame and prominence, Jackson thought the deceased mayor's greatest accomplishment was his ability to foster a significant coalition of African Americans, Orientals, whites, Hispanics, and Jews. Under Bradley's fair-minded and consistent leadership, according to Jackson's generous assessment, "they all found common ground." As for all the serious allegations of Bradley's involvements in varied conflicts of interest and other questionable practices, but without an indictment for any of these claims of wrongdoing, Jackson noted how Bradley's escape from prosecution had completely confirmed how a sharecropper's son had "walked through the fire and was never even singed by the smoke." Jackson's positive verdict of innocence may to some degree have been accurate, but Angelenos—looking for an honorable successor to Bradley—turned from selecting another African American Democrat to electing Republican Richard Riordan because, according to the *Economist*, "the golden age of black power is fast fading."[41]

Shifting Politics in Atlanta

While a mixed-race coalition with infusions of major inputs from a significant number of whites helped to elect an African American mayor in 1973 in Los Angeles, Atlanta, with a totally different combination of forces, produced a similar result. Unlike the California city with a clear legacy of de facto discrimination against both racial and ethnic minorities, a long history of de jure segregation epitomized Georgia's racial situation. Since the patterns found among people in Los Angeles typified demographic conditions of Western and Northern cities, covert injustices affected neither their growth nor their prosperity. On the other hand, Atlanta needed to advance and thrive, and the city's civic and business leaders began to recognize the importance of change as a catalyst to development. They therefore understood the need to work for greater inclusion of the city's African American residents. This desire for greater economic vitality led to a pragmatic recognition that Atlanta's negative reputation as the Southern citadel of Jim Crow practices must end and be replaced by a more positive image. As part of this remaking effort, Mayor William Hartsfield began boasting of a city "too busy to hate." Unlike civic rulers found elsewhere across the region, white moderates on race controlled Georgia's capital from the mid-1950s through 1973. During mayoral elections, with assistance from overwhelming African American voting pluralities, Hartsfield, along with successors Ivan Allen and Sam Massell, easily defeated challenges from blatantly reactionary candidates such as the committed segregationist Lester Maddox, an unapologetic racist whom Allen defeated in 1961.[42]

Maynard Jackson

As much as moderates administered the city, there was no African American presence on Atlanta's eighteen-member council before 1965. After the 1969 election, the number of African American aldermen increased from one to four, and in the same year Atlanta citizens selected Maynard Jackson as their vice mayor, thereby empowering a minority member with the city's second most powerful elective position. Having this particular person in a major office posed no threat to the status quo because Atlanta's leading entrepreneurs were familiar enough with his family background to have complete trust in his values. Jackson's father had for many years been the senior pastor of one of the major Baptist churches in Atlanta, and his mother had taught French at Spelman College. Massell and Jackson coexisted on good working terms until the vice mayor announced his plans to enter Atlanta's 1973 mayoral primary. Suddenly all traces of racial harmony seemed to vanish. Massell, now fearing that a significant threat had developed to his chances for reelection, responded with overt racist appeals to whites. Apparently it was the incumbent's hope that by instilling enough fear into white voters, he might galvanize them into a concerted backlash against a black mayoral challenger. "Atlanta's Too Young to Die"[43] was Massell's dire warning, but in the end this and other appeals to racism backfired on the mayor, however. One Atlanta editor, reflecting upon Jackson's primary and general election victories, put the city's political situation in a simplified but correct perspective: "Blacks have the ballot box and whites have the money."[44]

As a campaigner, Jackson declared that African Americans needed "a place at the table" and "a piece of the pie,"[45] but less than twelve months after his inauguration, these easily uttered promises collided with the much harder reality of governing a major city as complex as Atlanta. There were reasons for Jackson's inability to fulfill his earlier generous commitments. Within city boundaries African Americans represented a majority of residents, but Atlanta was most dependent upon five collar counties or the Standard Metropolitan Statistical Area (SMSA). Jackson quickly realized that if he were to push too much and too hard for African Americans within Atlanta's city limits, this would simply accelerate a white residential flight to the suburbs and force many businesses to relocate to outlying areas. As if these realities were not clear enough, he received a letter of warning. In a blunt message to the mayor, the president of Central Atlanta Progress (CAP), a powerful civic body that spoke for and represented the city's largest and most influential downtown businesses, threatened Jackson with eminent disinvesting in Atlanta's commercial and financial hub if his administration persisted in what the business leaders judged an anti-white agenda. A reiteration of basically the same message came to the mayor from elite members of the commerce community, who convened a forum for discussing Atlanta's apparent misdirection under Jackson. The mayor, apparently now sobered by what he had read and heard, began inviting top business moguls to confer with him every two or three weeks. A main result from these exchanges—known as Jackson's Pound Cake Summit sessions—was a solid commitment from CAP to continue its expansion and revitalization plans for downtown Atlanta. Jackson listened and adjusted; thus economic development pushed so hard by Atlanta's influential white power establishment assumed primary importance, and it became Jackson's top priority.[46] As analysts Clarence Stone and Carol Pierannunzi assess a change of mayoral direction, "the business sector in Atlanta has pulled city hall towards its agenda." Gone completely was a thrust found at the outset of the mayor's term to involve representatives from city neighborhoods extensively in municipal governance and in city decisions.[47]

Andrew Young

Jackson decided during his second term not to run for reelection, which meant the passing of power to a new Atlanta mayor. A primary offered city voters a choice between two African American candidates and one white hopeful. Of the black pair, very few observers gave Reginald Eaves much chance against the much better known Andrew Young. The favorite had assisted the Reverend Martin Luther King Jr., had served as a member of the House of Representatives, and, until a flap erupted over an unauthorized meeting with a representative of the Palestinian Liberation Organization, had been the American ambassador to the United Nations. State legislator Sidney Marcus pinned his hopes of winning on solid white support and enough African American crossover votes to emerge victorious. Although neither Marcus nor Young achieved a clear majority during the primary, experts more or less agreed that a runoff election would end in a landslide victory for the African American. In a contest demarcated along racial lines, results scripted out predictably; 55 percent of the electorate chose Young over Marcus.[48]

Even more so than his predecessor, the new African American mayor recognized what Clarence N. Stone has critically judged "the business elite is the coalition that works."[49] Young spoke of it as "public purpose capitalism,"[50] while offering business leaders open access to his office at city hall. Looking back at his two terms, the mayor reminisced fondly about completed downtown hotels and office towers, and he pointed with satisfaction to an expanded MARTA (Metropolitan Atlanta Rapid Transit Authority). In terms of disappointments, Young thought he had not done enough to provide affordable housing and combat crime. While these problems did have his sympathy as mayor, they never became anywhere near his main priorities. Not surprisingly, his strongest supporters were most often Atlanta's white corporate leaders, and his harshest critics were African American community activists. Developer John Portman noted how everyone in Atlanta "can feel proud of Mayor Andrew Young,"[51] but several residents did not find very much to praise. Urban Crisis Center head Charles King, economist Robert L. Woodson, and Susie LaBord—president of the public housing tenant association, were among critics who expressed public outrage and disapproval of Mayor Young's "trickle down" theory of progress because it "doesn't work for black people."[52] As the unofficial representative of people in her community, LaBord was particularly negative about mayoral neglect of poor residents and Young's lack of leadership: "So many times, things happen and we can't find him. If he is concerned, you'd never know it. This city hasn't moved forward. There ain't no better jobs and they are getting harder and harder to get. He should be doing more."[53] In many respects, Atlanta was like Los Angeles under Bradley. Minority interests in the Georgia capital—first under the leadership of Maynard Jackson and subsequently under Andrew Young—almost always seemed to be sacrificed on the altar of downtown developers and entrepreneurs. A witty and sarcastic critic, pointing to all these mayoral shortcomings, called the affliction "edifice complex." In the wake of Bradley's two statewide election failures, Atlanta's second African American mayor also tried and failed to win a statewide election. In the 1990 Democratic gubernatorial primary, Young polled less than 29 percent of the state vote against Zell Miller, the same candidate that, ironically, he had defeated in a 1972 House contest when King's former aide initially had won a seat in Congress.[54]

Maynard Jackson's Return

By 1989 white politicians more or less conceded that their chances of ever capturing another mayoral election in Atlanta were hopeless. The subsequent race for mayor became a contest between Jackson, making a return to city politics, and Michael Lomax, chair of the Fulton County Commission. Generally familiar with both African American candidates, the Atlanta electorate had to choose between an ex-mayor who allegedly opposed sacrificing more city neighborhoods to highway construction and claimed to reject plans for erecting a new domed baseball stadium at a site where poor African Americans resided and the county official who favored road building and the new sports complex. As the election drew near, polls were indicating Lomax would lose by a significant margin. In a gamble to win, the county leader launched new political commercials with implications that Jackson during his earlier two terms as mayor had demonstrated a tendency to be soft on crime. Although Lomax was, like Jackson, an African American, many black voters judged the underdog candidate's campaign advertisements to be racial profiling; therefore, they backfired. Sensing a defeat two months before the election, Lomax withdrew his candidacy, thereby leaving fiery Hosea Williams as Jackson's only opponent. Sharp contrasts between two remaining contenders were immediately apparent to voters. In an obvious pitch to transect racial lines, the former mayor directly aimed his campaign message at middle-class residents. In an appeal intended for an obviously different audience, Williams tried to capitalize on a career built around his efforts to help low-income African Americans, but the equally difficult dual tasks of first mobilizing a population segment without much political savvy and then trying to solidify this element of the city into an effective movement behind a candidate proved impossible. The consequence was an overwhelming victory for Jackson; he won with 79 percent of the total vote. Williams received only 16.5 percent, and an assorted group of fringe candidates in the mayoral race combined for 4.5 percent. Once more in Atlanta, the winner of the mayoral election had demonstrated enough capacity for apparent interest in both neighborhood issues and city development to emerge with sufficient voter support.[55]

William Campbell of Atlanta

Groundwork laid by Jackson and Young's combined five Atlanta mayoral terms allowed their successor William "Bill" Campbell to glide smoothly and easily into commanding city hall in 1993. While a youngster growing up in North Carolina, Atlanta's newest mayor had gained notoriety in 1960 as one of the integrators of Raleigh's public schools. Nonetheless, in 1993, Campbell's becoming the third different African American mayor of Atlanta did not have any pacesetting elements. An observant and compliant man, Campbell understood the elements that had always worked effectively for his black predecessors. He knew as well as anyone the negative results of upsetting the white business leadership with an overly ambitious agenda aimed at uplifting Atlanta's downtrodden underclass. In other words, he recognized that using revenue derived from a sharp raise in property taxes on commercial real estate holdings to help alleviate poverty would not be acceptable. Already during Atlanta's budget crisis in the summer of 1994—one that threatened the city with a lower bond rating—proof of Campbell's awareness of consequences was noticeably evident. Rather than request a tax increase from council members, he ordered cost-cutting measures. It was Campbell's advice to net major targeted revenue savings from reducing all garbage-truck schedules and suggesting early retirement for high-ranking police officers. The African American mayor understood and acknowledged CAP's preferences for cutting back municipal services and eliminating experienced law officers from the city payroll as better political alternatives to raising taxes.[56]

Also in 1994 but with a very different response, the mayor met with determination an equally serious crisis that demanded financial resources. In January, three water mains broke, causing not only a critical shortage of water but also a repair bill of $500 million. These ruptures, it turned out, represented a much larger municipal infrastructure problem. Parks, bridges, viaducts, and many other public assets, according to Campbell, were "crumbling and eroding in front of us. It's like the old television commercial [for changing to a particular brand of motor oil] where either you pay now or pay later." To perform the necessary repairs and to provide upgrades, the mayor backed a referendum for an authorization of bonds to fund the work. Thus, on one hand, he requested a one-half mill rollback on property taxes, while on the other hand, he sought to obtain Atlanta taxpayer approval of long-term funding through a public offering of new municipal securities. Editorially the voice of the African American community, the *Atlanta Daily World* favored passage, and across racial lines, Campbell gained support for bonds from two diverse community groups which did not always agree about such matters, RIOT (Rollback Increase On Taxes) and CARE (Committee for Atlanta's Revitalization and Enhancement). Voters approved the referendum on July 19, 1994; an impressive 73 percent of them backed the mayor's assessment of need for an issuance of bonds to provide infrastructure improvements.[57]

After less than one month at city hall, Campbell denied accusations that during Atlanta's preparations for hosting the Super Bowl, police were under mayoral orders to sweep homeless people from the capital's streets. According to rumored reports, Campbell wanted undesirable elements removed from view in order to enhance the city's image. "Absolutely not. Never happened. A figment of somebody's imagination. I met last week with a number of homeless groups and homeless individuals and the buck stops here. We're treating the homeless with dignity. I have no idea where this notion comes from. It's been perpetuated to the point where people believe it's true." All Campbell freely admitted was a personal command for a police crackdown against what he considered "obnoxious" panhandling.[58]

Whether Campbell wanted police to rid Atlanta of homeless people during Super Bowl week or not, such action was consistent with his stated first priority as mayor, that is, to "make Atlanta a safer city." On the eve of taking the oath to become mayor, he noted that this goal could be achieved from the implementation of additional walk and beat patrols. In addition, Campbell intended his administration "to [be] running government like a business and saving [money for] taxpayers." To reporters gathered for his pre-inaugural press conference, Campbell also declared that he favored the establishment of city enterprise zones and the revival of "Sweet Auburn," the once thriving but now quickly decaying African American neighborhood of Dr. King's Atlanta childhood.[59]

True to his pledge, fighting crime developed into an administrative priority. At least it was a favorite topic of the mayor's speeches. Campbell used the designation of April as Youth Month to announce his six-point program directed at preventing youth violence in Atlanta. The plan included "Tickets for Kids," a distribution of free admissions to concerts and other events. As an essential key to reducing street crime, Campbell emphasized a need for greater police visibility through more bicycle and beat patrols, but in his view, a much greater long-lasting effect in the struggle against criminal activity would come from parents instilling moral values in their children. As he put it, considering the relationship between parental responsibility and cutting crime: "our children simply need more care, guidance and direction. We'll never solve the problem by giving longer prison terms and building more jails."[60] A substantial grant, courtesy of the Clinton administration, proved helpful in Atlanta's battle to make the city safer. Georgia's capital was only one of four American cities placed in a pilot program with federally funded strengthening of the police force; Atlanta's share was $1.5 million. Other law-enforcement actions also resulted. With mayoral preapproval, Atlanta police swept through several zones on August 24, 1994, in raids that led to 157 arrests on 357 charges ranging from drug trafficking to prostitution and weapons violations. After this night of sustained and coordinated action against criminal activity, Campbell noted, the police had fulfilled his campaign promise "to be tough" on criminals. As Atlanta prepared to host the 1996 Olympic Games, residents often heard Campbell pledge his unwillingness to compromise with criminal activity. The mayor committed this when he spoke to residents in May 1996: "Atlanta will be a safer city . . ., the safest place on the globe."[61]

In following his agenda of law and order, Campbell pledged to undertake something that proved difficult to fulfill immediately. This was his promise to stop "Freaknik," which, in 1986, had started locally in a city park as a spring "freedom picnic" by partying students from Atlanta University, a historically African American university, but had evolved into a large annual pilgrimage to the capital of Georgia. By 1993, when Campbell became mayor, the event was generally attracting more than two hundred thousand African American young people. Now called "Freaknik," it demanded so many municipal resources to control that it upset many daily activities across Atlanta. Whites were particularly worried about the possible results of so many African American youths congregating in the city, and many Atlanta businesses owners were not fond of the presence of so many young people in the capital because shoppers were reluctant to venture downtown. Commuters objected to artery obstructions created by youthful drivers cruising city streets, one car slowly after another. Hence, to many upset residents' satisfaction, Freaknik was entered on Campbell's "hit list" as a costly menace in need of targeting for quick elimination. Speaking on his behalf as the mayor's chief of staff, Steve Lebovitz was adamant about plans for either curtailing or stopping altogether the event. As he put it, "The general party atmosphere with people just running around with impunity is not going to happen. The laws of the city are going to be enforced." As much as people inferred from this the mayor's intention to end Freaknik completely, abatement did not occur at once. Until 1999 and the event's finale, the number of African American young people arriving in Atlanta for spring break did not diminish. Arrest records show that Freaknik had become infiltrated by thugs and criminals; from all police indications, bad elements had arrived in Atlanta with the primary aim of generating trouble and causing harm and mayhem. In fact, the final end of this tradition of Atlanta hosting an annual spring break for African American collegians had more to do with the combination of numerous fights, the brutal rape of a female student, and many acts of vandalism and shoplifting than with a clampdown from the Campbell administration.[62]

Inasmuch as it was unruliness in 1999 more than Campbell's initial resolution in 1994 that ultimately figured into Freaknik's demise, the mayor did better at keeping other election promises during his first complete year in office. In July, under mayoral direction, his office applied for and gained status as a federal empowerment zone. The area of Atlanta covered by a rehabilitation loan was a blighted section measuring roughly nine square miles that skirted the downtown. Among residents at the proposed site, 57.4 percent lived below the national poverty level. Since the zone's location surrounded Atlanta's main commercial center, developers were anxious to act upon a great opportunity to expand downtown Atlanta. Excitement existed among real estate interests eager to receive approval to begin planning for the erection of tall glass-and-structural-steel office buildings on several acres of condemned and cleared slum property. Consent from the U.S. Department of Housing and Urban Development and its hundred-million-dollar appropriation arrived late in 1994 and thereby opportunistically opened up one of Atlanta's most deteriorated and impoverished sections to construction and revitalization.[63]

During the last quarter of 1994, Campbell fulfilled another commitment. As a candidate he had promised to hire people without regard to gender, race, ethnicity, and religion. At the end of October, the mayor appointed Beverly Harvard as Atlanta's new chief of police. Her selection for this position was a real breakthrough because no other African American woman had ever received an opportunity to run a major American city police department. In December Campbell followed Harvard's appointment with the naming of Kathy J. White as Atlanta's chief financial officer. Thus, by the end of the mayor's first year in office, he had passed to women two vital positions that had always gone to men.[64]

As an African American politician, Campbell discovered some of the dangers associated with seeking high office in Atlanta and serving as the city's mayor. While a candidate in 1993, he had received several threatening telephone calls along with a bouquet of dead flowers. After the election someone sent him a fake bomb. Before it was found to be harmless, bomb-defusing experts ordered the evacuation of city hall. Unlike Maynard Jackson, Campbell showed only casual nonchalance about threats to his safety. As a money-saving measure he dismissed as unnecessary a nine-member security detail, which during his predecessor's term had had the special assignment of protecting Jackson.[65]

As the threats against Campbell show, he made enemies, but these were not always white racists disgruntled about another African American mayor taking charge of Atlanta. Most police officers at the beginning of 1996 were angry with him because of his decision to reactivate the Civilian Review Board. Campbell's unpopular action with cops followed a fatal police shooting of an unarmed young man at a motorcycle shop. The officer accused of firing his weapon at the victim claimed self-defense, but several eyewitnesses contradicted this, asserting a complete absence of danger to the policeman.[66]

Decisions made at the beginning of 1996 against police judgments of their fellow officers—and another that would ultimately pit the municipality's most important elected official against the Atlanta Police Department—represented a prelude to the roller-coaster year Campbell experienced in 1996. The mayor discovered that several decisions involved with Atlanta hosting the Olympic Games during August were fraught with potential disappointments. His office faced the difficult tasks of selecting worthy builders capable of completing jobs to specifications and on schedule for the opening ceremonies. In addition, Campbell's administrative staff, charged with screening all potential applicants and then signing contracts with the most reputable vendors, contended with difficult, subjective responsibilities that were certain to incur protests of favoritism. The necessity of closing off and blocking streets, along with the need to redirect traffic, irritated Atlanta motorists inconvenienced by the changes. Inevitable as conflicts were, several examples of unfair choices made by Campbell's team ultimately led to a discrediting of his supervision of the international games.

Under the Atlanta Committee for the 1996 Olympic Games (ACOG), Shirley Franklin had the responsibility of guaranteeing contractual roles for minorities and women in every phase of planning, building for, and hosting the world's biggest sports spectacle. She supervised the awarding of $155 million in contracts to minority firms. Referring to her accomplishment at ACOG and its implications, Campbell both commended her and showed hesitancy. As he cautioned, "the ultimate test of whether the Olympic committee has left a legacy for minority businesses is if firms continue to get quality contracts without it being mandated."

Compared to the Bradley administration's "dismal record" in not awarding enough contracts to minorities for the 1984 Games, Paula M. White, writing for *Black Enterprise*, praised Campbell, Franklin, and ACOG's efforts because they allocated a "big slice of the Olympic pie" to women and African Americans.[67]

Published four months before the Atlanta Games' opening ceremony, however, White's positive judgment proved prematurely optimistic about how fairly ACOG had distributed responsibilities and contracts to African Americans. For one thing, a lawsuit brought by the Black Vendors Association (BVA) alleged that ACOG showed favorable preferences toward some favored minority-owned businesses. Campbell endorsed a leasing plan for vendors proposed by Munson W. Steed, B. G. Swing Games Management Company's black president and a generous campaign contributor to Campbell. Steed sold vending permits at prices ranging from ten to twenty thousand dollars. The mayor admitted to appreciating Steed's proposed managing of vendors. Openly in Campbell's judgment, "It was an innovative plan for the city of Atlanta to make money without risk to the taxpayers." BVA members opposed Steed, because his assessing of exorbitant prices for favorable sites had the consequence of forcing them to accept only undesirable locations. Many upset minority vendors excoriated mayoral-favorite Steed's greed and considered him guilty of "helping himself at the expense of other blacks." As bookkeeping records at the end of an Olympian fortnight clearly show, BVA members were correct about the unfavorable conditions. Results for the vendors forced to sell their merchandise and food away from areas of heavy pedestrian traffic show them experiencing losses totaling several million dollars.[68]

As less fortunate African American vendors fretted about the undesirable sales locations assigned to them, Campbell seemed oblivious to their complaints. Rather than respond directly to concerns about fairness, the mayor preferred to gloat over how his staff had succeeded and how his office's administrative actions had "created new entrepreneurs and strengthened existing entrepreneurs." In his words, his team had taken several steps for "minorities and women— particularly those who have not been a part of this mainstream before—[to] be included in the economic prosperity." In preparation for showcasing Atlanta to the world during the Olympic Games, Campbell touted "Operation Clean Brush" as another notable achievement worthy of mention. Through an agreement first initiated and later negotiated by the mayor's office, Sherwin Williams (the paint producer), and A. L. "Mike" Monroe, the president of the International Brotherhood of Painters and Allied Trades (IBPAT), arranged to redecorate the exteriors of some 250 houses around several Olympic venues. Valued at $1.5 million, the major collaborative effort involved IBPAT personnel as the work-detail coordinators and supervisors of painting performed by a work crew consisting of a dozen public housing residents, twenty unemployed Atlanta citizens, several Job Corps youths, and a volunteer team of union painters. For use on the project, Sherwin Williams donated 4,200 gallons of paint.[69]

From his 1993 inauguration through the Olympics, Campbell's reputation as an efficient administrator of a prospering city grew so much nationally that during late August, Democrats honored him with the privilege of renominating Vice President Al Gore at the party's national convention in Chicago. Then months later, after President Clinton's reelection, rumors began to circulate that the nation's chief executive might possibly be tapping Atlanta's mayor as the next secretary of Housing and Urban Development. In the end, Campbell noted a lack of personal interest in becoming a cabinet officer. In denying any plans to resign the mayoralty, Campbell explained how serious thoughts of leaving Atlanta for an executive department appointment had never crossed his mind because he "love[d] Atlanta and love[d] her people."[70]

From all indications, poverty and homelessness among Atlanta's ghetto population embarrassed Campbell. Just as during the preparations for the 1994 Super Bowl, before the Olympic Games city police again had orders to harass and arrest vagrants. Criticisms resulted from police crackdowns, but they represented only one side of how Campbell handled minorities. He accomplished more as mayor promoting affirmative action and Minority Contract Set-Asides than either Jackson or Young had done. On February 29, 1996, the mayor's Office of Contract Compliance (OCC) hosted Minority and Female Business Enterprises, a free conference designed to benefit attendees with personal one-on-one counseling with OCC specialists. Then in April 1996, during a convening in Atlanta of the National Conference of Black Mayors, Campbell angrily lashed out at critics of affirmative action, noting how "sick and tired" he was with all the contemporary discussions and arguments about the program outliving its usefulness. Its foes thoroughly disgusted the Atlanta host because "we all know that . . . [it] is right. And we all know that there's discrimination out there." Campbell's adamancy about extending mandates continued through his second mayoral term, and his outspoken stand on this issue—one that was generally unpopular with whites—caused even more disfavor as a result of a mayoral suggestion that the entire metropolitan area should apply Atlanta's rules for affirmative action.[71]

After Campbell's departure from office at the start of 2002, serious probing into his personal and professional activities began, which resulted in a federal grand jury indictment on August 30, 2004. Allegations involved racketeering, bribery, and wire-fraud charges. After a five-year federal investigation, jurors indicted the ex-mayor on charges of possible corruption between 1994 and 2002. Federal prosecutors showed how the official had used city contractors as "human A.T.M.s." In the process, they cross-examined WSB-TV news anchor Marion Brooks about a philandering mayor and allegations of her extravagant extramarital affair with him that included expensive gifts and trips to casinos. According to evidence, Campbell used illegal kickbacks to finance his relationship with Brooks. On March 10, 2006, despite strong evidence, a federal jury in Atlanta returned a verdict of not guilty on every impropriety charge. A courtroom acquittal did not fully exonerate Campbell, however. He still faced charges of criminal federal tax evasion. Subsequently, in a separate decision, a federal court found him guilty of deliberately failing to declare income. On June 13, 2006, U.S. district judge Richard Story sentenced Campbell to a thirty-month prison term for cheating on his income taxes. Judge Story mandated that following Campbell's prison sentence, the disgraced former mayor would spend another year on probation. The judge also ordered Campbell to pay more than $66,000 in fines and unpaid income taxes. On August 21, 2006, after failing to secure an appeal bond, Campbell entered a federal prison in Florida where he remained until 2008.[72]

W. Wilson Goode in Philadelphia

Having a background more similar to Tom Bradley's than those of Atlanta's trio of African American mayors, W. Wilson Goode became Philadelphia's mayor in 1983. For him, as for the Los Angeles mayor, early childhood was characterized by poverty rooted in Southern sharecropping. Family migrations brought both young boys from rural to urban settings, one to residence and education in Southern California and the other to Pennsylvania. Early in their lives and school experiences, these African American students, as minority members of society, entered white-controlled settings in different ways. Bradley awkwardly coped as a young African American teenager and young adult in high school and at UCLA, while Goode's first real experience of a personal challenge with outsider status came while a graduate student at the University of Pennsylvania's Wharton School. Nevertheless, these early successes at competing academically with white pupils bolstered both men's confidence and made their future contacts with the majority race easier and smoother.

Goode spent the first six years after his 1961 graduation from Morgan State University frequently changing jobs. He went from working as a probation officer to soldiering, to adjusting insurance claims, and finally to supervising for a building-maintenance firm. Obviously restless and unsettled, with a driving ambition to acquire a more personally rewarding career, Goode enrolled in a graduate degree program in government administration, which led to a master's degree from Wharton in 1968 and to an appointment as executive director with the Philadelphia Council for Community Advancement. As its head, Goode's job was to revitalize deteriorated neighborhoods as well to promote affordable housing for poor people. Goode earned praise and recognition for excellently handling these tasks, and knowledge of his superb managerial achievements reached Governor Milton Shapp, who coincidentally in 1978, was on the lookout for an individual with good credentials to serve on the Pennsylvania Public Utilities Commission (PPUC).

When Shapp offered Goode this opportunity, the Wharton graduate did not hesitate to accept the appointment to such an important regulatory body with oversight over some seven billion dollars in metered charges, rung up by a variety of different entities ranging from utilities to taxi operators. On October 13, 1978, or only a few months after Shapp's selection of the Philadelphian as one of five PPUC members, Goode's colleagues named the African American chair of the state regulatory body. In this capacity, Goode made two unpopular decisions, and he dealt with the Pennsylvania agency's greatest challenge. He returned unspent PPUC funds to the state treasurer, which angered his fellow agency members, and he caused more grumbling and complaining among his colleagues by ending PPUC reimbursements for their travel to annual meetings of the National Association of Regulatory Utility Commissions. His greatest challenge followed the dangerous accident on March 28, 1979, at the Three Mile Island Nuclear Generating Station. This presented the chair with two unenviable tasks. Goode had supervisory responsibilities over the investigations into the cause of the near-disastrous meltdown, and it was he who had the individual responsibility of reassuring Pennsylvanians about the safety of atomic energy.[73]

By handling a public relations nightmare in a professional manner, Goode attracted much favorable attention. Politicians began to notice him and to imagine how they might benefit from an African American with a flair for smooth intelligence under tough questioning. Meanwhile, in Philadelphia, months after the near catastrophe at Three Mile Island, campaign aids for Democratic mayoral hopeful Bill Green (without consulting Goode) leaked through several city-desk reporters their candidate's intention to tap Goode as city managing director. Motivating the circulation of the rumor through clandestine channels of information was a hope of gaining key African American leaders' support for Green. In his autobiography, *In Goode Faith*, Goode claims that his initial discussions with Green about an appointment to the important city post did not occur until three weeks after the mayoral election.[74]

Already by the time of the leaks, some activist-minded Philadelphian African Americans had expressed concerns about Goode's suitability for their city's second most powerful position. They viewed him as being against unions and for urban development at any price, positions that militants across the city considered antithetical to their own. So adamant was district union president Earl Stout's opposition to the naming of Goode that the labor leader ordered a wildcat strike as a protest against Green's selection. Behind the decision to request a work stoppage was Stout's complaint about the mayor-elect's reneging on a spoken promise to appoint another, more acceptable African American to the post.[75]

After two years as Philadelphia's managing director Goode's actions, it seemed, had justified critics' early doubts about his fitness for the job. A combination of both his supervisory decisions and his recommendations resulted in orders to downsize the municipality's police and fire departments, limit personal usage of city cars, withdraw municipal-issued credit cards from many employees, and initiate training programs for department heads on how to draft performance-based budgets. Under Goode's tight management, a tradition of municipal budget deficits ended, and city ledgers began showing surpluses. Since so many of the director's spending cuts were hitting the blighted African American neighborhoods hardest, ambivalence toward Goode developed. Proud and glad as many African American residents were with having this "black voice" at the mayor's cabinet sessions, they still felt dissatisfactions with Goode's major role in reducing personnel. To the poorest African American Philadelphians, Managing Director Goode symbolized achievement for the race more than any tangible results for the minority. At no time was this conclusion more apparent than after an officer fatally shot a young African American man. As a crowd assembled at a district police station to protest the shooting grew increasingly unruly, Goode appeared with stern advice for everyone to disperse. When the noisy demonstrators ignored his pleas, he left for home.[76]

Near the beginning of Green's final year as mayor, Goode began considering two options about his future. One was to remain loyal and helpful to the incumbent mayor as he prepared a quest for a second term; the alternative was to bolt from Green and contest him for mayor. As matters evolved, the managing director never had to choose between these possibilities because the mayor decided against a reelection bid. Green's announcement vaulted the city managing director into the role of favorite as the mayor's logical heir. Many city business and civic leaders displayed particular enthusiasm about the eventuality of the African American official becoming Philadelphia's next political leader, because of the benefits they anticipated from his leadership and his cost-effective, efficient management. Candidate Goode wisely entrusted his campaign activities and strategy to William Miller, because early in the mayoral race the advisor decided that it would make sense to avoid "your typical 'black campaign.'"[77] Rather than portraying Goode as an African American brother, Miller's emphasis went to characterizing his candidate as the "man of the future who can bring the city together."[78]

With a completely opposite resolve in the Democratic mayoral primary, Frank Rizzo contended with a racist appeal against his black opponent. Goode staffers used diverse statistics to remind Philadelphians of their city's decline during ex-mayor Rizzo's two terms. Beside all the tangible, negative evidence of poor leadership from the ex-mayor who had once served as chief of police in Philadelphia, his candidacy, claimed Goode's team, represented "the past, [the] divisive, living image of what we are not proud of, a politics of corruption and political demagoguery."[79] In contrast to Rizzo's use of blatant race baiting, Goode's commercials and flyers acclaimed a candidate who truly reflected his motto for the city, "Philadelphia's on the move."[80] Goode and his key advisors realized from the outset the wastefulness of mobilizing resources and arranging campaign appearances in Philly's African American neighborhoods because of the existence of apparently strong galvanization and determination by their residents to Rizzo's defeat. His years of active opposition to civil rights and his accumulation of a race-baiting record had long ago made this man persona non grata among most African Americans. Analysis of how voting went in the primary confirms the wisdom of Goode's strategy; by crushing Rizzo in African American precincts and performing extremely well with central Philadelphia's Jewish residents, the racial minority candidate obtained 53 percent of the total vote.[81]

Ahead was a general election with two opponents running against Goode—Republican John Egan and Democrat-turned-Independent Thomas Leonard. Given GOP rival Egan's past experience as chair of the Philadelphia Stock Exchange, it is surprising that Goode appeared more an advocate of urban entrepreneurship than his opponent. The African American Democrat spoke clearly and specifically of his intentions to revitalize Philly's economy by reforming the city's tax structure and promoting greater efficiency in municipal government. As for race as a campaign factor, Goode avoided the subject as much as possible and rejected help offers from both local African American activists and such prominent outside civil rights leaders as Jesse Jackson. As Goode often liked to emphasize in his addresses to mostly white audiences, "We're not against anyone; we're for everyone who lives in the city." Although Goode's speaking style was "breathtakingly dull," he still connected with white listeners. Always to them, he liked to dismiss color as an "unimportant" factor in the selection of the city's next mayor, and apparently most of the electorate agreed, because Goode scored an easy victory. He won with 55 percent of the vote; Egan and Leonard managed to draw only 37 percent and 8 percent, respectively. On election night, with success obviously now assured for the successful son of sharecroppers, Goode spoke to happy supporters of his plans to bring unity to the City of Brotherly Love: "All of us from all neighborhoods, from all walks of life, white, black, Asian, Hispanic, all of us working together can solve the problems facing our city."[82]

Not unlike other winners before him, Goode promised benefits to many diverse interests. Following his inauguration, he prioritized programs and thereby disappointed the constituencies whose special needs had received his commitments during the campaign but whose requirements then dropped, after the election, to the bottom of the list of issues of urgent importance in the city council. Goode, described by Derek T. Dingle as a "low-key politician," began governing with an "Agenda for the First 100 Days in Office." Included in it was some eighty-one specific goals, but promoting business was uppermost in importance. During his first week in office, the mayor mandated a survey of Philadelphia's thirty-three thousand businesses in order to ascertain how city government might serve them better. Favorably impressed by how Goode had begun his mayoral term, one leading corporate executive concluded that the mayor was one public official who "sees himself as the head of a $1.6 billion corporation whose only job is to provide services." This was by no means an isolated positive opinion. Goode's pro-business, trickle-down approach to governing Philly clearly generated much enthusiasm and anticipation from Greater Philadelphia First Corporation, the chamber of commerce body of businesses. Because of reliable and consistent support from many corporate allies, Goode could point to noteworthy accomplishments after his first one hundred days as mayor. These included a cable television agreement, a war on graffiti, a summer jobs program for young people, approval for a new convention center, funds for the removal of abandoned cars, and city council money directed to shelter homeless people. Late in the "honeymoon" first year, negotiations brought a deal for keeping the Eagles—and pro football—in Philadelphia. Goode did not exaggerate very much in his State of the City report, when he boasted of many significant accomplishments. Unfortunately these did not distribute equally among the entire citizenry. Critics found grounds to accuse the mayor of doing nothing to encourage African American business development and of doing even less to fulfill his campaign promises to involve Philly's neighborhoods in decisions. Other taxpayers voiced their disapproval of generous incentives that resulted in keeping the Eagles NFL franchise in Philadelphia. Goode's initial fascinations with a zero-based budget plan and downtown development efforts—at the apparent expense of checking North Side ghetto poverty—gained almost no initial criticisms.[83]

In the mayor's second and third years in office, his prioritizing of downtown projects over everything else became so obvious that neighborhood activists finally began to complain loudly and bitterly. City planners and developers naturally welcomed and appreciated Goode's interest in turning downtown Philadelphia into a thriving center of dynamic growth and business activity. In the judgment of Barbara Kaplan, the executive director of the Philadelphia Planning Commission, Goode's "planning frame of mind" represented the best city program since Joseph Clark's efforts in the 1950s. By late 1984, after steady cooperation and work with ally and developer Willard Rouse III, the visionary and entrepreneurial-minded Goode was ready to push an ambitious master downtown plan for immediate implementation. It included, as its crown jewel, a sixty-one-story tower, One Liberty Place. Completed in 1987, the tall structure enhanced the Philadelphia skyline with absolute defiance of an old city tradition that nothing built downtown should ever tower above the William Penn statue atop city hall.[84]

Had not a momentous and horrible mistake occurred on May 13, 1985, Philadelphians might well have judged and remembered their pioneering minority mayor for his technocratic skills and entrepreneurial management of municipal government. But, on this fateful day, in the midst of a violent standoff with police and firemen at a heavily fortified house located in a once pleasantly tranquil African American middle-class West Philadelphia neighborhood, John Africa —the inner-city leader of MOVE, a small militant sect with a return-to-nature agenda—and a small band of loyal followers violently resisted all attempts by law enforcement to enforce an inspection order. Not long after Africa and his extended MOVE family had taken possession of the house three years before, in 1982, several neighbors had complained to city authorities about putrid-smelling, uncollected garbage and a loud, shrieking noise, but none of their efforts for corrective actions were successful in bringing positive responses from city authorities. In June 1984, matters deteriorated even further for neighborhood residents, when from a recently erected rooftop loudspeaker, MOVE members began blaring obscenity-laden messages. Although Goode later admitted to having initially learned of Africa and MOVE's antisocial tendencies in 1976, he had shown timid reluctance as mayor to act on residents' complaints.

Matters changed on the day of confrontation in May 1985. Police and MOVE members were in the midst of exchanging many ammunition rounds when a city helicopter dropped an incendiary bomb on the occupied fortress. The house immediately burst into flames. While a fire official watched, burning soon spread quickly to an entire block of houses. A final toll registered eleven dead—including children—in the police-torched house, and smoldering in ashes along one side of Osage Avenue were the ruins of sixty-one residences.

Disputed in the aftermath was responsibility for the decision to drop the device from the helicopter. At the hearings about the disaster that caused some 250 people to become homeless, the issue was who to believe. Versions varied from police claims implicating a mayoral role in the disaster to Goode's denial of any responsibility. To investigators and in his autobiography, Goode insisted that he had had no prior knowledge of a police plan to bombard the house with an explosive charge. Police commissioner Gregor Sambour, with collaboration from his managing director, remembered the day differently. As a precautionary prelude to ordering use of the bomb, Sambour claimed to have asked for and received the mayor's consent. Novella Williams' account of her telephone conversation with Goode a few minutes before the fatal explosion largely discounted the mayor's assertion of innocence. According to her recall of an exchange with Goode, he seemed worried more about being perceived as weak and ineffective than about the ultimate safety of residents. Here is how she remembered the dialogue with the mayor:

> Goode: "If I don't go in now I appear irresponsible."
> Williams: "There are babies inside! You can't do it! Don't do it!"
> Goode: "I thank you for your call. I really appreciate your call."[85]

As much as Goode wanted to escape ultimate blame and culpability for the deaths and destruction, a "scathing censure" of him followed.[86] Editor Chuck Stone of the *Philadelphia Daily News* dubbed Goode "Brown Bomber II."[87] Gone forever was Goode's skillfully crafted image of the ultimately consummate manager. From across the United States, 109 African Americans, disapproving of Goode's feeble defense, paid to place their critical response in the *Philadelphia*

Tribune. Under "Draw the Line," their disapproving message asserted that "when black elected officials use their positions of power to attack black people or to cover up for or to excuse such attacks they are no friend of ours and don't speak for or represent the interests of black people."[88] Goode's strongest defenders were law-and-order advocates and notable conservatives such as Attorney General Edwin Meese of President Reagan's administration.[89]

As for Goode's ambition to serve a second term as mayor, a key factor proved helpful in overcoming bitter memories of the bomb. This was the renewed presence of even more despised and distrusted Frank Rizzo. Now a Republican, he hoped to capitalize on Goode's unpopularity. Neither Rizzo nor the incumbent mayor conducted a campaign completely free of the usual vituperative charges and nastiness in their election efforts. Incumbent Goode called Rizzo a "liar," while the former Democratic mayor turned Republican candidate charged that his rival had chosen a dishonest African American contractor to rebuild homes on Osage Avenue. As Rizzo worded his most negative assessment, "I watched [Goode] and listened and watched a great city go down the drain." Confronted with the undesirable choice of two evils, the Philly electorate reluctantly re-elected a severely wounded mayor, but memories of the city's actions against MOVE continued to haunt Goode, rendering much of his second term not much more than a lame-duck experience. According to John F. Bauman's assessment, "Goode neared the end of his administration viewed as the wounded head of a black party."[90]

David N. Dinkins in New York City

Unlike other profiled municipalities, New York City presented unique challenges for any ambitious African American trying to break through a difficult color barrier to become the pioneering black mayor of Gotham. Most notably, the city's division into five semi-autonomous, politically independent, competitive boroughs increased the potential difficulties for any politician—African or Caucasian—to command more than just a localized power base. Overcoming a city population's diverse and often conflicting elements was a major challenge for any aspiring leader. In general, mayoral formulas for initial political success have seldom worked forever, either at pleasing the demands of a diverse electorate or at solving problems. Often working to foil mayoral ambition to remain in control of city hall indefinitely was the constant appearance of new crises. With problems engulfing elected officials, a difficult-to-please and often fickle electorate typically has responded restlessly and impatiently, wanting to quickly replace public servants with different leaders who might have fresher ideas and newer approaches to the city's challenges. In essence, as details of David Dinkins's victories in 1989 and subsequent defeat in 1993 clearly demonstrate, his one-term fate was pretty normal for Gotham with its ever-growing, constantly changing, unresolved problems as well as with its general voter frustrations with politicians. Accurate to a degree as the reason New Yorkers rejected his management of city affairs, this somewhat simplified conclusion can only partially explain why New York's first African American mayor did not survive longer than one term at Gracie Mansion. For Dinkins, unlike predecessors who had lost reelection bids, another key factor worked decisively against his winning a second term—an aroused racial consciousness among white New Yorkers.[91]

Years prior to seeking the Democratic nomination for mayor in 1989, David N. Dinkins had progressed through Harlem's political network—after World War II and service in the U.S. Marine Corps, graduation from Howard University, and receipt of a law degree from the Brooklyn Law School. As a fundamental contributor to a locally influential Harlem leadership organization consisting of persuasively powerful Percy Sutton, Basil Paterson, and Charles Rangel, Dinkins briefly represented a mostly African American district in the New York General Assembly; thereafter he became New York City's clerk. Mayor Abraham Beame tried to name Dinkins deputy mayor, but disclosure of the nominee's failure to file income tax returns forced a withdrawal of the nomination. Then in 1985, after his third attempt, Manhattan voters elected the ex-marine their borough president. As candidate Dinkins was winning an important office, the city electorate also provided controversial and confrontational Edward I. Koch with a third mayoral term.

Between 1985 and 1989, Koch's ill-advised actions and foolhardy reactions to widely reported racially motivated crimes almost completely destroyed the mayor's reputation for fairness and impartiality. Possibilities for unseating an increasingly unpopular mayor seemed now to increase because of his crude and inappropriate responses to Bernhard Goetz's vigilante-style shooting of four African American young men on a subway train; a white gang's senseless attack on three African Americans at a Howard Beach pizzeria; a racially motivated and vicious assault on four young African American men who had dared to venture into the Bensonhurst neighborhood of Brooklyn to examine a used car; and a brutal, multiple raping of a white jogger in Central Park allegedly by African American and Puerto Rican youths (who years later gained their freedom as a result of evidence implicating a serial rapist).[92]

The outspoken Koch had hurt himself with New Yorkers in other ways as well. He upset minorities with a contention that excessive attention in Democratic Party platforms to advancing Hispanics and African Americans was not good for the party; Koch expressed the opinion that official Democratic policies were responsible for causing white middle-class voters to flee the party and become Republicans. His arguing against his party's position upset and alienated many members of both minorities. Some damaging revelations of scandals involving Koch's closest political allies also worked at increasing the veteran officeholder's vulnerability in 1989. As the dissatisfaction with Koch mounted, he miscalculated the degrees of general unrest that had developed under his rule and of the extent to which two large minority voting blocs felt real anger and resentment toward him.

In contrast, Dinkins had a better understanding of New Yorkers' general displeasures and of the severity of African American and Hispanic disgust with Koch. From Gotham's political climate, the borough president surmised that there now existed an excellent opportunity to challenge and defeat the incumbent mayor in the Democratic Party primary. Dinkins certainly comprehended a great deal more about the situation; he also realized that any overt appealing to race would cost him white votes and the opportunity to beat Koch. With this in mind, Dinkins faced a problem of how to handle the Reverend Jesse Jackson because, for the moment, the civil rights leader's attempt in 1988 to win the Democratic Party's presidential nomination presented the mayoral challenger with both negative and positive repercussions. Jackson had energized thousands of New York City's African Americans to register to vote and to involve themselves directly in political affairs, but in the process he had alienated New York Jews with unflattering and anti-Semitic remarks. The key question for the New York politician was whether Jackson's possible involvement would refresh bad memories with Jewish voters or help Dinkins galvanize African American support. The Jackson factor presented a major dilemma for Dinkins.

At least, this was what the candidate pondered before the Bensonhurst murder of Yusef Hawkins, a young black man who was slain by whites while checking out a used car. In a show of anger about the brutal assault of this young black man, a large assembly of minority mourners responded with an organized protest march through the Italian American ethnic neighborhood in Brooklyn, while residents met the demonstrators' presence with hostility and verbal abuse. Apparently insensitive to the exceptionally strong demands from so many African Americans for the right to move freely and fearlessly anywhere in the city, Koch had sternly advised against the demonstration in this hostile Brooklyn enclave because a march there might exacerbate additional tension and further infuriate residents. In contrast to the mayor's advice, which many African Americans interpreted as Koch's caving in to white racist pressures, Dinkins appealed for calm and for the immediate prosecutions of the accused murderers. Wanting to appear fair and racially impartial, the borough president advised, at the same time, the imposition of equally tough justice on the youths charged with the physical assault and gang rape of the Central Park jogger. Dinkins's show of evenhandedness elevated his standing among many liberal, fair-minded whites. While assuming the role of racial healer with whites, the candidate also managed to raise his stature among African Americans to that of a civil rights champion.

Obviously, success or failure in a New York mayoral primary depended upon more than merely the reactions to events in Bensonhurst or a plea against mercifulness toward allegedly vicious rapists facing trial. Dinkins's campaign obtained a quick boost from an early July endorsement by the New York City Central Labor Council, an umbrella body with some 1.2 million workers from more than 500 affiliated local unions. Also, as the challenger began his campaign, former mayors John V. Lindsay and Abe Beame jumped onboard the borough president's bandwagon as ardent supporters. Also solidly behind Dinkins early on were noted New Yorkers Bella Abzug and Gloria Steinem. The two feminist leaders, together with many other high profile Dinkins backers, formed what they called a "Circle of decency for New York." Meanwhile, in the midst of many key endorsements for the challenger, *New York Amsterdam News* editor in chief and chairman of the board Wilbert A. Tatum, in a complete reversal of his previous opinions of the sitting mayor, advised readers in headlined front-page editorials on both July 3 and July 8 why "Koch must resign." The call had resulted from the mayor's racist remarks. The African American challenger did not win editorial support from every New York newspaper, however. Consistently negative coverage of Dinkins by the *New York Post* and the *New York Times* upset Tatum. These two newspapers backed Koch, and they provoked the black newspaper executive's ire most of all by concentrating their coverage of Dinkins on the Manhattan borough president's earlier income tax problems.[93]

During the final seven weeks leading up to the primary Dinkins and Koch did more to clarify their positions, and as they did so, additional endorsements followed. To sweep aside any concerns about softness toward criminals, Dinkins issued a policy statement in which he declared, "every crime must be punished" with "no excuses, no apologies." At a Harlem church the mayoral candidate elaborated what crime meant to him personally and to his family, noting how the city's murder rate and drug problem were personal sources of worry in his household. And he offered a solution; Dinkins proposed removing police officers from desk details and placing them on neighborhood beats and in subway cars. With just over a month to go before Democratic voters would select their nominee for mayor, Koch found himself in the midst of an embarrassing situation with disclosure contained in a report titled "'Playing Ball' with City Hall: A Case Study of Political Patronage in New York City." The report was a scathing investigation into acts of favoritism and irregular contracts allegedly committed by some high-ranking members of the mayor's administration. Dinkins jumped at this fantastic opportunity to take the offensive, using disclosures to reprimand the incumbent for allowing illegal actions during his management of city hall: "If he knew about it, he is disqualified for reelection. If he didn't know about it, it shows that he's too careless and too tired to merit four more years."[94]

Dinkins also had something constructive to offer New York's acute housing shortage for low- and medium-income families. In order to provide these residents with decent homes, the challenger suggested requiring city building contractors to construct more affordable dwellings. Seemingly for the borough president, no issue appeared too controversial for him to ignore completely; throughout the campaign, Dinkins appeared to have definitive responses for every problem. A good case in point was how he handled questions about a woman's right to choose. To diverse audiences Dinkins pledged that, as mayor, the city would never deliberately "stand idly by while the right to [a] legal abortion is under attack." As for dealing with Operation Rescue militants, the abortion foes who broke laws to prevent pregnancy interventions, he threatened not to "tolerate the harassment of women, the violent destruction of clinics. . . . We will not allow a return to the days of back-alley abortions." The challenger's positions on the protection of the environment also won him praise and support. For proposing to prevent lead poisoning, to save the city's waterfront, and to stop entries of nuclear waste into New York's ports, Dinkins received the Sierra Club's endorsement.[95]

Both directly and indirectly, race figured into the two Democrats' campaigns. In an overt attempt not to appear as the African Americans' candidate, the challenger made only infrequent campaign stops in New York's ghetto enclaves. Dinkins's "invisible" strategy of ignoring blacks caused him problems with some civil rights activists. While they considered his evasiveness of the race a snub and a denial of his minority membership, other civil rights movement leaders like Benjamin Chavis Jr. viewed matters differently. Chavis credited Dinkins with not "allowing the forces of racism to disrupt his outreach into all communities." Of course sooner or later, Dinkins as a most carefully restrained challenger on racial matters had to confront the most delicate issue of whom to involve in his campaign. Bringing in Jesse Jackson as a vocal spokesperson had the potential of inciting New York's African Americans to vote, but real worries also existed that encouraging Jackson's presence on behalf of Dinkins's candidacy might upset Jewish voters who remembered the gadfly minister's anti-Semitic remarks. In the end, the challenger gambled on a decision to enlist Jackson's assistance. As Dinkins finally decided to involve the civil rights leader in the campaign, "I recognize that some people said they will not vote for me because of Jesse Jackson. I suspect they would not vote for me even if Jesse didn't come." As for Koch and New York African Americans, the mayor had probably lost almost all creditability with the minority. Obvious evidence of the mayor's low standing came during his attempted appearance at the wake for Yusef Hawkins, the young African American victim of murder in Bensonhurst. After a hail of bottles and verbal abuse greeted the mayor as he entered the funeral parlor, fearing for his safety, Koch slipped out a side door. Looking at the Democratic primary race for mayor, U.S. Senator Ted Kennedy correctly assessed the two contenders in New Yorkers' minds. To them, Kennedy observed, Dinkins had seemed the "great healer," while, unfortunately for Koch, city residents had interpreted his role as that of the "great divider."[96]

Overcoming obstacles proved too much for the incumbent. By an impressive margin (51–43 percent), the black challenger "slam dunked" a three-term mayor. Assessing reasons for the victorious result, Dinkins believed it had resulted from the people of New York voting their "hopes and not their fears." Only in a limited way did election facts support this interpretation, however. Dinkins carried only those boroughs with large minority-voting blocs—Manhattan, Brooklyn, and the Bronx—while he lost to Koch in predominantly white Staten Island and Queens. Racially, the breakdown shows that the African American candidate received only about 25 percent of the white vote. Dinkins owed his victory to Hispanics, who gave him 55 percent of their votes, and to African Americans, who registered a 95 percent plurality for the borough president. Probably, hopefulness characterized the two most prominent minorities in New York as they entered polling stations because they were expecting better futures with an African American mayor. Oppositely, with more or less equal decisiveness, a great majority within New York's white electorate by its vote for Koch expressed considerable fear of having a minority member in charge of city hall.[97]

By winning the Democratic primary, Dinkins successfully overcame the first challenge to becoming mayor. As a joint choice, the Liberal and Republican parties ran Rudolph Giuliani, a former U.S. attorney whose notoriety resulted from his successfully prosecuting Mafia leaders. Although Gotham was an overwhelmingly Democratic city, several election analysts expected a close contest because it introduced race into municipal politics as a great unknown factor. From the outset of the general campaign, Democratic National Committee Chair Ron Brown promised "to spend as much time as it takes" to deliver a victory for Dinkins. At a major kickoff gala held for the Democratic nominee at Harlem's Apollo Theatre and attended by a who's who listing of prominent African American entertainers including Bill Cosby, Harry Belafonte, Spike Lee, and Quincy Jones, New York governor Mario Cuomo served both as a master of ceremonies and featured speaker.[98]

Less than a week into the campaign, race became an issue. Jackie Mason, noted Jewish comedian and devoted Giuliani supporter, complained to the *Village Voice* about how "Dinkins is surrounded by Anti-Semites" such as Jesse Jackson and Louis Farrakhan, men who "are like the Mafia." Adding to his vilification of Dinkins, the popular entertainer of Catskill resort audiences chided the Democrat for his priorities, claiming he "spends his whole life putting on shirts and jackets and parting his hair. Dinkins looks like a Black model without a job."[99] Coming to Dinkins's defense and praising the Democrat for having "taken the high and vague road" in his response to Mason's unwarranted personal attack on the African American candidate and unfair linking of him to the unsavory actions of others, a *New York Times* editorial wanted to ascertain if his Republican opponent "had decided to pander to racial fears and prejudice."[100] This apparently was Giuliani's general strategy because he was present to hear Mason's insulting reference to Dinkins as "Schvartzer [servant in Yiddish] with a mustache."[101] Like others in the audience that night, the Republican supposedly laughed at the mean-spirited characterization of Dinkins. Then, confirming further an intention to frighten New York voters away from electing the African American as their mayor, Giuliani selected Roger Ailes—a man who had gained attention during George H. W. Bush's 1988 presidential campaign for developing the infamous Willie Horton ads—as his chief media advisor. Countering racial smears, Dinkins did as much as possible to remove the race issue from the mayoral contest. He received praise in the *New York Times* for noting, at a breakfast attended by prominent Jewish leaders that "Our enemy is not each other" but, rather, it is the combination of "crack, AIDs, hate crimes, despair, homelessness, poverty."[102] Under pressure, Giuliani ultimately disengaged himself from Mason's slurs, but the Republican candidate never tired of trying to closely link Dinkins to Jackson and to African American extremists such as Robert "Sonny" Carson, a black nationalistic extremist known in New York for his anti-white views. The GOP nominee also did his best to subtly imply that Dinkins was personally dishonest. In reaction, one friendly supporter advised Dinkins to respond: "you must contain the hemorrhaging."[103] With two weeks to go before the day of decision for New York voters, everything was coming down to how successful one candidate would be at negatively characterizing his foe. Would the New York electorate prefer to have a "Reagan Republican," as the Dinkins camp called Giuliani? Or would it rather opt for a "Jesse Jackson Democrat," as the other side depicted Dinkins? If press endorsements were any indicator of how voters might answer the question, Dinkins had wrapped up an easy win. Editorials favoring his candidacy appeared in the *New York Times, Newsday, Village Voice, Daily News,* and the *New York Amsterdam News.*[104] Tallying more than 896,000 votes and receiving 51 percent, Dinkins won what Giuliani conceded was a "historic achievement." Joyful with the election result, the winning African American Democrat immediately pledged "to be mayor of all the people," and promised "a new coalition of conscience and purpose."[105] Brushing aside all of Dinkins's good intentions and optimism, the first post-election editorials to appear in both the *New York Times* and the *New York Amsterdam News* indicated skepticism concerning the real possibilities ahead for Dinkins in fulfilling these commitments and accomplishing much as the new mayor of New York City. Judging the winner as a person of "indecision and ambiguity," who too often "hid behind generalities," the *New York Times* editor seemed certain about only one fact concerning Dinkins: he possessed a "genuine concern for New York." Yet Dinkins faced a difficult future because, at Gracie Mansion, he "will have to tax more, spend less and make government more productive."[106] For a set of different reasons, the editor of the city's only African American daily newspaper, the *New York Amsterdam News,* also indicated grave concerns about Dinkins' future. As the writer warned readers: "David does not have a mandate," and, without "an enlargement of that coalition from where it is now to where it must be, governance of this city will be well-nigh impossible."[107]

As mayor-elect, Dinkins showed doubters every intention to fulfill his promises for fair-mindedness toward all constituents. His twenty-one member transition team consisted of one Asian, three Hispanics, five American Americans, and twelve whites—the latter group divided equally among Gentiles and Jews. In response to African American critics with concerns about this display of fairness, Dinkins responded with sound advice that upset those minority members who had expected more rewards and greater prominence in the new administration from a man whose win had come, in large part, from almost unanimous support from the African American electorate. As one of the mayor-elect's minority supporters responded: "Although our votes and our dollars served as the base for a Dinkins victory, back off him now. Allow him to jump start a city."[108] According to a *New York Times* editorial that appeared on January 1, 1990, Dinkins's inauguration day, already enough satisfactory evidence existed from the soon-to-be installed Gotham mayor that "he'll risk angering his black base to be evenhanded."[109] Dinkins indicated this much in his inaugural address. Reaching out to all groups in "the gorgeous mosaic" of New York, Gracie Mansion's newest occupant gave New Yorkers a reassuring commitment "to be the toughest mayor on crime this city has ever seen."[110]

Dinkins' absorptions were with issues both difficult and divisive. These included sheltering homeless people with AIDS; deciding budget priorities for a city beset with economic woes; satisfying gays who sought participation in St. Patrick's Day parades, a move in direct defiance of the Hibernian Order's strong opposition to homosexual involvement in its annual event; asserting some control in city council over Speaker Peter F. Vallone, while trying to avoid offense to his aldermanic allies; handling objections to Columbia University tearing down the Audubon Theater and Ballroom (a shrine, because of Malcolm X's assassination there); replacing a historic building with a new biomedical laboratory; and overcoming criminal activities by two aides.[111] What emerged as the most troublesome and durable headaches for the mayor, however, were issues with the police and with Hasidic Jews. Certainly more than everything else in the opinion of most white New Yorkers, these were the issues that contributed to Dinkins's downfall and failure as mayor.

As a candidate needing to shake serious white doubts about his commitment to fighting crime, Dinkins promised toughness toward criminals and avid support for enlarging the municipal police force. With budgetary deficits confronting both New York state and city, and with the whole nation in the grips of a recession, the mayor had problems finding the revenue to add cops to the New York Police Department (NYPD). Neither raising taxes nor cutting back on municipal programs was a popular choice either with residents or with city council members. Since it was at the outset of the Dinkins administration, he certainly did not want to choose an option that might provoke a council fight or upset specific citizen blocs that were dependent upon city services. Hence, the mayor's solution for financing an additional eighteen hundred police officers was a proposal to create a special fund by generating sales of municipal bonds. Despite the plan's merits and its apparent immediate painlessness for taxpayers, several of

the most powerful councilmen became obstinately obstructionist. Their alternative to bonds was for the mayor to implement a blanket hiring freeze across all
city departments. In the end, Dinkins won a Pyrrhic victory. Approval followed,
somewhat, according to his terms for the recruitment of candidates to begin
studies at the city's police academy. But unfortunately, most of their beat assignments, after the officers' graduation, reflected political considerations more than
areas with the highest crime rates. New York's murder rate reached record levels, and to many city residents it seemed that Dinkins's lofty-sounding pledge to
institute a program for "Safe Streets, Safe City" represented a major public relations fiasco that had failed to create tangible results. On the defensive about the
increasing number of homicides, the mayor tried in vain to explain that matters
"are not out of control, and this is not Dodge City."[112]

Concerns about murders and clashes over how to fund and where to place
additional police officers were only part of the law-enforcement problems that
afflicted a now besieged and overwhelmed mayor. Contract negotiations over
what to include in a new police pay schedule reached the point of impasse. To
facilitate a final settlement, Dinkins took an unusual step for a New York mayor;
on behalf of the city, he unwisely participated directly in arbitration sessions.
This personal involvement cost Dinkins support among police officers because,
at the hearings, he insisted that New York could not afford more than a 4 percent
salary increase. Already unpopular because of this, Dinkins then proceeded to
make matters worse for himself by taking a stand against equipping officers with
semi-automatic handguns. This provoked more animosity, and to make matters
even worse, he also favored the establishment of an independent civilian control
board with responsibilities to both investigate and supervise police behavior. Repeated charges of police corruption and officer brutality put the mayor between
NYPD members, who adamantly opposed the proposition of an independent
agency with monitoring responsibilities over their actions, and civil libertarians,
equally insistent on the need for an all-civilian review board to look into citizens'
allegations of officer wrongdoing. The suspicious death of a detained African
American young man, as well as indications of kickbacks to upper-echelon officers, led Dinkins to back the establishment of an outside body to oversee the
NYPD. The mayor's support ignited a sharp reaction from rank-and-file officers.
In a demonstration of unity, some ten thousand angry police officers gathered
outside city hall to protest the mayor's proposal for instituting civilian oversight.
The massive assembly of mean-spirited uniformed police officers, one observer
wrote, resembled a "post-modern lynch mob full of racial bigotry and hate." Instead of rising above the ugliness and ignoring altogether the police officers' barrage of racist slurs, the mayor felt a personal need to respond. He asked, "Some
of them out there who were calling out 'n-r,' why would the people in our communities have any confidence in them, that they would have the sensitivity to
handle a tense situation in the minority community?" After the police mob vol-

untarily dispersed from the steps to city hall, the beleaguered mayor worked valiantly but in vain thereafter to convince NYPD members of his sincere respect for them. A police board did result, but relations between Dinkins and a majority of the city's law enforcement officers remained tense and unpleasant.[113] Seventeen days after his inauguration, Dinkins learned about the difficulty of remaining neutral in interracial disputes. In the midst of an African American boycott of a Korean-owned grocery in Brooklyn, Dinkins tried to intervene as an arbiter, which caused him to be "caught on a tight wire between Black and White expectations."[114] The militant black strike leaders and their supporters expected the mayor to support their fight, and Caucasians generally sided and sympathized with the Asian shopkeeper. After making an impassioned plea for an end to bigotry, Dinkins crossed a picket line and entered the store to a chorus of angry responses from boycott participants. C. Vernon Mason typified the activists' bitter reaction to Dinkins's desire to serve all New Yorkers: "I could not believe what that Negro said last night. . . . he is a traitor. . . . he is a lover of white people and the system. And last night he bashed black people. He ain't got no African left in him. He's got too many yarmulkas in [sic] his head."[115]

In the minds of many New York Jews, Mason's harsh judgment of Dinkins was incorrect, despite the mayor's avowed anti-Semitism and pro-Israeli record. The stabbing death in 1990 of Australian doctoral student Yankel Rosenbaum in Brooklyn's volatile, multiracial neighborhood of Crown Heights heightened tensions between blacks and Jews, because the victim was Jewish and the alleged assailant and his accomplices were African American. Every attempt Dinkins made to foster harmony and peace between two hostile groups, it seemed, had little chance of success. Doomed as a no-win proposition, Dinkins's valiant efforts to end or ameliorate such deep-seated animosities produced little effect on matters in Crown Heights. To Jews living there and across the city, Dinkins was overly partial toward his own race. Members of the Lubavitcher Hasidim sect simply sneered at the mayor's plea for some demonstration of loving understanding toward their African American neighbors from the Caribbean islands, while blacks interpreted the mayor's counter requests for West Indian tolerance toward Jews as "Uncle Tom" behavior and betrayal.

Racial wounds opened wider on October 28, 1992, after Lemrick Nelson's acquittal by a mixed-race jury consisting of six African Americans, four Latinos, and two Caucasians. The black teenager—whom a court had indicted and tried for fatally stabbing Rosenbaum—was free. Prominent African American leaders did not help Dinkins's cause by celebrating the verdict. Again, an event trapped the mayor; angry Jews expected Dinkins to condemn the jury's decision, while jubilant African Americans wanted him to share their joy with the judgment. With his political future and reputation seemingly at stake, dependent as he was upon the impossible task of responding satisfactorily to both groups, Dinkins received an opportunity to clarify his position before the Council of Jewish

Federations. In an emotional address the mayor made "an impassioned plea for justice"—over the shouts of a hostile group of protestors led by Rabbi Avi Weiss. Their waving placards read "Wanted for Murder" and featured Dinkins's photograph.[116]

Matters worsened for the mayor in early December after a gang of Hasidic men severely beat a homeless African American man, again in Crown Heights. After a subsequent arrest and detention of one of the alleged assailants, Jewish supporters demanded his immediate release from custody. Asked for comments about the assault, Dinkins was quick to condemn what all the preliminary police releases had reported to be another example of an unprovoked vicious attack on a defenseless, helpless victim. Some Jews immediately reacted to the mayor's assessment as being completely incorrect and premature. Once more Dinkins found himself in the middle of a racial conflict, trying to compete with hecklers bent on drowning out the mayor's voice with shouts of "Jew hater." This outpouring of emotion occurred at a Democratic club in Queens on December 3, 1992. Meanwhile the assailants were explaining their reason for the assault. According to their version, the victim had in his possession tools stolen from the Jewish center; he was escaping the area when the confrontation occurred. The Jewish assaulters claimed their attack was defensive. The facts did not matter so much for Dinkins as Jewish reactions to his initial response. Even one political supporter who earlier had praised the mayor's "wonderful record on Jewish issues" now alleged that his honor "knee jerks any alleged incidents against blacks."[117] Others judgments of Dinkins were considerably harsher. One Jewish woman shrieked at Dinkins, "You are just as dangerous as Farrakhan. The only thing is that you are an elected official and you can cause me more harm."[118] In his own defense, Dinkins asked, "When an African American is lying beaten, alone, he's been beaten by someone. Then what am I supposed to do?"[119]

Thus began the end to Dinkins's political career. There is some justification for arguing that its demise started in 1991 when an out-of-control car driven by a Hasidic Jew hit and killed a seven-year-old African American child in Crown Heights. Hours later, in an act of apparent revenge, one individual from a black gang fatally stabbed Yeshiva student Rosenbaum. The jury's acquittal of the accused assailant and the overwhelmingly celebratory black reactions to the verdict inevitably caught Dinkins—predictably and inescapably—in a strong vise between Jews and African Americans, a hold that only tightened after the Hasidic assault on a defenseless man behind the Jewish center, and the mayor's quick condemnation of an apparently wanton attack. Dependent as the mayor was for electoral success on strong support from African American voters and moderately lukewarm assistance from a minority of Jewish residents, Dinkins, as a most embattled incumbent, entered the 1993 mayoral race with so many obvious uncertainties about viable prospects for rekindling what had been in 1989 a winning coalition of African American, Jewish, Hispanic, and liberal white supporters.

Already, by the end of 1992, another showdown with Giuliani was obviously imminent, and Dinkins was also about to face an announced Democratic primary challenge from city council president Andrew J. Stein. Both the incumbent's apparent intraparty challenger and a resurrected Republican foe had accumulated many millions of dollars. At a massive December rally for Stein, some seven hundred supporters in attendance heard from Adam Clayton Powell IV of East Harlem and from Rabbi Shea Hecht of the Lubavitch sect. From all early appearances, Dinkins faced a struggle just to remain the Democratic nominee, but before the end of May 1993, Stein realized the futility of trying to unseat an incumbent and withdrew. Still vying with the mayor for a Democratic nomination were Roy Innis, the national leader of the Congress of Racial Equality, and Eric Melendez, a somewhat unknown Hispanic leader. Neither of these in-party rivals was really able to cause Dinkins as much worry and concern as Republican Giuliani in his second bid for mayor. That the two Democratic rivals were never serious causes for mayoral anxiety became obvious from the results of the primary. Dinkins trounced both men. He outpolled the combined Innis-Melendez total by 68–32 percent, thereby insuring another showdown with his most formidable GOP opponent from 1989.[120]

With the Democratic nomination secured, Dinkins soon found that many party members and even some of his appointees were either backing him "very skittishly," not endorsing him, or worse, bolting to Giuliani. Fire Commissioner Carlos M. Rivera was typical of the mayoral appointees who went over to the Republican candidate. Among other things, Rivera accused Dinkins of an anti-Hispanic bias and of not prioritizing the fire department. Several aides to former mayor Koch also crossed party lines to lend their support and advice to the GOP challenger. The reason these former Democratic insiders turned outsiders was obvious; the defectors were bitter at their loss of political influence after Koch's defeat in 1989. Worse, the likelihood in 1993 was for much less enthusiastic African American support for Dinkins than he had received from the minority four years earlier. As one non-white analyst put this erosion of interest, "there is still disappointment that many of the dreams, hopes and aspirations that came with the election of a black mayor have not been realized."[121] But all the movements in the wrong direction for the incumbent had some potential to work favorably in the end for Dinkins's status now that he had become an underdog. As the *New York Times* indicated, a perception of Dinkins being "dumped on and persecuted by his critics" could possibly have offered the positive effect of benefiting the mayor as an African American victim.[122]

As for Giuliani's strategy, the Republican never needed to mention race directly. Circumstances allowed him to ignore it altogether in his speeches and advertisements as "one of the less significant issues" and to still benefit from its presence in the minds of New Yorkers. The true implications of the GOP candidate's mentioning and emphasizing so much the other issues such as safety,

crime, drugs, and welfare in speeches and political commercials subtly refer-
enced only one thing for white voters, and this was the poorly disguised message
with race written all over it. Professor Andrew Hacker recognized the subterfuge as well as most everyone else who was following New York's mayoral contest. One month before election day, Hacker, a Queens College faculty member,
stated why whites were planning to vote overwhelmingly for the GOP candidate: "Because they have decided that this middle-aged, middle-class gentleman
[Dinkins] represents black New York—black power, that this is going to be an
apology for black behavior, which so many white people, just not far beneath
the surface, feel is dragging the city down."[123] According to Hacker's assessment,
voters did not need to know much about Giuliani or his platform for the city because "they'll vote for him anyway because of what he's not."[124] A public opinion
poll published in the *New York Times* on October 5 confirmed the existence of
some serious doubts concerning both candidates. At the same time, however, the
survey clearly indicated how differently specific population segments evaluated
Dinkins and Giuliani's capacities for effective rule at city hall. An overall conclusion among white residents—whether Jewish or Roman Catholic—was that
having Gracie Mansion transition to the Republican challenger would no doubt
bring to the mayor's office someone with greater capabilities for solving New
York's problems than Dinkins.[125]

As the race for mayor came down to the final weeks, ugliness and smears came
from both sides. Brooklyn Baptist preacher William A. Jones, an avid Dinkins
supporter, crossed the line of decency with claims that Giuliani encouraged "fascist" elements.[126] Although the Democrat made some effort to distance himself
from this characterization of his rival, Dinkins showed no intention of repudi-
ating Jones's support. On the other side, the GOP city comptroller candidate,
Herman Badillo, was guilty of conducting a blatantly racist campaign, and often
during running mate Giuliani's many appearances before ethnic audiences, listeners heard the Republican candidate's references to the Dinkins administration's impact on the city as one where criminals "slaughtered" children and police
and where "streets are overwhelmed by drug dealers."[127] The challenger's call for
an immediate end to affirmative action and set-aside contracts for minorities and
women resonated with white voters because they accepted the Republican's argument that the two programs resulted in both waste and favoritism. During the
campaign, by most objective standards, members of the white media showed no
fairness toward Dinkins. Calling specific attention to their attacks on him, one
New York Amsterdam News editorial angrily charged that newspaper reporters
and several radio talk-show personalities had "systematically attempted to de-
mean and discredit" the incumbent. The black editor described many Caucasian
writers and broadcasters as "raw and hateful."[128] It was no wonder with an election campaign jaundiced by such degrees of vilification and harsh accusation
that one *New York Times* editorial described both Giuliani and Dinkins as "im-

perfect" candidates. Most reluctantly the newspaper's tepid endorsement went to the incumbent Democrat. As the editor explained an unenthusiastic recommendation of Dinkins, "damage controllers are appreciated only when they have been replaced by damage creators. The fear about Mr. Giuliani is that he might be such a person."[129]

Despite support at rallies from noted personalities like Jesse Jackson, Bill Cosby, and Robert DeNiro and Dinkins's valiant attempts at reviving the African American-Jewish coalition by his attendance the weekend before the election at a breakfast with four Jewish U.S. senators, the incumbent lost to Giuliani by more than forty-four thousand votes. In 1993, the African American mayor performed poorer with both Hispanics and major white subgroups than he had four years earlier. A general consensus existed among black analysts that racism had exerted the decisive role in the outcome, but in all probability, the financial effects of a national recession upon New York had an equally important influence on the result as well. These were the more obvious explanations, but Dinkins's loss also resulted from a spike in crime, his bad relations with the police, the city's loss of revenue, and Jewish perceptions of his prejudice against them in all the major media-profiled conflicts with African Americans.[130]

Freeman Bosley Jr. and Clarence Harmon in St. Louis

St. Louis in the 1990s—like Chicago during the previous decade with the election, administration, and legacy of Harold Washington—progressed from having an African American mayor who was popular with the minority but generally loathed by white residents to the victory of a Caucasian-backed but African American-perceived "Uncle Tom." Similar in many respects to Eugene Sawyer's temporary elevation in the Windy City, the Missouri river city's black interim mayoral choice lasted in office for only one term, when assertive white forces reclaimed city hall from minority control. Any understanding of St. Louis racial political realities through most of the twentieth century requires comprehending the basic circumstances there before the aberration of 1993 that elevated an activist-minded African American candidate into the city's mayoral office. Not unlike Chicago, in its racial climate and composition, coauthors Robert Huckfeldt and Carol Weitzel Kohfeld have observed that Missouri's largest metropolis is "one of the most racially segregated cities in America."[131] Outcomes in mayoral elections from 1945 to 1993 usually occurred on the basis of which candidate had pledged the fewest promises to African Americans. This applied even in 1985 for Vincent C. Schoemehl's surprising victory in the Democratic primary over incumbent Jim Conway, after the previous underdog's campaign pledge to black residents to reopen a recently shuttered north side ghetto hospital, which the eventual loser had ordered to close. On this matter and others, the outcome did not ultimately matter much for St. Louis blacks because no sooner had Schoemehl become mayor than he broke his promise to the minority to re-open the health facility.[132]

Similar again to Chicago, where Washington's Democratic victory resulted in large part from his rivals splitting the white vote, the astonishing emergence of circuit clerk Freeman Bosley Jr. was because he had clearly become the benefi-ciary of white infighting. When St. Louis Democrats went to vote in the city's mayoral primary on March 2, 1993, Bosley's rivals on the ballot were three Cau-casians. Instead of concentrating their pitch on the threat from a black candidate, St. Louis aldermanic president Thomas A. Villa and Missouri state representa-tive Anthony Ribaudo wasted most of their energies exchanging personal insults with each other. Ex-alderman Steven C. Roberts, taking the role of gentleman, remained above the fray—expressing personal indignation and anger at both his white rivals and advising everyone to "end this petty family squabble and re-turn our full attention to the people."[133] In the end, decisively solid bloc voting from the predominantly black north side of St. Louis delivered a primary victory to Bosley. This success by the African American contender generated the most racially divisive general election in St. Louis history, one that climaxed aston-ishingly one month later in a victory for the African American candidate. An influential factor behind why Bosley had obtained enough white votes to emerge victorious had been his often-stated opposition to using either cross-town or city-county busing to bring about a desegregation of St. Louis's racially imbal-anced public schools.[134]

On a regular basis, almost from the moment of Bosley's move to city hall, con-troversies as well as negativity began swirling around him in sharp reaction to many of his administrative decisions and methods. Perhaps symbolically, soon after an April 20, 1993, inauguration, smelly, dirty floodwater from an overflow-ing Mississippi River inundated St. Louis. Old Man River's rampaging water, it seemed to white residents, was a bad omen of what might follow now, with a devil-be-damned African American in control of what they considered to be their city. During the summer of 1993, a few months into Bosley's four-year term, two frightful indications of future disenchantments with him occurred. First in June, he shocked and dismayed many residents by appointing a vocal gay-rights activist to the city's civil rights panel. Then two months later, in August, he urged city council members to raise the municipal sales tax by two cents. Sparking criticism, these two actions exemplified for whites what kind of mayorship they might expect from Bosley. Yet the reactions to these two early inputs from the new mayor were tame if they are compared to what followed. In May 1994, news reports disclosed the mayor's rift with Clarence Harmon, the police chief. Unlike previous disputes between St. Louis mayors and cops over policy differences, the current problem, according to the *St. Louis Post-Dispatch*, was altogether "per-sonal." As the first African American chief of the St. Louis Police Department (SLPD), Harmon gained an excellent reputation for working tirelessly to overcome a municipal legacy of discriminating against hiring and promoting minorities. He was popular because of his personally ordered investigations that ended in discharges and criminal trials for several SLPD members accused of involvement in kickback schemes and other illegal activities.[135]

Harmon's sweep against officer corruption included a reassignment of Mayor Bosley's personal bodyguard. The removal of the policeman from this detail resulted from an apparent linkage of the officer to a moonlighting scandal involving unauthorized off-duty security work. Also as part of the chief's direct intervention in corps reform, Harmon personally arrested two detectives who were close friends of the mayor; their alleged crime was the shakedown of a motorist for three hundred dollars. One of the two men removed by Harmon's actions from the SLPD had had the assignment of protecting state senate majority leader J. B. "Jet" Banks, a close political ally of Bosley and an individual involved in a long running feud with Harmon.

At stake behind the chief's actions was more than a desire to clean up a corrupt police department; also involved was a power struggle over ultimate control of the police force. Bosley made known his desire for a major jurisdictional overhaul that, if enacted, would have removed responsibilities for the SLPD from the state to the mayor's office. An absolute majority of the current police officers, SLPD retirees, and Chief Harmon all strongly voiced their opposition to home rule. In arguing on behalf of it before the state legislature, the municipal lobbyist representing Bosley's position insisted that St. Louis residents always looked first to the mayor's office and city hall for their protection and not to Missouri state government. In opposition, Deputy Chief Raymond Lauer feared that a shift of police authority to Bosley would position the mayor to discipline both the chief and all district commanders and to "replace them at will."[136] Instead of a city solving its problems, then, bitter exchanges and personal differences, for approximately eighteen months, continued to command the attention of the two most powerful black public officials in St. Louis, and their grudging dispute held up progress on several more pressing matters.[137]

The Bosley-Harmon dispute ended with the chief's resignation on November 10, 1995. Nearly tearful on this memorable occasion, as he glanced out over the podium in the direction of his officers—in attendance to hear a momentous speech from a man whose promotion in August 1991 had elevated him as the first person of his race to be named as chief of police in St. Louis—Harmon was there to announce his future employment as a company vice president of United Van Lines. As for his reasons behind a departure, Harmon explained that his resignation followed some irreconcilable differences with Bosley: "In the end, I recognized I couldn't stay under these circumstances, with a (St. Louis Police Board) I can't work with."[138] Harmon's resigning swiftly brought mixed reactions. Shortly before his announcement, a group of African American officers who were loyal to Bosley had expressed a lack of confidence in their police chief, claiming that under his leadership minority force members "have not been treated fairly."[139] This was not the view nationally and among the many varied neighborhood organizations in St. Louis; the overwhelming consensus was that the outgoing head of law enforcement had gained favorable reviews for instituting and championing community policing (Harmon's innovative program was designed to prevent crime by involving local residents in cooperative work with officers). In the end, the state legislature refused to approve local control of St. Louis police; thus the police department remained under the supervision of an independent state board, and Missouri governors continued to select four of its five appointed members.[140]

Other controversies plagued Bosley's attempt at unifying St. Louis residents behind his administration. A takeover by the mayor's office of the St. Louis Housing Authority met with only superficial opposition, but a series of scandals involving mayoral aides and close associates rocked the city, adding more evidence to the negative conclusions of so many St. Louis whites concerning the mayor's performance and fitness for office. When $133,000 went missing from Bosley's much ballyhooed "Midnite Basketball" program for youngsters, he felt especial personal embarrassment since he had so often championed it as an effective deterrent to youth crime. An administrative crackdown on municipal workers residing outside city limits caused considerable negative reaction. Most of these protests came from white municipal employees, because they were the targets as the ordinance's primary offenders. Finally, if there were any need among a majority of whites for additional reminders of Bosley's alleged racial bias against Caucasians, there followed the wave of publicity surrounding his active participation in Muslim militant Louis Farrakhan's Million Man March in Washington, DC on October 16, 1995. For many white residents of St. Louis, Bosley's presence at a march organized by an advocate of African superiority confirmed suspicions concerning the mayor's prejudice against whites.[141]

As many had feared from the outcome of the 1993 mayoral election, their city seemed now more racially polarized than it had been in recent years. Despite what appeared to whites as an apparent setback in interracial progress and harmony, Mayor Bosley continued to enjoy strong support from fellow African Americans. In the view of so many citizens of his race, he remained the ideal role model who had never lost "touch with his roots and the neighborhoods." St. Louis white residents generally had a totally different opinion of Bosley's impact. Polls indicated the majority was disgruntled at losing a voice in city hall decisions and in the development of urban priorities. Residents tended not to forgive or to forget Bosley's actions that had led to Harmon's resignation. Thus, in general, the white residents' response was primarily positive to speculation that was surfacing about Harmon possibly challenging Bosley in 1997. On the other side, local NAACP leaders were not at all enthusiastic about a Harmon candidacy. On September 5, 1996, or some six months before the city's mayoral primary, the civil rights body released a damaging report about the ex-chief. It chastised him for supposedly maintaining a double standard of punishment for white and African American SLPD police officers, with the latter allegedly more severely disciplined than their Caucasian counterparts for similar violations. Members of the NAACP leadership also cited Harmon for having failed to offer African American citizen complaints the same investigative attention as he had provided white residents' pleas for police assistance.[142]

Thus, the stage was all set for an intra-racial bloodbath, and the only uncertainty was whether Harmon would go ahead and contest Bosley for mayor. The first sign of this occurring came on July 18, 1996, with the formal registering of a "Harmon for Mayor" exploratory campaign committee. His agreeing to allow its formation indicated, for potential supporters, the ex-police chief's serious thoughts about making a run for mayor. Then during the weekend after Labor Day 1996, Harmon increased his followers' hope for a bid by hinting more directly of eventual plans to do so. Possibilities for candidacy came in twenty-six hundred letters mailed to friends and potential backers. Harmon wrote to inform people of tentative plans to contest the incumbent. Both actions—a mid-July filing of an exploratory body and Harmon's act in early September of posting to supporters an announcement of tentative mayoral ambitions—shocked, surprised, and disappointed Marit Clark. Many months earlier, on February 6, 1996, Harmon had endorsed the alderwoman as "the better of the announced candidates," and he had announced then his plans to host a February 21 fund-raiser for her. As he stated at the time in his support of her candidacy, "She can really get housing initiatives going in the neighborhoods."[143] In Clark's response to gaining an ex-cop's premature endorsement, she replied confidently how the two of them "share a similar philosophy of government and public service."[144] Asked in February to respond to the backing by Harmon of Clark, Bosley found a contradiction in his rival's action: "Harmon claims politics drove him out of office, and now he wants to play politics. This will go down as the biggest flip-flop of 1996."[145]

Here was one of the milder examples of Bosley's reactions to Harmon's direct involvement in St. Louis mayoral politics. As their campaigns eventually progressed toward primary day on March 4, 1997, exchanges between the incumbent and his nemesis became increasingly personal and vituperative. In their treatment of Harmon, neither the mayor nor his supporters showed much restraint. They were particularly nasty with their choice of descriptive terms for the ex-police chief. Referring to Harmon as "a rented Negro," Freeman Bosley Sr.—a veteran St. Louis alderman and the mayor's father—broadened the parameters for how to treat his son's rival, but the younger Bosley was quick to distance himself from racial comments, asserting "this election is not about who is blacker."[146] Yet verbal barrages against the challenger continued with only the most minimal efforts to curtail unkind racial inferences and without seemingly a serious attempt to reprimand supporters for publicly calling Harmon an "Uncle Tom."

In this, an ugly personal campaign, accusations surfaced about how early in his police career Harmon had monitored protesters in civil rights demonstrations, and Bosley's staff also tried to pin a charge of nepotism on the ex-police chief for his promoting an allegedly undeserving son, Steven, to sergeant in 1993 ahead of twenty-seven more qualified candidates. At countering the incumbent and his entourage of unbridled supporters, Harmon was not any more restrained in his characterizations of his foe. Negativity abounded on both sides during this campaign. As the ex-police chief liked to note for audiences, "Race is being used as the stalking-horse for (Bosley's) demagogic ambition, to support the status quo."[147]

Although the issues never seemed of top priority in this election with all its vitriolic exchanges and insulting charges, the two black mayoral contenders did occasionally stick to matters of importance and did provide information about their plans for actually improving their city. Seeking to find out how they might differ in their approaches to running St. Louis, the *St. Louis Post-Dispatch* solicited responses from each candidate to a series of relevant questions, and the St. Louis paper then published the candidates' unedited answers a few weeks before the city primary. The result showed basic accord on almost everything. Bosley used the opportunity to emphasize how his administration had worked tirelessly to make the city a better place, and he pointed to how his past invaluable experiences at the head of municipal government would have significant and positive impacts on the city's future. Harmon, without benefit of a record of accomplishment in public office, could only promise strong intentions and a personal commitment to outperform the current mayor at governing St. Louis and for offering fairness to everyone in St. Louis.[148]

On March 4, 1997, five days before the primary, the *St. Louis American* editorially announced its choice for mayor. Ever since Bosley's triumph four years earlier, an old guard of St. Louis business and civic leaders, warned the editor, had planned and plotted a recapture of political power by running Harmon as their surrogate. For this reason, the African American newspaper preferred the incumbent. In sharp contrast to the *St. Louis Post-Dispatch* editors' depiction of Bosley as a leader hurt by "allegations of cronyism and petty corruption,"[149] the *St. Louis American*'s view was that the challenger was no more than a stooge and stand-in for disgruntled, displaced white politicians and their affluent corporate sponsors who wanted only to regain lost influence and authority. To the *St. Louis American* editor, the Bosley-Harmon election represented a "referendum on whether this city/region is ready to move forward beyond modest reform and resist those who want to return to a discredited untenable set of past arrangements."[150]

On primary day, March 9, 1997, as the results definitely demonstrate, the city's racially divided electorate viewed two African American candidates most differently. In an odd contest won easily by Harmon (56,926–43,346), voting results reflected the degree of the city's racial polarity. By ratios as lopsided as 52–1, the ex-police chief carried white south side wards. The example of the Sixteenth Ward shows a completely lopsided result indicative of the citywide African American-Caucasian split. Here the challenger registered 6,678 votes to only 199 for incumbent Bosley. With the predominantly white south side having more than 8,000 registered voters than the overwhelmingly black north side, the only requirements for victory were unity behind a candidate and a strong white turnout at the polls. Simply put, white voters possessed a clear electoral advantage in St. Louis political races. In Democratic committeeman James Wahl's accurate assessment of the vote of the overwhelmingly white Sixteenth Ward, pushing Harmon was "an easy sell in our neighborhood. People see him as a man with a reputation for honesty, who can represent all of the city. Our people really felt that Bosley excluded them."[151]

In contrast, a strong feeling of fatal resignation characterized the incumbent's supporters. As Pearlie Evans summarized initial reactions to her candidate's defeat, "We did all that it was possible to do. It just wasn't enough to overcome the 'counterwork.'"[152] Both Wahl and Evans understood the reasons that the outcome had gone so decidedly in Harmon's favor. But still, the main point, according to St. Louis Post-Dispatch reporter Gregory Freeman, why a reality hit had come to Bosley had occurred some months before the election, when the incumbent had begun grasping the harsh realities of his chances for winning reelection. Bosley's campaign strategists' efforts at depicting challenger Harmon as not "black enough" were certain to backfire For many St. Louis whites, Bosley was "too black." All along, the incumbent—as mayor of a mostly segregated and polarized city, one where the distribution of white and black residents was almost even—sensed an entrapment by the split in the city's populace. Bosley put his predicament this way, "When you do something for white folks, the black people are mad at you. When you do something for black folks, the white folks are mad at you."[153] As he succinctly assessed after losing the city's primary, it was "a simple reminder that St. Louis is a diverse city and that candidates who try to appeal to a citywide audience, rather than to one race or another, stand to fare better."[154]

Compared to his often slanderous intra-racial struggle with Bosley to emerge as the Democratic Party mayoral nominee, Harmon's bid in the general election to outpoll two opponents—independent Marit Clark and Republican Jay Dearing—became a relatively easy task. A revolt by the outgoing mayor's upset supporters never materialized. In a concession announcement, Bosley generously put aside all personal bitterness by stating an intention to support the Democratic candidate. The Bosley-Harmon goodwill during the mayoral campaign vanished quickly, however. Days before the ex-police chief's inauguration on April 15, 1997, the lame-duck mayor, taking advantage of his powers of appointment, rushed through council some forty-seven selections to municipal commissions and boards. Embittered that Bosley had snuck these people into offices, Harmon naively wondered what his old rival's motives had been for doing something like this. As the new mayor expressed his negative reactions to reporters, "In the spirit of cooperation, you would have thought he would have given me the opportunity to make these appointments."[155]

With much more to concern the new mayor, Harmon quickly set aside his irritation caused by Bosley's last-hour elevations. Politically inexperienced, he soon found himself engulfed in bigger, more divisive issues. Effectively running St. Louis required political savvy and consistency—qualities Harmon lacked. After only six months in office, his critics had nicknamed him "Mayor Waffle," for his tendency to frequently change positions on pending issues. Problems with members of the city housing authority arose, and Harmon received but ignored several warnings about benefits to "front companies" from a proposed mayoral shift on minority firms. The mayor did not grasp how skeleton organizations—without actual minority ownership—could easily front as minority businesses by offering a minority figurehead. These were among the earliest indications that the job of St. Louis mayor was too difficult for Harmon to manage efficiently. As the *St. Louis Post-Dispatch*'s Freeman commented on October 12, 1997, Harmon's propensity for making so many ill-advised decisions had "raised political eyebrows" to such extent that he was becoming politically isolated and left without much support either among Democrats or in the city council. Even when he assumed a reasonable position, the key groundwork necessary to push a proposition through to a positive conclusion was generally absent. Harmon's efforts to challenge a state statute that banned local governments in Missouri from enacting their own gun-control measures illustrate Harmon's failure to appreciate the daily applications of give-and-take politics. He made no efforts to ally with powerful state legislators from other Missouri municipalities in order to form a favorable bloc for change, and his stand on this local-control matter died in the state general assembly.[156]

With the coming of the 2001 mayoral contest, one conclusion was obvious for a majority of St. Louis whites. From their perspective, "experimenting" with African American mayors had resulted in two failures; for future control of city hall, they were now ready to embrace and select only a white candidate. As the *Economist* understood the mood in St. Louis among the majority race, the city "appears to be on the verge of following New York, Chicago and Los Angeles in one thing. It is about to replace a black mayor with a white one." Apparently even a minority of African American residents had doubts about the wisdom and feasibility of backing a mayoral comeback of Freeman Bosley Jr. Thus victories by Francis Slay in both the primary and the general election seemed inevitable, and true to predictions, not only did Slay become the next mayor of St. Louis, but his election meant the city had reverted to having a white person at its helm.[157]

The two African American ex-mayors reflected on their terms, noting accomplishments as well as obstacles. It was almost a year before Clarence Harmon could offer an honest self-appraisal of his four turbulent years as the mayor of St.

Louis. To make this appraisal he chose his public administration class at Southern Illinois University in Carbondale, where he had become a faculty member. Looking back, Harmon most of all blamed personal indecisiveness as his major shortcoming. "I was an administrator," he confessed, "not a mover and shaker." Then in an indirect reference to the general problems facing ambitious African Americans, he backed into confessing how racism remained active in the forefront. As he gingerly put its apparent consequences, "There's something about rising above where people think you ought to be. It makes people uncomfortable."[158]

In summarizing African American mayoral experiences from the profiled cases, certain patterns and experiences existed. Only in Atlanta—a city where African American residents had the advantage of majority-minority status—was there continuous African American mayoral rule after what one might describe succinctly from a Caucasian perspective as an "experiment" in interracial political empowerment. Whether in Los Angeles after five terms by Tom Bradley, Philadelphia with Wilson Goode, New York's David Dinkins, or St. Louis through the consecutive terms of Bosley and Harmon, majority-majority electorates consistently rallied in each instance behind white replacements for returns to what white residents often considered the comfort zone of old-style, traditional political alignments. Even to a degree in Atlanta, Shirley Franklin's election in 2001 represented the prevalent pattern where electorates have turned more conservative to want a return to less conscious concern about and attention to minorities.

Although Peter K. Eisinger's scholarship predated all but a first half of Bradley's tenure, his sobering conclusions are true to some degree, nevertheless: African American mayors have only a minimal impact. He was writing in 1982, before victories by the most profiled mayors in this study except Bradley, Jackson, and Young, but Eisinger has nonetheless offered a premonition of the consequences. Although he limited his sampling to only a few cases, his analysis accurately demonstrates what winning mayoral elections have meant for African American candidates. Their triumphing, as such, represented "not a merely symbolic prize for minority groups to capture." In a most modest way, these results also afforded some possibilities for an urban "redistribution of existing resources." Disturbingly, some eight years after the publication of Eisinger's essay, William E. Nelson Jr. found that not much had changed. In Nelson's critical judgment, it was the "failure of black leadership and organization [that] has prevented the process of black incorporation from translating itself into major gains in the private sector." Even earlier—one year after Harold Washington's 1987 death—Abdul Alkalimat, writing for *Black Scholar*, provided a somewhat cynical conclusion about African American mayors. Their winning, he felt, "benefited certain professional administrators, consultants, and businesses but . . . often meant little other than symbolism for the masses of black people." Unfortunate, but no doubt a reality nevertheless is the apparent fact that each one of these three assessments contains truthful elements. African American mayors were unable to deliver on the miracles that their strongest and most ardent supporters had expected. Through control of resources and finances, whites in every city continued to hold onto the real power and authority. Thus black politicians had to accept the often temporary satisfaction of winning largely meaningless mayoral elections, which offered titles and large city hall offices but only on rare occasions really provided minority officeholders with the authority necessary to alter municipal priorities.[159]

Defying All Odds

African Americans Winning Statewide Elections

Whenever African Americans have embarked upon efforts to win elections for state offices, the act of being the first to do so would immediately become important. In every case, their resumes came with figurative asterisks to indicate their roles as the pioneering members of their race either to seek a particular position or to receive a party's nomination to run for one. Whether by their opponents' insinuations or officially for the record, race would matter enough to emerge as an important—and perhaps *the most important*—defining characteristic. In particular, among these pioneering minority candidates with hopes of winning election to political office, those who were dependent upon receiving sufficient votes from outside narrowly construed African American-populated districts gained special notice and notoriety. Often, therefore, other more relevant qualifications were pushed aside for those African Americans who had to campaign for white support. There was no escaping electorates' continuing fascination with skin color. It was rare for racial awareness not to creep into discussions and be present in assessments. Pigmentation always appeared as the characteristic that counted most of all as the final determiner in how majorities of voters—Caucasian and African American—would choose among the candidates running for a particular statewide office. But there is one other factor that needs elaboration for several black politicians who have competed against whites: their opponents' baggage. It could be a scandal or a resonating issue such as their party's connection to a recession.

From 1966 through 2008, black candidacies occurred across the United States for various statewide elective offices. Overall, African American office seekers who failed to garner enough white support to politically succeed outnumbered those with successful campaigns. No doubt a major factor contributing to the reason so few minority candidates had convinced white majority electorates to entrust them with public offices was the polarizing effect African American legislative caucuses had on white voters. By focusing most of their agendas and attention in general assemblies and city councils on obtaining as many benefits as possible for African Americans, these special interest groups in many instances prejudiced white voters to infer that members of the minority were the only ones to really gain from bestowing upon African Americans the commonweal that accompanies public offices. In essence, the absolute lesson whites took away from having blacks elected to important political positions ultimately came down to more representation, power, and privileges going to a minority at the expense of the white majority. Interracial contests often, therefore, turned into "us-versus-them" campaigns that thus became virtually unwinnable for African American candidates competing in political races with whites. Therefore as electable as Tom Bradley had been in Los Angeles, Andrew Young in Atlanta, and Norman Rice in Seattle, the African American trio badly faltered as serious contestants in the respective gubernatorial races of California, Georgia, and Washington. When judged locally, the three mayors had gained fine reputations for fairness and competence, but across their states a first aspect of importance and relevance about each one of these contenders for governorships became their skin color and not their impartiality. Hence white political opponents in every instance forced Bradley, Young, and Rice's evolving campaigns to disintegrate into defensive efforts, which clearly disadvantaged these three African American Democrats. As much as they might have desperately tried to center their predominantly white electorates on accomplishments and issues more substantial than race, their political foes and the media never allowed this to occur.[1]

Unsuccessful Campaigns of Roland W. Burris in Illinois and Ken Blackwell in Ohio

African American mayors were not the only minority members who experienced major difficulties at succeeding to governorship—records showcase several more instances of defeat in their attempts at obtaining higher offices by ambitious African Americans holding less prestigious state offices. In two notable cases from 2002 and 2006, Roland W. Burris and Ken Blackwell lost campaigns that would have elevated them to state leadership positions in Illinois and Ohio, respectively. The Illinois comptroller from 1979 to 1991 and later the state attorney general from 1991 to 1995, Burris was a relatively soft-spoken, conservative Democrat with the usually beneficial advantage of downstate Centralia roots in a state noted for its rural prejudice against Chicago. He had served Land of Lincoln residents with distinction. Even so, this cautious African American official, with a successful and scandal-free record in two relatively obscure statewide elective offices, lacked sufficient appeal with Illinois' Democrats to win a primary election over the less experienced Rod R. Blagojevich in 2002, and hence the opportunity to be his party's gubernatorial nominee. In a similar outcome four years later in Ohio, Blackwell was an unsuccessful Buckeye Republican choice for governor. Among active GOP elected officials in his state, Blackwell's conservative credentials certainly compared favorably to officeholders in his party. Two years before he lost the chance for the governorship while secretary of state, the national leadership of the ultra-rightist American Conservative Union had honored the African American Republican elected official; the organization had chosen Blackwell for its prestigious John M. Ashbrook Award in recognition of his "steadfast conservative leadership."[2]

Harvey Gantt in North Carolina

The two failed senatorial bids by Harvey Gantt of North Carolina provide a more spectacular and direct example of racism's effect on electorates. In the contests to continue representing the Tar Heel State in the U.S. Senate, Jesse Helms—the ultra-conservative GOP incumbent—encountered serious challenges both in 1990 and 1996 from Gantt, a courageous civil rights pioneer who had desegregated Clemson University in 1963 and, who twenty years later, had served as Charlotte's first African American mayor. On August 29, 2001, after Helms announced plans to retire from politics, a critical review of his senatorial career appeared in the *Washington Post*. Columnist David S. Broder took sharp exception to assessments of the North Carolinian that appeared in two other newspapers. A *New York Times* editorial demonstrated overt generosity, according to Broder, when it characterized Helms as "a conservative stalwart for nearly 30 years." An appraisal of the retiring Republican senator as "an unyielding icon of conservatives and an archenemy of liberals," as the *Boston Globe* put it, was equally too kind in Broder's judgment. As much as these two characterizations stressed certain elementary truths about a veteran North Carolina lawmaker's political philosophy, the senior staff writer for the *Washington Post* rejected these short phrases as inadequate descriptions of what the senator had truly been and represented in American political history. "What really sets Jesse Helms apart," Broder emphatically declared, "is that he is the last prominent unabashed white racist politician in this country."[3]

After two attempts at defeating the very mean-spirited incumbent, Gantt probably agreed more than most people with Broder. The defeated African American candidate had firsthand personal experience with how Helms had exploited racism in order to survive two reelection challenges. In no campaign after the passage of the Voting Rights Act of 1965 had any white candidate with an African American opponent relied more directly on the race card—with greater tenacity and effect as the key negative factor—than North Carolina's formidable five-term Republican archconservative senator. Twice, in order to persuade white Tar Heel voters of a desperate need to defeat Gantt, Helms resorted to frightening gullible Caucasians with possible negative personal consequences of affirmative action. In a photographic sequence to connect for whites what an unpopular civil rights program would have as an alleged ramification if Carolina voters elected Gantt, Helms used a television advertisement that began with a white hand holding an unopened envelope; shown next was the same hand crumpling a letter found inside the envelope as an unseen speaker offered without elaboration these sobering words as a reminder of what would likely transpire from a Gantt victory: "You needed that job. And you were the best qualified. But they had to give it to a minority because of a racial quota."[4]

Harold E. Ford Jr. in Tennessee

Just how much a candidate's racial identity can maintain a lingering presence in a key political campaign is demonstrated by what occurred in Tennessee during the 2006 U.S. Senate contest. After the two major parties had chosen their nominees in state primary elections, the contest pitted Representative Harold E. Ford Jr., a light-skinned African American Democrat, against Robert "Bob" Corker, an ex-mayor of Chattanooga and a Republican. Obviously worried (and with good reason, after a number of statewide public-opinion polls indicated a Ford victory), Coker, following the Republican tradition of Jesse Helms, turned to racism in order to gain momentum against a photogenic, Ivy League-educated bachelor opponent. The two candidates had taken almost identical stands on the issues and nothing of any substance had separated a pair of conservative candidates until a vicious television campaign advertisement highlighted the only major distinction. In the ad, a sexy blond woman gave Ford a suggestive personal invitation to contact her. Immediately this most despicable commercial engulfed the Democratic candidate in an awkward defensive position. Suddenly to white voters, it mattered little that the congressman from Memphis had described himself as "a different kind of Democrat." Now the important thing was his visit to the Playboy Mansion in California; that visit, in the alleged company of scantily clad or naked women, served as the basis of insinuations about Ford's character and the commercially exploited white female acquaintance whom Ford had supposedly met while there. The Coker campaign used her tantalizing voice and image to produce the desired negative effect on the African American candidate and reversed his previous references to the importance of religion in his life; for many righteous and religiously fundamental Tennesseans, the Democrat now appeared no more than a self-serving hypocrite. Confronted by George Stephanopoulos of ABC-Television News about the appropriateness of implying that Ford was really a two-faced "hypocrite," Corker replied that "I don't use words like that, but he's certainly running as somebody that he's not."[5] In looking for the main reason behind the Democrat's defeat, one can decide between two crucial factors. Did the loss result more from the effects of the sexually implicit advertisement or from the much-publicized legal troubles associated with alleged corruption involving other prominent members of the Ford family in Memphis? In all likelihood, both matters had equal significance, and each explanation for Ford's defeat was related to race. Still present in the minds of so many white Tennesseans, any suggestion of miscegenation remained for them morally wrong and repulsive, and all African American candidates seeking white votes had to adhere to a much higher standard of personal integrity than white office seekers. The outcome of the Senate race was a decisive Corker victory (929,911–879,976). No matter which factor carried greater weight, it was the winner's willingness to inject race into the campaign that definitely produced a profound effect on the election.[6]

Successful Senate Bids

A decade before Ford's defeat in Tennessee and just prior to Gantt's second loss to Helms in North Carolina, a book edited by Huey L. Perry appeared, titled *Race, Politics, and Governance in the United States*. In an attempt to determine if "deracialization" or "New Black Politics" accounted for minority candidates' victories, Perry assembled a collection of essays on this topic by different political scientists. Each scholar examined the final results of different white-African American elections. In the editor's introduction to the anthology, readers discover that Perry "defines deracialization as minimizing or avoiding racial issues in electoral campaigns in order to attract white support." As evidence suggestive of it working effectively, Perry points to 1989 as "the watershed year of deracialization"; there were, he claims, nine noteworthy examples during that year of the formula working beneficially on behalf of African American candidates' bids for white votes in either elections or reelections.[7] In the cited cases, the onus for deracializing campaigns always seemed to rest more with the minority office seekers than with their white opponents.[8] Evidence suggests, though, that the responsibility lies in the other direction. When white adversaries of African American candidates allowed issues to dominate elections or when they altogether bungled using the race card by either overplaying or exaggerating it, African Americans seeking election to public offices tended to fare better in interracial contests.

Edward W. Brooke III in Massachusetts

In statewide political races featuring African Americans pitted against whites, it was liberal-leaning Massachusetts—where African Americans accounted for less than 3 percent of the total population—that nationally pointed the way as the pioneering state in an election where the majority-majority overlooked the racial factor enough for a black candidate to defeat a Caucasian opponent in a significant statewide contest. The breakthrough occurred in 1966 when Bay State voters decided on a "Negro" Republican to replace Leverett Saltonstall, a veteran lawmaker who was retiring from the U.S. Senate. Edward W. Brooke III set an example as a winning pioneer and as the first African American since Reconstruction to achieve the honor of serving a state in the nation's upper chamber. Coming from neither rural Southern poverty nor ghetto deprivation, Brooke was the talented son of an attorney for the Veterans Administration in Washington, DC. After graduating from Howard University, he entered the army where he advanced to captain in the all-African American 366th Combat Infantry. As a soldier, he received several military decorations for his heroic service against fascist forces in the Italian campaign of World War II. Following an honorable discharge after the war, he studied law at Boston University and graduated with an LL.M. degree in 1949. Without any employment offers from established legal firms, Brooke began practicing law as a self-employed attorney. He interrupted his legal practice numerous times to enter politics as a candidate for several offices, but all of his early efforts to win elective positions ended in losses. Not one to surrender, Brooke finally won in 1962 when he defeated Eliot Richardson in the Republican primary and then Democratic nominee Frank Kelly in the general election for attorney general. Forces supportive of Kelly in the latter contest had conducted a dirty campaign against the African American contender, referring to Brooke as a "pushy nigger." Half-intoxicated, flashily dressed, ill-mannered black stooges were sent into suburbs in old cars laden with Brooke campaign stickers with an assignment to ask suburban white residents about houses that the Republican candidate might purchase. In the end, all these unethical tactics failed. Brooke overcame the dirty tricks and sabotage to collect more than 1.1 million votes. An analysis of the result reveals that the winning Republican collected fewer than 25,000 votes from the state's insignificant African American population. Speaking to reporters in response to his secured victory, the newly elected attorney general claimed he had not been "asked more than five questions on civil rights in the last two months." Columnist Carl Rowan offered an interesting explanation for why whites in Massachusetts had elected Brooke. Their votes, Rowan reasoned, represented for an overwhelmingly white electorate a relatively easy "expiation of sin." By supporting Brooke, "proper Bostonians" ridded and expunged themselves of "guilt feelings about race" in obviously a less painful manner than "letting a Negro family into the[ir] neighborhood or shaking up a Jim Crow school setup."[9]

As the Commonwealth's attorney general, Brooke achieved an enviable record along with a considerable reputation for independent thinking. In 1964, the year of his reelection and conservative Barry Goldwater's presidential campaign, the African American officeholder refused to endorse the ultra-conservative GOP nominee. As attorney general, Brooke also rejected calls for personal involvement in civil rights, excusing himself by claiming that his participation would only harm and destroy the political opportunities of African American candidates in search of necessary white support for triumphs. As he put his reluctance for any direct involvement, "If I did confine myself to Negro problems alone, there would hardly ever be another Negro elected to public office except from the ghetto, and justifiably so."[10]

Into a second term as attorney general, Brooke decided to seek the soon-to-be-vacated Saltonstall seat in the U.S. Senate. Hints he was possibly planning to go after this high office occurred twice during early 1966. For *Atlantic*, he wrote "Where I Stand," an article published in March. It was a synopsis of an earlier released work, *The Challenge of Change: Crisis in Our Two-Party System*. The latter study, a book-length revelation of ideas, represented the African American officeholder's thoughts and ideology on social-welfare programs as well as his harsh critiques of what he branded the 1964 GOP "aberration"[11] of nominating Goldwater and of his political party's overreliance on personalities. Brooke's specific suggestions included legislative initiatives such as extending Medicare-plan benefits to younger people, instituting a negative federal income tax, improving the quality of management of War on Poverty programs, increasing the minimum wage and its coverage, and developing a "giant transportation network."[12] As for Goldwater's nomination in 1964, Brooke judged it "a deviation from anything resembling traditional Republican values and virtues." For the party to regain a stronger position with the electorate, Massachusetts's attorney general advised the GOP to avoid such "glamorous personalities [as] military heroes, former film stars, and other celebrities, [along with] 'going it alone' Republicans."[13]

An early indication that Brooke was no diehard Republican had come in the Bay State during the senatorial race between John F. Kennedy and Henry Cabot Lodge in 1952. Italian-born and–raised wife Remigia, attended an afternoon-tea, fund-raiser for the Democratic challenger. Some fourteen years later, when he was questioned about her presence at this function—what many observers might judge an apparent faux pas—not overly partisan Brooke quipped that she "was there counting the Democrats for us Republicans." A considerable asset, who charmed her audiences with accented English, Remigia played an important role in her husband's campaigns. She became a valuable contributor to Brooke's campaigns, especially among the many Italian-Americans living in Boston's North End neighborhood.[14]

After Brooke's selection as the Republican nominee to fill Saltonstall's seat in the Senate and the Democrats' choice of Endicott Peabody, some immediate active bidding for votes began, and the hard campaigning continued until the election. Peabody's campaign was very rare for its almost complete absence of any references to race. Fear-mongering did not figure at all in the Peabody-Brooke election. All across Massachusetts, residents certainly were aware that Brooke was an African American, but only 5 percent of polled whites believed the

Republican was pushing too hard on behalf of African American equality. In the Brooke-Peabody contest, unlike what Perry has described as political deracialization or the deliberately orchestrated effort by a black office seeker to woo white voters by ignoring civil rights and minority issues, both the men running in this statewide election made conscious, concerted efforts to completely deracialize their campaigns in order to concentrate on issues of greater benefit to Massachusetts and the nation. Examples of how the African American Republican and his opponent attempted a focus on matters other than race included Brooke's bold plan for improving conditions for senior citizens and Peabody's concerns about "the alarming rise in the national crime rate."[15] Solutions followed in both cases; Brooke advised increases in social security benefits and in the earning maximums allowed without penalty taxes for the recipients, and Peabody proposed adding more officers to police departments. Both men offered plans for bringing more industry into the Bay State, and of course, partisanship certainly had a role in the two campaigns. As a member of the party not in control of the White House, Brooke exploited this to his advantage by leveraging a charge of "wasteful spending" on the "inadequate, uncoordinated and misdirected" programs of Lyndon Johnson's administration.[16] As a result of their alleged lack of cohesion and value, Brooke liked to emphasize to his audiences that need existed for a much greater Republican presence in the U.S. Senate because increasing GOP numbers in the chamber would offer the best means of insuring considerably more than "little progress in ending the habitual and endemic ills affecting Boston and virtually every major urban center."[17]

Unlike on other matters, the two liberal Senate candidates—Attorney General Brooke and Governor Peabody—differed sharply on what they considered to be the most desirable Vietnam policy and strategy. Although both candidates believed that the United States should not abandon altogether its military commitments to Southeast Asia, Brooke opposed escalation of the effort; he favored United Nations-sponsored negotiations as a preferred alternative to increasing troop deployments. Bringing the two warring sides to a peace conference under the auspices of the international organization, the Republican argued, would provide the best means for finding a lasting, peaceful resolution to the conflict. In contrast, Peabody remained a steadfast supporter of the Johnson administration's handling of the war. Thus, to the loyal Democrat, serious peace talks would only follow an escalation of the war and the continuation of American heavy aerial bombardments of North Vietnam. Brooke's views on Vietnam did not sit well with conservative Republicans. Their suspicions of him arose for two other reasons as well. His securing an endorsement from the Americans for Democratic Action did not go over well with party right wingers, and Brooke's favorable view of Johnson's social-welfare programs was another source of irritation. These controversial stands further alienated members of the GOP right; and their memories of his criticizing the party's nomination of Barry Goldwater remained fresh enough to remind them that he was too liberal a Republican candidate for them to accept and support. Also unhelpful at winning over party conservatives was Brooke's advice to Republicans to "go out to the highways and byways . . . and not to the country clubs" to find support.[18]

With the two campaigns primarily centered on issues and policy, race did not figure into the contest. Peabody's record on civil rights was stronger than Brooke's, and the Democrat refused to encourage a white backlash. After covering this campaign and reflecting on several previous Senate races, *Boston Globe* reporter Timothy Leland concluded that the Brooke-Peabody election not only had been "clean," but had represented "one of the quietest Senate contests in memory." True or not, the 1966 campaign did have meaningful consequences for both political parties. Republicans worked hard to reestablish themselves after their debacle in 1964, while Peabody as President Johnson's "gung-ho" supporter was important not only to the current administration but also to Democrats. All in all, the campaign of these two men vying for a Senate seat ultimately became "one of the country's most closely watched elections." Brooke's win by a sizable plurality (more than 300,000 votes) turned into a major national news story.[19]

As senator-elect, the African American Republican became the first member of his race in this position since Reconstruction—an accomplishment that blacks actively involved in civil rights greeted with mixed reviews. His critics—viewing Brooke negatively, as a nonparticipant without any notable public association with the movement and its campaigns for integration and equality—saw him more as the passive beneficiary of other people's sacrifices than as an important contributor to better conditions for African Americans. Disparaging the GOP politician even more, in the opinions of several activists, were his justifications and excuses for a lack of direct personal involvement. Thus, one Harvard University political scientist who had observed Brooke for several years reached the conclusion that Brooke is "more white than many white persons in this state in appearance, mannerisms, and philosophy. I don't know if you could even call him a Negro candidate. He didn't raise any of the issues that normally would be brought out with a Negro running for office."[20]

Rejecting what Brooke's biographer John H. Cutler referred to as "the role of lionized Negro," the independent-minded Massachusetts Republican entered the U.S. Senate in 1967 for two terms of unpredictable service. Unlike later-day GOP partisans and conservative ideologues Gary Franks and J. C. Watts, who both had deliberate intentions to follow their party's leaders carefully on most every important issue before the House of Representatives, Brooke dared to act with much greater independence. Jacob Javits, a New York liberal Republican, almost immediately became the African American senator's acknowledged mentor, and he continued in this role throughout Brooke's twelve years on Capitol Hill. The New Yorker taught his charge that taking a maverick stand on the side of righteous, moral causes was much better than obediently and blindly following an erring GOP majority.[21]

The Javits-Brooke tandem was especially independent throughout Richard Nixon's tumultuous presidency. Before judging three presidential nominees' suitability to serve on the Supreme Court, Brooke thoroughly examined each candidate's credentials in order to ascertain from background information their judicial philosophies and records. Between 1969 and 1971, from Brooke's personal and staff investigations into how judges Clement F. Haynesworth Jr., G. Harrold Carswell, and William H. Rehnquist had handled lower court civil rights cases, the GOP senator discovered similar patterns in the trio's recalcitrance and obstruction. Brooke, as a result, thrice rose from his seat on the Senate floor to list separately at different times why none of these three judicially conservative appointees should gain a confirmation for the highest court. In the case of Rehnquist receiving Nixon's appointment to replace John Marshall Harlan Jr. as a justice, Brooke feared the conservative nominee's potential "press to move the Court from its commitment to equal protection and opportunity" and to place "property rights [a] rank higher than human rights."[22]

Differences also occurred with Nixon over the president's Vietnam War policies. By the summer of 1972, Brooke had become a most irksome foe of American participation. On July 24, 1972, he pushed, unsuccessfully, to amend a military procurement bill. His objective was to restrict the employment of all weapons (procured through congressional authorization) on the twin tasks of guarding and protecting withdrawals of American ground, air, and sea forces from Indochina. Brooke's amendment also required a full evacuation from Southeast Asia operations within four months of the legislation's adoption. Although his initial efforts failed at forcing the administration to abandon its mission in Vietnam, the senator showed no signs of relenting. A personal inspection tour of the embattled Asian nation during the spring of 1973 confirmed Brooke's conviction that the war was futile and led him to renew efforts to cut off defense funding for the conflict.[23]

As evidence accumulated, in 1973, with increasing disclosures of criminal and unethical wrongdoing on behalf of Nixon's reelection campaign, Brooke was among the first GOP senators to favor the appointment of a special prosecutor to check into the allegations. Then with the astounding revelations of a possible presidential cover-up, the maverick Bay State senator added his name to a growing list of lawmakers who were demanding further investigations into possible wrongdoing. Thereafter, through the public Watergate testimonies before the Senate and Nixon's eventual resignation, Brooke consistently remained behind unrelenting efforts to explore everything related to the scandal. Brooke did not condone Gerald Ford's pardoning of his predecessor. Like Robert C. Byrd of West Virginia, the black senator considered Ford's action both wrong and inappropriate, because the presidential pardon should not have occurred until "after the judicial process has run its course."[24]

Unlike most Republican senators on many issues, Brooke was as much a libertarian as a liberal. With dissent growing on college campuses against both the domestic and international policies of the administration, Nixon's White House began to consider surveillance and purging campaigns against university professors with leftist ideologies. Any thought of the government's clearing people to teach offended Brooke. He was forceful in his case against censorship; "We are talking about the education of grown men and women, fully able to think for themselves."[25] He cautioned, "The notion of some political or ideological check on scholars engaged in free inquiry and instruction is alien to the entire concept of a university, wherever it functions."[26] Again, as further evidence of Brooke's courageous roles as a free political thinker and fearlessly independent Republican, one finds the senator's defense of a woman's right to choose abortion. Although the senator represented a predominantly Roman Catholic state, this fact did not impact his open support of freedom of choice. Even while battling hard in 1978 for reelection, Brooke openly praised Supreme Court justices for their *Roe v. Wade* decision legalizing women's right to abortions. The senator's willingness to confront this question directly reflected in many ways his much larger fight and disagreement with conservative Republicans concerning female rights and the empowerment of women. Unlike GOP right-wingers generally, Brooke was vocal in his support of the Equal Rights Amendment; to the senator its ratification represented a "personal magna carta" for women and was a desirable culmination to their long struggle for fairness and justice. As he emphasized, "They seek nothing more than equality. . . . and deserve no less."[27]

On a variety of social, economic, and educational issues, Brooke consistently aligned with activist senators who sought, like him, an expanded federal government role in assisting the nation's most disadvantaged citizens. Brooke, for example, was the only Republican among twenty-three senators who were against dissolving the Job Corps in 1969. Also in that year, he was equally proactive in his reactions to the report of the National Advisory Commission on Civil Disorders. From a study of the document, Brooke found two unmet problems in need of immediate legislative attention. First of all, he pointed to "paradoxically and inexcusably . . . the area of equal employment by Federal, State, and local governments" as examples of how laws intended to promote greater opportunities for everyone were failing to achieve intended results. As another matter to overcome, Brooke cited the need for an "expansion and encouragement of minority entrepreneurship." Both shortcomings could be eliminated, he thought, if Congress passed better, more effective legislation.[28]

Throughout Brooke's twelve-year Senate career, assistance to poor people—through an advocacy of and support for programs—remained key commitments on his to-do list. As a way of eliminating a backlog of cases responsible for "growing disrespect for law" and "frustration and despair," he argued forcefully in 1969 for his fellow congressmen to appropriate additional federal funds to the Equal Employment Opportunity Commission. With Javits and a coalition of liberal

Democrats in 1972 and 1973, Brooke went on public record as favoring the establishment of a Federal Full Employment Board, but bills designated for this purpose failed to emerge from the Committee on Labor and Public Welfare. Rather than becoming personally discouraged from his various failures to effect changes, the African American senator through the end of his tenure on Capitol Hill remained steadfast in his determination and support for pushing legislative attempts to make employment a guaranteed right. Also important was his crusade against hunger both nationally and internationally. He consistently expressed avid support for the Food Stamp program and for several initiatives to end global starvation, and he matched these efforts with a concern for eliminating the major causes of malnutrition both in the United States and around the world.[29]

For Brooke, the most fundamental way that the United States could resolve the country's most pressing social and economic problems was to equalize educational opportunities for all American children. During his second year on Capitol Hill, when federal Title I dollars were granted to the nation's rich school districts, the senator judged this appropriation absurd and unjustified, for in his opinion the entire appropriation needed to "go exclusively to communities in which 10 percent of the school-age children qualify as disadvantaged students."[30] Although his common-sense argument emerged early in his career in Washington, Brooke continued to advocate on behalf of underprivileged children until his departure from office at the end of the 1978 session. His fight took on several forms, including his courageous defense of busing in order to achieve racial integration. Assuming a position that was extremely unpopular with many, if not most, of his constituents, Brooke laid down a challenge to his congressional colleagues. With the aim of overcoming school segregation caused by racially restrictive residential patterns, Brooke advised his colleagues to come up with a better alternative than transporting children to achieve integration and improved educational opportunities: "what tools can be used to further our Federal antisegregation policies; how much discretion must be vested in HEW to facilitate accomplishment of these worthwhile policies; what is the impact of limitations, through amendment, on our ability to achieve equality." Brooke's reference is to an amendment offered by Senators Thomas Eagleton and Joseph Biden; it was the two Democrats' intention to preclude the Department of Health, Education, and Welfare (HEW) from acting remedially against any instances of school segregation that might have come from the existence of racially unmixed residential patterns. Eagleton and Biden did not want HEW to have responsibility for rearranging neighborhoods in order to achieve school integration.[31]

Brooke's defense of busing represented a clear case against his often repeated claims that racial identity had no influence on him; he denied any personal impact of race on his actions in order, apparently, to reassure white voters in the midst of both his early losing as well as his later winning candidacies. Despite the often repeated personal words of denial and downplay of race in several of his campaigns for political offices, Brooke's self-serving oratory should not be the judge of his tenure in the U.S. Senate. Although he defied his campaign pledges often as an officeholder, campaigner Brooke certainly was not Senator Brooke, despite what so many contemporary political observers, unsympathetic critics, and friendly biographer John H. Cutler might have incorrectly concluded about the politician.[32] A great deal of "foolin' master" played out in the Senate career of Edward William Brooke III.

To find another Republican senator with a more consistent record on civil rights and with overall African American interests more in center focus than Brooke, one must almost revert back to the period of Radical Reconstruction. Brooke's activities varied from backing home rule and congressional representation for the disfranchised residents of the District of Columbia to cosponsoring legislation for sickle-cell anemia research. He showed no timidity in positioning himself favorably behind both the Congressional Black Caucus (CBC) and colleague-besieged Adam Clayton Powell. Speaking after the death of Harlem's controversial representative, Brooke, in a eulogy, offered unqualified praise. His tribute, incidentally, was the only one given in the U.S. Senate. Also in 1973, when Richard Nixon and several other leading Republicans were ignoring the CBC's presence on Capitol Hill and the organization's list of demands, it was Brooke who announced boldly how "pleased [he was] to work with . . . the Congressional Black Caucus."[33] Having a definite call-to-action perspective that was very much at odds with the increasingly conservative GOP leadership, Brooke never quit trying to sway the GOP in a different, more progressive direction. In one desperate plea, during March of what would become Brooke's final year in the Senate, he tried nudging his fellow Republicans to adopt a dynamic agenda with several more programs reflective not only having a stronger commitment to the free enterprise system but also of other ones for removing all "our children and grandchildren . . . out from under the stigma of dependency, freed from the welfare line, able to feel the joy of independence, of a good job, and the ability to feed, clothe, educate and house our families."[34]

Changing party affiliation could have absolved Brooke from suffering political alliance and association with personally alienating right-wingers, but obviously the senator remained a convinced believer that the Republican Party needed his moderating influence in order to offset the many excesses of conservatives. An example of sobering a party that was moving decisively in direction opposite to his ideology occurred as the Poor People's March, led by the Reverend Ralph D. Abernathy, approached Washington, DC. Speaking to his colleagues, Brooke requested their "saneness, caution, calm thinking, and reasoning" in their reactions toward these marchers on their way into the nation's capital. He pled on their behalf because in his mind their activity was a reflection of "a right guaranteed to them." Adding to this, he admitted to believing the protesters' ambitious goals represented "a useful focus for all members of Congress concerned with the elimination of poverty and hunger in America . . . and [with the] full participation [of every citizen] in our society."[35]

Brooke's support of improving the lot of African Americans, more or less, followed a theme. He was not radical enough to favor overhauling or overthrowing the economic system, but he did think it needed expansion to include all minorities. His plan for making the lives of African Americans generally better revolved around their inclusion. In particular, Brooke's plan took three main forms during his tenure. He encouraged minority entrepreneurship by favoring a plan that established a targeted federal-credit reservoir for loaning black applicants entrepreneurial start-up money through the Small Business Administration. To increase the overall viability of minority-owned banks, he advocated a mandated directive to require all federal departments and agencies to channel and deposit a percentage of their funds through these institutions. As his means of promoting and increasing opportunities for home ownership by African Americans, while in the process, working to end neighborhood segregation, he assumed a leadership role in the fight to win congressional passage of the Fair Housing Law of 1968. And in the struggle to enforce its greater compliance, he sponsored a bill for much tougher law enforcement through a combination of increasing appropriations for the expansion of the regulatory staff and stiffening penalties and fines for the law's violators. On the subject of residences, Brooke backed efforts to provide "decent and suitable living accommodations for low-income families." To the success of this objective, he favored appropriating more federal dollars for public housing, and he sought the enactment of a rent-subsidy program.[36]

For civil rights legislation due to expire without congressional action to renew it, Brooke actively fought to ensure the continuations of these programs. Unlike a majority of Republicans in the Senate, who like Nixon obviously followed their party's Southern Strategy, Brooke, as the Bay State junior senator, chose to associate in 1969 with Northern Democrats in order to back that year's ill-fated Omnibus Civil Rights Bill. Negative votes coming from a combination of Southern Democrats and Republicans on the Committee on the Judiciary enabled Chairman James O. Eastland of Mississippi to block the proposal from ever reaching the full Senate. Thus no floor action and vote followed on a comprehensive four-part package that included increasing equal employment opportunities for every American worker, guaranteeing no prejudicial jury selections, extending the 1965 Voting Rights Act to 1975, and removing the ceiling set in 1968 on appropriations for the Civil Rights Commission. Subsequent efforts by Brooke and a bloc of other liberal-minded senators did result in renewing federal suffrage protections and in continuing the activist role of the Commission on Civil Rights.[37]

In foreign affairs, Brooke's chief interest was Africa. In early 1968, he went on a three-week tour of twelve African nations. He was mainly interested in economic development and regional political conditions. While there, he checked to ascertain how American aid, the Peace Corps, and private investments were functioning, and he examined American programs in Africa to see how they were comparing to the efforts of other countries. From discussions with heads of state, the senator discovered that the United States had "three political assets" to build upon in its dealings with Africans: no legacy of colonial power, the presence of several million African descendants in America, and his nation's "own democratic revolution." From conversations, Brooke discovered that his country was not successful in leveraging its advantages in order to improve relations with the African nations.[38] After returning home, Brooke did not lose interest in African affairs. During the Nigerian Civil War, the senator worked with Republican colleague James B. Pearson of Kansas to channel emergency relief supplies into the strife-torn nation through international humanitarian organizations. As for taking sides, Brooke advised caution, lest enemies construe favoritism as American interference or partiality. Later, with the indigenous population of colonial Rhodesia's (now Zimbabwe) demands for independence growing, Brooke authored Senate Bill 174, banning imports of Rhodesian chromium and imposing trade sanctions against the white regime. The bill passed the Senate (66–26). The African American lawmaker also became one of Capitol Hill's harshest and most vocal critics of South Africa's apartheid-enforcing minority government. After the death of African National Congress activist Steve Biko while in police detention, for example, Brooke made a passionate public plea to President Jimmy Carter to respond with some "effective measures against the Republic."[39]

For African American causes, his harshest critics sneered, Brooke was an active promoter of only symbolic endeavors. This judgment is unfair. His role provided whites with a respected African American leader's opinions of and reactions to several contemporary events. As noteworthy examples of his quiet behind-the-scenes efforts, Brooke, with Senator Hugh D. Scott Jr. of Pennsylvania, cosponsored Senate Bill 14, authorizing and funding a "Commission on Negro History and Culture." Brooke's efforts on behalf of this agency began in 1968, and his tireless pursuit continued into 1970. The Massachusetts senator was also one of the initial Capitol Hill backers who suggested honoring Martin Luther King Jr.'s birthday, January 15, as a federal holiday. Brooke singled out for acclaim the musician and composer Isaac Hayes for contributing to the development of American music as well as for establishing the Hayes Foundation, a philanthropic organization devoted to ending "suffering wherever and whenever possible."[40] After the riots following King's assassination, as well as the violent unrest at the Attica State Prison in New York, Brooke exerted an active role as an African American spokesman with a rational understanding concerning the assessments of causes along with advice for preventing future racial outbreaks. The senator expressed no great surprise at the occurrence of a violent outbreak of insurrection among inmates. There were too many African Americans held in detention at the overcrowded maximum security facility, and Brooke presented reasons to explain their presence in such disproportionate numbers, directly attributing the higher rate of incarceration among black people than Caucasians to several factors, including "less educational opportunities, poorer quality education, more substandard housing, less income, and . . . greater discrimination." As for why the uprising had occurred at Attica, Brooke blamed it on the facility's "dehumanization" of its residents.[41]

Much misunderstanding and some unfair charges followed the request from Mississippi civil rights leader Charles Evers for Brooke to visit Jackson State College for the purpose of the senator conducting a personal inquiry into the fatal shootings of two students by police officers. Unlike the unsavory accounts of Brooke's campus tour made by several other minority members of Congress, and especially the allegations that the Mississippi governor had successfully duped a naive black visitor from Massachusetts, Brooke placed his version of the fact-finding mission to Jackson in the *Congressional Record*. His account notes two reasons for his presence on the blood-stained, bullet-riddled campus: to personally inspect the shooting site and to collect student testimonies. In the senator's assessment, the police assault against unarmed students had resulted without provocation and warning. In addition, his published report on the police action expresses considerable disappointment with Nixon and ascribes a degree of blame both to the president and to many of Brooke's congressional colleagues for demonstrating so much more concern about the white students' deaths at Kent State University than for those at Jackson State. As Brooke stated his outrage at the disparity of concern in the *Record*, "the present challenge is to leave no doubt that black lives are as precious as white lives."[42]

Having in effect bolted his party and Nixon through an active defiance of the Southern Strategy by reelection time in 1972, Brooke met almost no challenge in his bid for a second senate term. From an analysis of opinion polls, the *Boston Globe* reported on November 3 that the incumbent senator was a "lopsided frontrunner" who benefited from an anticipated campaign-fund surplus of some $200,000. Therefore, during the next five days, the largest circulating newspaper in the state did not cover the race. Prognoses of Brooke's chances for an easy victory were correct; the senator smothered Democrat John J. Droney, a Middlesex County district attorney, by "an overwhelming margin." The winner's immediate reaction to hearing the expected election result was a pledge of independence to the residents of Massachusetts; Brooke promised only to "support the President where I think he's right and disagree where I think he's wrong."[43] More elaboration came one day after the election. Speaking of his party's leadership, it "ought to have," Brooke advised, "liberal moderate thought." As for the circulation of rumors spreading that the African American senator might contemplate a run for higher office in 1976, Brooke refused to rule out the speculation about a presidential bid because "Mr. [Spiro] Agnew is not the heir apparent." On the issue of too much federal power shifting from Congress to the executive branch under

Nixon, the recently reelected senator agreed with critics who were declaring it "wrong, and it doesn't matter who is in the White House."[44]

As much as winning had not been difficult in 1972, gaining support six years later proved much more arduous. Democrat Paul Tsongas was an engaging opponent; and a contentious, tell-all divorce as well as a Senate Ethics Committee investigation into allegations that the senator had illegally altered his financial records combined to tarnish Brooke's once-admired reputation. During the final days of the 1978 campaign, Brooke panicked and acted confused. Asked to comment on the merits of the United States developing a neutron bomb, for example, the GOP incumbent showed inconsistency, giving both positive and negative responses. In an October 31 attempt to woo conservatives he was in favor of its development, but he reversed his position two days later during an address to the League of Women Voters. Clarifying, he explained his earlier support as a complete misunderstanding of his true position; what he had meant was that the United States' possession of this weapon would give America "a bargaining chip against the Soviet Union."[45] This was not the only contradictory side to Brooke's troubled reelection bid. In a statement of beliefs and intentions, he left out all mention of support for affirmative action and civil rights. Yet on the basis of his support for both, Coretta Scott King, Clarence Mitchell, and Jesse Jackson campaigned enthusiastically for the incumbent. In 1978, unlike in all previous campaigns, Brooke showed greater duplicity on race; that is, he denied it as an important issue when addressing white voters and tried to capitalize on its significance when seeking African American support. As he warned one large minority audience, "There is a lot more at stake here than just Ed Brooke."[46] Unlike his Republican opponent, Tsongas completely deracialized his campaign—a fact that Brooke later acknowledged as a most admirable feat in his concession statement. The defeated outgoing incumbent senator was gracious enough to praise his Democratic foe "for the quality of his campaign and for the honorable manner he has conducted the campaign."[47]

Different political experts, seeking answers for the winner's plurality of 201,665 votes, have provided a variety of explanations for Brooke's landslide defeat. No analysis, however, did better at reasoning through the factors for this loss than the *Boston Globe*'s perspective given two days after the Tsongas victory. The newspaper's analysis explained how Brooke's demise as a popular public figure had resulted from six months of troubles. What earlier had galvanized an effective coalition of support from liberals, African Americans, Jews, WASPs, Italians, and Irish Catholics became "snarled" in mixed messages. His reelection chances also suffered from the development of a considerable disenchantment with Brooke by philosophically conservative Republicans; what irked and alienated the GOP right wing so much about the senator was his support of the Panama Canal treaty, of women's rights to abortions, of the Equal Rights Amendment, Medicaid, and busing. A *Black Enterprise* editorial found that Brooke deserved both praise and recognition for daring to take these stands and for showing so much political independence from his party. In this editor's opinion, the senator was truly a most tenacious fighter "for the rights of the underdog—blacks, women, the elderly, the poor, and youth."[48]

Fair and factual, this brief assessment countered the ill-informed negative judgments that critics had offered Brooke long before the completion of his twelve-year Senate career. Perhaps the nastiest of the many premature evaluations came from the militant right wing in 1967, and two years later from Chuck Stone. One negative assessment described the then-freshman Republican senator as a "NASP" (Negro Anglo-Saxon Protestant), while in 1969 Stone described Brooke as "a colored Honkie."[49] Black critics who disapproved of the Bay State senator cited as their reasons for negativity his "white tastes," which included passions for opera and for tennis, his membership in the Episcopal Church, his preference for tea over coffee, and the fact that he owned a vacation home on Martha's Vineyard. In Brooke's defense, making these choices was more evidence of his sense of equality than evidence of a desire to act white.[50]

In 2007 Rutgers University Press published *Bridging the Divide*, Brooke's long-awaited autobiography. Filled with personal explanations for his legislative positions and with few regrets, the account by the ex-senator from Massachusetts confirms why he had increasingly become an aberration in his party. Any person reading the book can definitely deduce from his words a personal conviction that the Republican Party had begun to leave him with its nomination in 1964 of Barry Goldwater for president and thereafter with its subsequent shift to the extreme right. Implicitly Brooke offered sound reasoning for his decision after World War II to declare himself a Republican. "In those days, moderates dominated the Republican Party, both nationally and in Massachusetts. . . . It was [in this state] a Republican governor and a Republican legislature that enacted antidiscrimination laws, and Democrats who resisted them."[51]

Carol Moseley-Braun of Illinois

A most unusual episode by an African American office seeker unfolded in Illinois in 1992. Sensing how strong the feelings of women were running against incumbent Alan Dixon because of his support of Clarence Thomas's appointment to the Supreme Court, Carol Moseley-Braun, ignoring the advice of Senator Paul Simon and many other prominent Illinois Democrats, mounted a primary challenge against Dixon. It soon became apparent that her efforts to defeat a well-known incumbent senator were more about gender than about race. Female charges against Dixon began during Senate Judiciary Committee hearings on the Thomas selection, coming as they did after attorney Anita Hill's allegations of sexual harassment. Testifying under oath against the confirmation of her former boss, in a sworn testimony given before a bipartisan panel of senators, Hill charged Thomas with on-the-job, annoying insistences of a relationship. Asked to respond to a serious claim of misconduct and sexual harassment, Thomas completely denied its truthfulness. Thus confronted with a decision of whom to believe—Hill or Thomas—the male-dominated Senate faced a tough confirmation decision. The key question came down to whether President Bush's appointee had indeed acted improperly according to Hill's claims or whether Thomas had become the victim of an angry woman's lies and professional envy. In an apparently complete rejection of Hill's veracity on the witness stand and of her allegations of most unpleasant encounters with the appointee, Dixon, like a majority of senators, opted to believe Thomas and not Hill, thereby uniting feminists, nationally, with both outrage and resolve.

Like Anita Hill, Carol Moseley-Braun was an educated African American woman with a law degree, and her resume from the start appeared excellent for a bid to unseat Dixon in the Democratic nomination. In order to acquire strong female support for her candidacy, Moseley-Braun did not claim to have been a victim of sexual harassment, but she was able to address the problem with so much familiarity and contempt that, all across America, irate women began to identify with the Illinois woman and make her their choice as a prospective U.S. Senate champion against male oppression and misogyny. Before Hill's testimony and Moseley-Braun's candidacy, not many people in Illinois and across the nation had ever heard of or known Dixon's challenger. After completing law school at the University of Chicago in 1972, Moseley-Braun worked for five years as a federal prosecutor. She continued working in the U.S. attorney's office until 1977 and the birth of her son, Matthew. Thereafter, from a Chicago district that included liberal Hyde Park, the female lawyer ran for and won an election as a representative to the Illinois General Assembly. During ten years in Springfield, she experienced some success as a lawmaker. Her greatest achievement was the filing and winning of a reapportionment case; it affirmed the principle of "one man, one vote" in Illinois. She also became the floor leader in the state's lower house for Chicago mayor Harold Washington. Impressively, each year of Moseley-Braun's tenure, the Independent Voters of Illinois, a reform organization, awarded her its "Best Legislator" accolade. In 1987 she ran for and became the recorder of deeds for Cook County. During her four years in this elective position, she garnered both criticisms and praise for how she handled her administrative responsibilities. Moonlighting activities then as a lobbyist and a lawyer brought charges of impropriety against her, but on a positive note, her determination to phase out an antiquated Torrens system implemented by the county in the aftermath of the Great Chicago Fire of 1871 as a guarantee of ownership of land and its physical parameters netted her the appreciation from real estate interests, because old rules had the effect of bogging down the conversion of rental apartments into condominiums. Her administering the records office overall brought needed beneficial reforms for more operational efficiency and less bureaucracy.[52]

Regarding the primary fight to become the Democratic Senate nominee, most political experts considered Moseley-Braun's election a very long shot. Not only did she face in Dixon a veteran incumbent with strong downstate support, but the contest also included Albert Hofeld, a multimillionaire attorney from Chicago. Moseley-Braun struggled as well with other obstacles. The state's leading Democrats endorsed Dixon's reelection. Simon, for example, told voters that the incumbent was "the guy I want fighting for me and all the people in Illinois in the Senate."[53] Even Roland Burris, the only African American holder of a statewide office in Illinois, backed Dixon. Adding more discouragement to Moseley-Braun's chances for electoral success were fund-raising woes, staff dissension, and pessimistic results of several public opinion polls. Pollsters reported her trailing far behind the incumbent. On the other hand, she benefited from one important advantage; Dixon and Hofeld, as conservative Democrats, allowed their female opponent to coalesce support among the Illinois electorate's liberal-minded citizenry and among African American Democratic voters.[54]

The underdog female contestant never relented, barraging Dixon with harsh criticisms at every campaign stop. For instance, in Chicago at Children's Memorial Hospital, Moseley-Braun labeled as "shameful" her chief male opponent's nonparticipation in Senate health-care hearings. With "no record on health care," Dixon, she felt, "should be ashamed."[55] In contrast to his noninvolvement—which contributed to the reason there was no soliciting of ordinary citizens' testifying led to "stealth hearings,"—she promised to fight so the general public could have input on matters of vital concern to the citizenry. As for finding campaign funds, Moseley-Braun's staff resorted to some unusual strategies. On February 16, 1992, for example, an exclusive hair salon became the setting for a group of Moseley-Braun supporters. In exchange for a substantial contribution to her campaign, guests sipped wine and ate hors d'oeuvres while receiving expert hair-style advice and facial demonstrations. The underdog challenger gained no other editorial endorsements for her candidacy than from Chicago's two African American newspapers. With or without explanations, *Crusader* and *Defender* articles urged their readerships to cast their votes for Moseley-Braun.[56]

As unlikely as winning had once seemed with her entry in the primary contest, an upset occurred on March 18, 1992. Moseley-Braun rose from the relative obscurity of a county elective office to stun political experts and pollsters, thereby making national headlines with an astounding victory over Dixon and Hofeld. Having just gained 38 percent of the Democratic primary vote, the winning candidate—who certainly had gained more identification as a female office seeker than as an African American Democrat—had won by waging a vigorous campaign that inspired significant national support from feminists. Moseley-Braun's win surprised almost everyone, outpolling as she had both an affluent attorney and an incumbent. Hofeld netted 27 percent of Democratic votes, while Dixon attracted 35 percent. Certainly not a mandate from Illinois Democrats,

Moseley-Braun's victory resulted from her collecting some 51 percent of her entire electoral total from Chicago precincts. Looking even worse for the future, she carried only 7 of Illinois's 102 counties. At a post-election press conference, the joyful winner "attempted to steer away from race and gender analogies by stressing [other] issues."[57] In an obvious move to broaden her appeal across Illinois, Moseley-Braun attributed success to her supporters' door-to-door efforts. It certainly was not, she laughed sarcastically, because of her large campaign budget; she had spent $375,000, whereas Dixon and Hofeld had combined to flush $2.5 and $4 million, respectively, into their losing efforts. Her commentary explained how a shortage of money had not greatly mattered. "They said we didn't have the money and the organization to win. We showed them we had the votes."[58] To the media and to Illinois residents, Moseley-Braun also had something to say about a poor downstate showing. "Where I did campaign . . ., the numbers show I did better. Remember, I didn't have the access to the media down there like my opponents." Regarding what she must assemble in order to fabricate a winning strategy for November, the African American Democratic woman noted vague plans to capitalize on her strongest asset, her "merits."[59]

Unimaginable as Moseley-Braun's victory appeared at first, political commentators offered a variety of explanations. The *Chicago Crusader* offered one of the earliest accounts, claiming "the key nail in Dixon's coffin" was the outrage he had caused among women by helping to confirm Clarence Thomas. Moreover, while her foes in the race concentrated on mudslinging each other, Moseley-Braun's message consistently stressed "substance over sound bytes."[60] Agreeing with this assessment but supplementing it somewhat, Tom Krish, a freelance writer for the *Chicago Defender*, attributed Moseley-Braun's success in part to what the analyst sensed had been an electoral "'throw the rascals out' sentiment." Many members of both the Illinois and national electorates, according to Krish, had developed such disgust with incumbents' "lack of sensitivity to public concerns" that in many instances across the nation "they will be swimming against the tide this November." Speaking to a weekly Saturday morning audience at Operation PUSH and comprehending the meaning of the election in much the same way, but contextualizing the result somewhat differently, Jesse Jackson characterized Moseley-Braun's success as "one light of hope to challenge a whole area of darkness."[61] Finally, Bill Crotty, a political science professor at Northwestern University, concluded his analysis with a brief description of the winner as an "articulate" politician with a tremendous advantage as an African American office seeker. Crotty viewed Moseley-Braun as "nonthreatening to white people, to other women, to Republicans."[62]

Certainly not taken as a serious challenger for the nomination, Moseley-Braun was aware now, as the official Democratic nominee, how matters would change. She realized that enlisting as much outside assistance as possible would prove most valuable to her in her aim to win the general election. She was running against Richard Williamson, a wealthy Republican opponent who could depend upon his party's deep reservoir of financial resources for aid in the campaign. Days after her win, in appeals for advice and monetary commitments, Moseley-Braun traveled to Washington, DC for consultations with influential Democratic senators. With the staff at the *Chicago Defender* before her departure for the capital, she discussed an intention to confer in Washington with such important party leaders as majority leader George J. Mitchell, Charles Robb of the Democratic Committee to Elect Senators, chairman Ronald Brown of the Democratic National Committee, and District of Columbia mayor Sharon Pratt Kelly. In addition to these prominent figures, Moseley-Braun anticipated calling on the headquarters of numerous national women's organizations in order to obtain their moral support as well as some monetary pledges.[63]

Unlike Dixon's dismissal of her entry in the primary as no more than an inconsequential challenge, her surprising receipt of the Democratic nomination opened up her entire life history to scrutiny. Digging by Williamson's staff into her past revealed what looked like a grossly illegal deal. Discovered was an allegedly fraudulent windfall inheritance for Moseley-Braun's mother, an elderly woman dependent upon Medicaid. Serious cheating had occurred by the Democratic candidate, Republicans charged, because neither she nor her mother had reported any details either to the Internal Revenue Service or to the Illinois Department of Public Aid of information about a sale of timber for $28,000 from the Moseley family's 7,100 acres in the South. With a proper disclosure to authorities, the candidate's mother would have lost her eligibility to remain in a nursing home at taxpayers' expense. Almost immediately after the disclosure by the Williamson campaign office of what appeared as criminal intent to defraud the state, Moseley-Braun responded to the serious accusation, stating emphatically that her family had not defrauded anyone. With neither investigative reporters nor Williamson willing to allow a messy matter to die, Moseley-Braun finally put an end to the dispute by "voluntarily" paying the Illinois treasury office $15,000. Then, apparently as her way of diverting attention in another direction from a scandalous activity, she went on the offensive against Williamson, demanding an explanation as to why he belonged to a North Shore golf club that barred memberships to minorities and Jews and that placed a ceiling on its number of Roman Catholic members. The Democrat asked some other awkward questions for her Republican opponent to answer. In particular she wanted his response to why he remained "an apologist for 12 years of Reagan-Bush failure." Reacting to what Illinois voters knew about Moseley-Braun, the *Chicago Crusader* supposed that state authorities had assumed to have caught her hand "in the proverbial cookie jar, though it has not been proven that wrongdoing actually occurred." More important, countered the newspaper's editor, the episode involving Medicaid, an elderly parent, and an inheritance confirmed a need to examine more diligently the content of her platform because it included provisions advising more help to older Americans. In Moseley-Braun's own defense, she noted the existence of national health insurance, as she advocated as an important legislative priority, would relieve a person's eligibility for care based solely upon "absolute destitution."[64]

The 1992 Senate race in Illinois involved more than mudslinging exchanges; it evolved into what the *National Review*'s John R. Coyne Jr. described as a "happening" in the "year of the woman." Through the National Organization of Women's Political Action Committee's "Women For a Change," feminists gathered at the Conrad Hilton Hotel in Chicago in June to confer about and develop strategies to bring about victories for female candidates in several upcoming electoral campaigns. To benefit targeted candidates such as Moseley-Braun, the assembled women launched what evolved into a well-organized national grassroots "get out the vote" and fund-raising network. A good example of the help this effort would provide to the Illinois gender-conscious Democrat occurred in New York. There, in the luxurious Manhattan apartment of socialite and activist for women's rights Sherry Bronfman, her prominent guests included politicians Mario M. Cuomo and David Dinkins and female activists Betty Friedan and Gloria Steinem; they were there to meet and greet donors at Bronfman's exclusive cocktail party that collected $68,000 for Moseley-Braun. In response to the crusading women who worked so hard for the election of female candidates, Pate Phillips, the notoriously outspoken GOP leader of the Illinois State Senate, ill-advisedly referred to these enthusiastic campaigners as "frustrated divorcees."[65]

Moseley-Braun—unlike other African American office seekers who, in their searches for white support, tended to ignore members of their own race—devoted a considerable portion of her campaign schedule to appearing before predominantly African American audiences. On the occasions when she spoke to minority gatherings, her addresses often contained class-conscious messages. For example, in one of these appearances, she told listeners, "We don't need any more rich boys in the Senate. It is time for change and that's what this election is all about." Even her campaign commercials broadcast by radio stations with predominantly black listeners suggested a rich-poor dichotomy and stated emphatically that Moseley-Braun's intention in the Senate was to become the representative of oppressed people—or as she liked to deride the upper chamber —"the millionaires club." Media consultant Gerald Austin hammered the point home in one of the radio advertisements aired and paid for by the Moseley-Braun election team; the point of the message was to tell listeners how Beatrice Foods had rewarded CEO Williamson with a golden-parachute severance package worth one million dollars at the same time as the company was handing pink slips to thousands of hourly workers. "That's Reagan/Bush/Williamson economics in action. Haven't we had enough?"[66]

Short on taking specific stands on particular issues, Williamson and Moseley-Braun's campaigning seldom focused on how either candidate, if elected to the

Senate, would vote on currently unresolved legislative proposals. The Republican supported school choice, while his opponent labeled it "a bad idea that most Americans oppose." She considered vouchers so "misguided" that they "would be the destruction of neighborhood schools."[67] As a practicing Roman Catholic, Moseley-Braun noted that she could never consider having an abortion, but she supported the legal right of every pregnant woman to choose to have one. Williamson, after having made a reversal on the subject of legal abortions, changed his position, disappointing much of his conservative base. During the course of his campaign for the Senate, he moved from opposing the termination of pregnancies to advocating something similar to Moseley-Braun's pro-choice position.[68]

Chicago's two African American newspapers, the *Crusader* and the *Defender,* both rallied to support Moseley-Braun, offering her strong editorial endorsements. The *Crusader,* as its primary justification for backing the Democrat, cited "her long history as a progressive with ideas that help people," whereas the editorial staff of the much better circulating *Defender* reached the harsh judgmental conclusion that "Williamson's record, his past political associations and his running a 'dirty' campaign" qualified him as a "NUT."[69] Inasmuch as Illinois voters were probably kinder in their personal judgment of the Republican candidate than editors at the *Defender,* a majority still decided for the Democratic candidate whom political scientist Katherine Tate would later describe as possessing "double liabilities" of race and gender. Moseley-Braun not only won the popular vote, but she outpolled the total tally for Bill Clinton in Illinois, easily surpassing the winning presidential candidate's total of 2,408,817 votes by 177,776. Altogether, the female Democrat carried 57 of Illinois's 102 counties.[70]

Chicago's African American press hailed her winning result as a great victory, while commentators and political analysts attributed Carol Moseley-Braun's triumph to several factors. Attested by "supporters from a vast array of socioeconomic and racial backgrounds" at a victory celebration, the *Defender* judged the Democratic female winner "a candidate of mass appeal."[71] To the *Crusader,* it was Carol Moseley-Braun's "upbeat image" that contrasted so sharply to Republican Williamson's "constant mudslinging."[72] As for how she interpreted the result, it was, in her opinion, because the Illinois electorate had decided that 1992 represented a "time for change." Elaborating further, Moseley-Braun concluded that "people are tired of the many problems we face in today's society which include health care and unemployment. The people . . . were ready for change and women became the change agents in many regards and that's one of the messages of this election."[73]

Moseley-Braun's popularity ranking sank almost immediately after the election, because of some bad judgment calls. Her campaign manager and fiancé, Kgosie Matthews, was clearly at the core of the senator-elect's first problems. For his supervision of her senatorial bid, he earned a monthly salary of $15,000, but it was not this large outlay that caused early reverberations after the election. The major problem was ironic, since she had waged so much of her efforts against Dixon on the senator's alleged insensitivity to women that now Matthews would become front and center of sexual-harassment complaints made by Moseley-Braun's female campaign staffers. Completely satisfied that an investigation had cleared her future husband of all these allegations, Moseley-Braun, who had so harshly criticized Dixon in the primary, now seemed satisfied to accept Matthews's innocence—much as the defeated incumbent senator had confessed to being satisfied with Thomas's denials.

Adding to the public-relations fiasco for the new senator were some blatant examples of her ill-advised extravagance after a great election victory. Almost immediately, she purchased both a condominium along Chicago's lake front and an expensive automobile. This was not all. As a widely reported climax to this flaunting and conspicuous consuming, senator-elect Moseley-Braun and fiancé Matthews boarded a Concord airliner for visits to his native country of South Africa as well as several other African nations. Thus Illinois's newly elected lawmaker vacationed in Africa while every other incoming senator was receiving important orientations to Senate rules and protocols. This fact was closely observed and harshly criticized by a legion of curious followers of the black woman's meteoric rise to political fame. A footnote emerged to her extravagance and to an apparent disregard for her constituents' best interests. As much as the opposition during the female candidate's run for the Senate tainted her reputation for failing to disclose an inheritance, Moseley-Braun's standing as an honest person did not improve after revelations about her campaign finances. Examining auditors uncovered an unexplained debt of approximately $500,000. Considering that the candidate had collected more than $6 million from donors, questions as to where and to whom the money had gone caused the recently elected official both legal concerns and negative publicity.[74]

Arriving late to the Senate with many Illinois supporters shaken by her excesses, Moseley-Braun ignored criticisms, deciding instead to concentrate her attention on all the causes and issues that had received special emphasis during her campaign. More than all other matters on the Senate docket during the 103rd through the 105th congresses, Moseley-Braun's greatest interests and preoccupations were issues that involved protecting and promoting children and women's rights. Seemingly whenever the floor debate centered on abortion, the Illinois senator arose to enter discussions with her defense of keeping all procedures legally available to every woman. Consequently, in 1996, while abortion opponents were attempting to cut off all federal funding of the practice for federal female government employees as well as for women serving in the armed forces, Moseley-Braun forcefully argued to continue their full access to coverage. Moreover, after the murders of several abortionists and after a series of attacks on abortion clinics, the first-year senator fervently argued for stronger protection and a jurisdictional move to federal courts for the indictment and prosecution of all suspects accused of these crimes.[75]

Women's health was another of Moseley-Braun's concerns. In speeches before the Senate during her first year in office, Moseley-Braun noted why she was sponsoring legislative-funding programs to study women with HIV and to research lupus. Since nine of ten sufferers of the latter affliction were women of child-bearing age, her amendment called for appropriating $20 million to the Public Health Service Act for a scientific inquiry into why the occurrences of lupus were so much more frequent among this special group. Funding research, Moseley-Braun reasoned, might uncover the responsible factors. Early in her Senate career, she also joined a bipartisan group of senators in resolving to include both obstetricians and gynecologists as vital primary caregivers to women with insurance coverage from a variety of federal health programs. She consented to cosponsor legislation to approve a land-title conveyance to Columbia Hospital for Women, and she worked (without any tangible results) to provide residential support services to pregnant women at high risk for miscarriages due either to personal histories of substance abuse or their youthful age.[76]

The general welfare and protection of women also gained Moseley-Braun's attention and advocacy. She focused on specific crimes against women such as spousal abuse and female genital mutilation; she championed both causes because they were of great importance to her. Concerns led her to address the consequences of these deplorable acts against women, and she introduced appropriate legislation for dealing harshly with these abusive practices. Although laws seldom came about as a result of her activism, she at least battled to bring awareness among her male Senate colleagues of the degree and variance of female suffering.

Two other feminist causes of special interest to the Illinois senator were equal rights and better legal protections for all women. Whether it was a reduction of the allowable number of monthly hours of work by flight attendants or the tearing down of the thick "brick wall of pension law that prevents women from investing enough for their future," Moseley-Braun became the chief spokesperson in the Senate of these gender-specific causes. She demanded equal treatment of women through revision of the Higher Education Act of 1965. Most forcefully on behalf of female athletes, she presented arguments why any fair interpretation of the law's Title IX should require equal fund distributions for men and women's intercollegiate athletics. Thus, in a most unprecedented way for a member of the Senate, Moseley-Braun became a most unusually strong advocate for women and a leader of drives aimed at improving both their legal status and their opportunities.

Moreover, she was a supporter of others who shared her vision. This meant she defended Joycelyn Elders, after conservative opponents had balked at her becoming the surgeon general. The pro-feminist African American senator from

Illinois also commended Ruth Bader Ginsburg's "pioneering work in the area of gender discrimination." Included among Moseley-Braun's many (largely symbolic) gender-related actions were efforts to have the Senate designate every March the "Women's History Month," and she coaxed the body into honoring all female veterans of the armed forces with specially minted commemorative coins.[77]

Closely related to Moseley-Braun's drives to single out women and to assist, protect, and promote their rights were endeavors on behalf of children and family values. During the 1993 term, her inaugural year, she spoke on multiple issues. This was either to sponsor legislation or to address the reason need existed in the States. She spoke for a national, compulsory, family-leave program to mandate parental work leaves after both births and adoptions; for significant improvements in the delivery of child-welfare services; for a major raise of the assets limit for recipients of Aid to Families with Dependent Children who were in the process of developing enterprises; for preventative actions to reduce fetal alcohol syndrome; for discrimination-free adoptions; for educational programs to protect against and to prevent child abuse; for a tough federal law to enforce court-decreed child-support payments; for guaranteed education access for all children in detention centers; and for parental responsibility for acts of juvenile delinquency.[78]

Recognizing that her primary obligation was to women, Moseley-Braun also grasped the importance of devoting considerable attention to her African American base. After all, she owed her victories in 1992 primarily to these two electoral elements. The black female senator knew why showing gratitude to and assisting both groups was important, but if she had to prioritize between gender-related causes and African Americans, then helping women almost always gained more of her attention. Whether her interest in female matters resulted from fears of a white-voter backlash or something else, she never offered an explanation. Her record in the Senate indicates that fighting for gender- and family-related issues accorded with a plan to maintain as much feminine support as possible. This was despite the fact that paying greater attention to these matters came at the expense of African Americans on her agenda. So much is clear from examining the *Congressional Record*, but on closer scrutiny of Moseley-Braun's Senate term, a record of her steady involvement and accomplishment in minority affairs is also evident. Of her efforts on behalf of blacks, none carried more importance for her than continuing affirmative action. To the senator from Illinois, this program was all "about equal economic opportunity." Mandating contracts to minority-owned enterprises and directing federal agencies and departments to use minority-operated banks were among her earliest recommendations for legislative action by the Senate. Moseley-Braun believed so strongly in the federal government's responsibility to boost minority entrepreneurial activity that she let out an angry outburst after the high court's ruling against set-aside programs. She was livid on June 14, 1995, in response to the Supreme Court's decision in *Adarand* v

Pena. Not mincing words, the African American senator not only criticized the legal outcome, she severely chastised the five majority justices, referring to their action as "bad law" and a vivid reminder of "the infamous Dred Scott case."[79]

Her outburst of emotion against a court ruling was not the only occasion when the female lawmaker turned feisty with a passionate response to a racial issue. In July 1993 an attempt by Carolinians Jesse Helms and Strom Thurmond to renew a patent held by the Daughters of the Confederacy for the Confederate flag insignia roused her to fight. Before she began issuing her strong objections, none of the other Senate members had opposed passing an extension. For Moseley-Braun, the flag symbolized an era of chattel slavery, and therefore it represented for her and so many other African Americans bitter reminders of an unhappy period in the lives of their ancestors. Her protestations led to a loss in the Senate of the Helms-Thurmond bill for the patent's renewal, 75 votes to 25. No doubt without her fiery negative reaction, it surely would have won approval.[80]

On other issues of interest to African Americans, Moseley-Braun contributed testimony, but not much commitment. These included statehood for the District of Columbia, funds for midnight basketball, the abatement of redlining practices, penalties for owners of toxic-waste dumps located near African American neighborhoods, and reaction to a court ruling against the use of race as the basis for redistricting. Hate crimes such as the gruesome one occurring near Jasper, Texas, roused her, but then again such acts of racist savagery horrified every senator. The brutality of avowed white racists who had dragged an African American man to his death behind a pickup truck in east Texas found no defenders in Congress.[81]

Moseley-Braun, like liberal and conservative African American congressional members both before and after her tenure, introduced resolutions for and spoke kindly about various African American contributors and institutions. These included her mention of the anniversaries of Hiram Revels's Senate election and the fiftieth year anniversary of President Harry Truman's use of an executive order to integrate the armed forces. On the Illinois senator's designated list for notable honors for personal and collective achievements of African Americans were these proposals for monuments, museums, and highway markers: a memorial to Martin Luther King in Washington, an African American museum at the Smithsonian Institution, a national historical park devoted to jazz located in New Orleans, and markers to denote specific stops and safe havens found along the Underground Railroad. Additionally, Moseley-Braun resolved to proclaim 1994 "The Year of Gospel Music," and one by one from the Senate floor, she praised the educational accomplishments of the historically African American colleges and universities and the civil rights achievements of Thurgood Marshall and the Reverend George "Ed" Riddick of Operation PUSH. Finally, as Moseley-Braun's personal tribute to Dr. King's legacy, the senator favored the creation of a national service day in his name.[82]

Steadfast as the first-term senator was to all her campaign commitments to women and African Americans, a variety of other issues naturally commanded her attention in the Senate, too. On miscellaneous matters, her positions were not necessarily consistent, crossing as they often did a wide political spectrum from libertarian to conservative. Moseley-Braun referred to herself as "a different kind of senator" who could not "escape the fact that I came to the Senate as a symbol of hope and change."[83] Critic Ruth Shalit did not appreciate this side of the senator and proclaimed instead her effectiveness "as a pork-barrel pol[itician]" whose only true interest was "identity mongering."[84] And the charge was valid to a degree. Any attempt at assessing with fairness the black female senator's career must focus to some extent on her obvious inconsistencies and desires for attention. In essence, therefore, one can make a strong case both for the pioneering lawmaker's personally flattering self-assessment and for Shalit's harsh critique.[85]

On free trade and foreign affairs, Moseley-Braun moved from being a traditional laissez-fair liberal to an interventionist. Unlike so many other Democratic senators who sought identity as pro-union opponents of the North American Free Trade Agreement (NAFTA), she saw herself as friendly to organized labor, but on this particular issue, she was at odds with a majority of union sympathizers. She went on record speaking favorably of a plan to lift most commercial American barriers with Mexico and Canada. Therefore, on a vote to ratify or reject the proposed North American free-trade zone, she bolted from a majority of Democratic senators to join Republicans in support of the treaty. In some respects her action favoring duty-free trade represented a philosophical turnabout for her, because regarding how the United States should handle problems in Somalia, Moseley-Braun offered passionate arguments for adopting an active policy of involvement and direct intervention. She joined several fellow Democrats as a cosponsor of Senate Joint Resolution 45, a proposal authorizing use of American military forces in the African nation. Even a tragic, humiliating loss of several American lives in Mogadishu did not change her mind about the disputed merits of continuing to deploy Operation Restore Hope troops in Somalia; it remained in her judgment "a noble undertaking" that aided "our specific national interests."[86]

An equal amount of confusion resulted on domestic matters. Despite once proclaiming a reluctance "to tinker with the Constitution," Moseley-Braun aligned with senators who favored a balanced-budget amendment. As opposite from organized labor as she was on NAFTA, she joined Howard Metzenbaum of Ohio as a joint supporter of Senate Bill 55—their attempt at amending the National Labor Relations Act with provisions to prohibit managerial discrimination against a worker's participation in labor unrest and against a permanent hiring of strikebreakers. It did not pass. Like so many other lawmakers from urban areas, the senator from Chicago favored restricting the ownership and sale of guns. On both the possession of assault weapons and the transferring of guns to juveniles, she supported prohibitions. Moreover, in her judgment, the Bureau of Alcohol, Tobacco, and Firearms, through hiring additional agents, could begin to exercise more effective control over gun dealers. According to a plan she proposed, the necessary funds to hire more personnel could come from increasing from $10 to $1,125 the annual licensing fee paid by authorized weapons sellers.[87]

Moseley-Braun also had a libertarian side. Her expressions on the proper treatment and judgment of homosexuals were the most emphatic and zealous revelations of this characteristic. When controversy divided Congress about the right of gays and lesbians to serve in the military, the female senator showed her fearlessness, asserting in her Senate speech of February 4, 1993, that a person's sexual orientation in no way should enter into qualifications and eligibility to perform in uniform. Here is how she advanced her position: "The military has no more of a rational basis for banning gays and lesbians in 1993 than it did for segregating African-Americans in 1943."[88] She was similarly bold after a personal fight against the Defense of Marriage Act in 1996; to Moseley-Braun, it was unconstitutional and "mean-spirited legislation." Moreover, the African American lawmaker took a position in favor of stronger federal laws to guarantee and protect the employment rights of gays and lesbians. Sensitive as Moseley-Braun was to discrimination, her reaction to a senatorial attempt to bar illegal aliens from state legislative impact assistance grants (SLIAG) was most predictable. During her first year on Capitol Hill, a heated debate on a legislative proposal to force such denials roused her ire enough that she requested an opportunity to address the Senate on the subject. Thereupon, the freshman female solon brazenly and passionately argued against such barring with the bill's major defender, veteran lawmaker J. James Exon of Nebraska.[89]

Campaign finance reforms and welfare reform emerged as commanding congressional issues during Moseley-Braun's term. During a Senate floor debate on how best to deal with the divisive subject of reforming campaign finances, the novice African American senator spoke on June 17, 1993, in defense of spending limits. She advised changes, claiming a legislative goal should be "to ensure that voters, and not money, determine election results." While maintaining that the system should become "more open and competitive" with "tough spending limits . . . [becoming] the cornerstone of reform," she exempted union-funded and women-funded PACs from all the intended changes to the financing of future elections. As for lobbying activity, she defended it as an example of free speech, for which she did not believe in restrictions. Her vote on the subject together with ones from fifty-nine others resulted in the passage of Senate Bill 3; it was a weak bill with only marginal corrections aiming only superficially at the end of potentially corrupting and compromising election donations.[90]

After Labor Day and the summer recess of 1995, Moseley-Braun and ninety-nine Senate colleagues returned to Washington, DC. Topping their autumn work schedule was a comprehensive and controversial reform suggested three years earlier during the 1992 election by centrist Democratic presidential candidate Bill Clinton. His campaign pledge then had been to "end welfare as we know it," and now some three years later a proposal was under review. As a senator with so many of her supporters living on welfare checks, Moseley-Braun had a grave responsibility to weigh a major legislative reform's social and economic consequences, both negative and positive, before passing judgment. As much as the senator from Illinois possibly agreed with the goals of the Family Self-Sufficiency Act, worries persisted. In particular one of her principal concerns was the change's effect on children. Upon a closer look at the bill, she wondered if it did not offer too inadequate state provisioning for job training. As she expressed her grave fears, "We [Congress and the federal government] will not be there to help out with State efforts to create jobs. We will not be there to help out with child care. We will not be there to help out with the administration of whatever the State response is. That is a fundamental problem I think with the underlying bill." In order to insure and protect vulnerable children and force states into funding job-training programs with federal block-grant allowances, she insisted her support would depend entirely upon whether or not suggested proposals for sweeping welfare-reform legislation incorporated basic guarantees for children and education. Taking a personal responsibility for these, Moseley-Braun acted by introducing two safeguarding amendments. These went nowhere, however; led by a Republican majority in the Senate, colleagues overwhelmingly rejected her sincere attempt at ameliorating weaknesses in the legislation. In the summer of 1996, President Clinton signed into law a welfare-reform bill without Moseley-Braun's protective provisions.[91]

Finally the senator, while campaigning for Dixon's seat, stated some clear positions on health and education. Her perspectives on these topics did not change after the election. For example, Moseley-Braun's opposition to vouchers remained steadfast. Unlike their advocates who imagined private institutions posing competitive challenges to public school administrators either to begin providing school children with improved educational experiences or start facing lost financial support, Moseley-Braun continued to assert that "our responsibility [remains] to fix them [public schools because they] "are the glue that has held our society together." It was the senator's opinion that in addition to public education's longstanding social benefit on the nation, another invaluable reason existed for why taxes should go exclusively to the support of public institutions. She feared putting government money into private schools would invite "fly-by-night operators" to open "fraudulent private schools [just] as they have done in higher education."[92]

Moseley-Braun and America's first family—President Bill Clinton and First Lady Hillary Rodham Clinton—sought expansion of health-insurance coverage to all Americans. As a senatorial candidate in 1992, Moseley-Braun set a goal of working in Congress to provide universal coverage as one of her highest legislative priorities. Therefore in August 1994, with the administration's plan "in danger frankly of being outshouted [sic] by the special interests," the female legislator from Illinois became one of the program's most consistent and vocal defenders. On August 19, she challenged the fear mongers with their emotional claims about the horrifying consequences of "socialized medicine." Rather than using the scare tactics of opponents to alarm Americans about possible dire results from the presidential plan, she dared foes to debate her about the ramifications of not having universal health care for every American. Instead of her fellow lawmakers heeding all of the awful warnings from lobbyists about the consequences of tinkering with the status quo, she urged members of the House of Representatives and her fellow senators to "put a ribbon around the energy in this Chamber and achieve real, viable, doable health care reform that meets the expectations of our people and meets the requirements and the demands of our country as a whole."[93]

Finally, "with grandstanding for the home folks," Carol Moseley-Braun displayed as much skill as any other congressional member. Since Jews had supported her generously during both the primary and general election, expressions of her appreciation followed with a carefully worded congratulatory resolution to the Anti-Defamation League on its ninetieth anniversary and a second one that designated two spring weeks in 1993 and 1994 as "Jewish Heritage Week." The senator was also mindful as a Roman Catholic that followers of her faith often constituted the most prominent Christian group in several Illinois communities. Thus after a diagnosis had revealed the existence of a fatally malignant cancer in Cardinal Joseph Bernardin's body, the senator responded with a "call for the prayers of the American people in behalf of his eminence," the spiritual leader of the Chicago Archdiocese. As an astute politician, Carol Moseley-Braun naturally offered Illinois constituents something more than congratulations and demonstrations of concern. In response to property damage brought on by Mississippi River flooding in 1993, the lawmaker from Chicago joined other regional senators in sponsoring legislation for a study of levee conditions to ascertain where weakened locations were in urgent need of repair as well as for a recommendation for additional flood-control measures. With plans proceeding several miles north of Chicago for Fort Sheridan's closure, Illinois senators Carol Moseley-Braun and Paul Simon together with John Warner of the Senate Armed Forces Committee assumed the tasks of overseeing the sale and reuse of the military base. Her basic instinct for politics taught her to demonstrate special passion for and interest in matters of concern to the people back in Illinois. Moseley-Braun's inclination for correct responses showed up in 1995 when Congress had under consideration some major cuts to Department of Agriculture programs and subsidies. She protested these reductions, claiming "the net effect of the overall bill is to tighten the economic vise on rural America."[94]

Six years after a successful challenge to Senator Alan Dixon in the Democratic primary and an almost complete Senate term, the record on Capitol Hill of the

African American female incumbent clearly reflected her promises to Illinois voters in 1992. Her stated priorities included placing women first and African Americans second, and the senator definitely fulfilled both of these commitments. Therefore, had accomplishing objectives solely served as the basis of her bid for reelection, the Illinois electorate would have given her a second term in a landslide win. This was not the case, however. Her life outside the Senate became a greater focus than her Capitol Hill activities. Thus with her possession of all the advantages of incumbency together with her accumulation of a much larger campaign treasury than her obscure Republican opponent, great disadvantages worked against Moseley-Braun's reelection, nevertheless. Neither money nor experience could assist her at overcoming personal mistakes. Republican adversaries and their candidate Peter Fitzgerald were relentless in their personal vilifications of Moseley-Braun. With no letup, they flashed back and emphasized every unsavory episode in the senator's entire public career. Witty conservative columnist George Will likened the female incumbent to a typical crooked Chicago Democrat, and even a *Chicago Defender* editor admitted early in the bid for reelection that her greatest campaign problem would amount to overcoming what the newspaperman considered a series of "minor faux pas." After several opinion polls had put the Democratic senator as many as fifteen points behind her opponent, increased desperation began to follow from the Moseley-Braun campaign. Rather than running on a strong record on behalf of women and consistent loyalty to the Clinton administration, Moseley-Braun resorted to besmirching Fitzgerald as a dangerous right-wing radical whose views were contradictory to mainstream values. During a joint appearance with him in Chicago on WBBM radio, the incumbent challenged her GOP opponent with the following proposition "If you stop lying on me, I'll stop telling the truth about you." Although Hillary Clinton and Gloria Steinem each visited Illinois in attempts at assisting the senator's flagging reelection, the benefits of their appearances on behalf of Moseley-Braun quickly diminished after the candidate's appeals for votes assumed an increasingly racial tone. Unintentionally, by traveling across Illinois on the senator's behalf, Jesse Jackson projected this effect on her reelection bid. Adding to this impression were television cameo shots of Chicago's flamboyant African American councilwoman Dorothy Tillman urging on fellow minority voters to "turn out her base in full force." Her endorsements injected a negative subliminal message in the minds of Illinois's white voters. From them listening to Tillman warn African Americans about what they would lose as a result of a Fitzgerald victory, one need not speculate about the negative effects of such rhetoric on Moseley-Braun's chances.

Editors made Fitzgerald their overwhelming choice for endorsements. The most read and largest circulating newspapers in greater Chicago—the *Daily Herald,* the *Chicago Tribune,* and the *Chicago Sun-Times*—all backed the GOP challenger. Downstate, in a sharply contrasting editorial assessment, the *St. Louis Post-Dispatch*—a popular publication with a wide readership across the

Mississippi River in southwestern Illinois—proclaimed unequivocally the black female senator's valuable impact on Capitol Hill "both symbolically and substantively to women and African-Americans." The Missouri newspaper urged Illinois voters to return her to the Senate. Despite Moseley-Braun producing a record consistent with what she had set out to accomplish in the Senate, a plurality of Illinois voters decided that the senator's personal follies counted for much more than individual accomplishments on Capitol Hill. Despite Fitzgerald's pledge after the victory over Moseley-Braun to represent everyone equally, his promise failed to convince Barack Obama, a member of the Illinois state senate; what stood out about Fitzgerald in Obama's memory was how the GOP victor opposed "vigorously the programs, policies, and issues that are interests to the people of my [inter-city] district." Carol Moseley-Braun, undoubtedly possessed with much remorse as she recalled a "good and noble fight," observed regretfully how her defeat would leave African Americans without a true representative in the Senate.[95]

Successful Gubernatorial Bids:
Lawrence Douglas Wilder of Virginia

After Brooke's 1978 defeat, eleven years elapsed before another African American contender won a significant statewide office, and then the victory occurred in the most unlikely of places. In a most astonishing turn of events—at the root of American slavery and the capital of the Confederate States of America—a majority of Commonwealth of Virginia voters in 1989 chose Lawrence Douglas Wilder to be their next governor. Noting the location of this stunning election feat, two pertinent questions require answers. Who was the victorious African American politician? And how did he accomplish such an amazing triumph?

Born in Richmond during the Great Depression on January 17, 1931, the second youngest of eight children, young Douglas first showed an interest in politics as a teenager while listening to adults discussing current political topics and world affairs at a neighborhood barbershop. After high school and his graduation from Virginia Union University with a degree in chemistry, Wilder was drafted into the army for eventual active service in Korea. A battle hero, he was awarded the Bronze Star for his bravery in rescuing injured American soldiers. Returning home at the conclusion of his military duty and in preparation for a legal career, Wilder studied law at Howard University. Then as an attorney in race-conscious Richmond, he gained a reputation for courage and an unusual public demeanor. While in the courtroom, Wilder defiantly refused to obey what a segregated, caste-ridden society demanded of him; the brazen African American lawyer often demanded more respectful treatment from presiding judges on behalf of clients. In 1969 this attorney—known for his "bushy Afro hairstyle and an apparently confrontational attitude" that white Virginians likely viewed as the "epitome of the angry young black"—won a hard-fought campaign to gain a senate seat in the state legislature. By winning the election, he thereby became the chamber's first black member since the years of Radical Reconstruction.[96]

From the very outset of Wilder's political career in 1970 as a state lawmaker, in contrast with Brooke's career some ten years earlier as the attorney general of Massachusetts, the black Virginian was a fearless, outspoken activist, who established a strong record for a robust battle on behalf of civil rights. In his maiden speech from the senate floor, Wilder passionately advised the legislature to repeal the state song—"Carry Me Back to Old Virginny"—because he, like many other sensitive African Americans, felt its three lyrical references to "old darkeys" to be offensive and racist. Although Wilder's appeal went nowhere in the legislature, the issue never completely disappeared from his agenda; the fight to drop the song, after decades of emotional debating, ultimately succeeded in 1997 when Virginia's general assembly changed its status to "state song emeritus." During Wilder's fifteen active years as the most courageously outspoken member of the Virginia legislature, numerous instances of his involvement in civil rights issues and causes occurred. These included introducing several bills, some for the benefit of low-income residents and others in support of equality. During the mid-1970s, Wilder began a campaign to designate Martin Luther King's birthday as an official state holiday, and finally in 1984, after almost a decade of his advocacy for this cause, the general assembly enacted a bill for this purpose. One year later, Virginia voters, in a landslide election, chose Wilder as the state's next lieutenant governor, a historic first in the modern era for an African American politician anywhere in the United States.[97]

Wilder's winning came from a number of factors. First of all, he succeeded in obtaining almost every vote cast by African American Virginians, a category of voters that constituted only about 18 percent of the commonwealth's electorate. Second, he was superb at convincing whites of his sincerity as a truly fair-minded person; this and a talent for drawing enough of a doubtful majority to him resulted in 44 percent support from whites. Of course, there were also other reasons why they had placed confidence in Wilder. Excepting his lead in a senate fight to make King's birthday a state holiday and his vote against capital punishment, Wilder had deliberately made a supreme effort to form a key alliance with Democratic Party centrists. Another thing that resonated well with whites was his up-by-the-bootstraps message to blacks. The state's majority appreciated his advising minority members that for them to be looking "anywhere but to yourselves [for improvement] is a mistake."[98] Also during the 1985 general election, as a black candidate needing white votes to win, Wilder enhanced his position with whites by emphasizing his support for fiscal prudence and tougher anti-crime measures. Thus, his careful and deliberate strategic decision to ignore almost completely all issues of special interest to Virginia's African American residents made it easier for the whites in Virginia's electorate to forget that Wilder was an African American candidate seeking their votes. His slighting of the minority became so apparent that one black ministerial alliance refused to endorse the state senator. Whether related to the candidate's calculated disinterest in or the reoccurring problem of general apathy by many African Americans in politics, their voter turnout during the gubernatorial election was low, but Wilder did extremely well among the politically engaged black electorate, receiving 97 percent of the minority's votes.[99]

Holding the Commonwealth's second highest office, as the lieutenant governor, Wilder viewed himself as a "principled pragmatist."[100] After three trade missions to Taiwan, he began looking forward to 1989 and making a determined bid for the governorship. In order to avoid controversies that might lose him white support deemed so necessary in efforts first to gain the Democratic nomination and then to succeed in a general election, Wilder was careful to assume only moderate positions on almost everything. Since he comported himself most acceptably, without making many references to race or discrimination, the state party bosses purposely began discouraging all other potential candidates from seeking the gubernatorial nomination; leaders urged all other hopeful contenders to step aside for Lieutenant Governor Wilder. As a result of promises and persuasion, opposition vanished within the Democratic Party, and Wilder became the undisputed nominee. Meanwhile, contenders in the Republican primary engaged in a bitter, often personalized struggle for the right to represent the GOP against Wilder. A divisive, nasty contest left Republicans in such shambled disarray that party leaders desperately tried to reunite and rally disparate elements for a triumph over the unchallenged African American Democrat. J. Marshall Coleman, the GOP's wounded choice for governor, waged two battles, one for the support of the upset backers of his two rivals for the nomination and another for votes from the Virginia electorate.[101]

Similar to all three of the opponents who had contested Brooke during his senatorial races of 1966, 1972, and 1978, and despite his staunch conservative credentials, Coleman avoided the temptation to inject any element of race into his campaigning against Wilder. Thus, once again, the major responsibility for deracializing a political contest came from the white candidate and not the African American contender. The absence of race stirrings left an electorate with making an election decision untarnished by the one factor that could have divided it emotionally. The result was that the Virginians decided which person— a conservative Republican or a moderate Democrat—had the better credentials for governing the Commonwealth effectively. Coleman and Wilder campaigned hard to gain the trust and support of the majority, and they offered two different stances on several issues, but to the credit of both candidates, the contest never focused specifically on race. In this contest—unlike others waged later among neighbors to the south, in North Carolina in 1990 and again in 1996, that would reward Jesse Helms's despicable behavior against challenger Harvey Gantt with a pair of ugly election victories—Virginians surprisingly did not witness anything comparable from Coleman.

The only emotional commotion roused during the Wilder-Coleman contest for control of the state house in Richmond resulted from the candidates' complete differences on abortion. The Democrat supported women's rights to control their bodies, and Coleman judged as murder any and all medical interventions to terminate fetal development. In order to distort and exaggerate an opponent's record, both sides used political commercials that emphasized aberrations and inconsistencies. Coleman, for example, tried to exploit people's fear of crime, claiming that Wilder on three occasions as a defense attorney had petitioned judges to allow the questioning of rape victims by accused assailants and their attorneys. Overall, the Republican focused his run on Wilder's character and not his race. As much as Coleman did not capitalize on color, reporters covering the contest and citizens following it both expressed degrees of curiosity about how Wilder viewed race as a factor in his life. The Democratic candidate, as a comparatively light-skinned African American, never made any attempts to deny the effects of race on his development. In answer to one person's question about his identity, he noted, "How can I not think of myself as a black man? I shave."[102] Even though race was not the major decisive factor in the election, white Virginians still faced the decision on Election Day in 1989 of how to respond to the Democrat seeking their votes. Since a concern about Wilder's racial background had not emerged as a key issue during the campaign, many voters familiar with Wilder's earlier activist reputation on civil rights more than likely did some pondering about whether he had truthfully undergone a complete metamorphosis from his time as the most spirited, racially conscious senator to an even-tempered politician who now as a black Democratic candidate for governor preferred, if pressed, to discuss racial issues only in "soft, almost dulcet tones."[103]

As Election Day approached, some questions arose about the accuracy of opinion polls. To African American pollsters, white respondents apparently were reluctant to indicate support for Coleman. In contrast it appeared that "undecided" responses from both African American and white voters might in fact suggest opposition to Wilder. Thus guessing the election's final outcome was difficult because of how close it appeared and the apparent unreliability of voter surveys. It was no real surprise that Wilder's margin of victory over Coleman was slim; he won by fewer than seven thousand votes, a feat as remarkable for its rarity as for its accomplishment. The fact that Wilder won and as a result became the first African American ever to be elected to a governorship is even more fascinating if one considers where this victory occurred. After all, it was in the Commonwealth of Virginia where white residents had once been so desperate to stop their schools from integrating that they had engaged in a court fight to end public education altogether. Analyzing vote totals by gender, race, age, locale, and various other factors reveal just how the African American Democratic candidate amassed enough white support to triumph in a Southern state known politically for its staunch traditions and conservatism. Social scientist Alvin J. Schexnider painstakingly examined the 1989 gubernatorial vote from several different perspectives. Favoring and aiding Wilder's bid, the researcher found, were some major shifts and changes in the state's population and demography. "Approximately 44% of Wilder's voters," Schexnider observes, "spent most of their childhood years outside of the state as compared to only 38% of Coleman's supporters." Moreover, the black voter turnout of 73 percent was greater than that of whites at 65 percent, and Wilder was the recipient of almost every vote cast by the African American electorate. Coleman's adamant anti-abortion position apparently hurt him decisively with both female and younger voters. On ticklish racial matters, the Democrat had been careful to distance himself from civil rights activists such as Jesse Jackson and had been smart to reach out to all Virginians "with a mainstream, centrist appeal."[104] No analyst put the true reason behind Wilder's victory better and more succinctly than the winner; "Jesse runs to inspire, I run to win."[105]

Like other winning minority candidates before and after Wilder, the Virginian quickly discovered that gaining office was somewhat easier than retaining support and popularity as an elected official. There was, first of all, a smoldering intra-party feud. The governor and Charles "Chuck" Robb—the son in-law of Lady Bird and Lyndon Johnson—neither trusted nor liked each other. What began as a power struggle among Democrats for control over the party would escalate in 1988 after Robb acquired a secretly taped Wilder political discussion with a trusted crony. Although Robb denied all responsibility for the surreptitious recording, the lieutenant governor did not believe him. Then, as governor in 1991, Wilder refused to use his power to halt embarrassing personal investigations into Robb's role as an alleged witness of cocaine use and into his rival's supposed philandering affair with Tai Collins, a former Miss Virginia. Commentator Fred Barnes, writing of tit-for-tat infighting for the *New Republic*, explained that the animosity would never end, because Wilder was "an obsessive grudge-bearer" and Robb was "a political klutz."[106] Now with Robb's severely damaged reputation and his political career clearly in jeopardy, a pundit remarked how Robb's future in public life was "sinking faster than Saddam Hussein's navy."[107]

Wilder's clumsy handling of opposition to the confirmation of Clarence Thomas's appointment to the Supreme Court angered Roman Catholics both in Virginia and nationally. Pointing to the religion of the nominee, the governor had wondered, "How much allegiance is there to the Pope?" Mention of the question implied that Thomas's Catholicism would prevent his judicial independence. Right-winger Gary Bauer, founder and head of the Family Research Council, surmised, "it was deliberate to have a Southern black governor raise this issue to get these Southern Democratic senators off the hook. And it would be very dangerous for us to let this pass."[108]

Occasionally Wilder upset African Americans. As a gubernatorial candidate, he had made a commitment to equalizing school-district expenditures, but once in office, he did not fulfill this campaign pledge. The governor's failure to act opened a rift between him and Jesse Jackson, because the civil rights leader had intervened in the battle to guarantee expenditures that would be equal for every Virginia schoolchild. As a result of this apparent interference in state-funding matters, Wilder subsequently accused Jackson of sabotaging public education in the Commonwealth by organizing protests. After a clemency plea from Jackson's Operation PUSH, the governor further irritated the civil rights activist when he failed to stay the execution order of an African American man convicted of murdering a gas-station attendant. Wilder's frugal handling of the state's fiscal crisis through a significant reduction in state jobs and programs countered activists' advice to him; unlike the praise Wilder received from bankers and investors, the state's liberals rebuked the governor for not raising taxes as a way to retain workers. On the other hand, on May 12, 1992, *Financial World* singled out Wilder for recognition, praising him for deft management of a budget crisis; his major role resulted in the magazine's selection of the Commonwealth as the nation's best-managed state.[109]

On behalf of the rights and positions of women and minorities, as well as on libertarian issues generally, Wilder offered more positive than negative leadership. By an executive order issued on July 23, 1992, he demanded the painting of American flags on Virginia National Guard airplanes as replacements for the Confederate stars and bars. Regarding a gender controversy surrounding the emotional debate about the pros and cons of admitting women to the Virginia Military Institute, Wilder initially wanted to avoid taking a stand, but ultimately through the governor's reluctant leadership, efforts led to the entry of the first female cadets in 1993. His most decisive action on behalf of liberty came five months after his inauguration. Wilder used an executive order to require every state-operated agency and institution—including every state college and university in Virginia—to divest at once all financial interests in firms having ties to South Africa. In many cases, these investments were substantial. For example, more than 50 percent of state retirement system holdings along with University of Virginia assets valued at approximately $16 billion were in companies with major financial interests in the rogue nation. Wilder explained his action in a commencement address at Norfolk State University: "I'm sending a message not just to schools and institutions in Virginia but also around the country and world about how we feel about freedom-loving people [across] the world."[110] Throughout Wilder's one term as governor, the African continent remained a special interest for him. For example, in 1992, the governor headed a trade and cultural mission there; the high point for him was a visit to the slave market—Maison des Esclaves (slave house)—at Goree, Senegal.[111]

Overall, the Wilder administration did more for African Americans in Virginia than any previous regime. No former Commonwealth governor could match Wilder's exemplary record of appointing members of the minority to major positions. Altogether, he could proudly and justifiably boast of having had responsibility for the fact that two cabinet posts, seventeen state agency heads, two deputy secretaries, and more than six hundred reappointments and new appointments to state boards and commissions went to African Americans. James Dyke, Virginia's first black secretary of education, was among these appointees. Moreover, at Wilder's insistence, Virginia raised its public-assistance budget to families with dependents by $15 million, extended basic Medicaid coverage to include both children and pregnant women, and revamped food-stamp deliveries to make them more expeditious. Of the sixteen designated state communities for acceptance in 1992 as first-class participants in the Virginia Tourism Accreditation Program, Wilder carefully and deliberately chose several areas with significant black populations. Also, he made a practice of inviting many talented African Americans to his office and to the state mansion in Richmond as his way of bringing them to the state's attention. For example, in August 1992, he hosted a welcoming ceremony for jazz legend Dorothy Donegan where he honored her contributions. Donegan's presence typified how the governor enjoyed promoting notable African American achievements.[112]

Until a startling announcement came out in the news, public opinion polls were showing general support for Wilder. A significant plummeting in his popularity occurred during his fifth quarter as governor. It was then that Virginia's somewhat unpredictable politician announced plans to seek the Democratic presidential nomination. The decision to run, he noted, was the result of a personal conclusion about the nation needing a person with his talents in the White House in order to correct what Wilder considered as a correction of President George H. W. Bush's "fiscal follies" and "divisive" racial policies. Elaborating on his decision to run, Wilder explained: "As someone who has fought for positive change and the American dream for all these years, I cannot stand on the sidelines while the country I love stumbles further backward."[113] Shortly after the governor spoke out about the nation moving in the wrong direction and about its bleak future with Bush's occupancy of the Oval Office, a pollster surveyed Virginians for their reactions to the governor's plans. Their responses were overwhelmingly negative; of all those people quizzed for reactions, the polling results showed now a Wilder approval rating of 23 percent for his leadership and performance as the Commonwealth's governor. All across the nation, the electorate demonstrated equally little enthusiasm for Wilder's presidential ambitions. Mindful of the hopelessness of a run for the Democratic nomination, Wilder withdrew his name from the race during his January 1992 State of the Commonwealth Address. As an excuse, he cited a need to concentrate attention on what he said were Virginia's Bush-induced fiscal woes. Withdrawing, the governor assured anxious Commonwealth residents, became vitally necessary because "President Bush's policies have weakened our national economy and made [both Wilder and Virginia] vulnerable. Yet at the same time, the weak national economy has made it all the more difficult for me to make my case while tend-ing to ever more pressing obligations at home."[114] What Wilder did not mention in his justification for dropping his attempt at the nomination was the real reason. Wilder had not raised enough money for a campaign. Simply put, he found himself totally unable to ignite much excitement and interest across racial lines—and especially among African Americans. Without the legal opportunity to seek reelection (because the Commonwealth of Virginia had a law that barred successive gubernatorial terms), Wilder had no choice but to retire from the governorship in 1994. His legacies for the Commonwealth were more and better employment opportunities for black Virginians both in state government and in the redistricted congressional jurisdictions. A remapping of congressional jurisdictions meant that the victory of African American Robert C. "Bobby" Scott to the U.S. House of Representatives in 1992 had then become possible from a reconstituted third congressional district. Meanwhile, after the governorship and his four-year residence at the state mansion in Richmond, Wilder temporarily retired from public life with his acceptance of a law and government professorship at Virginia Commonwealth University. Then, almost eleven years later, on November 2, 2004, the former governor received about 79 percent of the Richmond vote in a campaign to become the capital city's first elected mayor in sixty years; previously city council members had assumed the responsibility of selecting municipal leaders for the city. Choosing retirement over a bid for reelection in 2008, at seventy-seven years of age, Wilder announced plans to leave politics for a second time and to surrender his tenure as Richmond's mayor.[115]

Deval Patrick of Massachusetts

Public television news reporter and author Gwen Ifill devotes an entire chapter in *The Breakthrough: Politics and Race in the Age of Obama* to Deval Patrick's successful bid to be Massachusetts' first African American governor. In 2006 victory came to fifty-one-year-old Patrick, a politician raised in a single parent household on Chicago's South Side and a life-changing beneficiary of a prep-school scholarship to Milton Academy in the Bay State. There, among privileged blue-blooded white boys and subsequently at Harvard, the Chicago native had adapted so well to these environments that his sister, Rhonda, pointed out disparagingly to her brother, "You talk like a white boy." In 1982 after receiving a Harvard Law School degree, the graduate accepted employment with the NAACP Legal Defense Fund. After four eventful years involved in civil rights litigation, he joined Hill and Barlow, a most prestigious Boston law firm. Patrick's tenure practicing law as one of two African American attorneys for the law partnership ended in 1994 when President Clinton appointed Patrick to serve as assistant attorney general in charge of 250 lawyers at the Justice Department's civil rights division. His main responsibilities in this position were twofold: "to mend, not end affirmative action" and to prevent mortgage-lending discrimination. Winning a $45 million suit against the Denny's restaurant chain for its prejudicial dealings with minority patrons represented for Patrick both his most controversial and his most significant accomplishment while at the Department of Justice. After a two-year stint in Washington, DC, Patrick returned to Boston for a position at Day, Berry, and Howard, a large New England law firm. Thereafter, he served as general counsel at the Coca-Cola Company; there he rose to become this corporation's most powerful African American executive. Then, Patrick joined the board at ACC Capital Holdings.

As satisfying and rewarding as his legal activities were, the attorney surprised not only his wife, Diane, but many of his closest friends as well when he announced an ambition to become the Commonwealth's next governor. Senator Barack Obama of Illinois was among the small circle of acquaintances whom Patrick consulted about running. The two black Harvard Law School graduates conferred in a Chicago coffee shop, and Patrick came away from their informal meeting with encouragement and with an agreement that his bidding for the highest state job in Massachusetts would make sense. Not everyone involved in Bay State politics shared this enthusiastic opinion, but their objections were not enough to discourage the neophyte African American political hopeful. The result of the Democratic primary held in September was a relatively easy defeat of Thomas Reilly, who as the state attorney general had been for many partisan insiders the anointed choice to run in the general election as the Democratic nominee for governor. Facing Patrick in November as his Republican opponent was Lieutenant Governor Kerry Healey. Healey ran a racist campaign with political advertisements linking her opponent to the defense of a parolee whom a jury in 2002 had convicted of rape. True as the public record indicates, Patrick, in a concerted effort to exonerate the person accused of the crime, had in fact contributed $5,000 to a defense fund for a DNA test that ultimately and ironically would solidify the prosecutor's case of the man's guilt. Patrick did not necessarily impress black voters in Massachusetts, but at less than 7 percent of the state's residents, they did not account for a significant portion of the electorate. Many of their clergy were against Patrick because of his open support for both gay marriage and abortion, two positions that many black preachers found objectionable. As Gwen Ifill concludes from her investigation into how the African American Democrat managed to obtain 56 percent of the vote in the race for governor, he was "not the sort of black man who might scare anyone."[116] As with similar beneficiaries of racial crossover wins elsewhere, Patrick had secured victory from "putting whites at ease without alienating blacks." Quoting Wayne Budd, an African American attorney with years of activity in Massachusetts politics, Ifill concurred that Patrick had run a most successful political campaign with whites that had been so completely dependent upon the black candidate's receipt of their overwhelming acceptance. According to Budd's reading of the victory, "Maybe it's a part of the old Ed Brooke genre. He [Patrick] was very fresh, very alive, very articulate, very charismatic, and people saw him not as a black candidate. They clearly did not."[117]

Chapter 5

The Political Pinnacle

Barack Obama's Presidential Victory

The culmination of African American candidates' seeking offices where dependence upon white votes was necessary for success came on November 4, 2008. Senator Barack Obama's victories first in grueling primary and caucus battles for the Democratic nomination and then in the presidential election have raised many questions for examination. Most important, did the victory imply a move away from race as the salient characteristic of voting? What began, in the judgment of most political experts, as a long-shot political exercise against insurmountable odds—as he was competing against favorite and better-known Hillary Rodham Clinton as the Democratic Party's choice for president—ended on election night in an emotional victory that brought tears of joy and pleasant disbelief to many African Americans. But how did the Obama campaign succeed at winning over such significant segments of the white electorate? Did his triumph occur because of momentous attitudinal changes on the part of many white voters, or had the electorate become so disgusted with the Republicans and George W. Bush that the race factor did not figure prominently in voters' decisions? Did enough deracialization really occur among white voters in this election to offset race's ultimate effect on the outcome? On the other hand, if race had entered the contest as a factor, what mitigated against it taking hold and changing the outcome? As for the matter of campaign strategy, and its role in Obama's efforts to undermine the obvious factor of racialization during the primaries and in the general election, did Obama's key political advisors and strategists David Axelrod and David Plouffe have a better understanding of the Democratic electorate than the people closest to Senator Clinton in the primary elections? Did the Obama team direct a better campaign in the general election than the Republican operatives around Senator John McCain?

As the self-described "skinny guy with a funny name," Obama naturally could not avoid his physical characteristics, but how was this candidate able to relegate race to a less important status than other issues in the minds of so many ordinary white voters? Obama's race did receive considerable attention during the primaries and in the general election—he and his wife, Michelle, were forced on several occasions to answer questions about it during the two years running up to the November election—but for reasons analyzed in this chapter it never resonated as the crucial factor in the final outcome. Ultimately, then, did Obama's landslide victory represent a revolutionary triumph of societal deracialization in American politics or something much less spectacular? In other words, was this election the final chapter of racial politics and the start of post-racial America?

Berkeley's chair of African American studies, Charles P. Henry, characterizes two distinct categories of how blacks sought political offices. In cases where the minority dominated the electorate, the University of California professor credits an "insurgent strategy [resembling] a social movement" as generally successful at gaining election victories. In a number of instances recently with whites clearly in the majority, Henry notes African Americans succeeding in bids for elective offices by employing a "deracialized strategy that avoid[ed] racially divisive issues" and that "promote[d] nonthreatening images of racial cooperation."[1] It will become evident in this chapter which course Obama followed in pursuit of the presidency.

For America's highest office, an absolute curiosity about race occurred after Illinois' African American senator's announcement of his candidacy for the Democratic presidential nomination. Beginning on February 10, 2007, at the Old State Capitol in Springfield, Illinois, with Obama's public declaration of plans to enter state primaries with this goal, media reports framed the candidate's race as the salient feature of his striving after the nation's highest office.[2] On February 14, 2007, a panel consisting of Clarence Page, Debra Dickerson, and Bobby Rush assembled for discussions on an important question for National Public Radio (NPR) listeners. Their responsibility was to answer, "Is Obama black enough?" Months later on July 9, 2007, for this same radio network, it was the turn of Obama's wife, Michelle, to answer questions about her husband's candidacy and race. None of the other declared Democrats in the presidential nominating derby—or for that matter, potential Republican nominees—ever had to face queries as to whether they were white enough or how their whiteness might affect their candidacies. Among several prominent black leaders, loyalty to and past performances by Obama's rivals for the nomination trumped race as the most important criteria in their choice of whom to support. As a result it was Bill Clinton's popularity that earned Hillary Clinton the early support of civil rights legends Andrew Young and John Lewis, Mayor Michael Nutter of Philadelphia, and Congressman Charles Rangel from Harlem.[3]

The carryover effects of race on candidacies would have its ultimate test in 2008 at the first serious possibility that an African American might become a major political party's nominee for president. Announced presidential candidacies by members of the minority had indeed occurred in the past, but in the cases of Shirley Chisholm, Jesse Jackson, Douglas Wilder, Alan Keyes, Carol Moseley-Braun, and Al Sharpton, their hopes for successful bids had been unrealistic—because of either a lack of campaign funds or the general indifference of other African Americans and influential white political leaders. For Chisholm, Jackson, and Sharpton (in the Democratic presidential primaries of 1972, 1984, 1988, and 2004) and for perennial Republican hopeful Keyes (a fixture in his party's contests from 1992 to 2008), one might view these bids more as attempts to publicize various concerns. In other words, for the trio of African American Democrats, these bids were a way to force upon white party leaders brokered deals to ensure the inclusion in the final drafts of party platforms some specific planks for greater protection of minority rights and for additional financial assistance to underprivileged residents. In Jackson's case, his bid was perhaps to induce more African Americans to register to vote. As for the reason why the black GOP candidate was always running, one can surmise it was because he clearly wanted to focus national attention on an ultraconservative moral agenda. Several members of the Congressional Black Caucus criticized Chisholm for what they viewed as being a harmful distraction to their political party's chances for victory in 1972, and Jackson (the winner of seven primaries in Southern states and a handful of caucuses in 1988) did not win the backing of many prominent black Democrats. As for Wilder in 1992 and Moseley-Braun, their efforts to gain political traction were largely stillborn. The Virginian withdrew immediately after sensing the futility of attempting a serious bid for the Democratic nomination. The ex-senator who had lost a reelection bid in 1998 declared her presidential candidacy in February 2003, only to grasp four days before the January 8, 2004, Iowa caucuses the hopelessness of her continuing, and thus the Illinois politician's nomination bid ended with her personal endorsement of John Dean.[4]

From the moment he officially entered the contest on February 10, 2007, Barack Hussein Obama had an experienced corps of political advisors behind him and, unlike his African American predecessors, a complete understanding of the key parameters necessary for a successful political effort fully dependent upon significant white acceptance. Obama's experienced campaign operatives were David Plouffe and David Axelrod, advisors who had developed excellent reputations for successful work with black candidates, having engineered several successful African American campaigns including Patrick's 2006 gubernatorial victory in Massachusetts. These two veteran managers knew from past experiences how to steer black candidates away from any concentration on race, to the more unifying election themes that promised greater acceptability to whites. And during their initial planning sessions with Obama more than two months before the senator's announcement to run, these two skilled operatives agreed to use all their knowledge and experience to apply basic deracializing principles to his presidential run in 2008. With meticulous detail, campaign manager Plouffe in *The Audacity to Win* reviews Michelle and Barack Obama's solemn evaluation of the consequences of seeking the presidency that preceded the freshman senator's decision to seek the nomination.[5]

Unique in several respects when compared with other blacks seeking multiracial support, Obama offered some special challenges. Born to a Kenyan father and a Caucasian mother from Kansas, and raised primarily in Honolulu, Hawaii, by his maternal grandparents without any paternal influence, this offspring of a biracial relationship carried into political campaigns neither the burdens caused by a family legacy of slavery nor any direct ties to the civil rights movement. As he freely admitted in his best-selling memoir, Obama began to discover vicariously the meaning of an African American heritage in the United States through a purpose-driven reading of black authors and history. As he learned early in life, his physical features were the factor that placed him ultimately among other people of color. As a result of his personal curiosity, several conscious decisions made deliberately during his young adulthood led this curious man to absorb the true consequences of blackness in the United States. First as a student at Columbia University when he devoted his leisure time to mentoring activities in Harlem, and later as a community organizer when he worked to improve the lives of struggling minority residents on Chicago's South Side, Obama more or less overcame his sheltered childhood spent growing up in a white household. Additional acclimation to his true personal identity as a man of color resulted from his marriage to Michelle Robinson, an exceptionally talented young woman from a working-class, inner-city Chicago family. Her deep roots in the African American community along with the influence her husband gained from joining and attending Trinity United Church of Christ, a congregation under its dynamic but controversially volatile pastor, the Reverend Jeremiah A. Wright Jr., placed Obama even closer to the inner workings and feelings of black Americans. Worship at and influence from Trinity, an activist, social-gospel church involved in community-outreach programs reflecting its slogan of "unashamedly Black and unapologetically Christian," exposed congregant Obama not only to the lessons of Wright's flamboyant sermons based upon black theology but also to Gospel music. Thus, for a Hawaiian native whose interracial background had fostered some degree of personal ambivalence about personal racial identity and a placement in society, answers to life's challenges began coming together after an undergraduate degree from Columbia University and a diploma from Harvard Law School. The confidence that had come from knowing himself better and from gaining an excellent education seemingly gave Obama ideal credentials for a successful debut in the racially bifurcated arena of American politics.[6]

A legal career as both a practicing attorney with a special focus on civil rights and a law lectureship at the University of Chicago preceded Obama's quest for a public office. When his decision came to run for office, Obama used the lessons of Harold Washington and Carol Moseley-Braun as his models. He had carefully observed their impressive victories in 1983 and 1992, and their influence molded his thinking about how to run and win. Just as with Washington's debut in elective politics years earlier, Obama's choice in 1996 to start a political career was a seat representing an Illinois state senate district. The district Obama chose spans several mostly black South Side neighborhoods, and it includes the upscale intellectual island of Hyde Park, a unique city section that is home to the University of Chicago's campus and represents an aberration in many respects by Chicago standards because of its residential integration. The opportunity for Obama to run opened up after a decision by the district's Democratic incumbent senator, Alice Palmer, to contest in the Democratic primary in order to become the party's nominee for a vacant House congressional seat. According to an informal deal with Obama, Palmer agreed to retire from politics if her primary bid should fail. However, with a faltering of her nomination campaign for Congress, she decided to renege on her agreement with Obama and seek reelection to the state senate. He refused to meet her request for a withdrawal. With Palmer's return to the field for the state legislature, Obama faced the daunting prospect of a better-known opponent who would benefit from support from such recognized community leaders as Representative Jesse Jackson Jr. As a determined response to stop the incumbent's reentry in the state senate race, supporters of challenger Obama looked for and found a flaw in Palmer's return to the state senate race. Suspicions arose about the legitimacy of many names on petitions for including her entry on the Democratic ballot; a subsequent investigation resulted in an election board ruling that Palmer's campaigners had indeed failed to secure the required number of approved signatures. As a result, Obama did not have to face her in the primary, and similarly successful challenges removed everyone but Obama from the primary ballot. Thereafter, in the general election, district voters elected him to support their interests in Springfield. But the win had repercussions. In the process of his defiant actions against the plans of Palmer—a popular African American progressive—Obama lost the respect and support of several of Bronzeville's most prominent black political reformers.

Once in Springfield, Obama earned a reputation among fellow senators for his ability and desire to work well with both Republican and Democratic members. This willingness did not necessarily seem an admirable achievement among a majority in the Black Caucus. There was one exception, however; the newcomer to Springfield pressed for and obtained help from the most influential African American senator, Democratic leader Emil Jones Jr., a state senate veteran, who liked Obama enough to guide him through the labyrinth of Springfield politics. Through Jones, the freshman lawmaker met and gained the assistance of a powerful contact, Dan Shomon, who proved an invaluable aide who introduced Obama both to people with political clout and to ordinary citizens throughout Illinois. Moreover, in the role of personal tutor, Shomon facilitated his pupil's adaptation to fellow legislators and helped the senator in the formation of important political alliances. Perhaps, even more important for an impressionable student's political future, the politically savvy instructor impressed upon his charge the valuable pragmatic lesson of always attempting "to adapt as best you can to the culture you are stepping into."[7] Frank and to the point, Shomon seldom hesitated to remind Obama of the very dangerous consequences of showing too much urbane sophistication or elitism; these and any overt displays of superiority, warned the advisor, were tendencies that, if coming from anyone with Obama's racial background, were certain to alienate working-class white voters. In noting instances of condescension, Shomon observed a problem others would also note about Obama.

Deceived by his initial electoral success and by a proclivity to look down at people, the state legislator in 2000 believed his positive qualities would translate into more than enough votes to unseat incumbent Bobby Rush in the Democratic primary, but the popular congressman easily trounced his challenger, obtaining two votes for every one going to his upstart rival. Examining the defeat in retrospect, several factors accounted for Obama's poor performance. Throughout the spring campaign, the portrait of Obama that emerged from Rush's speeches and political advertisements was of an opponent who was "not black enough" and who was so "overeducated" that he could not relate to the ongoing problems of the ghetto residents of the First Congressional District. Rush's popularity resulted from such achievements as his past leadership of the Illinois Black Panther Party, his service as one of Harold Washington's key supporters in the Chicago city council, and his outspoken defenses of constituents' personal interests. In a contest with Rush, Obama did not benefit from having Hyde Park as his base of support. The problem arose because of the neighborhood's unwanted reputation as being the location of African Americans in pigmentation only, out-of touch white liberals, and an elitist institution, the University of Chicago.

An intangible matter also hurt the challenger. Emotionally harmful to Obama's waging an effective campaign against Rush were the drug-related murder of the incumbent's adult son and the challenger's missed state senate roll-call vote on a tough handgun-control legislative measure. The Rush reelection team constantly reminded voters that the state senator's absence from Springfield had resulted from him prioritizing a family vacation trip to Hawaii over voting to protect people from such fatal shootings as the one responsible for killing Rush's son. Therefore, in final analysis, Rush supporters' unflattering description of Obama as a "white man in blackface in our community"—when coupled to the incumbent's superior name recognition and the effect of the assessment of blame on Obama for a senate disappearance after the Rush family's tragic loss—stuck home in the decisions of most voters.[8]

Humbled by defeat, Obama became more open to suggestions for developing an effective strategy. Above all, he learned that Americans "are hungry for a new kind of politics!" With the knowledge gained from losing to Rush and with awareness of incumbent senator Peter Fitzgerald's decision against a reelection bid and Carol Moseley-Braun's lack of desire to attempt a Senate comeback, opportunistic Obama sensed as early as 2002 that the time to move upward politically appeared to be at hand. As an initial step, he enlisted the advertising and organizing talents of David Axelrod, a man whom many experts in Illinois considered their state's most gifted political strategist as well as a major contributor to the successes of Harold Washington. In January 2003, or several months after the hiring of Axelrod, the ambitious state senator declared his intention to seek the Democratic nomination for the U.S. Senate. Although the future vacancy had drawn fifteen hopeful contestants from the two major political parties, the March primary result was not close. Obama obtained 52 percent of the Democratic primary vote total and easily surpassed the combined tally of all his intraparty rivals. His victory apparently set up a tough autumn contest with Jack Ryan, the GOP winner. Given the circumstances and his opponents, the victory on March 16, 2004, by the self-described "skinny guy from the South Side" was a most remarkable feat.

On further examination, Obama's success reveals the factors he had overcome in order to emerge with the Democratic nomination. Assessing the obstacles, the victor offered this initial analysis: "I think it's fair to say that the conventional wisdom was we could not win. We didn't have enough money. We didn't have enough organization." Dan Hynes, Obama's closest competitor with 24 percent of Democratic votes, at one time seemed the odds-on favorite to win because the Chicago Machine was in support of his candidacy, but as Noam Scheiber observed in a *New Republic* article, the winner possessed a reassuring quality that transcended race. "Obama is one of the very, very few African American candidates since the civil rights era to whom" alienation of moderate whites and dampened enthusiasm among African Americans and liberals just did not apply. Working favorably were the candidate's "speech [and] his unusual racial and cultural background." The result was an acceptable minority candidate about whom working-class voters "don't see . . . in terms of promoting black interests at the expense of their own." Obama was a person "who was not *stereotypically* African American."[9] Helping the primary winner as well was the undoing of his millionaire opponent, Blair Hull—whom media revelations had discovered to be the subject of an ex-wife's restraining order. Nevertheless, Obama summarized his appeal this way: Democratic voters were "more interested in the message than the color of the messenger" because it was their general conclusion that the black candidate's values were "essentially American values."[10] Yet, when pressed to clarify in an interview for *Essence* if these included any special responsibilities to African Americans, Obama emphasized for reporter Nicole Saunders that never in Congress would his intention include "bashful[ness] about being an advocate on behalf of our communities."[11] Clearly, however, Obama never did want the white electorate across Illinois to perceive him as *Businessweek* had done weeks after the primary—to be considered "The Great Black Hope," as the magazine article headline put it, did not fit strategically into the Democrat's plans for winning the general election.[12]

During the summer lull between the primary and the fall campaign, one event occurred that changed and tainted the race for the U.S. Senate. About four years earlier, in 2000, in an ugly divorce proceeding, Jeri Ryan had accused her husband, Jack (the politician who eventually would become Obama's slated rival for the vacating seat), of taking her to sex clubs, over her strong objections. Sealed and considered safe and private, every document pertaining to the couple's ugly, fiercely contested child-custody dispute leaked to the press, thereby destroying Jack Ryan's moral reputation and run for office. Although Ryan wanted to remain the GOP candidate, the party leadership decided his removal from the ticket would serve the best interests of the party. The decision to drop Ryan led to a frantic search for his replacement.[13]

Meanwhile, key members of the Democratic National Committee realized that, in the Illinois state senator, their party had someone special and worthy of promotion and elevation. The result of their favorable impression was an invitation to Obama to deliver the keynote address at the Democratic National Convention in Boston. To delegates and most everyone else, questions arose about this selection and about the designated speaker, but in reality, choosing men and women without much prior national exposure for this task was not especially unusual. Both political parties had introduced relatively unknown individuals of promise and expectation to the nation at their quadrennial gatherings. Four years before Obama's opportunity to speak, conventioneers and a national audience had heard Harold Ford Jr. Before him, Jesse Jackson, Barbara Jordan, and Bill Clinton had addressed conventions. In 1936 Arthur Mitchell caused a walkout of several white delegates from the South because the Democratic National Committee had offered its podium to the black congressman as a way of regenerating the party and Franklin Roosevelt's renomination with excitement. Nevertheless, as Obama admitted jokingly about his previously unknown identity before delivering a memorable speech at the Fleet Center in Boston, people, he laughed, were "calling me Alabama and Yo mama." His attentive audience, whether delegates on the convention floor or the millions of viewers in front of television sets all across America, might have stumbled with the speaker's name, but his phrases catapulted their interest and emotions into high gear. Especially memorable about the address was Obama's inclusive assessment that "there's not a liberal America and a conservative America—there's the United States of America." After Obama had delivered what was by almost all accounts a brilliant oratorical performance on July 28, 2004, questions arose at once about the speaker's willingness and potential as a future presidential candidate—a possibility he dismissed as both "flattering and silly." Quizzed to name someone whom he especially admired among Democrats, Obama offered Hillary Rodham Clinton, because she was "a workhorse, not a show horse."[14] Meanwhile, back home in Chicago, the two major daily newspapers expressed both pride and favorable impressions in how the Democratic candidate for the Senate had performed in his national debut. The *Chicago Tribune* headlined its reporting of the address with simply "The Phenom," and the *Chicago Sun-Times* proclaimed how Obama "wows crowd."[15]

Analysis of the African American orator's appeal followed elsewhere as well. A *New York Times* article offered an excellent explanation for Obama's cross-racial popularity. It was a special ability he had to cause voters not to "look at him stereotypically." In particular, in his role as keynote speaker, Obama sounded more like an immigrant than an African American; according to the *Times*, it was his point that in "no other country on earth is my story possible." The article made special reference to Orlando Patterson who had examined the state senator to ascertain what it was about him that removed race as a factor in how Americans were viewing the emerging politician. The Harvard University sociologist considered positive responses to Obama as being part of "a transcending culture [that emphasized] an American identity and not a racial one."[16]

The African American Democrat's ascendance to national prominence did not make the task of finding a replacement for Ryan any easier for Republicans. First choices included Mike Ditka and Orion Samuelson, but neither the successful, candid ex-coach of the Chicago Bears nor the popular WGN-Radio broadcaster of Midwest farm news expressed any desire or interest in an opportunity to run against Obama. Finally, on August 8, 2004, forty-four days after the GOP had pressured Ryan to withdraw from the Senate race, the Republicans found a candidate in Maryland resident and twice-failed contender for the GOP presidential nomination, Alan Keyes. In order to contest Obama, Keyes agreed to establish residency in Illinois so as to qualify for the challenge. It was an unusual but direct consequence of the Marylander's consent to move to Illinois to run that, for the first time in election history, a pair of African Americans received the two major political parties' nominations for the U.S. Senate.[17]

Three other stories emerged in August. One involved Justin Warfel, a young Ryan agent who had been employed to stalk Obama and video record his every move. On August 2, 2004 (months after being employed on a two-week tracking assignment for Ryan in May), Warfel shared with conservative reporter Matthew Continetti some explicitly detailed objections to Obama's candidacy. The stalker's comments appeared in the extreme right-leaning *Weekly Standard* and stated that Illinois voters had not had exposure to an accurate or truthful account of Obama's agenda. Labeling the African American Democrat "a runaway freight train," Warfel stated that the Illinois electorate should beware of electing Obama. He had accumulated "a left-liberal voting record" that included support for partial-birth abortions, gun control, tax increases, and a greatly expanded government role in health care.[18]

As much as Obama kept his message racially opaque, it was black nationalists who expressed concerns. They wanted to exclude him as a legitimate minority candidate because, above all, none of his ancestors had suffered as slaves. With bitterness remaining from Obama's 2000 challenge, Bobby Rush was one black leader who refused to support the Democratic nominee for the Senate. In Kenya, the homeland of Obama's father, none of the hostility and negativity received any attention, however. In the East African nation, "Obamania" swept through the general populace in much the same way as John F. Kennedy's presidential candidacy in 1960 had touched people in Ireland.[19]

Entering the final weeks of the campaign, Obama came into focus increasingly as being more than a candidate for the U.S. Senate. Both backers and opponents surveyed his record as a state legislator to find helpful or harmful evidence to use for or against him. Without much to glean from his speeches on his views of the state of racism in America, Barbara Ransby, in an exclusive interview for the *Progressive*, sought some answers. The candidate candidly replied without hesitation that he not only supported affirmative action but had addressed in the state senate the problem of racial profiling. "So, no," he attempted to reassure the reporter's concerns about where he stood, "I don't believe racism has somehow gone away. We have to be vigilant in eradicating all forms of discrimination, but I also think that some of our biggest challenges have less to do with race and more to do with the educational and economic barriers that all poor people are experiencing."[20]

Obama came under increasing scrutiny as the campaign unfolded in October. As he and Keyes spoke to voters and reporters, a clear separation was apparent on many key social issues. Their differences highlighted the fact that minority status was about the only thing they had in common. Keyes enthusiastically supported the right-to-life movement and reminded the Illinois electorate that abortions for any reason must be judged immoral and therefore must be opposed as murders of unborn infants. Obama believed in a woman's right to choose. Opposing views resulted on school prayer, stem-cell research, and legalization of same-sex unions. Keyes agreed with so-called moral conservatives on these issues, whereas Obama sided with liberals. Critics of the Democrat charged him with having a general softness on crime and with opposing a citizen's unrestricted rights to gun ownership. Occasionally the attacks forced Obama to defend his legislative record and positions. Most of all, he was defensive when charged with somehow sympathizing with criminals: "I voted for, or co-sponsored myself, over 100 bills that strengthened criminal penalties for everything ranging from sex offenders to drug dealers to domestic violence abusers. It would be very hard to argue . . . that I somehow have been soft on crime." As for issues of partisanship and philosophical inflexibility, the Democratic candidate maintained that during his terms in the state senate he had achieved a most commendable record of showing a willingness to "work both sides of the aisle."[21]

A statewide-carried radio debate between Keyes and Obama on October 12, 2004, demonstrated a sharp contrast between the two men's positions on a variety of topics. They clashed over abortion, with the Republican accusing the Democrat of infanticide for opposing the Born Alive Infant Protection Act, an effort that disallowed late-term abortions. Their distinctive positions on the Iraq War also emerged. Keyes viewed the American invasion as "the correct thing," while Obama cited President George W. Bush's use of faulty evidence as grounds for an unnecessary military engagement. Obama chided the current administration for offering tax breaks to companies guilty of moving jobs away from the United States. In the Democrat's judgment, financial benefits should go exclusively to employers who invested their profits in America.[22]

Entering the final weeks of the election, polls showed Obama running away from Keyes. One survey of voters indicated the Democrat capturing 66 percent and his conservative foe only 19 percent of the electorate. With seemingly a victory already locked up and a massive sum of accumulated campaign funds, Obama decided on assisting fellow Democratic office seekers in need of his support. Having already raised $4.19 million by the end of the third quarter of 2004, the Illinois state senator had more than tripled the amount collected by his feisty opponent. The Democrats' keynote speaker began bankrolling fellow party members. By mid-October, one estimate indicated his donations at $268,000. Monetary recipients included Senator Tom Daschle, who was in a tough reelection battle in South Dakota; the Democratic Party hopeful for president, John Kerry; and Melissa Bean, who was in an uphill campaign to capture a congressional seat in a traditionally Republican suburban Chicago district where veteran House member, Philip Crane, had represented residents for many terms. Obama supplemented political donations with personal appearances on behalf of fellow Democrats in Milwaukee, Los Angeles, and Denver. To a Wisconsin political rally gathered on behalf of Russ Feingold's bid for another Senate term, a master of ceremonies introduced the guest from Chicago as the "young man [who] has set Illinois on fire and set America on fire."[23]

In a third and final broadcast debate, Obama and Keyes addressed economic problems and solutions but with very different perspectives and answers. Ultraconservative Keyes was certain that easing poverty would never result from public efforts and legislation, because he was not "obsessed with government" as a positive resource for helping poor people.[24] Responding to this disengagement of any public responsibility for improving citizens' lives, Obama countered with a call to action. As he stated his case for governmental involvement: "When a child doesn't have health insurance, they [sic] don't need a lecture. They need health insurance."[25] This exchange was one reason that explained why the Democrat resonated with the Illinois electorate and his negative-minded opponent did not. The size of crowds gathered at political rallies for the two candidates illustrated as well as any factor which man was connecting with voters. Alan Keyes's emotional diatribes seemed to attract only fanatic Christian evangelicals. As an example of the Republican's problems, only "small but enthusiastic crowds in southwestern Illinois" were on hand to learn what Keyes was judging a "clear choice" between two senatorial hopefuls: "On every issue of moral concern to the future of this country, he [Obama] has taken the position that corresponds to the wrong choice instead of the right one, to the wicked choice instead of the good one, to the evil choice instead of the choice that is compatible with American principles and American conscience."[26]

Although both candidates were African American, Obama was the one who connected decisively with the minority. According to a *Chicago Tribune*/WGN-TV jointly completed survey released on October 30, 2004, the Democrat could expect to receive 93 percent of the state's African American vote. This minority segment of the Illinois electorate was in general agreement with Obama's message of positive government, and it rejected Keyes's view of a "moral crisis" in need of fixing.[27] As for repeated criticisms that Obama did not legitimately belong as a member of the black community, he waited until the close of his last week of campaigning before finally addressing the matter. To explain himself on this delicate issue, Obama elaborated on his childhood experiences under the guidance of a white mother and grandparents. He told of how they had imparted in him positive images of African Americans. "And there was no reason to think that the stereotypes that I would learn subsequently about African-Americans that were still rampant, and to some extent are still rampant, ever applied to me."[28]

Lopsided in Obama's favor as the election appeared to voters, the Democrat also had the advantage of gaining editorial endorsements from the two Illinois newspapers with the largest circulations. Just as in February before the Democratic primary, on October 15, 2004, the editorial staff of the *Chicago Sun-Times* repeated its endorsement of the state senator, but the paper was not altogether unqualified in its support. His stands against the Iraq War and such "other left-leaning positions" as opposing NAFTA and other free trade agreements were reasons for concern, but favoring Obama's candidacy was his proven ability to work well with both Republicans and Democrats. "A man for all ethnic seasons, he stirs our optimism and most assuredly gets our support."[29] With even greater enthusiasm and less equivocation, members of the editorial staff at the traditionally Republican *Chicago Tribune* supported Obama over Keyes in their October 24, 2004, endorsement. In what seemed like a general agreement with most residents from across Illinois, the editorial board took a positive view of Obama, a candidate whom it described as "someone who is able to rise above ethnic and racial divides and political partisanship and find the best in people, find common ground and solve problems." As a candidate possessing the "tongue of a statesman" and the "touch of a commoner" and as a leader who swells in most every resident across the Land of Lincoln a sense of pride that "such a person hails from Illinois," Obama received unqualified editorial backing from the "World Greatest Newspaper."[30]

Only an hour after polling ended, the prediction of a landslide victory by Obama was fulfilled. When all the votes were counted, the results showed the Democrat's victory. For a U.S. Senate seat, Obama's landslide win represented the largest margin of victory in Illinois electoral history. The final tally showed the victor with 3,425,074 votes or 70 percent and his hapless, overwhelmed opponent with 1,319,920 or 27 percent. On closer inspection of the tabulation, an analysis indicates that Obama triumphed everywhere and with almost every voting category. As shown in the following table, the only apparent exception to the rule occurred among "White Protestant Conservatives":

Table 4

Voter Category:	Obama	Keyes
African Americans	92%	8%
White Protestant Conservatives	18	77
Catholics	75	23
Vote by Region:		
Chicago	88	11
Cook County Suburbs*	75	23
Collar Counties	65	32
Northern half of Illinois	62	35
Southern half of Illinois	61	36

Note: *Obama carried every suburban township, gaining in these 724,221 votes to Keyes's 225,176.[31]

By winning so easily on November 2, 2004, and in his success across so many divisions of Illinois's diverse electorate, Senator-elect Obama became an immediate political celebrity who was "embraced by a party hungry for new faces."[32] Only hours after the victory in the Illinois race for the U.S. Senate, Democrats proclaimed the African American winner a "rising star." Avid reporters looking for news even questioned Obama to ascertain if he might not now have future national political ambitions. To these suggestions, he was adamant: "I am not running for president in four years. It's a silly question."[33] Not receiving encouragement from Obama, media representatives turned to Axelrod, but again denials of interest in higher office resulted: "I don't think we're trying to dampen expectations. We're trying to douse them. We're trying to pour as much water as we can find on them. . . . It's just not healthy for him." With revelations of the full dimensions of Obama's victory, a *Chicago Tribune* editor did not venture any contemplation of Obama's eventually seeking a national office, but the newspaperman did try to interpret the hopeful meaning of the Democrat's victory for Illinois residents: "Blessedly, Barack Obama has no IOUs except to the people of Illinois." Thus, the great challenge facing the victor, cautioned the editor, will be "to live up to his promise of bipartisanship."[34]

Immediately after the Obama victory, its dimensions and possibilities stretched beyond Illinois to become a national story covered by all three major weekly news magazines. On November 15, 2004, Amanda Ripley for *Time* in partnership with CNN provided her lengthy assessment of the meaning of the African American's win and of its effects on his personal life, his political future, and his party. Democratic strategist Donna Brazile who ran Al Gore's 2000 campaign for president was somewhat afraid of what might occur for Obama in the U.S. Senate. "My greatest fear for Barack," she expressed, "is that he'll be in the background, another black face in the sea of whiteness." With this possibility in mind, she advised that "he doesn't have to become the next black leader," but he should "become a great Senator from the state of Illinois." Ripley cited Representative Gwen Moore of Milwaukee who, like Obama, went to Congress after the 2004 elections. In the new congresswoman's assessment, "He's all of us! He's not black! He's not white!" Moreover, observed Ripley, Obama's "background resonates because it proves his points" because he "doesn't sound like a civil-rights-era politician." Rather than accusing Americans of not following the nation's highest ideals, he challenged them to do better. To the point of Obama's effect on his audiences, Ripley quoted an African American barber who put his reactions to Obama this way: "When he talks, you don't think about his color."[35] As one of the racially seamless politician's key mentors at Harvard Law School, Laurence Tribe remembered a gifted student who had "the surest way of calmly reaching across what are impenetrable barriers to many people."[36] Not surprisingly for Obama after an overwhelming landslide win for the U.S. Senate some fourteen weeks after delivering a most electrifying keynote address, *Gentleman's Quarterly* in December named the senator-elect from Illinois and extroverted real estate mogul Donald Trump to share the magazine's accolade as Men of the Year for 2004.[37] Aware of the attention Illinois's new senator was attracting as a possible presidential candidate in 2008, six-year-old daughter Malia asked her father innocently after the Senate swearing-in ceremony, "Daddy, are you going to be president?"[38]

If any two other African Americans had a chance with enough white voters to win the highest office in 2008, they were Obama and popular television personality Oprah Winfrey. Asked for her intentions in an interview on CNN's *Larry King Live*, the popular female entertainer stated on September 30, 2006, that she had no personal interests in running herself, but she expressed a strong desire to bolster the candidacy of Illinois's junior senator.[39] A generally respected impartial syndicated columnist from Chicago, Clarence Page explained what he saw occurring across racial barriers to the detriment of African Americans: "Of course, the irony is that the quest to elect a symbol of how America has moved beyond race means that Obama, [Secretary of State Condoleezza] Rice, Winfrey, [comedian Bill] Cosby, etc. must be judged at least in part on the color of their skin, not the content of their character, as Martin Luther King Jr. [had] dreamed." Page considered this grossly unfair to these individuals and also not at all beneficial: "This effectively reduces them into something less than the individuals they strive to be. Such are the ways of modern politics, which pit one media-created image against others. But they also help explain why Obama, among others, has good reason to avoid jumping into the presidential ring too soon, if at all."[40]

With so much focus on Obama and his future decision about whether to make an attempt at a national office, he again stated his commitment to the more pressing immediate role of serving Illinois residents in the U.S. Senate. Ranked ninety-ninth according to seniority rules, the lone African American member of Congress's upper chamber had few opportunities to influence legislative developments. Despite his status as newcomer, Obama promised to provide some impact on how the nation would be governed. Both children and elderly Americans, in particular, would gain his devoted attention because he wanted "to make sure that we create the kind of nation that these children and your children and your grandchildren deserve."[41] In order to quickly gain as much knowledge about the Senate as possible, Obama turned to Peter Rouse, a Washington veteran who had been ex-senator Tom Daschle's top aide. Obama devoted much of his first year to handling routine constituent matters and to gaining international experience through excursions to Russia, Eastern Europe, Israel, and Iraq. The off-year elections of 2006 afforded Obama almost unlimited opportunities to raise money and appear on behalf of Democratic candidates. On several occasions he spoke in support of their elections. As the credits from these personal appearances were building for the young senator, he became more circumspect about getting involved in anything very controversial. Tracking what in all probability represented a deliberate effort to throw off future critics, Senator Obama, according to observer David Mendell, understood that if the lawmaker "had larger ambitions, his team believed he could not be fitted too comfortably with a liberal straitjacket." Weighing the choice between irritating a core of liberal backers and suffering the possible negative effects of having a pigeonholed reputation as an unacceptable ideologue for moderate voters, Obama opted for the politically safer option of somewhat alienating the former group. Despite all his carefully adept maneuvering away from extremist causes, the Illinois politician's first-year floor votes remained with his party 95 percent of the time.[42]

As much as roll-calls seemed indicative of partisanship, individual actions reflected more of the same willingness on Obama's part to reach across the aisle to work with Republicans in the U.S. Senate as he had shown earlier during his tenure in the Illinois State Senate. Obama worked with Richard Lugar to bring down stockpiles of conventional weapons and joined with other GOP members to propose immigration reform with Florida's Mel Martinez. He also cooperated with Oklahoma Republican Tom Coburn for improved supervision of Hurricane Katrina relief contracts.

The closest Obama came to taking risks as a freshman member of the Senate was his willingness to assume a "self-imposed role of racial bridge-builder."[43] Wary advisors urged him not to attempt this because they feared he might alienate both whites and blacks. Boldly choosing to ignore his aides' advice for caution, Obama, as the most powerfully positioned black in America's government, felt an obligation for more direct involvement after Hurricane Katrina's devastating toll on African Americans. Soon after the full impact of the disaster had become known, a reporter asked Obama to comment about the correctness of hip-hop artist Kanye West's assessment that "George Bush doesn't care about black people." The black senator measured his words carefully to answer that "passive indifference" rather than blatant racism characterized the problem of what had occurred to the minority in New Orleans.[44] This reply was not what civil rights activists wanted to hear. The subtlety of Obama's choice of words had the predictable effect of annoying veterans of the civil rights movement. Jesse Jackson, for one, was livid at Obama's suggestion that class and not race explained the Bush administration's woeful treatment of flood victims: "I think Barack chooses to walk a very delicate balance, but sometimes it is not your walking that is the issue, it is what is beneath your feet. The right wing radically shifted the earth."[45]

With advice divided about whether to seek the Democratic presidential nomination in 2008, the junior senator from Illinois decided his chances for a successful bid were better than skeptics such as Page supposed them to be. Confirmation of Obama's decision to run occurred on a bitterly cold day at the Old State Capitol in Springfield. There on February 10, 2007, where Abraham Lincoln had once stood, the freshman senator referred to the sixteenth president when announcing his plans to seek the nation's highest position. In quick succession thereafter, the number of declared Democratic contenders for their party's top honor swelled to ten candidates, and the African American lawmaker was definitely the least experienced of the group. John Edwards had been the party's vice-presidential nominee in 2004, Joe Biden and Christopher Dodd had achieved notoriety during many years in the U.S. Senate, Governor Bill Richardson had served the nation in several diverse high-ranking posts, and frontrunner and favorite Hillary Rodham Clinton was familiar to most Americans because of her active roles as First Lady and presently as New York's junior senator. It was she and not Obama who attracted public backing from such prominent African Americans as former U.N. ambassador and retired Atlanta mayor Andrew Young, veteran civil rights activist and House member John Lewis, Philadelphia mayor Michael Nutter, and Harlem's powerful, veteran congressman Charles Rangel. Generally dismissed at the outset with no better chance to succeed than Obama, the other four announced contenders—Tom Vilsack of Iowa, Mike Gravel of

Alaska, Evan Bayh of Indiana, and Dennis Kucinich of Ohio—did not figure as serious hopefuls in the nominating process. Unable to raise much interest or adequate funding, the Iowan and the Hoosier dropped out days before the Iowa caucuses—the official beginning of the hunt for convention delegates—on January 3, 2008. On the other hand, to the astonishment of many veteran political observers, Obama was performing well. In Plouffe's judgment, "doing well in Iowa was essential because Hillary Clinton had to be disrupted early in the primary season for us to have any chance of derailing her."[46]

Obama's first charge toward a leadership position among all the candidates came on November 10, 2007, with a rousing address to a partisan gathering at the Iowa Democratic Party's annual Jefferson-Jackson Dinner in Des Moines. On this occasion the senator delivered a speech that injected adrenaline into his supporters and won new converts to his bid. Columnist David Yepsen of the *Des Moines Register*, commenting on Obama's crowd-stirring oration, predicted that, as a result of it, "Saturday's dinner will be remembered as one of the turning points in his campaign here."[47] As for Clinton, she had earlier demonstrated an element of self-destruction during a televised debate with the other candidates, when the moderator asked her to comment on New York governor Eliot Spitzer's controversial proposal to offer eligibility for driver's licenses to illegal aliens. Caught off-guard by the question, she fumbled at first through a veiled endorsement before sensing that a shift to her opposition would play better with voters. Almost instantly, in response to her equivocating, campaign opponents capitalized on her evasiveness to such a degree that the former First Lady now appeared guilty of "talking out of both sides of her mouth" on this issue.[48] Early in the battle for caucus votes, Obama's capable organization gained on her and on everyone else. His staff showed more creativity and greater imagination at using the Internet to find donors and volunteers. His promising to bring about change resonated well with Iowans who were tired of the current Republican administration and the seemingly never-ending war in Iraq. In the final week before Iowans would gather at caucuses throughout the state, the Reverend Al Sharpton indicated, without any stated purpose, his intention of coming to Iowa. Fears gripped Obama's top staff members that the boisterous civil rights leader might be contemplating an announcement of support for their candidate, and this backing from Sharpton was certainly something the Obama camp did not desire.[49] Coming from him, it might racialize the campaign because whites overwhelmingly disapproved of Sharpton. In the end, as a courtesy and as a reflection of Obama's wishes, the reverend canceled his appearance.

The results from the Iowa caucuses surprised Clinton and Edwards. Both candidates had expected a contest between the two of them, but Obama astonished the early frontrunners, along with many political observers. Of the forty-five delegates tied to results from the January 3 caucuses, Obama collected twenty-seven, or 38 percent of his party's caucus vote. With 93,952 Iowa Democrats making open their declarations for him before both neighbors and friends, the African American senator easily eclipsed Edwards and Clinton with their respective totals of 74,377 and 73,663. An assessment of Iowa's unique system of choosing delegates showed the winner doing especially well with youthful, first-time caucus goers. Biden and Dodd, reacting to their dismal showings in Iowa, immediately suspended their presidential campaigns before the New Hampshire primary set for January 8.[50]

With the Democratic presidential field thinned out to three major contenders and three improbable hopefuls, attention turned to unpredictable New Hampshire. Fiercely independent Granite State voters traditionally do not follow Iowa's lead by supporting the same candidates. With only twenty-two convention delegates at stake, this state's primary offered more symbolic value than an actual effect on two political parties' nominations of presidential candidates. Yet in efforts to influence a favorable outcome, candidates Obama, Clinton, and Edwards each spent considerable time, energy, and money with personal efforts in the New England state. The junior senator from Illinois also had something important to prove; Obama sought a demonstration of how well his message of change would appeal with New Englanders after its enormous success a few days earlier in the Midwest farm belt. Although he did well in the nation's first Democratic primary with 104,815 votes or 37 percent, Clinton did better. She amassed 112,404 votes or 39 percent. Edwards trailed the two leaders, gaining only 48,699 votes or 17 percent of the total vote. Taken together, Richardson, Gravel, and Kucinich were nonfactors, accounting for no more than 6 percent of the Democratic vote total.

The outcome in New Hampshire was remarkable because polls had pointed to an Obama victory. Left for pondering and understanding was the motivation behind the apparent shift. As a group of analysts surmised, the move to Clinton from Obama occurred in the privacy of voting booths because this was where white voters—who, with sheepish reluctance to admit truthfully to pollsters their true intentions of never backing a black presidential candidate—could tell the truth of their preferences. Another school of thought attributed the unexpected shift to a rare show of emotion on the part of Clinton. Initial fears had been that her shedding tears in public might prove a liability, but instead this turned into an asset. As Dan Balz and Haynes Johnson conclude in *The Battle for America 2008*, her public crying represented "a break in Clinton's steely exterior that let a glimmer of her humanity peek through for all of New Hampshire, and the world, to see." Hillary's display of passion, when added to perceptions of her as the recipient of her two male opponents' verbal assaults and of Obama's spontaneously condescending remark about her being "likable enough," made her the victim in the minds of many New Hampshire women and thereby thrust forward into play her gender as decisive factors on primary day.[51]

Although the schedule showed Michigan theoretically as the next state to hold a primary, none of the major candidates dared to campaign seriously there. The problem behind the boycott was Michigan's violation of Democratic Party rules by pushing forward the date of its primary election to January 15, a move that cost residents their voice in the nominating process. Clinton's name remained on ballots, but Obama had never acted for inclusion. Thus, voting in Michigan lost all of its relevance and legitimacy. For similar reasons, Florida held an equally meaningless "quick-start" primary on January 29. As with Michigan, the Democratic National Committee refused to accept voting results from Florida. Democrats had opportunities to vote for both Obama and Clinton in the Sunshine State, but unfortunately for the New York senator, the unrecognized and meaningless result of a decisive victory for her did not count. Until a few days before the opening of the party's convention in Denver, the DNC's credential committee had not decided whether to seat Michigan and Florida delegations. Thus possibilities existed for exclusions of these two maverick states from all proceedings. In the end, after the credentials committee's harsh rebuke for violating party rules and not following a correct order for holding primaries, Democrats from Michigan and Florida gained last-hour reprieves and permission to participate fully in all convention proceedings. Unlike Clinton's wavering from the outset of the dispute because an acceptance of results from the pair of dissident states would have favored her, Obama had decided early to abide by party rules. He had opted against having his name placed on Michigan ballots, and he had refrained altogether from campaigning for votes in the Florida primary.

Despite Hillary's triumph in New Hampshire, her election team was in shambles as she began preparations for Nevada, the next sanctioned primary. Infighting over the most effective strategy to use against Obama and personality clashes among staffers poisoned any chances of unity developing among the highest tiers of her campaign advisors. As early as March 2007, chief strategist Mark Penn had advocated using a negative attack against Obama, one that would have questioned his "American roots," but he found little support for this approach. In title only, Patti Solis Doyle was the campaign's manager until her dismissal for suggesting that Clinton consider withdrawing her candidacy. As a consequence, when Nevada Democrats went to the polls on January 19, 2008, to select their convention delegates to Denver, destructive undercurrents of jealousy and factionalism had already disrupted any joint sense of purpose and resolve among Clinton's closest advisors. Since these problems were not occurring in view of the electorate, the important matter at hand for Clinton became a task of convincing Democrats why they should vote for her. With the number of contenders in Nevada reduced to Obama, Clinton, and Edwards, the major uncertainty revolved around which person from the trio had the best chance of scoring with the state's large Hispanic voting bloc.[52] After a tally of all the ballots, the ex-First Lady was the clear victor. Of participants in Nevada's Democratic primary, 51 percent of them chose her, while 45 percent selected Obama. Edwards barely survived as a viable candidate for the nomination after a poor showing; he received only 4 percent of the total primary vote. At this point, the only factor responsible for keeping him in the race was a fleeting hope for success in his native state of South Carolina. To turn around a stalled campaign, he pinned everything now on his favorite-son status there. He realized after Nevada that, if he were to fail in his home state, any efforts at continuing to bid for support elsewhere would make no sense.

South Carolina Democrats staged their primary on January 26, and unlike in three previous contests, it was crucial to obtain the African American vote. The election also figured to test the popularity of Obama and the contention of whether he was really "black enough" in the minds of the minority. Bill Clinton, described in 1998 as America's first black president by Nobel Prize-winning novelist Toni Morrison, had attracted a number of prominent African American leaders to his wife's side. Certainly of equal or perhaps even greater significance, Congressman James Clyburn, the state's most influential African American politician as a result of his duty as the Democrats' Whip in the House of Representatives, remained neutral, refusing despite pleas for endorsements to support either Clinton or Obama.

The start of the Illinois senator's push for Palmetto State votes began on December 9, 2007, in Columbia at the University of South Carolina's Williams-Brice Stadium. On hand for a major campaign rally in the state capital were Oprah Winfrey and Barack and Michelle Obama. In an energetic speech that celebrated the courageous battlers for civil rights during the 1960s, who had demonstrated determination to "stand up," the candidate ended with a plea, "Don't let them tell you we've got to wait. Our moment is now."[53]

When it was clear that his wife, Hillary, was not electrifying the African American electorate as Bill Clinton had assumed her campaign should, he allowed apparent frustration with what he considered the minority's lack of appreciation for all his administration had done for race relations to overtake his better judgment about injecting race into the campaign. Instead of being an asset, now, the former president turned into a serious liability. Moving from what Balz and Johnson have called "the ultimate surrogate," Bill ended up costing his wife votes and future endorsements while damaging his own reputation. On Obama's record of opposition to the Iraq war, the ex-president dismissed it as "the biggest fairy tale I've ever seen."[54] Moreover, he drew a direct comparison between Obama's appeals to South Carolina African Americans in 2008 to Jesse Jackson's efforts there during his 1984 and 1988 presidential campaigns. Unspoken—but certainly implied—was the suggestion that Obama's primary source of strength came as an African American candidate. As if damage from her husband's ludicrously unsavory characterizations and assessments were not bad enough, Hillary then credited Lyndon Johnson's responsibility for civil rights legislation as being more important than that of Martin Luther King. In a bitter reaction to the pair's denigrating and incendiary comments and the ill-advised conclusions, once-neutral

Clyburn turned livid, reprimanding both Hillary and Bill Clinton for their dashing the "hopes and dreams" of African Americans. Chastising did not appear to have any immediate effect, however; the New York senator listened and offered no rebuke to Black Entertainment Television founder Robert Johnson's derogatory remarks about her rival. While accompanying Mrs. Clinton at South Carolina political events, the African American billionaire entrepreneur compared Obama to a Sidney Poitier-portrayed character in the film "Guess Who's Coming to Dinner?," and with innuendo poked fun at the rival candidate's drug use during his teenaged years in Hawaii, a matter already confessed by Obama in his best-selling memoirs.[55]

The nasty tone of the Clinton campaign and its racial overtones upset Senator Ted Kennedy of Massachusetts. His worry was in part because prospects existed for divisiveness over race carrying over into the general election in November, and in a telephone conversation he did not hesitate to remind the former president of his personal displeasure. Race, the veteran lawmaker from one of America's most famous political dynasties warned, is always "a-burning," that is, lurking close to the surface. As he reminded the forty-second president, "You know it and I know it. . . . Let's get back and talk about heath care. Let's get the hell off this thing." Stung by the charges against them, the Clintons announced an end to subtle injections of race into their campaign against Obama, noting in the process how they and he "are on the same side."[56] Contrition came too late for Caroline Kennedy and Uncle Teddy, however, because on primary day in South Carolina and the next day, first Caroline and then Ted endorsed the Illinois senator. In terms of having an effect on Democratic voters in the Palmetto State, support of Obama from the veteran senator and his niece came too late, but their help was not needed. Obama captured 55 percent of the vote, thereby dwarfing Clinton's 27 percent and Edwards's 18 percent. After this dismal showing in his home state, Edwards withdrew from the race, leaving it as a two-person battle of historic significance involving race pitted against gender.

With the scorecard from contests to date reading one primary win and a caucus triumph for Obama and two primaries for Clinton, attention and interest turned to Super Tuesday—scheduled for February 5. Much was at stake in a one-day event that featured battling over convention delegates in twenty-two states and American Samoa. Cumulatively involved in all these contests on one day were more than half of all credentialed convention attendees. The combination of six populous states—California, Georgia, Illinois, Massachusetts, New Jersey, and New York—alone accounted for 620 delegates. Obviously neither Clinton nor Obama could effectively campaign everywhere, and as a consequence of the logistical impossibility of making personal appearances in so many places over a short period of time, the total amount of available advertising revenue became a crucial factor. Here was where Obama's campaign definitely had an advantage. His team, through a clever use of such Internet sites as Facebook, received donations from millions of small contributors, while it was enlisting an active army of thousands of enthusiastic volunteers capable of reaching millions of Democratic voters spread across all the states voting on the most important day of the primary and caucus season. Unlike the decision of the strategists working for Clinton who had opted to avoid devotion to the caucus states on Super Tuesday, David Plouffe engineered a completely comprehensive plan for Obama, which conceded nothing anywhere to Clinton. Although she was successful at gaining more votes than her rival in New York, California, Massachusetts, and New Jersey, while also doing better in American Samoa, Arkansas, Tennessee, Oklahoma, and New Mexico, none of these contests were winner-take-all elections. Complex party rules proportioned out delegates in each state—both according to the statewide vote and by congressional districts. Thus after a completion of all vote tallying, Obama's triumphs in thirteen states, together with shares where Clinton had gained more popular votes but where the loser nevertheless garnered delegates, left Obama with 847 delegates to 834 for his rival. Therefore, odd as it might seem, Clinton, though winning the overall popular vote on Super Tuesday, 8,081,748 to 7,987,274, still lost ground to Obama.

After February 5, 2008, her campaign went into a downward tailspin as her much better organized opponent secured eleven straight victories over the next fortnight. During an eleven-day span from February 9 through February 19, Obama rolled to consecutive wins in both primaries and caucuses. The most impressive triumphs in terms of delegates were those of Washington state, Virginia, and Wisconsin. At the end of this round of contests, Obama had what in the view of most political analysts looked like an insurmountable edge over Clinton, because in all, the results of contests to date had already awarded him 2,200 delegates. With approximately 1,000 regular delegates remaining for voters to choose and some 800 super delegates—a mixing of elected officials and party leaders—with automatic voting privileges at the Democratic Party Convention, the contest for the nomination appeared to have ended. Making matters even worse for the New York senator's efforts to win, bickering left Clinton's staff in dissolution over how to proceed. Despite setbacks and losses, she did not lose her will to fight to the end. Remaining ahead were large states like Ohio, Texas, and Pennsylvania, and Clinton was a resilient optimist who hoped victories in these would convince super delegates of Obama's lack of electability in the general election against Senator John McCain, the likely nominee of the Republican Party.

Polls were indicating blue-collar whites in industrial states found reasons to suspect the African American Democrat's patriotism and religion. Constantly unfounded rumors circulated about his secret Islamic beliefs and his disloyalty. According to rumor mongers and distracters, Obama was a closet Muslim who attended a *madrasah* (Islamic school) during a childhood spent in part in Indonesia. Citing the Islamic background of the candidate's father and the son's middle name of Hussein, worriers suspected the candidate's involvement in an elaborate terrorist plot that included a scheme of secretly foisting Obama on the American electorate. Also circulating was the unfounded contention that the senator had taken his oath of office with a Koran and not with his left hand on a Bible. The latter charge about his disdain for the United States stemmed from a photograph of him supposedly not placing his right hand over his heart during the Pledge of Allegiance; in actuality he was standing at attention during the playing of the national anthem. Obama's detractors also doubted his eligibility for the presidency because in their view he had not been born in the United States.

Then just about the moment the furor over Bill Clinton's race-baiting remarks was fading from front pages, others in Hillary's circle of prominent supporters re-injected Obama's color as an issue. This time the primary culprit was former vice-presidential candidate and Clinton aide Geraldine A. Ferraro. According to her assessment, "if Obama was a white man, he would not be in this position" as a leading contender for the Democratic nomination.[57] Negative responses were immediate. Reverend Al Sharpton quickly answered with a rebuke of the ex-president, Ferraro, and Clinton supporter Governor Edward G. Rendell of Pennsylvania for their apparent roles of reintroducing race as a factor in the election. What was particularly upsetting to the civil rights leader from New York City was Hillary Clinton's lack of stated contrition for the divisive statements of her supporters. As Sharpton put his displeasure, "When you hear the lack of total denunciation of Ferraro, when you hear Rendell saying there are whites who will never vote for a black, one has to wonder if the Clinton campaign has a Pennsylvania strategy to appeal to voters on race."[58]

Tony Rezko's trial on corruption charges was another distraction for Obama to counter. More than just an acquaintance, the developer had contributed significantly to the Chicagoan's campaigns and had once sold the candidate a small parcel of land adjoining the Obama's Hyde Park home. A question about the two men's true relationship naturally arose for the politician to explain. For having failed to deal with Rezko before the opposition could capitalize on possible wrongful connections between a person under indictment for fraud and the candidate, Plouffe blames himself in his account of his service as Obama's campaign manager.[59] News of this story was occurring when further encouragement came to Clinton from a release of her most effective television advertisement entitled "3 a.m." It showed children asleep in their beds with a worried mother pondering over a response to the question of who would you want in the White House answering the phone at this hour? By implication, Obama's lack of experience represented a serious problem if a crisis were to arise for his attention.

Primary votes from Ohio, Rhode Island, and Texas on March 4, 2008, seemingly confirmed the doubts about Obama's abilities to connect with a crucial element of the white electorate, union members. In Ohio, Clinton's efforts had benefited from Governor Ted Strickland's support. Voters in the first two named states gave her impressive pluralities. Texans, in a most unusual electoral setup, used both a primary and a caucus to select their delegates; Clinton won the first battle but lost in the second part, providing in the process a slight gain for Obama in the struggle for convention delegates. Meanwhile in the Ocean State, Rhode Islanders' favorite was clearly the female senator from New York. Further north in New England, Vermont Democrats overwhelmingly decided for Obama. During the next week momentum swung back for Illinois's junior senator. On March 8, Wyoming caucus goers gave their support to him, and then African Americans and a minority of white voters going to the polls in Mississippi on March 11 definitely preferred Obama to his female opponent; the result of their lopsided voting surged the Chicagoan to victory by a large margin, 255,809 to 155,686.

With a loss in Ohio and a Mississippi win resulting from an apparent effect of Obama's race, the media's fixation with this became increasingly evident. News reports almost always broke down primary election results into voter profile analyses based on color, and more than earlier in the judgment of Obama strategists, Clinton's advisors employed this as evidence to publicize why she could win in November and why her African American rival would lose the general election. Obama refuted Clinton's claims this way: her "campaign has talked more during the course of the last few months about what groups are supporting her and what groups are supporting me and trying to make a case that the reason she should be the nominee is that there are a set of voters that Obama might not get. And that seems to track in a certain racial demographic."[60]

Days after the Mississippi triumph, Obama began suffering through the worst two months of his bid for the Democratic nomination. Compounding some errors by his campaign staff was a personal connection that left the candidate in a precarious position. Appearing before national television audiences on March 14, 2008, to Obama's total embarrassment, was his pastor, the Reverend Jeremiah Wright, blasting the United States with "God damn America!" and holding the nation's past responsible for the terrorism of 9/11. Here on video was Obama's spiritual advisor and the religious leader who had married him and Michelle, and later had baptized their daughters, Sasha and Malia. As much as Obama had wanted to move well beyond reminders of his mixed biological heritage by offering a post-racial message of unity, everything related to all the ugly controversies of the black-white divisions in American society blazed now suddenly front and center. Plouffe and Axelrod admitted their culpability for allowing Wright's tirades to emerge so late in the primary season. Even before the senator's announced candidacy for the Democratic nomination for president, Obama's campaign manager in *The Audacity to Win* admits to having suspected a potential for trouble from the pastor. Plouffe had known from reading an article about the minister's vitriolic views in an article published in *Rolling Stone*, but just as with the Rezko relationship, at the time the staff manager had failed to confront a potential menace before its discovery by personally looking at tapes of Wright's sermons.[61] As much as Obama claimed to have never heard Wright utter such accusatory conclusions about the nation, dodging race altogether was no longer an option for the African American presidential hopeful. In an eight-paragraph statement about personal reactions to Wright's scathing assessments of the United States, Obama not only condemned the pastor's remarks as "inflammatory and appalling," but he also commended Wright for a personal role in contributing to a positive Christian experience.[62] After a brief appearance on MSNBC with these reactions to Wright, Obama decided his best course of action would be a major address on race in America. Although some staffers were uncertain about the advisability of him speaking about so delicately emotional an issue as race, the candidate felt that he must "deal with this squarely." Rather than relying on a speech writer to compose his words, Obama preferred for this address to express his own impressions on a most touchy subject.[63]

Completed in the early morning hours of March 18, 2008, Obama's speech, "A More Perfect Union," was ready for delivery later that day at Constitution Hall in Philadelphia. Then in a calmly reassuring tone, Obama described how Wright's comments were "not only wrong but divisive." The candidate characterized a more positive side of his pastor, noting how his spiritual convictions had been responsible for introducing a faithless man to Christianity. As for explaining Wright's offensive remarks, Obama dedicated a greater part of his address to dealing with what he considered a generational gap among African Americans and how it separated older people such as his pastor who had lived and suffered sacrifice during the 1950s and 1960s from a younger group of blacks, the beneficiaries of more positive experiences resulting from greater opportunities and a more inclusive society. He ended his convincing presentation with the story of Ashley Baia, a twenty-three-year-old white supporter from Florence, South Carolina, who had looked beyond her skin color to comprehend how citizens of both races and from diverse backgrounds shared a common stake in working for "a more perfect union."[64] Although Obama's presentation received generally positive reviews, the effects of his relationship to Wright remained without a definitive resolution. As brilliantly as the speaker framed his response to the preacher, doubts still lingered about the probability of the senator's ability to recover from his connection to a hateful man and then to muster enough support from white voters to win in future primaries.[65]

Just as the ramifications of this episode were fading, the frontrunner for the Democratic nomination jeopardized his standing further with white working-class voters. On April 6, after a fund-raising event in San Francisco, Mayhill Fowler, a citizen journalist for the *Huffington Post* and an Obama donor, heard and recorded what amounted to denigration of small-town residents from the senator:

"You go into some of these small towns in Pennsylvania, and like a lot of small towns in the Midwest, the jobs have been gone now for twenty-five years and nothing's replaced them. Each successive administration has said that somehow these communities are gonna regenerate and they have not. So it's not surprising then that they get bitter, they cling to guns or religion or antipathy to people who aren't like them or anti-immigrant sentiment or antitrade sentiment as a way to explain their frustrations."

Wrestling for five days with what to do with an unfavorable analysis, Fowler finally decided to post Obama's comments on an Internet blog.[66] Within a few hours, fifty thousand viewers read what certainly had appeared a most derogatory slap at average Americans by an arrogant snob. Considered ammunition to discredit whatever appeal Obama might have had with working-class Pennsylvanians, Clinton now had her rival's own words to support a claim that she truly was the champion of the state's suffering middle class.

Coming as the revelation had after the Wright debacle, Obama's ill-advised commentary caused new worries for him and his staff because new questions about the candidate's alleged true identity popped up on cable television broadcasts, and his faux pas provided conservative talk radio personalities with more fodder, one more reason to attack the liberal Illinois senator's presidential aspirations. Quick to respond to the unfortunate episode before a friendly audience in Indianapolis on April 12, Clinton pounced on a golden opportunity to chastise Obama and to characterize his remarks as those of an "elitist and [someone] out of touch." She assured listeners that his sentiments were not "reflective of the values and beliefs of Americans" she knew.[67] In response to Hillary and to all the generated negative publicity, Obama had no choice but to attempt to make amends with a public apology for his clumsily worded characterization captured clandestinely on tape. Irritated by Clinton's continually reminding her audiences at every campaign stop of a most careless indiscretion, Obama fired back, calling Clinton a modern Annie Oakley "packing a six-shooter" because of her sudden defense of a citizen's right to gun ownership.[68]

In a contest beginning to look more like a tit-for-tat series of errors by both candidates, Clinton obliged with the next misstep. Embellishing her trip to Bosnia as First Lady, she described how snipers had greeted her arrival with a barrage of gunshots. A review of video coverage of the event showed her deplaning to a reception by children presenting a famous visitor from the United States with flower bouquets. With evidence disproving any presence of danger, Hillary and Bill were left with an embarrassing retreat from a falsely described heroic depiction of her travels to a Balkan war zone in the 1990s. In an attempt to connect with blue-collar workers, Obama's campaign bus stopped at a Pennsylvania bowling alley in order to give the candidate a photo opportunity. His anticipated effort at connecting with working-class voters went totally awry, however; his rolling a thirty-seven with several gutter balls only confirmed for everyone his lack of previous bowling experiences. Obama then followed up this debacle with a final debate with Clinton on April 16, 2008. For Obama's appearance and demeanor at this event, Balz and Johnson describe the mood of the Illinois senator as "foul" and his attention as "distracted."[69] The debate moderators offered no help: Charles Gibson and George Stephanopoulos of ABC News concentrated their grilling of Obama by asking him about his previous campaign mistakes and by reintroducing such annoyances as his "bitter" remarks captured in San Francisco; his relationship to Reverend Wright; his exact association with Hyde Park neighbor William Ayers, the convicted ex-Weather Underground radical who several years earlier had served with Obama on a foundation-sponsored board dealing with reforming Chicago public education and who had hosted a fund-raiser for neighbor and state senate candidate Obama; and his explanation for allegedly refusing to attach a flag pin to his suit-coat lapels. Sensing the one-sidedness in the questioners' discussion topics, the candidate performed poorly at fielding these tough inquiries.[70]

Without support from Governor Rendell and Mayor Nutter, Obama lost the Pennsylvania primary on April 22 by more than nine percentage points. In many ways, the worse part of this defeat for him was the revelation of a demographical analysis of the vote. Clinton had asserted that blue-collar white Democrats would not support her opponent in a general election, and now the results of her victory seemed to affirm these suspicions because her plurality among the state's white voters was 26 percent. Moreover, exit polls taken on Election Day showed her obtaining a forty-point advantage among whites who had never attended college. Without any apparent impact on changing minds and perceptions, Obama's concentrated effort of dedicating seven weeks to canvassing Pennsylvania for votes and his primary campaign's record-smashing expenditure of $11 million on television advertisements had not caused any shift among one of the most important elements of the Pennsylvania electorate. According to the *Economist*, the candidate's disconnect with a large segment of the state's Democratic voters caused alarm, because "These people are the heart and soul of the old Democratic Party. They hold the balance of power in a swathe of big industrial states that the Democrats simply have to win in November to take the White House." Certainly encouraging for many Clinton backers, as state primaries were winding to an end, was the apparent influence of the ugly conspicuous specter of race in the voting decisions of many white voters.[71]

Race emerged in many contexts as the focal point of Obama's bid for the Democratic nomination. In a historic battle projected to bring to the top of a major party's ticket either a woman or an African American, Senator Clinton was unwilling to capitulate, despite her hopelessly trailing Obama in the delegate count. She based her continuing on what seemed correct indicators that voting decisions made in the industrial states of Pennsylvania, Ohio, and Indiana by blue-collar whites would prevail at the convention. Thus considerable optimism existed among Hillary Clinton's avid supporters that the votes cast by hourly wage earners would have considerable effect upon super delegates at the convention. Some ill-advised statements made by both Barack and Michelle Obama had not helped their cause with the white working class. Her comment months earlier that "for the first time in my adult lifetime, I am really proud of my country," and his remark captured at a private fund-raiser in San Francisco about middle-class Americans "clinging to guns and religion" fueled campaign advertisements that reminded ordinary white Democrats of the Obamas' alleged elitism and anti-Americanism. In the opinion of director Andrew Kohut of the Pew Research Center, "Race intertwined with a broader notion that he [Obama] is not one of us. They [whites with twelve or fewer years of education] react negatively to people who are seen as different."[72] Freelance and independent Democratic pollster Peter D. Hart reached a similar conclusion, but with a different slant. To this surveyor of public opinions, a major question about Obama persisted continuously after his announced bid for the Democratic nomination: "Is he safe? Safe in terms of both the cultural values that he has, and about whether he is strong enough to be commander in chief."[73] In what conservative editor and opinionated commentator Bill Kristol was characterizing as a "rollicking demolition derby," Clinton and Obama operatives bashed their rivals with increasing openness.[74] Of equal significance for this particular study in the not-so-subtle case against Obama was the contention that he had become to many voters just another "black candidate."[75]

As if the meaning of the election result were not bad enough for Obama, Jeremiah Wright reemerged three days after the Pennsylvania debacle. In three different appearances over a span of three days, the flamboyant pastor was Bill Moyers's guest on public television, an honoree at an NAACP dinner, and a speaker at a National Press Club breakfast in Washington, DC. At none of these opportunities did Wright show any remorse or inclination to recant his harsh, outlandish assessments of the United States, which he had attacked in sermons. Initially, to the onslaught from Wright, about the only thing a shocked Obama could think to utter about the renewal of vituperation from his pastor was a bland statement that "He does not speak for me." Then after having conferred with senior staff members, Obama responded with a much stronger denunciation of Wright, as well as with the announcement of his planned withdrawal of membership in Trinity Church of Christ.[76] Nevertheless, as two *Washington Post* staff writers, Shailagh Murray and Peter Sleven, concluded, the pastor, by resurrecting at this particular time in the campaign the controversies surrounding his personal relationship with a key congregant, once again became a major "headache for the Obama campaign."[77]

After the Keystone State primary, seven more contests remained on the docket. Of these, Indiana and North Carolina received the greatest press coverage. The matter most in doubt was the effect of race on voting. As much as Obama tried to distance himself from this disruptive issue, it would not disappear. Losing results from Ohio and then Pennsylvania along with Wright's reappearance brought to the surface a consciousness that had been missing months earlier when Iowans went to caucuses to state their preference for the Democratic nomination. With the issue of race being the only significant difference separating Clinton and Obama and with its overall importance looming larger now as the key factor in the contest, more than it had earlier, political analysts watched anxiously to see how it might tilt voting in Indiana. Opinion polls were not especially helpful as some foresaw a large majority for Hillary, while others were predicting a close outcome because of Indiana's proximity to Illinois and because of the large African American voting blocs located in Lake and Marion Counties. After all the votes were in and tallied, pollsters who had expected a tight race were correct; Clinton received 641,734 votes, and Obama had 623,294. The bigger election surprise on May 6 occurred in North Carolina where the Illinois politician astonished almost everyone by scoring a landslide victory, 887,391 to 657,669. With the Tar Heel State win, Obama inched closer to acquiring the necessary number of pledged delegates for a sealed-up Democratic presidential nomination. Thus after a most difficult, trying period that included dealing again with the troubling effects of his former pastor's obvious bid for attention, Obama sensed a reinvigoration of hope. On the night of May 6, 2008, in a direct response to Clinton's remarks delivered before the two primaries, the Illinois senator gave the following perspective: "There were those who were saying North Carolina would be a game changer in this election. What North Carolina decided is the only game that needs changing is the one in Washington, D.C."[78]

Clinton took something entirely different from the two primaries. Disturbingly and to a degree desperately, she read the results as being evidence of her opponent's serious vulnerability in the November general election. In an exclusive interview published by *USA Today* one day after the Indiana and North Carolina primaries, the female candidate expressed her fears again of unspecified negative consequences for the Democratic Party from an Obama nomination. Comprehending herself to have "a much broader base to build a winning coalition on," she cited exit polls from the two states "that found how Obama's support among working, hardworking Americans, white Americans, is weakening again, and how whites in both states who had not completed college were supporting me. There's a pattern emerging here."[79] Most reactions to Clinton—even from some of her strongest supporters—were generally negative. Under a sensational headline "Desperate Hillbillies threaten to break up party," *New York Post* columnist Charles Hurt offered this pithy commentary in response to her assessment: "Well, now these racial politics have spilled out into the public and are splintering longtime, devoted Democrats into separate camps. It's become the 'working-class whites' versus the 'eggheads and African-Americans.'" In Hurt's view, the New York senator had unfortunately "gone nuclear" and was "getting kookier by the minute."[80] This was true to a degree, but in all fairness to Clinton, her comments in reality only reflected what media reports had noted almost incessantly from the beginning of Obama's surge toward the nomination.[81]

Vandalism and overt acts of racism directed both at the black candidate's campaign and his supporters increased as the inevitability of his success became more apparent. In Indiana, a state where the Ku Klux Klan had thrived during the 1920s, Obama volunteers encountered both hostility and derogatory name-calling. For example, in the southwestern town of Vincennes on the eve of the primary, vandals broke a large plate-glass window at the Illinois senator's local campaign headquarters and spray-painted on the building several nasty personal references to the Reverend Wright. One message proclaimed "Hamas votes BHO [Obama's initials]"; another indicated, "We don't cling to guns or religion. God-damn Wright."[82] A *Newsweek* polling of the electorate confirmed that racism was a significant obstacle for Obama to overcome. According to the weekly news-magazine's Racial Resentment Index, the greatest likelihood for strong negative reactions to him came from white citizens without college degrees, voters over the age of sixty, and Caucasians living in the South.[83]

With a winding down of primaries after Indiana and North Carolina, discussions of race and American politics increased. In order to obtain varied perspectives on this hot topic, Jeffrey Brown of PBS's *NewsHour* on May 7 hosted a three-member panel for assessments about how well the media was tackling race during the Clinton-Obama campaign. The moderator began by asking panelists to grade reporters' coverage. Each guest agreed news commentators had shown degrees of general awkwardness and discomfort in dealing with the subject of race. Of the three discussants, director Kathleen Hall Jamieson from the Annenberg Public Policy Center at the University of Pennsylvania was the most critical of news reporting on race. As she emphasized her criticisms of tendencies to oversimplify complex trends: "When the media focus on 'the black vote,' 'the white vote,' and then they start to particularize the white vote within that, they invite us to see race as a defining category of analysis. That simplifies, distorts, and heightens a concept that probably is best left not discussed in this broader, complex arena, because it's missing a whole lot of what's happening with this electorate."[84]

From the perspective of the *Economist*, as much as Obama tried to present "himself as admirably post-racial," not all voters wanted to look beyond race. With roughly 90 percent of the African American vote going to him in North Carolina and Indiana, the "colossal gap can hardly be attributed to the policy differences between the two candidates, which are small." The Illinois senator's candidacy offered an unprecedented opportunity for blacks to demonstrate how much race "matters. He gives our children hope. He's a role model." In sharp contrast, for many members of the majority the thought of Obama becoming president was a frightening prospect. If pressed for an explanation of their fear, whites often cited Obama's failure to place his right hand over his heart during the pledge of allegiance, and they mentioned his religious mentor's disdain for the United States.[85]

Without suffering a complete collapse brought on by a scandal or a major desertion of the super delegates, Obama had wrapped up the nomination. Despite what the numbers indicated, Clinton remained feisty, refusing to concede defeat. On consecutive Tuesdays, May 13 and 20, overwhelming support came to her from West Virginia and Kentucky voters. In the former state, the final tabulation showed Hillary with 177,159 votes to Obama's 109,248. Among Kentucky residents, Clinton succeeded even better, dwarfing Obama, 459,124 to 209,778. In both these instances, reports from election analysts emphasized white voters' unwillingness to back an African American candidate. On the same day that Kentuckians were marking so many of their ballots for Hillary, an altogether different outcome unfolded in Oregon. There in the Northwest where black residents represented only a miniscule fraction of the electorate, Oregonians favored Obama by an impressive margin, 375,385 to 259,825. The last primaries occurred on June 3, but the election outcomes from South Dakota and Montana had long ago lost significance. Hillary carried South Dakota, while Barack picked up a win in Montana. On June 7, four days after the final voting, the candidate who had almost broken through the so-called glass ceiling for female politicians appeared at the Pension Building in the nation's capital and delivered her concession speech. In it, Senator Clinton advised her loyal supporters to turn their efforts toward electing Obama the forty-fourth president, and she personally committed to "work my heart out to make sure that Senator Obama is our next president."[86] Her decision to quit the race was in part due to Congressman Rangel's advice that he could no longer support her bid. With defeat so imminent, the defection of a key African American supporter serves as a reminder of Jesse Jackson's campaigns, first in 1984 and then in 1988, when a number of prominent minority members urged the civil rights leader to acknowledge the reality of lost bids and to offer his backing to Walter Mondale against Reagan and four years later to Michael Dukakis in a contest against George H. W. Bush.

As for explanations as to how the African American candidate emerged victorious over more experienced and better-known opponents, analysts have emphasized several views. To put it simply, Obama ran a better campaign from start to finish. Clinton's staff lacked unity and direction, whereas the Obama team worked almost without mistake throughout the campaign. Balz and Johnson offer a concise explanation that resonates correctly with what transpired at every crucial moment: "Obama found . . . the combination of message, strategy, innovation, and discipline to prevail."[87] The mood and desires of a majority of the Democratic electorate also played an important role. From the Iowa caucuses on through the Montana primary, voters showed considerably more interest in leadership than in experience. The senator from Illinois stuck to a theme of change, and this offered a promise of something different to many citizens disgruntled with the policies of President Bush. Hurting Clinton as well was the possibility that her presidency might be a return to the tumultuous years of her husband's presidency.[88] According to Mark Penn's reflections on the nomination race, Clinton waited too long to attack Obama. Moreover, he contended, the press had shown considerable favoritism toward her opponent. In terms of what the Obama team understood and incorporated imaginatively into an action plan, clearly nothing was more impressive than the way the staff harnessed the Internet to the basic requirements of a political campaign. Exploiting this to a greater extent than any previous national campaign had ever done, the black senator raised more money from more individual donors and engaged a greater number of people to volunteer than all earlier candidates for their party's presidential nomination. Finally, Obama's effort concentrated on fighting for delegates and not on winning the popular vote. Overall, this controversial strategy ended in a generally closer than normal accumulative tally of voter preferences, but clearly not in what mattered most for gaining the Democratic nomination.[89]

Analysis of Obama's success at winning the contests for delegates cannot ignore the issue of race. Political analysts, journalists, bloggers, the Clintons, and Jeremiah Wright never allowed the issue to fade into obscurity as the African American senator had certainly desired from the outset. As much as he could not alter his physical appearance, Obama could and did steer his campaign away from any overtly racial message and appeal.[90] Advisors Axelrod and Plouffe knew from past experiences how to avoid turning their man's campaign into a referendum on colorblindness, and Obama had learned this lesson as well as a successful candidate for the U.S. Senate in Illinois. Therefore, from the start in Iowa to the final primary, this pair of skilled political handlers maintained their intention to conduct a race-neutral effort, although factors beyond the control of the Obama team intervened at times to render deracialization more or less impossible. Whether it was remarks by Bill Clinton, the strong support of African Americans for Obama in South Carolina, or the release of the white voter profiles from primaries in Ohio and Pennsylvania, many questions began to center around the likelihood of an African American's electability in the general election against a Republican opponent. Calmly, but evasively, when giving doubters his calculated responses, Obama liked to emphasize what united Americans and noted an overriding need for change. Wright presented an altogether different problem for the candidate because it was so personal. Therefore, Obama had no choice but to offer a direct confrontation to his preacher's scathing sermons. The result was an Obama speech that focused on three objectives; in the clearest possible terms, he sought to distance himself from his pastor's obnoxious conclusions, to emphasize why need existed for more openness about race relations in America, and to demonstrate the unifying effects his bid for the nomination had on both races. In a serene and reassuring presentation, and through the use of skillful explanation, Obama pointed out how and why many members of Wright's generation tended to hold onto bitterness and harsh judgments of the United States. By following this approach to a difficult challenge, he managed not only to separate himself from an older minister's vilifying conclusions but also, more importantly, to return the focus of his campaign to the deracialized messages of unity and change.

With the completion of the primaries and an African American almost assured of his party's nomination, race remained at the center of political discussions. At the heart of Obama's problems was the contention that neither he nor Michelle could be considered as truly "authentic Americans." In this line of absurd reasoning, having a genuine American identity results only from a clear association with a European background.[91] With a November presidential election likely to pit Senator John McCain of Arizona against Obama, a *Washington Post*-ABC News poll surveyed a sampling of Americans to ascertain their views on race. Polling confirmed that three in ten people were candid enough to acknowledge "feelings of racial prejudice" and suggested that degrees of racial bias would have a profound effect on their assessments of the Illinois senator. In general, 60 percent of African Americans rated interracial relations as either "not so good" or "poor." In sharp contrast, 53 percent of whites viewed them in a more positive context. A more discouraging discovery was that over half of polled whites judged Obama a "risky" choice for the White House, and two in every ten surveyed white Americans worried that an Obama presidency would no doubt "overrepresent the interests of African Americans."[92]

Unlike customary past lulls between the settlement on party presidential candidates and national party conventions, election year 2008 was unusual. Obviously the difference was the presence of an African American as the Democrats' likely nominee. A reoccurring question he had to address was how he would deal with the minority. It was a no-win proposition that he could not avoid. When the Reverend Jesse Jackson chastised Obama for his alleged "talking down to black people" about personal responsibilities, an embarrassing faux pas occurred for the outspoken civil rights activist. Assuming someone at the controls had turned off his microphone after a speech, when it was in fact still on, Jackson uttered for the nation to hear how much he would like a chance to "cut [Obama's] nuts off."[93] Although not intended to help Obama, this crude suggestion coming from a man many whites despised proved beneficial to the Democratic nominee. Discussions of race resulted again from McCain and Obama's separate appearances on August 1 and 2 at the Urban League's annual convention in Detroit. Although both politicians and their backers engaged in "ongoing finger-pointing over race," militants in attendance at the session demonstrated a greater impatience with Obama than they had done a day earlier with the conservative Republican. Heckling the Democratic hopeful for president throughout his address, demonstrators tried to make the point with loud jeers and boos that Obama had consistently shunned all issues of importance to his race. In their judgment, this failure to discuss a specific agenda for assisting the minority indicated a deliberate attempt of denial on his part; according to the rude individuals complaining with boisterous protests during Obama's speech to the Urban League, the candidate had not shown sufficient pride in his African American roots.[94]

Obama in one way found himself entrapped by who he was. If he mentioned his racial identity, he found himself at the center of accusations that he was "playing the race card." If he abstained from saying anything about it, critics wondered where his pride and loyalties were. An excellent case in point occurred in an Obama response to McCain. In this instance, the Democrat pointed out how he was "different" than previous candidates for president. As most irrefutable evidence, he cited an odd-sounding name and an appearance unlike the chief executives on the one- and five-dollar bills. His seemingly innocent remark brought forth an immediate response from Republicans that McCain's Democratic opponent had intentionally injected race into the 2008 presidential contest. Commenting about the charge on PBS's *NewsHour*, syndicated columnist Mark Shields called the criticism absurd. According to him, anyone looking at Obama would at once be able to recognize that he was definitely different and an African American just as any person observing Hillary Clinton would see that she was a woman and not a man.[95]

Given the number of words written and spoken about the racial issue during primaries and about the pioneering achievement of an African American candidate, the *New York Times* headlined an article in its Sunday magazine supplement for August 17, 2008, with a suggestive proposition about a new era in American political history. Matt Bai, in "Is Obama the End of Black Politics?" began a lengthy probe of this question with comments from Congressman James Clyburn. From incarceration forty-seven years earlier in Columbia, South Carolina, for leading protesters in a march against segregation, the veteran civil rights activist and lawmaker went on to become the majority whip in the House of Representatives and the highest-ranking black in Congress. He, like many other members of the Congressional Black Caucus, acknowledged that he had had preliminary doubts about Obama, "with," according to Bai, "his nice talk of transcending race and baby-boomer partisanship." Too young to have experienced firsthand all the struggles in the South against segregation and for equal voting rights, Obama often found himself encountering among older African Americans in leadership positions the judgment that he was less worthy of their support than Senator Clinton. A generation gap existed within the minority. As a thirty-eight-year-old pollster working for Obama summarized the split: "I'm the new black politics. The people I work with are the new black politics. We don't carry around that history. We see the world through post-civil-rights eyes. I don't mean that disrespectfully, but that's just the way it is."[96] The older generation was prone to criticizing Obama for not being "black enough" because his father "came to America on scholarship, not in chains." Of equal importance, Clinton also held onto her support until the bitter end of her struggle to become the Democratic nominee from younger leaders like Michael Nutter, the African American mayor of Philadelphia. He rejected suggestions that his support should automatically go to Obama as purely "presumptuous" reasoning. Frequently asked as an African American official to explain his nonsupport of Obama in Pennsylvania's primary, Nutter cited an incorrect assumption about his race. The mayor complained that a "completely monolithic . . . lockstep" did not exist within the minority any more than it did among whites. "I mean, I don't remember seeing *John Kerry* on TV and anybody saying to him, 'I can't believe you're not for Hillary Clinton.' Why?"[97]

With Republican and Democratic nominations already solidified by the time of the two national party conventions, both gatherings followed well-orchestrated scripts without suspense or major surprises. John McCain's choice of Governor Sarah Palin of Alaska as his running mate came as a shock, before the arrival of GOP delegates in St. Paul, and only few conventioneers knew much about the Alaskan official. Once exposed to Palin, party faithful found enough in her acceptance speech to find encouragement about her potential for a positive impact on the Republican ticket. Obviously more than willing to accept the traditional vice-presidential candidate's role of attacking opponents, Palin as McCain's surrogate aggressor seemingly relished the assignment of emphasizing why the Obama-Biden team and Democratic liberal programs were inconsistent with American values. At least, this was her responsibility in the campaign. Meanwhile earlier, at the end of August, delegates to the Democratic National Convention arrived in Denver in a celebratory mood. The climax of their festivities came symbolically at a filled football stadium on the forty-fifth anniversary of the "I Have a Dream" speech by Dr. Martin Luther King Jr. It was in this open-air setting during Obama's acceptance of his party's presidential nomination and his acknowledgement of a historic occasion that he concentrated on telling Americans why electing McCain would represent nothing more than a third term for George W. Bush.

To the Republican nominee's credit as a consistently loyal supporter of an increasingly unpopular lame-duck president, McCain did not waver much from a pledge not to make race an issue in the election. Officially, Palin's repeated attempts to connect Obama with his neighbor, convicted anti-war bomber William Ayers, were as close as McCain's official campaign team came to besmirching their opponent's character. As noble as this refrain from bringing up Pastor Wright and race might have appeared, Republicans working outside of McCain's direct control performed some dirty campaign work for him, nevertheless. Weeks before Obama's official receipt of the Democratic nomination, three sensationally negative published accounts of the candidate's rapid movement upward to political prominence surfaced as warnings to voters why they should not elect an allegedly dangerous black man as president. At the same time and throughout the autumn, a hard core of Internet bloggers and zealous ex-official McCain supporters—not bound at all by the Republican nominee's promise—did their best to spread fear and alarm about the dire consequences that would result from an Obama presidency. In one completely misunderstood case (not intended to help McCain), a caricature of Barack and Michelle Obama appeared on the cover of the *New Yorker* for July 21, 2008. The cartoonist had obviously intended the work to be a sarcastic indictment of the believers of total falsehoods about the black candidate, and it was printed certainly without malice or intent to harm the chances of victory by Obama, but the cartoon became a most popular image among his detractors. It portrayed Barack as a Muslim religious leader and Michelle in a full Afro dressed in military fatigues as an automatic-weapon-toting black militant extremist.[98]

Through November 4, 2008, the alleged effects of race on the presidential election continued to fascinate pollsters and journalists. A major Associated Press-Yahoo News voter poll conducted by Stanford University noted how "lingering racism may hurt Obama" more than all the gigantic obstacles facing McCain.[99] According to Professor Paul Sniderman, a respected political scientist at the California institution, "There are a lot fewer bigots than there were 50 years ago, but that doesn't mean that there's only a few bigots." The survey revealed that one-third of white Democrats held negative opinions of African Americans; as a result of their feelings, these persons were unlikely to vote for the Illinois senator.[100] The gloom of this forecast was partially offset by a poll cosponsored by *USA Today*, ABC News, and Columbia University. For African Americans who expected McCain to defeat Obama, only 13 percent considered that racism would result as the key contributing factor. On the other hand, in a positive contrast, only 5 percent of whites with predictions of a Republican win on November 4 pointed to prejudice as the most compelling reason for the Democrat's defeat. The response of a white stay-at-home mother from Tucson, Arizona, typified the reactions of solicited interviewees in this polling. In her personal evaluation of the upcoming presidential election, she viewed it as "a big breakthrough," one in her evaluation that "doesn't matter if you're a man or a woman, black or white, or whatever race you are—it's the ideas you have for the country and who supports you on them."[101]

No matter how much some polls were showing voters' intentions to select Obama, reasons existed for skepticism concerning their reliability. Doubts centered on what political analysts since the surprising result of the 1982 California gubernatorial race had dubbed the "Tom Bradley effect." Major polls had shown the Los Angeles mayor running several points ahead of his Republican opponent, but Bradley suffered a devastating loss nevertheless. The most generally accepted explanation for such a surprising loss was the reluctance of the people polled to admit their true preference. Once more—as had occurred with voters polled in 1982 about their preferences for either Bradley or Deukmejian—did respondents truthfully indicate to pollsters who their real presidential choice would be? When the desire was not to appear racist by favoring McCain, the question was, Could enough of the favorable responses for Obama indicate another subterfuge and bring into serious doubt, the accuracy of the numerous opinion polls with definitive predictions of a landslide victory? McCain disbelieved racism would have a measurable impact on the election.[102] Appearing on CNN's *Larry King Live* less than a week before the election, and reported in the *Washington* Post, the Republican expressed his complete confidence in Americans deciding on whom to support with their votes "for the best of reasons, not the worst of reasons." Elaborating why so few people would react negatively to the Democrat due to his skin color, the Republican claimed, "people are hurting too much now. I mean, they're worried about staying in their homes, keeping their jobs."[103]

As much as McCain tried to show optimism and an upbeat demeanor during his interview with King, subtle indicators were coming from the GOP nominee that he was expecting to lose. Too many signs pointed in the direction of an Obama victory for the Republican candidate to ignore the inevitability of an election defeat. As much as McCain tried to separate himself from George W. Bush's presidency, the heroic Arizonan could not dodge a voting record of more than 90 percent agreement with the unpopular president. What had seemed at the time a smart choice for a running mate quickly turned sour on McCain and showed up as a bad choice of desperation and insufficient vetting. As soon as Palin had exposed her general ignorance of global and domestic issues during several television interviews, McCain's claims that she had greater experience and better judgment than Obama caused serious doubts about the Republican nominee's own superior wisdom. Yet, in final analysis, nothing would hurt the McCain candidacy more than his mishandling of bad economic news. With the nation already reeling into an obviously deepening financial crisis in September, the Republican insisted on the national economy's "fundamental soundness." Then in the midst of Congress's consideration of a Bush request to approve a $700 billion bailout for the nation's largest financial institutions, McCain looked even more ridiculous. For suspending his campaigning because, he said, he wanted to devote all his energy and time to a leadership role in finding solutions, the candidate showed bewilderment. The fact that he then did nothing of the kind became so evident to everyone following his actions at this point that the Republican presidential nominee appeared in a complete state of confusion about the economy. With the economy surfacing as the number-one topic on the minds of the American electorate, negative perceptions of the GOP candidate decidedly helped Obama to overcome McCain's superior experience on matters of defense and international affairs.[104]

It is not surprisingly, then, that across America so many media endorsements and positive judgments went overwhelmingly to the Democrat. Altogether, 240 major newspapers endorsed Obama, while only 114 key publications chose

McCain. An investigation of editorials favorable to the election of the African American revealed the reason these editors supported Obama by a margin of more than two to one over McCain. Looking foremost for evidence of vision and change, the writers of opinion columns found these in Obama's message. The *Economist* offered one of the better statements for its selection of Obama. It found so much evidence of McCain abandoning himself that the generally conservative British weekly newsmagazine could not find a good reason to back his candidacy. Despite such known liabilities as his age, sharp temper, and hastily made decisions on important matters, the ex-prisoner of the Vietnam War had "bravely taken unpopular positions—for free trade, immigration reform, the surge in Iraq, tackling climate change, and campaign-finance reform." Favorable as well was the Arizonan's "long record of working with both Democrats and America's allies. . . ." "That, however, was Senator McCain; the Candidate McCain of the past six months has too often seemed the victim of political sorcery, his good features magically inverted, his bad ones exaggerated." As more than sufficient evidence of this change in the wrong direction, the editorial had unqualified praise for Senator McCain as a onetime courageously independent fiscal conservative foe of Bush's unaffordable tax cuts but then found nothing but rebuke for his reversal to endorse even deeper tax reductions. From the individual who had once denounced the religious right as "agents of intolerance," the nominee again bowed to expedience in 2008 to embrace what the weekly newsmagazine dismissed as "theocratic culture warriors." Finally, but no less important, McCain's selecting "Sarah Palin epitomized the sloppiness" that so characterized his generally abysmal candidacy. For "his most important appointment," he had decided on her after only two brief meetings. With some reluctance and reservation, editors of the English weekly publication opted for the Democrat: "In terms of painting a brighter future for America and the world, Mr Obama has produced the more compelling and detailed portrait. He has campaigned with more style, intelligence and discipline than his opponent. Whether he can fulfil [*sic*] his immense potential remains to be seen. But Mr Obama deserves the presidency."[105]

Voters agreed on November 4, 2008. Obama amassed 349 Electoral College delegates to McCain's 163 and accumulated 62,443,218 votes (52 percent) to his Republican challenger's 55,386,310 (46 percent). Most definitively, this verdict did not result because a majority of the electorate miraculously had lost its race consciousness. Reminders of Obama's minority status abounded on the Internet, during television and radio news broadcasts, and in publications. He never escaped the notoriety of being the first African American aspirant ever to secure a major political party's presidential nomination. In the news reporting of the primaries and later during his bid against McCain, from his succeeding early in 2008 at the Iowa caucuses to the historic victory on the night of November 4, commentaries about Obama's identity and how it was either helpful or harmful had dominated. These constant reminders had weighed against the winner in some cases, but he possessed an important attribute that proved in the end more decisive than the color of his skin. Of greater impact, Obama was not a Republican at a moment when having any connections to the GOP was proving more fatal than people's concerns about a nominee's race. Summarizing the condition of the nation when Americans had decided so favorably for a black presidential candidate, a November 5, 2008, editorial in the *Jackson Clarion-Ledger* all but conceded that "an economic meltdown" had contributed to Obama's victory. Noting that never "since the Great Depression has the nation faced such a disastrous mix of financial markets in distress, major jobs producers . . . in distress, the housing industry collapsed, and adding to it the nation in a war on two fronts."[106] Although this had been candidate Bill Clinton's summary of problems facing the United States in 1992, "it's the economy, stupid," this also applied as the simplified assessment of why Obama's promise to bring "change" had generated so much more meaning to a desperate nation than his biracial heritage. But turning again to the Mississippi newspaper's editorial, some sobering caution followed: "The content of Barack Obama's character, intellect, ideas, and ability to unite the people will be tested to the utmost."[107]

In an exhaustive breakdown of voting in the blue and red states, NBC News directors Chuck Todd and Sheldon Gawiser examined the electorate's decision for Obama from many different angles. Most revealing were their analyses of seven battleground states won by Obama. Several factors accounted for Colorado transitioning from red to blue, but Todd and Gawiser claim it had been "Obama's performance with white college graduates [that] put him over the top." McCain's neglect of Florida along with the severe economic slide in home construction and tourism cost the Republican enough votes to lose the Sunshine State. More or less similar factors were favorable for Obama in Indiana; while he and his staff worked hard with Hoosiers to win their support, his opponent waited altogether too long to invest campaign resources and time in an electorate misjudged as one considered totally impervious to Democratic efforts. Yet nine in ten residents expressed worries about where the economy was heading, and McCain was not present enough in Indiana to reassure people and to argue against perceptions that his election would represent a continuation of Bush policies. Not too differently, Iowans knew more about Obama's promises than they did about his opponent. McCain made the mistake of irritating the state's corn producers by failing to support federal government subsidies for the production of ethanol. In North Carolina, as in several other key states lost by the GOP nominee, it came down to his overconfidence. When it became apparent to Republican strategists that the Tar Heel State was literally up for grabs, their input was already too late to alter the outcome. Among all the question-mark states, Ohio certainly represented a significantly greater challenge to predict accurately than the others. As yet undetermined was whether economic woes could trump race in the voting decisions of many blue-collar residents. Obama demonstrated that they would, because his result among whites was the best of any Democratic presidential candidate since

Bill Clinton's reelection in 1996. Finally, in Virginia, it was the economy together with McCain's neglect that resulted in victory for the senator from Illinois.[108]

Captured images on both digital and television cameras from Chicago's tightly packed Grant Park on the night of Obama's historic victory told in graphic detail the meaning of the occasion for African Americans. Cameramen scanning the crowd found tears of joy running down the cheeks of famous people such as Oprah Winfrey and the Reverend Jesse Jackson Sr., and on the faces of several thousand anonymous other people in the huge crowd. The scene of momentous political triumph represented an extraordinary moment in the long journey from second-class citizenship to freedom, and this gathering was an occasion with special meaning for many older blacks with bitter memories of segregation and discrimination; they could recollect so many sacrifices that had forged significant changes to American society. From their respective childhoods in Mississippi and South Carolina, Winfrey and Jackson, like so many others in attendance, had good reasons to weep as they witnessed a symbolic breakthrough in the civil rights crusade. They were joyous observers of what was certainly a most impressive visible political achievement in African American political history. John Lewis—a legendary contributor to the civil rights movement of the 1960s, and in 2008 a veteran congressional member from Georgia—was "overwhelmed" with a sense of joy. In an MSNBC interview, he expressed his feelings: "I never imagined, I never even had any idea I would live to see an African-American president of the United States." With tears in his eyes he commented on a historic day in the life of the nation: "We have witnessed tonight in America a revolution of values, a revolution of ideals. There's been a transformation of America, and it will have unbelievable influence on the world."[109] In conceding the election to Obama, McCain was a most magnanimous loser who noted that he "recognized the special significance" of the Democrat's victory for a minority.[110]

In an open letter to the president-elect, Pulitzer Prize-winner Alice Walker on November 5, 2008, eloquently offered both her reflections on the culmination of a long struggle and her personal advice to Obama. The black novelist gave his victory an interesting perspective:

> You have no idea, really, of how profound this moment is for us. Us being the black people of the Southern United States. You think you know, because you are thoughtful, and you have studied our history. But seeing you deliver the torch so many others before you carried, year after year, decade after decade, century after century, only to be struck down before igniting the flame of justice and law, is almost more than the heart can bear. And yet, this observation is not intended to burden you, for you are of a different time, and, indeed, because of all the relay runners before you, North America is a different place. It is really only to say: Well done. We knew, through all generations, that you were with us, in us, the best of the spirit of Africa and of the Americas. Knowing this, that you would

actually appear, someday, was part of our strength. Seeing you take your rightful place, based solely on your wisdom, stamina and character, is a balm for the weary warriors of hope, previously only sung about.

Walker's counsel was for Obama to realize that he "did not create the disaster that the world is experiencing." Instead of assuming every burden and taking "on other people's enemies," he should, she advised, "cultivate happiness" and follow the biblical command to "hate the sin, but love the sinner."[111]

The various different reactions and responses to the victory are important, because the possibility of an African American's being elected to the presidency appeared thoroughly improbable as late as Obama's ambitious announcement on that wintery day in 2007. Thus, a question worthy of more than passing consideration becomes, How did the son of an African goat herder and a white mother from Kansas succeed? One factor was his immediate opposition to an American invasion of Iraq. He predicted that going to war would result in an unfortunate military action "of undetermined length, at undetermined cost, with undetermined consequences." Also working most advantageously in his favor was an unwillingness to become "trapped by black politics." Like Massachusetts's Governor Patrick and Philadelphia's Mayor Nutter, according to the *Economist*, Obama "embraced post-racial politics." He did not waver with his twin campaign messages of "change" and "hope," and these catchwords reached an electorate at a time of intense frustration and open desperation. Without offering too many details, Obama promised to restore government to the people. Describing reluctance to allow others to pin him into corners, he confessed to wanting an appearance of a "blank screen" devoid of many specific details about an overall political strategy. Equally important was his "essential pragmatism." What this meant for Obama, according to the *Economist*'s pithy assessment, was that "At every stage of his career he has calibrated the balance of political forces and adjusted his behaviour accordingly." Helpful with voters was Obama's personal style that "prefers compromise and conciliation to confrontation." Not to be minimized was his extraordinary talent for organization. At almost every step during an extended primary season, his people completely and effectively outperformed Clinton's team. Instead of avoiding a racially mixed heritage, he hinted in subtle terms how a "transformational figure" in a divided society such as himself, could, as the *Economist* projected, "make amends for the country's racist past." His trusted friend Deval Patrick translated the lessons of his experiences of running for Massachusetts's highest office into some unsolicited but valuable advice for Obama to follow as he campaigned. The African American governor told his close friend the presidential candidate to avoid a role as "black oracle." Obama—ever conscious of the grave risks of attempting too much as an African American politician in need of considerable white support—probably never had to receive this warning more than one time.[112]

In an essay titled "The Ambivalent Embrace of Barack Obama," Maulana Karenga challenges the African American victor to offer real change domestically and internationally. In order to make a meaningful difference, Obama, chides Karenga, cannot attempt a racial "self-concealment [by not acting 'too black'] or disappearance." As much as the candidate "tried to 'transcend race' and avoid racial references, hoping his fellow Americans would do likewise," the essayist notes, "racism is too rooted in this country to be sidestepped." As Karenga views a most impressive victory by an African American in 2008, it "is clearly a historical moment of considerable meaning, but it is not conclusive proof or automatic promise of significant social or systemic change."[113]

Whether through his intuition or through knowledge gained from his keen interest in African American history, Obama's quest for victory evidenced lessons gained from the successes and failures of other minority candidates who were also dependent upon making inroads across racial divides. All winning minority politicians shared in common a general avoidance of noting plans for the specific commitments of public resources to helping other African Americans. For Bradley, Goode, Dinkins, and Bosley, their campaign pledges were to treat all constituents equally—and, more importantly, to provide primary assistance to downtown business development and real estate interests. These African American mayors also had the good fortune either to follow or to compete against unpopular and divisive individuals who had contributed in some degree to harming the reputations and images of their cities. Yorty in Los Angeles, Rizzo in Philadelphia, Koch in New York, and Schoemehl in St. Louis had each become an easy target for criticism because of their demeanor and blatant unfairness. Although blacks had emerged as a majority in Atlanta, the situation there was not dissimilar to those in Los Angeles, Philadelphia, New York, and St. Louis. After a presentation of harsh economic realities to Maynard Jackson early in his first term by representatives of Central Atlanta Progress, the mayor reoriented his priorities to place downtown interests first, and each successor acknowledged and followed this example. Unlike the overall successes with whites generally enjoyed by Jackson, Young, and Campbell in Atlanta; Bradley in Los Angeles; and Goode to a considerable extent in Philadelphia, the dissipation of support occurred quickly for Dinkins and Bosley. In both of these instances, enough white voters began to perceive from their minority mayors so much alleged favoritism toward African Americans that both incumbents failed in reelection bids.

Representatives Franks and Watts also provided Obama with an element that resonated with whites. As spokespersons of conservative family values, both these Republicans lectured African Americans about assuming greater personal responsibility for their lives and children. Their advice was well received by whites who were of the opinion that too many minority members relied altogether too much on exonerating themselves by placing all blame for the woeful plight of large numbers of African Americans on the majority race. Franks and

Watts were also critical of black men who abandoned their paternal responsibilities and of the minority women who gave birth to so many thousands of babies out of wedlock.

Brooke, Wilder, and Moseley-Braun set concrete examples for Obama of how to succeed with white voters. In each case involving the African American trio—two triumphant contests for senator and one for a governorship—victories occurred as the result of downplaying racial issues and of concentrating on what mattered most to their respective electorates. As an Illinois resident living on Chicago's South Side in 1992, Obama was a particularly keen observer of how his Hyde Park neighbor Carol Moseley-Braun had surprised almost everyone by winning the Democratic primary with smart, effective maneuvering that capitalized on passionate feminine disgust with an incumbent's unapologetic support for Clarence Thomas. During both this contest and later in the general election, Moseley-Braun emphasized her gender at the expense of a focus on African American affairs. Then, like others with strong interests in Illinois politics, Obama was witness to how the female incumbent had developed the reputation of an office-holder with more regard for minority problems and Africa than for questions of more general importance to the majority of Illinois residents.

Governor Wilder's earlier implosion as a serious presidential candidate was a showcase of how not to proceed. The governor's alleged favoritism toward members of his race early in the Wilder administration hurt the chief executive in Virginia, but it was his foolhardy entrance into national politics that might have imparted particularly important lessons for serious political strategists, of how not to proceed nationally with a campaign for a presidential nomination. Expecting, as Wilder had anticipated, a gigantic groundswell of African American support as an unsatisfactory substitute for first having secured financial resources and a dependable professional organization, the Virginian quickly found out what mattered most were money and a team with political savvy. Wilder had withdrawn his name from any consideration even before the first primary.

Of the highlighted African Americans who preceded Obama, Brooke offered the best example for the Illinois senator to follow. Light complexioned and criticized often by black nationalists for embracing both "white tastes and values," the GOP candidate for senator from Massachusetts had learned from early political setbacks, as Obama would later learn from losing to Bobby Rush. Brooke grasped that any electoral success in the Bay State could result only if he appealed to whites. He was most fortunate during two victorious senate races that he was running against opponents who did not resort to exploiting race in their campaigns against their black opponent. In 2004, when Obama was pitted in a contest against Keyes for the U.S. Senate, racism certainly could not arise as a negative factor because both he and a Republican opponent belonged to the same minority group. Moreover, just as Obama would express negativity toward the United States going to war with Iraq, Brooke became one of the earliest critics of American involvement in Southeast Asia. Coincidentally, of equal importance for two African American politicians dependent upon white support, neither Brooke nor Obama had any significant associations with civil rights protests or organizations before the launches of their statewide campaigns. As senators, both men were outspoken supporters only of legislation of general benefit to large majorities of their constituents, and the two senators were reticent about pushing or sponsoring bills that might irritate white voters in their states. Simply put, both Brooke and Obama understood what to support and what to avoid.

During John F. Kennedy's final months in the White House and before the civil rights legislation of 1964 and 1965, if a soothsayer had predicted a victory by an African American candidate for president within forty-five years, few people would have believed such a prophesy. Yet, in succession before Obama's 2008 triumph, significant victories had occurred as stepping-stones. Whether these were known or perceived by the Illinois senator and his political strategists as they devised their plans to win the hearts and votes of enough white voters to secure the presidency is not altogether clear. The considerable accomplishments by the ten black predecessors singled out in this study, for example, were in several ways both indirectly and directly helpful to Obama in fulfilling what skeptics as late as the Iowa caucuses had judged an impossible achievement.[114]

It did help the minority candidate that many whites viewed him more as a first-generation American than as an African American. Perhaps, if John McCain had chosen a strategy to spoil this perception by hammering Obama with negative race-baiting campaign advertisements aimed at connecting his Democratic opponent to the Reverend Jeremiah Wright, for example, chances are that the African American Democrat might have lost. To McCain's credit he, like Edward Brooke's first rival for the U.S. Senate in 1966, chose not to turn race into an issue and, in the process, probably aided the presidential ambitions of "the skinny guy with a funny name." In terms of a direct bid aimed at blue-collar white voters, about the closest Palin and McCain ever came to tailoring their campaign message to this group were their constant references to Samuel Joseph Wurzelbacher, the man who became better known to voters as "Joe the Plumber," the GOP's overworked symbol of working-class distrust of Obama.

In final analysis it was the economy and McCain's lack of understanding of its depth that trumped the race issue. The Obama campaign reminded voters repeatedly of the Arizonan's disastrous recommendations for and inaccurate assessments of the recession's severity. The first questionable advice from McCain came on March 25, 2008, when the Republican war hero advised "removing regulatory, accounting, and tax impediments to raising capital." As for the faltering national economy, Obama's opponent wrongly judged on September 15, 2008, that "the fundamentals of our economy are strong." The harsh reality of worsening economic conditions and the obvious causes for them forced McCain into retreat from his premature and ill-advised judgments. Seeking to win office on merit and experience and not on overtly racist appeals, the Republican candidate found himself doomed by his obviously wrong conclusions, evidence of his connections to a most unpopular president blamed for the recession, and his gentlemanly unwillingness to frighten whites with race. The result was a landslide win by a calmly confident black aspirant whose opponent allowed him to state his case for the office of president without the emotional distraction of race. Thus in many ways, the obvious success of Obama's presidential candidacy mirrored that of Brooke's victory for the U.S. Senate more than four decades earlier. In the words of representative Maxine Waters, the 2008 presidential election was won by the senator from Illinois because "he found ways to say it [assisting African Americans] that make people feel comfortable, that make them feel safe. He has . . . developed a style and a language and a way of presenting himself that causes people to stop and listen."[115] If one statement can give an overall view of successful African American candidacies with white voters from Brooke in Massachusetts in 1966 to Obama's primary and general election victories of 2008, it was that pluralities dependent upon multiracial support were possible through an applied combination of correct conditions and a deracialized message. Another factor hurting McCain was his inability to generate excitement among conservative Republicans. Among their representatives, nobody expressed more disappointment with the Arizonan becoming the GOP presidential nominee than Rush Limbaugh. Throughout the primaries and then during the general election, he urged his followers to support anyone but McCain.[116]

In assessing the win for which he could claim partial credit, David Plouffe ignores the advice he and David Axelrod certainly offered Obama about the need to skirt the racial issue as much as possible. Instead of focusing on this obvious factor for a historic victory, the winner's campaign manager cites seven other reasons in *The Audacity to Win*. First was recognition of the Internet as a valuable resource for informing and involving people on Obama's behalf. Second was the maintenance of a consistent message. Third was internal control of the campaign's progress instead of a dependence upon the reliability of outside opinion polls. Fourth was the placement of "a real premium on discretion," in order to prevent leaks to the press of "internal discussions and business." Fifth was the implementation of a management style that emphasized "clarity, calmness, conviction, and collegiality throughout the ranks." Sixth were the people, "our army of volunteers, real people who brought Obama's message and ideas to their neighbors, co-workers, and fellow citizens." Finally, seventh was the candidate himself, a person whom his "supporters knew in their hearts and in their guts . . . treasured and respected their involvement and leadership in their communities."[117]

As much as race had factored into Obama's bid for the presidency, it also had an effect upon one debate after the election. One controversy reopened by his victory was the question of a continuing need for the Voting Rights Act of 1965 (VRA). For a vociferous core of conservative opponents, the election of an African

American president certainly represented sufficient proof for why Congress should repeal the law. Section 5 of the law became the focus of their drive. This part of the legislation was responsible for special monitoring of specific voting districts with notorious past reputations for disenfranchising minority voters. Leading the onslaught against renewal were longtime foe Abigail Thernstrom, noteworthy African American politician and spokesperson for GOP conservative causes Ken Blackwell, and syndicated right-wing columnist George Will. Each in a different way essentially argued against VRA reauthorization on the grounds that the 2008 presidential election did not revolve around race as the decisive factor in the outcome.

Thernstrom, a scholar known best for her methodical dissections of liberal civil rights positions, maintains in *Voting Rights—and Wrongs* that votes against Obama in areas covered by the VRA had less to do with his race than with his platform and statements. The Democratic candidate's liberal domestic positions on such issues as mandatory health care for all Americans, and his lack of military experience had more to do with tilting an overwhelming majority of white voters in section 5 districts than Obama's skin pigmentation. It was Thernstrom's conclusion that John McCain received a large plurality of votes across the area because of his opponent's perceived weakness on national defense and his alleged open advocacy of a major redistribution of wealth. And unlike decorated war veteran John Kerry who had not had to deal in his presidential bid of 2004 with the equivalent of the Reverend Jeremiah Wright, Obama preferred to emphasize the need for alternative sources of energy at the expense of the South's extensive dependence on coal-burning power to generate electricity, and equally unpopular, the Democrat dared to imply a challenge to right-to-work statutes found throughout the region. "Reasons other than race," in Thernstrom's opinion, "may well account for the Kerry-Obama gap in white support" (Kerry's advantage among white voters from section 5 jurisdictions was six percentage points). As she concludes in her case against continuing VRA, "we need much more compelling evidence before we conclude that race played a decisive role in the choices that white voters made in 2008."[118]

Also like Thernstrom, with openly acknowledged support from the American Enterprise Institute, a conservative think tank, Charles S. Bullock III and Ronald Keith Gaddie studied VRA's impact on minority voting. In order to ascertain the results of the law, they looked individually at each state in the South covered by section 5 and then at the ones in the region without Department of Justice monitoring. Developing from their exhaustive investigation were some definitively positive conclusions. As they put their basic sanguine assessments, "The initial goals of the VRA—removing barriers to black registration and turnout—have long since been attained. The more recent goal of facilitating the election of candidates preferred by minority voters has also achieved great success." Bullock and Gaddie found difficulty with distinguishing "a racial vote from a party vote." In their judgment, the reality of whites voting for Republican candidates and

African Americans choosing Democrats "does not rise to the level of unconstitutional discrimination." In sum, the coauthors judged what has emerged politically in the South as a political pattern "more alike than different" from the rest of the nation.[119]

Injury to the cause of continuing the push for civil rights was another ramification of the Obama victory. With the election of an African American to the presidency, conservatives began asserting that strong evidence existed that the United States had reached a post-racial era. Thus, the election negated requirements for additional protections and legislation to assist blacks in their drive for equality and fairness. As Psychologist Thierry Devos warns, "voting for Barack Obama may give some White voters the moral capital that affords them the opportunity to be less concerned about racial biases in other contexts, perhaps even including future elections."[120]

In a much more exhaustive examination of the voting jurisdictions under the Section 5 watch by the Department of Justice, a trio of distinguished professors, in an article published in 2010 by the *Harvard Law Review*, disagreed with the general premise of the conservative advocates who were arguing on behalf of rescinding the VRA on the basis of Obama winning the presidency. The authors— Stephen Ansolabehere, a government professor at Harvard, Nathaniel Persily, a law and political science professor at Columbia Law School, and Charles Stewart III, head of the political science department at MIT—methodically looked at the presidential vote in each covered voting district and concluded that the election results from the monitored areas generally confirmed the existence among white residents of a continuing pattern of latent hostility toward the concept of supporting black candidates for major offices. To the regret of the three investigators as they conclude in their summary of research, "The 2008 election did not indicate a disruption of well-known patterns of race, region, and vote choice. If anything, Barack Obama's higher vote share among minorities and his uneven performance among whites suggest those patterns are quite entrenched."[121]

Kristen Clarke, co-director of the NAACP Legal Defense and Educational Fund's Political Participation Group, added her perspective to the debate on VRA's renewal. In an article appearing in the *Harvard Law & Policy Review*, she offers doubts about Obama's win as an example of what some optimistic observers have considered the "beginning of a 'post-racial' era in which race bears less significance or consequence." As positive as the result might seem, it did not signal an end to a justification for the VRA. In her words, "we have not yet moved beyond the problem of race, as careful analysis of the 2008 presidential election outcome reveals notable patterns of racially polarized voting, particularly in those jurisdictions covered by the special Section 5 provision of the Voting Rights Act."[122]

By any objective analysis, race was a conscious element in the 2008 presidential election. Whether it was Senator Harry Reid's private prediction that Obama had a chance to become the first black president because he was "light-skinned" and had "no Negro dialect, unless he wanted to have one," or it was Diane Fedele, a local Republican leader in California, who distributed a newsletter in 2008 with Obama's face surrounded by a watermelon, ribs, and a bucket of fried chicken, the factor of race was omnipresent in the minds of the electorate. David A. Bositis, a senior political analyst at the Joint Center for Political and Economic Studies, recognized its significance on the decisions of African Americans. In terms of their turnout and their choice for president, the voting statistics Bositis has cited for the minority demonstrate the degree of pride and partiality blacks had shown for Obama's candidacy. As an aspirant for the nation's highest office, the Democratic contender tried to follow his advisors' directions and defuse color as an issue in the campaign, but it always managed to percolate somehow into the electoral equation, whether among black or white voters. Throughout the primaries, analysts looked at results to ascertain how Obama was faring with white voters, and the conclusions were more or less the same. After three contests in the bidding for the Democratic nomination, political scientist Philip Klinkner reported a "ceiling" on white support for the senator from Illinois. Obama's victory over McCain represented a breakthrough in race relations, but it certainly was not the beginning of a post-racial society.[123]

Notes

Chapter 1

1. The Congressional Black Caucus receives full coverage in Chapter 2.

2. Stephan and Abigail Thernstrom, *America in Black and White: One Nation, Indivisible* (New York: Simon and Schuster, 1997), 286–302. Dr. Jack Kevorkian gained fame and prison time for advocating and participating in euthanasia.

3. Matthew Holden Jr., "Black Politicians in the Time of the 'New' Urban Politics," *Review of Black Political Economy* 2 (1971): 60.

4. Charles V. Hamilton, "De-Racialization: Examination of a Political Strategy," *First World* 1 (1977): 3–5.

5. Thomas E. Cavanagh, ed., *Race and Political Strategy: A JCPS Roundtable* (Washington, DC: Joint Center for Political Studies, 1983), *vii*, 2, 6, 14–15, 20, 24, 26, 28, 34, 36, 38.

6. Holden, "Black Politicians," 60; Linda F. Williams, "Beyond the Race Issue in American Politics?," *Congress and the Presidency* 21 (1994): 137; Katherine Tate, *From Protest to Politics: The New Black Voters in American Elections* (Cambridge, MA: Harvard University Press, 1993), 21–29; Carol M. Swain, *Black Faces, Black Interests: The Representation of African Americans in Congress* (Cambridge, MA: Harvard University Press, 1993), 37–140. In Paul M. Sniderman and Thomas Piazza, *The Scar of Race* (Cambridge, MA: Harvard University Press, 1993), race is described as "a red-flag issue" as a result of the prevalence of a white-imposed "negative characterization of blacks," 36. Writing some four years later with Edward G. Carmines, Sniderman in *Reaching beyond Race* (Cambridge, MA: Harvard University Press, 1997) discusses how both white and black Americans had come to see race in terms of "ominous trinity": worsening inequality, deepening white resistance to governmental solutions, and increasing belief in racial equality but not to changing public policy. In *Racial Trends in America: Trends and Interpretations* (Cambridge, MA: Harvard University Press, 1997), lead author Howard Schuman on pages 315–16 discusses why Colin Powell "appeared attractive as a presidential candidate to many white Americans." The conclusion is that "he did not ever suggest that he represented or would represent blacks as a collective political force." In another study, the Thernstroms have indirectly advised black office seekers through a collection of essays from like-minded scholars about the goodwill that awaits them if only they would understand what whites do not want to hear; see their edited *Beyond the Color Line: New Perspectives on Race and Ethnicity in America* (Stanford, CA: Hoover Institution Press, 2002); Wilbur C. Rich, "From Muskogee to Morningside Heights: Political Scientist Charles V. Hamilton." www.columbia.edu/cu/alumni/Magazine/Spring2004/hamilton.html.

7. William Julius Wilson, "Race—Neutral Programs and the Democratic Coalition," *American Prospect* 1 (1990): 74–81; essays gathered from Georgia A. Persons, ed., *Dilemmas of Black Politics: Issues of Leadership and Strategy* (New York: Harper Collins, 1993) include: Persons, "Introduction," 2–4 and her "Black Mayoralties and the New Black Politics: From Insurgency to Racial Reconciliation," 38, 45, 61, 63; Joseph P. McCormick II and Charles E. Jones, "The Conceptualization of Deracialization: Thinking Through the Dilemma," 68, 70–71, 76, 78–79.

8. Jane J. Mansbridge, "Should Blacks Represent Blacks and Women Represent Women?: A Contingent 'Yes,'" *Journal of Politics* 61 (1999): 629–31.

9. Zoltan L. Hajnal, "White Residents, Black Incumbents, and a Declining Racial Divide," *American Political Science Review* 95 (2001): 603–17. Bernard Grofman, Lisa Handley, and Richard G. Niemi share Hajnal's conclusion that an opportunity to hold office gives black elected officials a basis for building a positive "reputation that will earn them considerable crossover support." See their *Minority Representation and the Quest for Voting Equality* (New York: Cambridge University Press, 1992), 136.

10. Carol K. Sigelman et al. "Black Candidates, White Voters: Understanding Racial Bias in Political Perceptions," *American Journal of Political Science* 39 (1995): 245, 263.

11. Ronald Walters, "Two Political Traditions; Black Politics in the 1990s," *National Political Science Review* 3 (1992): 203.

12. Ibid., 198–208; Nayda Terkildsen, "When White Voters Evaluate Black Candidates: The Processing Implications of Candidate Skin Color, Prejudice, and Self-Monitoring," *American Journal of Political Science* 37 (1993): 1048; Pamela Johnston Conover and Stanley Feldman, "Candidate Perception in an Ambiguous World: Campaigns, Cues, and Inference Processes," *American Journal of Political Science* 33 (1989): 937.

13. Andrew Hacker, *Two Nations: Black, White, Separate, Hostile, Unequal* (New York: Ballantine Books, 1995), 201–13. See also, Richard L. Engstrom, "The Political Thicket, Electoral Reform, and Minority Voting Rights," in Mark E. Rush and Richard L. Engstrom, eds., *Fair and Effective Representation?: Debating Electoral Reform and Minority Rights* (Lanham, MD: Rowman and Littlefield, 2001), 11; Pamela S. Kaplan, "The Impact of the Voting Rights Act on African Americans: Second- and Third-Generation Issues," in Mark E. Rush, ed., *Voting Rights and Redistricting in the United States* (Westport, CT: Greenwood Publishing Group, 1998), 125; David T. Canon, *Race, Redistricting, and Representation: The Unintended Consequences of Black Majority Districts* (Chicago: University of Chicago Press, 1999), 5–12; Charles Cameron et al., "Do Majority-Minority Districts Maximize Substantive Black Representation in Congress?," *American Political Science Review* 90 (1996): 794–95, 809; Abigail M. Thernstrom, *Whose Votes Count?: Affirmative Action and Voting Rights* (Cambridge, MA: Harvard University Press, 1987), 35–81.

14. Myron Rothbard and Oliver John, "Intergroup Relations and Stereotype Change: A Social-Cognitive Analysis and Some Longitudinal Findings," in Paul M. Sniderman et al., eds., *Prejudice, Politics, and the American Dilemma* (Stanford: Stanford University Press, 1993), 58; Michael W. Giles and Arthur Evans, "The Power Approach to Intergroup Hostility," *Journal of Conflict Resolution* 30 (1986): 470–71; Canon, *Race, Redistricting, and Representation*, 41. See also Claudine Gay, "Taking Charge: Black Electoral Success and the Redefinition of American Politics" (PhD diss., Harvard University, 1997), 5, 8–9; Mary R. Jackman and Marie Crane, "'Some of My Best Friends Are Black . . .': Interracial Friendship and Whites' Racial Attitudes," *Public Opinion Quarterly* 50 (1986): 481–82.

15. Douglas Massey and Zoltan Hajnal, "The Changing Geographic Structure of Black-White Segregation in the United States," *Social Science Quarterly* 76 (1995): 536; Scott J. South and Glenn D. Deane, "Race and Residential Mobility: Individual Determinants and Structural Constraints," *Social Forces* 72 (1993): 147–67.

16. Mark Peffley and Jon Hurwitz, "Whites' Stereotypes of Blacks: Sources and Political Consequences," in Hurwitz and Peffley, eds., *Perception and Prejudice: Race and Politics in the United States* (New Haven, CT: Yale University Press, 1998), 62, 90.

17. Ibid.; Linda Williams, "White/Black Perceptions of the Electability of Black Political Candidates," *National Political Science Review* 2 (1990): 62, for quotation see 45–46; Edith J. Barrett, in "The Policy Priorities of African American Women in State Legislatures," *Legislative Studies Quarterly* 20 (1995): 243, assessed chances for blacks succeeding with white voters this way: "the successful modern black candidate must show a transethnic concern for the needs of all U. S. citizens. . . .; candidates must not appear to be concerned only with minority constituents." Overwhelmingly, as Williams noted, feared results from blacks in office show increases in direct proportion to the percentage of blacks in a population segment as the following studies stress: Mark A. Fossett and K. Jill Kiecolt, "The Relative Size of Minority Populations and White Racial Attitudes," *Social Science Quarterly* 70 (1989): 833; Donald Kinder and David O. Sears, "Prejudice and Politics: Symbolic Racism Versus Racial Threats to the Good Life," *Journal of Personality and Social Psychology* 40 (1981): 415; James M. Vanderleeuw, "A City in Transition: The Impact of Changing Racial Composition on Voting Behavior," *Social Science Quarterly* 71 (1990): 328, 336–37.

18. James Button and David Hedge, "Legislative Life in the 1990s: A Comparison of Black and White State Legislators," *Legislative Studies Quarterly* 21 (1997): 213–14; Hanes Walton Jr., "African American Foreign Policy: From Decolonization to Democracy," in Walton, ed., *African American Power and Politics: The Political Context Variable* (New York: Columbia University Press, 1997), 352–67; Theodore S. Arrington and Gerald L. Ingalls, "Race and Campaign Finance in Charlotte, N.C.," *Western Political Quarterly* 37 (1984), 578; on a broader basis, Robert C. Smith, in "Financing Black Politics: A Study of Congressional Elections," *Review of Black Political Economy* 17 (1988): 17, 23, confirms funding as a difficulty for blacks contesting white congressional incumbents.

19. Peyton McCrary, "Racially Polarized Voting in the South: Quantitative Evidence from the Courtroom," *Social Science History* 14 (1990): 507–31.

20. Hanes Walton Jr., "African Americans and the Clinton Presidency: Political Appointments as Social Justice," in Walton, ed., *African American Power and Politics*, 320–22.

21. Lani Guinier, "The Representation of Minority Interests," in Paul E. Peterson, ed., *Classifying by Race* (Princeton, NJ: Princeton University Press, 1995), 24; Ronald W. Walters, *Black Presidential Politics in America* (Albany: State University of New York Press, 1988), 52. Although its release came as George H. W. Bush was entering the White House, Edward G. Carmines and James A. Stimson in *Issue Evolution: Race and the Transformation of American Politics* (Princeton, NJ: Princeton University Press, 1989) offers evidence of estrangement's effects on partisan politics and white candidacies; Patricia Gurin et al., *Hope and Independence: Blacks' Response to Electoral and Party Politics* (New York: Russell Sage Foundation, 1989), 46–65.

22. Robert C. Smith, *We Have No Leaders: African Americans in the Post-Civil Rights Era* (Albany: State University of New York Press, 1996), 26, 30–41, 53–54, 79; *Economist*, August 6, 2005, 33; Gurin et al., *Hope and Independence*, 117, 174–75, 237.

23. CBS's *60 Minutes*, February 11, 2007; Paul Frymer, *Uneasy Alliances: Race and Party Competition in America* (Princeton, NJ: Princeton University Press, 1999), 164, 176–78; Michael Dawson, *Behind the Mule: Race and Class in African-American Politics* (Princeton, NJ: Princeton University Press, 1994), 3–8. Publishing before Jesse Jackson and Harold Washington's respective campaigns for office, William J. Wilson argued for social status or economic class as more important than race in determining black voting patterns, a thesis largely disproved by the overwhelming support given the aforementioned efforts to secure either the Democratic nomination for president or Chicago's mayorship of Chicago;

see Wilson's *The Declining Significance of Race: Blacks and Changing American Institutions* (Chicago: University of Chicago Press, 1980); Hanes Walton Jr. et al., "African Americans and the Resurgent Republican Congress: The Duality of Transformation," in Walton, *African American Power and Politics*, 321–35.

24. Guinier, "The Representation of Minority Interests," in Peterson, ed., *Classifying by Race*, 29.

25. Ibid., 24; Gurin et al., *Hope and Independence*, 46–47; Wayne A. Santoro, "Black Politics and Employment Policies: The Determinants of Local Government Affirmative Action," *Social Science Quarterly* 76 (1995): 794–96; Milton D. Morris, "Black Electoral Participation and the Distribution of Public Benefits," in Chandler Davidson, ed., *Minority Vote Dilution* (Washington, DC: Howard University Press, 1984), 277–84; Adolph Reed Jr., "Demobilization in the New Black Political Regime," in Michael P. Smith and Joe R. Feagan, eds., *The Bubbling Cauldron: Race, Ethnicity, and the Urban Crisis* (Minneapolis: University of Minnesota Press, 1995), 202–6; Lawrence Bobo and Franklin D. Gilliam Jr., "Race, Socioeconomic Status, and Black Empowerment," *American Political Science Review* 84 (1990): 377; Gay, "Taking Charge," 7–9.

Chapter 2

1. Dennis S. Nordin, *The New Deal's Black Congressman: A Life of Arthur Wergs Mitchell* (Columbia: University of Missouri Press, 1997); Mary R. Sawyer, "A Moral Minority: Religion and Congressional Black Politics," *Journal of Religious Thought* 41 (1983–1984): 57. Mention should be noted that Mitchell's success with white voters was not the first instance of this happening in Chicago politics; John W. E. Thomas had gained a seat in the Illinois General Assembly in 1876 as a result of whites voting for him, an African American candidate. See: David Joens, "John W. E. Thomas and the Election of the First African American to the Illinois General Assembly," *Journal of the Illinois State Historical Society* 94 (2001): 200–16.

2. James L. Cooper, "South Side Boss," *Chicago History* 19 (1990–1991): 66–81; Maurine Christopher, *America's Black Congressmen* (New York: Crowell, 1971), 185–93.

3. Charles V. Hamilton, *Adam Clayton Powell, Jr.: The Political Biography of an American Dilemma* (New York: Athenaeum, 1991), 5, 7; Lucius J. Barker et al., *African Americans and the American Political System* (Upper Saddle River, NJ: Prentice Hall, 1999), 87; David Hapgood. *The Purge that Failed: Tammany v. Powell* (New York: McGraw-Hill), 4, 10–16, 22, 25.

4. Christopher, *America's Black Congressmen*, 210–14.

5. Walters, *Black Presidential Politics*, 115; in fairness especially to Diggs and Hawkins, increased interest in matters of particular importance to blacks did occur after demographic shifts in the racial compositions of their districts. Thereafter Diggs coerced black congressmen to communicate minority concerns to the House's Democratic leadership about the Nixon Administration's dismantling of Great Society programs, and he led African American colleagues to Chicago for inquiries into the police slayings of Black Panthers Fred Hampton and Mark Clark. Hawkins was helpful to the CBC's formation by leading discussions on how it might be financed. For information on how Diggs and Hawkins had changed with their constituencies, see CBC leader William L. Clay's *Just Permanent Interests: Black Americans in Congress, 1870–1991* (New York: Amistad, 1993), 111–37.

6. Marguerite R. Barnett, "The Congressional Black Caucus," *Proceedings of the Academy of Political Science* 32 (1975): 34–35; Clay, *Just Permanent Interests*, 111–37; Gurin et al., *Hope and Independence*, 47–49.

7. Barnett, "The Congressional Black Caucus," 36; James B. Johnson and Philip E. Secret, "Focus and Style Representational Roles of Congressional Black and Hispanic Caucus

Members," *Journal of Black Studies* 26 (1996): 267. See also Abigail Thernstrom, "Black Republicans?," *Public Interest* 120 (1995): 109; Robert C. Smith, "Black Power and the Transformation from Protest to Politics," *Political Science Quarterly* 96 (1981): 442–43; Kweisi Mfume, *No Free Ride: From the Mean Streets to the Mainstream* (New York: Ballantine Books, 1996), 334.

8. Clay, *Just Permanent Interests*, 111–37, 142–43; Lucius Barker et al., *African Americans and the American Political System*, 88, 278–79; Mfume, *No Free Ride*, 319–20; Kathleen Bratton and Kerry L. Haynie, "Agenda Setting and Legislative Success in State Legislatures: The Effects of Gender and Race," *Journal of Politics* 61 (1999): 661, 672.

9. Barker et al., *African Americans and the American Political System*, 279; Walters, *Black Presidential Politics*, 47–48.

10. Barker et al., *African Americans and the American Political System*, 280–81; Walters, *Black Presidential Politics*, 47–48.

11. Barker et al., *African Americans and the American Political System*, 281–82; Katherine Tate, *Black Faces in the Mirror: African Americans and Their Representatives in the U.S. Congress* (Princeton, NJ: Princeton University Press, 2003), 96–110; Robert Singh, *The Congressional Black Caucus: Radical Politics in the U.S. Congress* (Thousand Oaks, CA: Sage Publications, 1998), 5; Walters, *Black Presidential Politics*, 48, 94–95, 105.

12. *Washington Post*, August 11, 1980; Gurin et al., *Hope and Independence*, 51–52.

13. Hanes Walton Jr., "The Political Context Variable: The Transformation Politics of the Reagan, Bush, and Clinton Presidencies," in Walton, ed., *African American Power and Politics*, 22–24; Barker et al., *African Americans and the American Political System*, 282–83; Frymer, *Uneasy Alliances*, 158–60; Gurin et al., *Hope and Independence*, 51–52; David Hatchett, "Parren Mitchell, *Crisis* 93 (1986): 36–37.

14. Gurin et al., *Hope and Independence*, 52, 55; Walton, "The Political Context Variable," 22–25; Manning Marable, "Reaganism, Racism, and Reaction: Black Political Realignment in the 1980's," *Black Scholar* 13 (1982): 8.

15. Keith Reeves, *Voting Hopes or Fears?: White Voters, Black Candidates and Racial Politics in America* (New York: Oxford University Press, 1998), 16; Mfume, *No Free Ride*, 311–19; Kenneth J. Whitby, *The Color of Representation: Congressional Behavior and Black Interests* (Ann Arbor: University of Michigan Press, 1997), 73–77; Richard Champagne and Leroy N. Rieselbach, "The Evolving Congressional Black Caucus: The Reagan-Bush Years" in Huey Perry and Wayne Parent, eds., *Blacks and the American Political System* (Gainesville: University Press of Florida, 1995), 130–61; Barker et al., *African Americans and the American Political System*, 283–84; Frymer, *Uneasy Alliances*, 160.

16. Mfume made his point to the press that CBC members did not intend to offer Clinton their support if the president did not respond favorably to the black congressional members' agenda.

17. Mfume, *No Free Ride*, 321–32; Donald L. Payne, "Introduction: The 104th Congress —The Perspective of the Chairman of the Congressional Black Caucus," in Walton, ed., *African American Power and Politics*, *xxvi-xxix*; Clarence Lusane, "Unity and Struggle: The Political Behavior of African American Members of Congress," *Black Scholar* 24 (1994): 20–21; Barker et al., *African Americans and the American Political System*, 229–31, 284–87; David A. Bositis, *The Congressional Black Caucus in the 103rd Congress* (Washington, DC: Joint Center for Political and Economic Studies, 1994), 125–47; Tate, *Black Faces in the Mirror*, 92–93, 96–110, 118–19; Singh, *The Congressional Black Caucus*, 178–98, 200–11; Frymer, *Uneasy Alliances*, 160–62.

18. California's Sanford Bishop and Indiana's Julia Carson were two more Democrats who represented predominantly white districts, an oddity so special it received Tate's mention in *Black Faces in the Mirror*, 68. See her also for divisions within the CBC and the

confidence African Americans have with leaders of their race, 113–42. Many other sources went into the aforementioned sweeping assessments and conclusions; these include: Singh, *The Congressional Black Caucus,* 1–5; Barker et al., *African Americans and the American Political System,* 49, 224–25; Mfume, *No Free Ride,* 79, 335–36, 345–51; Gay, "Taking Charge," 3, 11, 165, 167; Abigail Thernstrom, "Black Republicans?," *Public Interest* 120 (1995): 109; Walters, *Black Presidential Politics,* 88–92, 191; Ronald Walters, "The Imperative of Popular Black Struggle: Three Examples from Miami, Los Angeles, and Chicago," *Black Scholar* 24 (1994): 33–35; Barnett, "The Congressional Black Caucus," 48; Lusane, "Unity and Struggle," 16–67, 20–22, 25; Bositis, *The Congressional Black Caucus,* 13–21, 125–47; Sawyer, "A Moral Minority," 58–59, 63–66; Robert C. Smith, "The Black Congressional Delegation," *Western Political Quarterly* 34 (1981): 203–21; Gurin et al., *Hope and Independence,* 55, 63–65, 117, 126–27. Sample vignettes into the lives of three diverse CBC members can be found for Mike Espy in Frank Parker's *Black Votes Count: Political Empowerment in Mississippi after 1965* (Chapel Hill: University of North Carolina Press, 1990), 140–42; for Katie Hall in LaVerne McCain Gill's *African American Women in Congress: Forming and Transforming History* (New Brunswick: Rutgers University Press, 1997), 86–94; for Yvonne Braithwaite Burke in Pamela Lee Gray's "Yvonne Braithwaite Burke: The Congressional Career of California's First Black Congresswoman, 1972–1978" (PhD diss., University of Southern California, 1987), 2–191; and in Jeffrey M. Elliott's "The Congressional Black Caucus: An Interview with Yvonne Braithwaite Burke," *Negro History Bulletin* 40 (1977): 650–52.

19. Abigail Thernstrom has been a primary cheerleader for conservative black Republicans. See her "Black Republicans?," a review appearing in *Public Interest* 120 (1995): 106–10 of Michael C. Dawson's, *Behind the Mule: Race and Class in African-American Politics* (Princeton, NJ: Princeton University Press, 1994) and her "Racial Gerrymanders Come before the Supreme Court," *Wall Street Journal,* April 12, 1995. Across cyberspace on December 12, 2005, the Salon Media Group heralded the "new generation of black politicians"; in another instance, a *Wall Street Journal* headline proclaimed, "New Generation: Black Moderates Win at Polls by Targeting Once-Elusive Whites," a conclusion refuted by Paul Ruffin's "Interracial Coalitions," *Atlantic,* June 1990, 28–34. Publisher Willie A. Richardson of *National Minority Politics* looked to the future with optimism due to such successful black Republican candidates as Colorado's Vicki Buckley and Ohio's Kenneth Blackwell—winners in statewide elections as secretary of state and state treasurer, respectively. From Frank McCoy, "Black GOPers on the Rise?," *Black Enterprise,* March 1995, 24.

20. Elwood Watson, "Guess What Came to American Politics?: Contemporary Black Conservatism," *Journal of Black Studies* 29 (1998): 73–92; Reeves, *Voting Hopes or Fears?,* 8–9; Ruffins, "Interracial Coalitions," 28–34; Manning Marable, "Blacks and the Republicans: A Marriage of Convenience?," 150–52; "Black Conservatives, Shelby Steele, and the War against Affirmative Action," 212–21; "Clarence Thomas: Black Conservative for the Supreme Court?," 222–24, in *The Crisis of Color and Democracy* (Monroe, ME: Common Courage, 1992); Ezola Foster, *What's Right for all Americans: A Fearless Los Angeles Schoolteacher Challenges the Black Political Establishment* (Waco, TX: WRS Group, 1995), 13–16, 41; "Black, proud—and Republican," *Economist,* April 1, 1995, 54; Hanes Walton Jr. and Lester Spence, "African-American Presidential Convention and Nomination Politics: Alan Keyes in the 1996 Republican Presidential Primaries and Convention," *National Political Science Review* 7 (1999): 196–97; Lewis A. Randolph, "A Historical Analysis and Critique of Contemporary Black Conservatism," *Western Journal of Black Studies* 19 (1995): 155–61; Joyce Jones, "Racing toward the Finish Line," *Black Enterprise,* November 1996, 20; Walton, "The Political Context Variable," in Walton, ed., *African American Power and Politics,* 27; Marable, "Reaganism, Racism, and Reaction," 8–10.

21. Watson, "Guess What Came to American Politics?," 73, 76, 78–79; Ruffins, "Interracial Coalitions," 28–34; Reeves, *Voting Hopes or Fears?*, 8–9.

22. *Waterbury Republican-American*, November 1, 1990.

23. Ibid., October 18, 1990.

24. Ibid., October 24, 1990.

25. Ibid., November 5, 1990.

26. *Waterbury Republican-American*, October 2, 4, 8, 11–13, 17–18, 21–24, 26, 31, November 1, 4–5, 7, 1990; Gary Franks, *Searching for the Promised Land: An African American's Optimistic Odyssey* (New York: Harper Collins, 1996), *xxiv-xxv*, 13–71. For a generally constructive view of Franks's election, see Persons, "Introduction," 5 and her "The Election of Gary Franks and the Ascendancy of the New Black Conservatives" in Persons, *Dilemmas of Black Politics*, 194, 200, 204, 206.

27. Franks, *Searching for the Promised Land*, *xxiv-xxv*, 72–76; Ruffins, "Interracial Coalitions," 28–34.

28. Franks, *Searching for the Promised Land*, 77–80, 85–96.

29. *Congressional Record*, 102nd through 104th Congresses, 1st and 2nd sessions, February 27–28, March 13, May 21, July 11, October 2, 23, 1991, February 26, October 2, 1992, March 4, August 6, September 13, October 6, 19, 1993, March 24, September 23, November 29, 1994, February 22, 28, 1995, June 13, 18, 1996.

30. Ibid., 104th Congress, 1st and 2nd sessions, June 14, July 26, 1995, March 8, 1996. Arsonists had been responsible for the destruction of several black churches in the mid-1990s.

31. Ibid., 103rd Congress, 2nd session, May 4, 1994. An indicator of his stand had come October 12, 1993 in his speech to the first session of the 103rd Congress; see 1st session, June 18, 1993, for his Father's Day message supporting HR 892; Barker et al., *African Americans and the American Political System*, 98–99.

32. *Congressional Record*, 102nd Congress, 2nd session, June 3, 1992.

33. Ibid., 102nd Congress, 1st session through 103rd Congress, 2nd session, June 6, November 21, 26, 1991, May 12, June 3, July 22, 1992, January 20–February 3, 24, April 2, 22, May 13, 26, June 15, October 13, November 19, 1993, September 30, 1994; Franks, *Searching for the Promised Land*, 85–96.

34. *Congressional Record*, 102nd Congress, 2nd session, June 3, 1992.

35. Ibid., April 30, 1992.

36. Ibid., 102nd Congress, 1st session, May 9, November 6, 1991, 2nd session, April 30, 1992, 103rd Congress, 1st session, February 4, 1993.

37. Ibid., 102nd Congress, 1st session, November 6, 1991.

38. Ibid., 102nd Congress, 1st session, March 12, June 4, November 7, 1991; Franks, *Searching for the Promised Land*, 75–76.

39. Ibid., 103rd Congress, 1st session, June 30, 1993.

40. Ibid.

41. Ibid., August 4, 1993.

42. *Black Enterprise*, January 24, 1994; Franks, *Searching for the Promised Land*, 97–117; David T. Canon, "Redistricting and the Congressional Black Caucus," *American Politics Quarterly* 23 (1995): 160–89.

43. *Congressional Record*, 103rd Congress, 2nd session, July 20, 1994; Franks, *Searching for the Promised Land*, 129–40.

44. *Waterbury Republican-American*, October-November, 1992.

45. Ibid., October 6, 8, 16, 20, 27, 30, November 1, 6, 1996; Joyce Jones, "Out with the Old . . . .," *Black Enterprise*, January 1997, 22; "Anatomy of a Defeat: Republican Gary Franks," *Businessweek*, November 1996; Franks, *Searching for the Promised Land*, 96; Watson,

"Guess What Came to American Politics?," 81. As a postscript, Franks tried unsuccessfully to unseat Senator Chris Dodd; see Stuart Rothenberg, "Plenty of Problems for Connecticut's Gary Franks," Home News Analysis Community, www.cnn.com/ALLPOLITICS/1998/06/02/rothenberg.

46. Franks, *Searching for the Promised Land*, 168–71, 190–92.

47. *Tulsa Oklahoma Eagle*, November 3, 1994; Frank McCoy, "Thanks, but no Thanks," *Black Enterprise*, July 1995, 22; *Time*, November 30, 1998.

48. McCoy, "Thanks, but no Thanks," 22.

49. On June 7, 1998, near Jasper, Texas, three white supremacists secured Byrd, an African American man, to the rear of a pickup truck in order to drag their victim to gruesome death.

50. *Congressional Record*, 104th Congress, 1st session, September 29, December 12, 1995, 2nd session, June 13, September 17, 1996; 105th Congress, 1st session, April 9, 16, June 17, 1997; 106th Congress, 1st session, March 23, April 20, 1999; 107th Congress, 1st session, June 27, December 11, 2001, 2nd session, February 28, September 18, 2002; *Oklahoma City Black Chronicle*, March 25, 1999; *International Herald Tribune*, March 25, 1999.

51. Amy Waldman, "The GOP's Great Black Hope," *Washington Monthly*, October 1996, 34–35.

52. Ibid. See also Darcy O'Brien, "The Great Black Hope," *New Yorker*, February 10, 1997, 29–30; Constantina Petropoulos, "J. C. Watts, Jr.," *Current Biography Yearbook*, March 1999, 590–93.

53. Waldman, "Great Black Hope," 40.

54. Ibid. See also *Vital Speeches of the Day*, September 1, 1996; *Time*, November 30, 1998; O'Brien, "The Great Black Hope," 29–30; Oklahoma City *Black Chronicle*, February 18, 1999; Petropoulos, "J. C. Watts," 590–93; Andrew Phillips, "Black, Proud and Republican," *Maclean's*, August 11, 1997, 26.

55. Waldman, "Great Black Hope," 34–35; O'Brien, "The Great Black Hope," 29–30; *Vital Speeches of the Day*, September 1, 1996.

56. *Vital Speeches of the Day*, March 1, 1997.

57. *Oklahoma City Black Chronicle*, November 19, 26, 1998; Joyce Jones, "High Wattage," *Black Enterprise*, March 1999, 28.

58. Oklahoma City *Black Chronicle*, May 16, 1996, October 29, November 5, 1998; O'Brien, "The Great Black Hope," 29–30; Joyce Jones, "The Republican Way," *Black Enterprise*, June 1996, 38; Stuart A. Reid, "Watts Condemns Taxes, Gov't Spending," *Dartmouth*, April 8, 2005; *Tulsa World*, February 22, 2000; *USA Today*, February 22, 2000; *Congressional Record*, 104th Congress, 2nd session, May 9, July 24, September 26, 1996; 105th Congress, 1st session, September 9, October 31, 1997; 106th Congress, 1st session, June 22, 1999, 2nd session, October 26, 2000; 107th Congress, 1st session, May 15, 23, 2001; Kate O'Beirne, "Bread and Circuses," *National Review*, April 21, 1997, 21. In an autobiography, Watts discusses his opposition to affirmative action's end; see J. C. Watts Jr. with Chriss Winston, *What Color is a Conservative?: My Life and My Politics* (New York: HarperCollins, 2002), 254.

59. Watts, *What Color is a Conservative?*, with references on pages 50 and 149 as typical confirmations of this conclusion; the autobiography formed a backdrop to much of what has been discussed about Watts' career; see pages *x, xvi-xvii,* 69, 151–52, 156, 158, 179–81, 203, 206, 208, 250, 252.

60. Kenneth A. Jordan and Modibo M. Kadalie, "Prologue: The Conceptualization of a Variable," in Walton, ed., *African American Power and Politics*, xxxiv; Reeves, *Voting Hopes or Fears?*, 9.

Chapter 3

1. William E. Nelson Jr. and Philip J. Meranto, *Electing Black Mayors: Political Action in the Black Community* (Columbus: Ohio State University Press, 1977), 37–59.

2. Ibid., 68–112; Leonard N. Moore, *Carl B. Stokes and the Rise of Black Political Power* (Urbana: University of Illinois Press, 2002), 53–60; Saundra C. Ardrey, "Cleveland and the Politics of Resurgence: The Search for Effective Political Control," in Persons, *Dilemmas of Black Politics*, 112.

3. Moore, *Stokes*, 53–60.

4. Ibid., 53–99; Mfanya D. Tryman, "Black Mayoralty Campaigns: Running the Race, *Phylon* 35 (1974): 351–53; Steven F. Lawson, *Running for Freedom: Civil Rights and Black Politics in White America since 1941* (New York: McGraw-Hill, 1991), 145–80.

5. Nelson and Meranto, *Electing Black Mayors*, 143–320; Jon C. Teaford, "'King Richard' Hatcher: Mayor of Gary," *Journal of Negro History* 77 (1992): 126–30; Tryman, "Black Mayoralty Campaigns," 353–55.

6. Teaford, "'King Richard' Hatcher," 137.

7. Ibid., 130–38; Wilbur C. Rich, *Black Mayors and School Politics: The Failure of Reform in Detroit, Gary, and Newark* (New York: Garland, 1996), 57–63, 81–85; Edmund J. Keller, "Electoral Politics in Gary: Mayoral Performance, Organization, and the Political Economy of the Black Vote," *Urban Affairs Quarterly* 15 (1979): 51; Richard G. Hatcher, "Black Politics in the 70's," *Black Scholar* 4 (1972): 17–18.

8. Tryman, "Black Mayoralty Campaigns," 349–51; Rich, *Black Mayors and School Politics*, 97–123; from the author's memory of attending Operation PUSH when Bill Cosby responded with obviously tongue-in-cheek sarcastic humor to Gibson's victory in 1970.

9. Heather A. Thompson, "Rethinking the Politics of White Flight in the Postwar City: Detroit, 1945–1980," *Journal of Urban History* 25 (1999): 185.

10. Ibid., 189.

11. Ibid., 184–91; Carlito H. Young, "Constant Struggle: Coleman Young's Perspective on American Society and Detroit Politics," *Black Scholar* 27 (1997): quote on 39, but see also 31–39.

12. Huey Perry, "Black Political and Mayoral Leadership in Birmingham and New Orleans," *National Political Science Review* 2 (1990): 154–60.

13. Kelly Dowe, "Richard Arrington: Birmingham," *Southern Exposure* 12 (1984): 76.

14. Ibid.; Huey Perry, "The Evolution and Impact of Biracial Coalitions and Black Mayors in Birmingham and New Orleans," in Rufus P. Browning et al., eds., *Racial Politics in American Cities* (White Plains, NY: Longman, 1997), 179–200; Huey Perry, "The Political Reincorporation of Southern Blacks: The Case of Birmingham," *National Political Science Review* 3 (1992): 230–37; Huey Perry, "The Reelection of Sidney Barthelemy as Mayor of New Orleans," *PS: Political Science & Politics* 23 (1990): 156–57; Jimmy L. Franklin, *Back to Birmingham: Richard Arrington, Jr., and His Times* (Tuscaloosa: University of Alabama Press, 1989), 66–91, 139, 154–74, 209–45, 302; Dowe, "Richard Arrington," 76–78; Arnold R. Hirsch, "Race and Politics in Modern New Orleans: The Mayoralty of Dutch Morial," *Amerikastudien* 35 (1990): 461–84. Somewhat differently in 1983, the white-majority city of Charlotte elected Harvey Gantt mayor; his involvement in civil rights was more direct than most other black politicians; as a young man, he had participated in early sit-in demonstrations and desegregated Clemson University; see Lawson, *Running for Freedom*, 216–17.

15. Christopher L. Warren et al., "Minority Mobilization in an International City: Rivalry and Conflict in Miami," *PS: Political Science & Politics* 19 (1986): 626–34.

16. Sharon D. Wright, "Electoral and Biracial Coalition: Political Election Strategy for African American Candidates in Louisville, Kentucky," *Journal of Black Studies* 25 (1995): 749–57; Nancy Hartsock, "Feminists, Black Candidates, and Local Politics: A Report from Baltimore," *Feminist Studies* 10 (1984): 339–52; Gwen Ifill, *The Breakthrough: Politics and Race in the Age of Obama* (New York: Doubleday, 2009), 4–5. Arthur O. Eve, running in Buffalo's Democratic mayoral primary in 1977, sought votes primarily from black voters, and he won what would be a Pyrrhic victory because no matter that his campaigning in the general election had been directed almost exclusively at white voters, perceptions of him as the African American candidate stuck. See Paul Carton, "A Black Man Runs for Mayor: The Extraordinary Campaign of Arthur O. Eve," *Afro-Americans in New York Life and History* 4 (1980): 8–54.

17. Quintard Taylor, "The Chicago Political Machine and Black-Ethnic Conflict and Accommodation," *Polish American Studies* 29 (1972): 40–66; see also Harold M. Baron, "Black Powerlessness in Chicago," *Trans-Action* 6 (1968): 27, 28, 31.

18. Manning Marable, "Black Power in Chicago: An Historical Overview of Class Stratification and Electoral Politics in a Black Urban Community," *Review of Radical Political Economics* 17 (1985): 157–71; Marable, "Harold Washington and the Politics of Race in Chicago," *Black Scholar* 17 (1986): 22; Paul Kleppner, *Chicago Divided: The Making of a Black Mayor* (DeKalb: Northern Illinois University Press, 1985), 136–39, 151, 161–62; Gary Rivlin, *Fire on the Prairie: Chicago's Harold Washington and the Politics of Race* (New York: Henry Holt, 1992), 20; author's personal involvement in events leading to the 1983 primary campaign and his active participation in it for Washington.

19. Marable, *Black Power in Chicago*, 177–78; from working in white precincts for Washington and being a poll watcher for him, the author recalled tremendous hostility. Just spotting a "Washington for Mayor" button on this supporter's garments, racist whites responded with "nigger lover" or made dirty gestures and looks; Rivlin, *Fire on the Prairie*, 129–263; Kleppner, *Chicago Divided*, 191–207; Paul Kleppner, "Mayoral Politics Chicago Style: The Rise and Fall of a Multiethnic Coalition, 1983–1989," *National Political Science Review* 5 (1994): 152, 155–60.

20. Kleppner, "Mayoral Politics Chicago Style," 160–79; Pierre Clavel and Wim Wiewel, "Introduction," to Clavel and Wiewel, eds., *Harold Washington and the Neighborhoods: Progressive City Government in Chicago, 1983–1987* (New Brunswick: Rutgers University Press, 1991), 1–29; from this edited work, Doug Gills, "Chicago Politics and Community Development: A Social Movement Perspective," 34–61; William J. Grimshaw, *Bitter Fruit: Black Politics and the Chicago Machine, 1931–1991* (Chicago: University of Chicago Press, 1992), 164, 167, 172–73, 177, 179–80,185, 187–88, 193, 197–99, 206; Rivlin, *Fire on the Prairie*, 243–44, 263.

21. Mary Summers and Philip Klinkner, "The Election of John Daniels as Mayor of New Haven," *PS: Political Science & Politics* 23(1990): 142–45.

22. Mylon Winn, "The Election of Norman Rice as Mayor of Seattle," *PS: Political Science & Politics* 23 (1990): 158–59.

23. *Los Angeles Times*, May 30, 1973.

24. http://www.socialhistory.org/Biographies/bradley.html; John M. Allswang, "Tom Bradley of Los Angeles," *Southern California Quarterly* 74 (1992): 55–65; Raphael J. Sonenshein, *Politics in Black and White: Race and Power in Los Angeles* (Princeton, NJ: Princeton University Press, 1993), 59–60.

25. Allswang, "Tom Bradley of Los Angeles," 67–70; James A. Regalado, "Organized Labor and Los Angeles City Politics: An Assessment in the Bradley Years, 1973–1989," *Urban Affairs Quarterly* 27 (1991): 88–93; Raphael J. Sonenshein, "The Dynamics of Biracial Co-

alitions: Crossover Politics in Los Angeles," *Western Political Quarterly* 42 (1989): 337–42; Mike Davis, *City of Quartz: Excavating the Future in Los Angeles* (New York: Vintage, 1992), 126–29; Harlan Hahn et al., "Cleavages, Coalitions, and the Black Candidate: The Los Angeles Mayoralty Elections of 1969 and 1973," *Western Political Quarterly* 29 (1976): 512–13; Harlan Hahn and Timothy Almy, "Ethnic Politics and Racial Issues: Voting in Los Angeles," *Western Political Quarterly* 24 (1971): 721–27; Raphael J. Sonenshein, "Biracial Coalition Politics in Los Angeles," *PS: Political Science & Politics* 19 (1986): 585; Raphael J. Sonenshein, *Politics in Black and White: Race and Power in Los Angeles* (Princeton, NJ: Princeton University Press, 1993), 85–94; Richard L. Maulin, "Los Angeles Liberalism," *Trans-Action* 8 (1971): 40–51.

26. *Los Angeles Sentinel*, January 4, February 1, 1973.

27. Ibid., January 18, 1973; Allswang, "Tom Bradley of Los Angeles," 71.

28. *Los Angeles Sentinel*, March 1, 8, 22, 29, 1973; Allswang, "Tom Bradley of Los Angeles," 71.

29. *Los Angeles Sentinel*, May 17, 24, 31, 1973; "Play It Again, Sam?," *Time*, April 16, 1973, 17–18; "Return Match," *Newsweek*, April 16, 1973, 32; "Fear and Loathing in L. A.," *Time*, May 28, 1973, 31; "Bradley not Yorty," *The New Republic,* June 9, 1973, 8–9; "Los Angeles: A Black Mayor," *Newsweek*, June 11, 1973, 29–30; "Beating the Voter Backlash," *Time*, June 11, 1973, 17–18; J. K. Obatala, "White Workers Wise Up," *Nation*, June 18, 1973, 774; Cornish Rogers, "Tom Bradley and the Black Churches," *Christian Century*, June 13–20, 1973, 668; Sonenshein, *Politics in Black and White*, 107–8, 111; Allswang, "Tom Bradley of Los Angeles," 71–72; Sonenshein, "Biracial Coalition Politics in Los Angeles," 585–86; Sonenshein, "The Dynamics of Biracial Coalitions," 342–43.

30. *Los Angeles Sentinel*, July 5, 1973; Roger M. Williams, "The Blacks' 'Big Four!': A Status Report," *Saturday Review World*, May 4, 1974, 12–13.

31. Shana Alexander, ". . . And now, the Good News," *Newsweek*, July 23, 1973, 27.

32. "Creating Popularity Out of Restraint," *Time*, June 15, 1981, 32.

33. "An Interview with Mayor Tom Bradley," *Black Enterprise*, January 1974, 34–37; Davis, *City of Quartz*, 304; Bryan Jackson, "Black Political Power in the City of Angels: An Analysis of Mayor Tom Bradley's Electoral Success," *National Political Science Review* 2 (1990): 175.

34. Sonenshein, *Politics in Black and White*, 153–54.

35. Ibid., 210–26; Eric Mann, "The Poverty of Corporatism," *Nation*, March 29, 1993, 406–11; Tom Morganthau and Andrew Murr, "The Score: Gates 1, Bradley 0," *Newsweek*, April 15, 1991, 34; *Los Angeles Times*, November 15, 1991; Raphael J. Sonenshein, "Los Angeles," in Browning et al., eds., *Racial Politics in American Cities*, 46–50.

36. Michael Reese, "California Dreaming," *Newsweek,* April 8, 1985, 28; Thomas Banville, "Mayor Bradley Discusses Urban Education," *PTA Magazine*, October 1974, 18–9; Mann, "The Poverty of Corporatism," 410–11.

37. Stephen Gayle, "Tom Bradley's California Quest," *Black Enterprise*, May 1982, 46–49; Joan Didion, "Letter from Los Angeles," *New Yorker*, April 24, 1989, 88–99.

38. "Why the Sake Flows at Tom Bradley's Fund-Raisers," *Businessweek*, July 11, 1988.

39. Ibid.; Didion, "Letter from Los Angeles," 88–99; William Oscar Johnson, "A Flaming Olympian Mess," *Sports Illustrated*, June 26, 1978, 22–31; Allswang, "Tom Bradley of Los Angeles," 89–92; Jack Citrin et al., "White Reactions to Black Candidates: When Does Race Matter?," *Public Opinion Quarterly* 54 (1990): 74–96; "California Dreaming," *Time*, October 4, 1982, 36; Charles P. Henry, "Racial Factors in the 1982 California Gubernatorial Campaign: Why Bradley Lost," in Michael B. Preston et al., eds., *The New Black Politics: The Search for Political Power* (New York: Longman, 1987), 76–82, 90–91; Edward G. Carmines

and Robert Huckfeldt, "Party Politics in the Wake of the Voting Rights Act," in Bernard Grofman and Chandler Davidson, eds., *Controversies in Minority Voting: The Voting Rights Act in Perspective* (Washington: Brookings Institution Press, 1992), 133. Of interest, Norman Rice attempted a move from mayor of Seattle to governor of Washington in 1996 with the same result—a loss attributed to a racist effort by an opponent; see Oklahoma City's *Black Chronicle*, May 30, 1996.

40. Michael Reese, "L. A.'s Teflon Mayor," *Newsweek,* April 10, 198), 33; Eric Schine, "Bradley: Down and Nearly Out?," *Businessweek,* August 7, 1989, 29; Edwin M. Reingold, "Hard Times for Teflon Tom," *Time,* May 22, 1989, 35; Allswang, "Tom Bradley of Los Angeles," 95–97.

41. *Chicago Defender,* October 1, 1998; "Los Angeles Politics: The Fading of Black Power," *Economist,* May 16, 1998, 54, 59.

42. Peter K. Eisenger, *Politics and Displacement: Racial and Ethnic Transition in Three American Cities* (New York: Academic Press, 1980), 65–69; Clarence N. Stone, "Atlanta: Protest and Elections Are Not Enough," *PS: Political Science & Politics* 19 (1986): 618–25.

43. Eisenger, *Politics, and Displacement,* 67.

44. Ibid., 74.

45. Ibid.; Clarence N. Stone and Carol Pierannunzi, "Atlanta and the Limited Reach of Electoral Control," in Browning et al. eds., *Racial Politics in American Cities,* 164–75; M. H. Jones, "Black Political Empowerment in Atlanta: Myth and Reality," *Annals of the American Academy of Political and Social Science* 439 (1978): 90–117; Stone, "Atlanta," 623–25.

46. Stone and Pierannunzi, "Atlanta and the Limited Reach of Electoral Control," 175.

47. Adolph L. Reed Jr., "Narcissistic Politics in Atlanta," *Telos* 48 (1981): 99; Stone, *Regime Politics: Governing Atlanta, 1946–1988* (Lawrence: University Press of Kansas, 1989), 109,132,134, 159, 197–98, 208, 213; John V. Moeser and Christopher Silver, "Race, Social Stratification, and Politics: The Case of Atlanta, Memphis, and Richmond," *Virginia Magazine of History and Biography* 102 (1994): 534–36.

48. Stone, *Regime Politics,* 132; see also: Laughlin McDonald et al., "Georgia," in Chandler Davidson and Bernard Grofman, eds., *Quiet Revolution in the South: The Impact of the Voting Rights Act, 1965–1990* (Princeton, NJ: Princeton University Press, 1994), 85; Stone, *Regime Politics,* 109.

49. Moeser and Silver, "Race, Social Stratification, and Politics," 537; see also Stone, *Regime Politics,* 132.

50. Alton Hornsby Jr., "Andrew Jackson Young: Mayor of Atlanta, 1982–1990," *Journal of Negro History* 77 (1992): 175.

51. Ibid., 177–78; Stone, *Regime Politics,* 166–67.

52. Hornsby, "Andrew Jackson Young, 177; see also 159, 174–75, 177–78.

53. Marilyn Davis and Alex Willingham, "Andrew Young and the Georgia State Elections of 1990," in Persons, *Dilemmas of Black Politics,* 147–69.

54. Carol Pierannunzi and John D. Hutcheson Jr., "Electoral Change and Regime Maintenance: Maynard Jackson's Second Time Around," *PS: Political Science & Politics* 23 (1990): 151–53.

55. Pierannunzi and Hutcheson, "Electoral Change and Regime Maintenance," 152–53.

56. *Atlanta Daily World,* January 2, 6, July 24, 1994.

57. Ibid., January 25, February 13, March 3, 6, 8, 10, 13, May 5, 19, June 19, July 21, 1994.

58. Ibid., January 30, 1994.

59. Ibid., January 2, 1994.

60. Ibid., April 17, 1994.

61. Ibid., May 9, 1996.

62. Ibid., September 27, October 9, 1994, April 11, 25, 1996; *Atlanta Tribune*, June 5, July 3, November 1, 1995.

63. *Atlanta Daily World*, July 3, December 25, 1994.

64. Ibid., October 30, December 18, 1994.

65. Ibid., May 26, 1994.

66. Ibid., January 7, 1996.

67. Paula M. White, "Big Slice of Olympic Pie," *Black Enterprise*, April 1996, 15–16. Other premature praise resulted as well; see *Atlanta Tribune*, January 1, July 1, 1996; *Atlanta Daily World*, May 23, 1996.

68. Johnetta Dillard, "Streets Paved with Olympic Gold," *Black Enterprise*, July 1996, 130–32; *Atlanta Daily World*, June 2, July 25, 28, August 22, 1996; *Atlanta Tribune*, September 1, 1996.

69. *Atlanta Tribune*, July 1, 1996; *Atlanta Daily World*, July 14, 1996.

70. *Atlanta Daily World*, September 1, November 24, 28, 1996.

71. "Campbell, Bill," *Current Biography Yearbook* 1996, 66–68; Cynthia Brown, "Not so Peachy in Georgia," *The Nation*, July 15/22, 1996, 5–6; *Atlanta Daily World*, June 12, 1994, February 20, April 28, 1996; *Atlanta Tribune*, September 1, 1995.

72. www.ourgeorgiahistory.com/chronpop/1000028; *New York Times*, March 9, 2006; *Jackson Clarion-Ledger*, March 11, 2006.

73. W. Wilson Goode and Joann Stevens, *In Goode Faith* (Valley Forge, PA: Judson Press, 1992), 92–139.

74. Ibid., 142–47.

75. Ibid., 147–48.

76. Ibid., 149–51, 156–57; Joe Davidson, "Is This Any Way to Run a City?," *Black Enterprise*, February 1982, 79–84.

77. Bruce Ransom, "Black Independent Electoral Politics in Philadelphia and the Election of Mayor W. Wilson Goode," in Preston and others, eds., *The New Black Politics*, 265.

78. Ibid.

79. Ibid., 265–66.

80. Ibid., 268–69.

81. Ibid., 256–72.

82. John F. Bauman, "W. Wilson Goode: The Black Mayor as Urban Entrepreneur," *Journal of Negro History* 77 (1992): 149; see also Lenora E. Berson, "The Return of the Big Bambino," *The Nation*, February 19, 1983, 205–7; "A Black Mayor for Philadelphia?," *Time*, March 7, 1983, 43; Michael A. Lerner and Tom Morganthau, "A Philadelphia Story," *Newsweek*, April 11, 1983, 20; "Face-off in Philadelphia," *Time*, May 16, 1983, 19; "Another Big-City Black Mayor?," *Time*, May 30, 1983, 22; Frank McRae, "Black Power at the Polls," *Black Enterprise*, May 1983, 17; "Goode Show?," *Time*, November 7, 1983, 69; "Elections '83: A Winning Round," *Time*, November 21, 1983, 18; Goode and Stevens, *In Goode Time*, 167–86; Bauman, "W. Wilson Goode," 148; Ransom, "Black Independent Electoral Politics in Philadelphia," in Preston et al., eds., *The New Black Politics*, 265–78; Carlos Munoz Jr. and Charles Henry, "Rainbow Coalitions in Four Big Cities: San Antonio, Denver, Chicago and Philadelphia," *PS: Political Science & Politics* 19 (1986): 601; Richard A. Keiser, "After the First Black Mayor: Fault Lines in Philadelphia's Biracial Coalition," in Browning et al., eds., *Racial Politics in American Cities*, 76–77.

83. Derek T. Dingle, "At the Helm of the City," *Black Enterprise*, February 1984, 13; Munoz and Henry, "Rainbow Coalitions in Four Big Cities," 601; Ransom, "Black Independent Electoral Politics in Philadelphia," 278–82; Bauman, "W. Wilson Goode," 149–50; Keiser, "After the First Black Mayor," in Browning et al., eds., *Racial Politics in American Cities*,

76–77; Roger Biles, "Black Mayors: A Historical Assessment," *Journal of Negro History* 77 (1992): 120; Goode and Stevens, *In Goode Faith*, 189–205.

84. Bauman, "W. Wilson Goode," 151–52.

85. Jim Quinn, "MOVE v. The City of Philadelphia," *The Nation*, March 26, 1986, 441, 458–60.

86. Chuck Stone, "Goode: Bad and Indifferent," *Washington Monthly*, July/August 1986, 27.

87. Ibid.

88. Ibid., 28.

89. Ibid., 27–28; Goode and Stevens, *In Goode Faith*, 160–65, 207–51, 260–61; Mark Starr and Martin Kasindorf, "'A House is Not a Home,'" *Newsweek*, July 15, 1985, 25–26; Kenneth M. Jones, "Philadelphia Moves on," *Black Enterprise*, August 1985, 19; "After the Bomb," *Time*, October 28, 1985, 46; "Did I Make a Mistake? Yes," *Time*, November 18, 1985, 47; Larry Eichel, "Life after the Bomb," *The New Republic*, December 23, 1985, 13–15; Jim Quinn, "MOVE v. The City of Philadelphia," *The Nation*, March 26, 1986, 441, 458–60; Philip Weiss, "Goode, Bad, and Ugly," *The New Republic*, June 10, 1993, 12–13.

90. Terry E. Johnson, "Philadelphia's Bare-Knuckled Political Brawl," *Newsweek*, November 2, 1987, 59; Bauman, "W. Wilson Goode," 155; Goode and Stevens, *In Goode Faith*, 276–87.

91. For background of New York City politics, see: John Mollenkopf, "New York: The Great Anomaly," *PS: Political Science & Politics* 19 (1986): 591–97; Judson L. Jeffries, "The New York State Black and Puerto Rican Legislative Caucus, 1970–1988," *Afro-Americans in New York Life and History* 24 (2000): 7–40.

92. Patricia J. Williams, "Home on the Range," *The Nation*, November 4, 2002, 10. She described "intense, at times hysterical, public pressure to make New York safe for tourism" as responsible for the arrest and conviction of five young men who would later be exonerated of involvement in the rape.

93. *New York Amsterdam News*, July 3, 8, 1989.

94. Ibid., August 12, 1989.

95. Ibid, July 22; see also the following dates: July 29, August 19, 26, 1989.

96. Ibid., September 9, 1989; see also the following dates: August 5, 12, September 2, 1989.

97. Ibid., September 16, 1989; see also Gerrard Bushell, "The Politics of Fiscal Scarcity and the Mobilization of Political Power in New York City: The Electoral and Governing Strategies of New York City's First Black Mayor" (PhD diss., Columbia University, 2004), 141.

98. *New York Amsterdam News*, September 23, 1989.

99. Ibid., September 30, 1989.

100. *New York Times*, October 5, 1989.

101. *New York Amsterdam News*, October 7, 1989.

102. *New York Times*, October 13, 1989.

103. Ibid., October 26, 1989.

104. Ibid., October 5, 11, 13, 19, 22–24, 26–31, November 1, 4, 1989; *New York Amsterdam News*, September 30, October 7, 21, 28, November 4, 1989; Bushell, "The Politics of Fiscal Scarcity," 145.

105. *New York Times*, November 8, 1989.

106. Ibid.

107. *New York Amsterdam News*, November 11, 1989.

108. Ibid., November 14, 1989.

109. *New York Times,* January 1, 1990.

110. Ibid., January 2, 1990; for more on the transition, see *New York Amsterdam News,* December 16, 23, 1989.

111. *New York Times,* February 10, 21, July 26, 1990, April 6, September 25, 1991, January 5, 12, 25, March 25, July 12, November 5, 1992.

112. Ibid., August 6, 1990; for other details of Dinkins's dealings with law enforcement, see the *New York Times* for January 5, August 6, 1990, April 10, 23, 25, 1991.

113. *Chicago Defender,* October 6, 1992; for more details of the conflict over a police board and related police matters, see the *New York Times,* September 24, 1991, October 1, 3, 4, 9, 1992.

114. Bushell, "The Politics of Fiscal Scarcity," 250.

115. Ibid.

116. *New York Times,* November 12, 1992.

117. Ibid., December 6, 1992.

118. Ibid.

119. Ibid., December 5, 1992; see also December 2–4, 6, August 30, 1993; *New York Amsterdam News,* July 24, 1993.

120. *New York Times,* December 3, 8, 1992, May 29, September 4, 15, 1993.

121. Ibid., October 4, 1993.

122. Ibid.; see also September 1, 5, October 1, 2, 1993.

123. Ibid., October 4, 1993.

124. Ibid.

125. Ibid., September 29, October 5, 1993.

126. Ibid., October 1, 7, 1993.

127. Ibid., October 13, 1993.

128. *New York Amsterdam News,* October 30, 1993.

129. *New York Times,* October 24, 1993; see also October 1, 6, 7, 13, 18, November 2, 1993; and *New York Amsterdam News,* August 28, October 9, 30, 1993.

130. *New York Amsterdam News,* August 21, November 6, 1993; *New York Times,* November 1, 3, 4, 1993; Jim Sleeper, "The End of the Rainbow?: The Changing Politics of America's Cities," *The New Republic,* November 1, 1993, 20–22.

131. Robert Huckfeldt and Carol Weitzel Kohfeld, *Race and the Decline of Class in American Politics* (Urbana: University of Illinois Press, 1989), 19.

132. Ibid., 19–22; *St. Louis Post-Dispatch,* February 16, 2000.

133. *St. Louis Post-Dispatch,* February 17, 1993.

134. Ibid., February 17, October 3, 1993.

135. Ibid., December 12, 1993, June 19, 1994, February 23, 1997; for background into the SLPD's record with black police, see Eugene J. Watts, "Black and Blue: Afro-American Police Officers in Twentieth-Century St. Louis," *Journal of Urban History* 7 (1981): 131–68.

136. *St. Louis Post-Dispatch,* February 17, 1994.

137. Ibid., March 17, May 27, 29, June 19, 1994, March 31, November 9, 11, 1995.

138. Ibid., November 11, 1995.

139. Ibid., November 9, 1995.

140. Complete details of the dispute can be found in the *St. Louis Post-Dispatch,* February 17, March 17, May 27, 29, June 19, 1994, March 31, November 9, 11, 1995.

141. Ibid., February 23, 1997.

142. Ibid., September 6, 1996.

143. Ibid., February 7, 1996.

144. Ibid.

145. Ibid.; see also July 19, September 11, 1996.

146. Ibid., January 12, 1997; also see September 20, 24, 1996.

147. Ibid.; refer as well to February 13, 16, 26–28, 1997; *Economist*, March 8, 1997, 65; the *St. Louis American* gave the Bosley-Harmon race considerable coverage but with bias against the challenger; for examples see January 2–8, 9–15, 16–22, 23–30, February 5, 6–12, 13–19, 20–26, 27-March 5, 1997.

148. *St. Louis Post-Dispatch*, February 16, 2000.

149. Ibid., March 1, 1997.

150. *St. Louis American*, February 27–March 5, 1997 edition.

151. *St. Louis Post-Dispatch*, March 6, 1997.

152. Ibid.

153. Ibid.

154. Ibid.; for more on the election, see the *St. Louis Post-Dispatch*, March 5, 1997; *St. Louis American*, March 6–12, 1997.

155. *St. Louis Post-Dispatch*, April 23, 1997; for more on interim, see the *St. Louis Post-Dispatch*, March 6, 8, 14, 16, 28–29, April 11, 13, 16, 23–24, 1997; as an olive-branch offer, Bosley apologized to Harmon for characterizing during the primary the elevation in rank of his successor's son as a fraudulent action; the new mayor accepted the apology, thereby ending his libel suit against his predecessor. See the *St. Louis Post-Dispatch*, July 8, 1997.

156. Ibid., March 6, April 16, July 12, October 3, 12, 16, 21, November 7, 1997, February 9, 16, 2000, February 11, 13, 15, June 27, 2001, July 13, 2003; *St. Louis American*, March 13–19, 20-April 2, 3–9, 1997.

157. *Economist*, March 3, 2001, 48.

158. *St. Louis Post-Dispatch*, February 17, 2002, July 13, 2003.

159. Peter K. Eisinger, "Black Employment in Municipal Jobs: The Impact of Black Political Power," *American Political Science Review* 76 (1982): 391; William E. Nelson Jr., "Black Mayoral Leadership: A Twenty-Year Perspective," *National Political Science Review* 2 (1990): 194; Abdul Alkalimat, "Chicago: Black Power Politics and the Crisis of the Black Middle Class," *Black Scholar* 19 (1988): 45; see also Adolph Reed Jr., "The Black Urban Regime: Structural Origins and Constraints," in Michael P. Smith, ed., *Power, Community and the City* (New Brunswick, NJ: Transaction Books, 1988), 138–89.

Chapter 4

1. For studies of black state caucuses and lawmakers, see: Sharon D. Wright, "The Tennessee Black Caucus of State Legislators," *Journal of Black Studies* 31 (2000): 3–19; Robert A. Holmes, "The Georgia Legislative Black Caucus: An Analysis of a Racial Legislative Subgroup," *Journal of Black Studies* 30 (2000): 768–90; Carolyn M. Morris, "Black Elected Officials in Ohio, 1978: Characteristics and Perceptions," *Ohio History* 88 (1978): 291–310; Kerry Lee Haynie, *African American Legislators in the American States* (New York: Columbia University Press, 2001). For black mayors seeking governorships, see Chapter 2 as well as: Mylon Winn and Errol G. Palmer, "The Election of Norman B. Rice as Mayor of Seattle," 82–95, and Carol A. Pierannunzi and John D. Hutcheson, "The Rise and Fall of Deracialization: Andrew Young as Mayor and Gubernatorial Candidate," 96–106, both in Huey Perry, ed., *Race, Politics, and Governance in the United States* (Gainesville: University Press of Florida, 1996).

2. http://Wlss.townhall.com/columnists/KenBlackwell.

3. *Washington Post*, August 29, 2001.

4. Charles L. Prysby, "The 1990 U.S. Senate Election in North Carolina," in Perry, ed., *Race, Politics, and Governance*, 34; Addison Godel, "Did 'White Hands' Do Helms's Dirty

Work?: Reexamining the Final Days of the 1990 North Carolina Senate Race," a seminar paper submitted for Charles Bullock's Southern politics course at the University of Georgia in 1993 and found on Ummagurau.com; Ruth Ann Strickland and Marcia Lynn Whicker, "Comparing the Wilder and Gantt Campaigns: A Model for Black Candidate Success in Statewide Elections," *PS: Political Science and Politics* 25 (1992): 205–10; Kathleen Hall Jamieson, *Dirty Politics: Deception, Distraction, and Democracy* (New York: Oxford University Press, 1992), 81, 94–100; Zaphon Wilson, "Gantt versus Helms: Deracialization Confronts Southern Traditionalism," in Persons, *Dilemmas of Black Politics*, 176–91; Charles S. Bullock III and Ronald Keith Gaddie, *The Triumph of Voting Rights in the South* (Norman: University of Oklahoma Press, 2009), 208–9.

5. Ed O'Keefe, "Harold Ford Eyes Senate Upset, Denies Being a Playboy," *ABC News*, October 15, 2006.

6. For more on Ford's background and the election, see Ibid.; Dana Milbank, "Harold Ford Jr. Storms His Father's House," *New York Times Magazine*, October 25, 1998, 40–43; Mike Batistick, "Harold E. Ford, Jr.," *Current Biography*, November 1999, 204–6; "Featured Democratic Speakers—Rep. Harold E. Ford, Jr.," NPR's Election 2000 Coverage: Democratic National Convention, August 18, 2000; Linda Feldman, "All Eyes on South's Big Race," *Christian Science Monitor*, October 25, 2006; Bullock and Gaddie, *The Triumph of Voting Rights in the South*, 296–97, 300.

7. Huey L. Perry, "An Analysis of Major Themes in the Concept of Deracialization," in Perry, ed., *Race, Politics, and Governance*, 1.

8. Ibid., 1–6; see also in the same edited volume, Robert B. Albritton, George Amedee, Keenan Grenell, and Don-Terry Veal, "Deracialization and the New Black Politics," 179–92.

9. John H. Cutler, *Ed Brooke: Biography of a Senator* (Indianapolis: Bobbs-Merrill, 1972), 146.

10. Ibid., 148; for more details of Brooke's early background and first political efforts, see same source, 13–14, 48, 51, 72–76, 89, 92, 117–18, 139, 146, 148; *Time*, February 17, 1967; for background on race and politics in Boston, see Toni-Michelle C. Travis, "Boston: The Unfinished Agenda," *PS: Political Science & Politics* 19 (1986): 610–16.

11. Martin F. Nolan, "The Junior Senator from Massachusetts," *The Reporter*, December 1, 1966, 46.

12. Ibid.

13. Ibid., 48; for more on Brooke's criticisms, see Edward W. Brooke, *The Challenge of Change: Crisis in Our Two-Party System* (Boston: Little, Brown, 1966); Brooke, "Where I Stand," *The Atlantic*, March 1966, 60–65. Brooke also lectured about GOP shortcomings to members of the Publishers' Publicity Association on March 16, 1966; for coverage of his address, see "What's Wrong with the Republican Party," *Publishers' Weekly*, March 28, 1966), 37–39; *Time*, February 17, 1967.

14. *Boston Globe*, November 1, 1966.

15. Ibid.

16. Ibid., November 4, 1966.

17. Ibid. For more on the election, see *Boston Globe* articles for November 1, 3–5, 1966; "The Power of the Polls," *Trans-action*, June 1968, 4–5.

18. Cutler, *Ed Brooke*, 165; see also pages 162–63. Clarification is needed on Brooke's view of the war; his 1967 trip did not cause him to believe in an unconditional pullout of American forces. As a result his views clashed with those of Martin Luther King and others who were demanding an immediate end to American participation. See "Senator Brooke and Dr. King," *Nation*, April 10, 1967, 452–53.

19. *Boston Globe*, November 6, 9, 1966.

20. Cutler, *Ed Brooke*, 3, 175, 194, 206; As *Time*, February 17, 1967, noted, Brooke's presence on the floor of the Senate became a Capitol Hill tourist attraction" that drew gallery spectators to "crane their necks, gawk and buzz excitedly."

21. Ibid., 209–210; *Congressional Record*, 90th-95th Congresses. To the Republican National Convention on August 5, 1968, Brooke advocated a liberal agenda for the party in an address entitled "To Forge a New Unity"; for a copy of this speech, see *Vital Speeches of the Day*, September 1, 1968, 691–93.

22. *Congressional Record*, 91st Cong., 1st sess., November 17, 1969, 2nd sess., February 25, 1970, 92nd Cong., 1st sess., December 7, 1971. Brooke passionately fought Haynsworth and Carswell's confirmations, see Cutler, *Ed Brooke*, 323–30. It should also be noted that Brooke had equal reservations about confirming Griffin Bell as Jimmy Carter's attorney general after a surfacing of revelations about the appointee's membership in an exclusive, white-only private club; see 95th Cong., 1st sess., January 25, 1977.

23. Ibid., 92nd Cong., 2nd sess., July 24, August 22, 1972, 93rd Cong., 1st sess., January 4, May 14–15, 29, July 18, October 10, 1973. Brooke opposed Nixon's proposals to fund MIRV (multiple independently targetable reentry vehicles) and SST (supersonic transport) commercial aircraft; see Cutler, *Ed Brooke*, 354, 357.

24. Ibid., 93rd Cong., 1st sess., May 31, 1973, 2nd sess., September 12, 1974.

25. Ibid., 91st Cong., 1st sess., June 9, 1969.

26. Ibid.

27. Ibid., 92nd Cong., 2nd sess., March 22, 1972; for more evidence of Brooke's agenda, see 93rd Cong., 2nd sess., March 22, 1974, 95th Cong., 1st sess., July 19, November 29, December 7, 1977, 2nd sess., September 27, October 12, 1978.

28. Ibid., 91st Cong., 1st sess., January 10, April 25, May 5, 12, June 12, 1969.

29. Ibid., 90th Cong., 2nd sess., March 29, May 23, 1968, 91st Cong., 1st sess., September 24, November 5, 1969, 2nd sess., April 10, 1970, 92nd Cong., 2nd sess., August 17, 1972, 93rd Cong., 1st sess., May 3, 1973, 2nd sess., October 1, 1974, 94th Cong., 1st sess., June 11, 1975, 2nd sess., April 6, 1976, 95th Cong., 1st sess., September 27, 1977, 2nd sess., October 11, 1978.

30. Ibid., 90th Cong., 2nd sess., April 17, 1968.

31. Ibid., 90th Cong., 2nd sess., April 17, 1968, 91st Cong., 1st sess., June 9, 1969, 2nd sess., December 17, 1969, 92nd Cong., 1st sess., April 22, October 1, 1971, 2nd sess., February 24, October 10, 1972, 93rd Cong., 2nd sess., November 19, 1974, 94th Cong., 1st sess., May 20, September 17, 19, October 7, 1975, 2nd sess., May-June, October 1, 1976, 95th Cong., 1st sess., June 28, 1977, 2nd sess., August 23, September 7, 1978; for Brooke's favorable support of the Philadelphia Plan, see *Congressional Digest*, March 1970.

32. Such words of comfort to whites as "I'm not running as a Negro" were a trademark of Brooke, a seeker after a majority's votes, and they fooled more than the Massachusetts electorate. The list of people who accepted this denial included Boston mayor Kevin White, syndicated columnist Roscoe Drummond, and Cutler; see Cutler's *Ed Brooke*, 48, 54, 117–18, 148, 175, and 209–10.

33. *Congressional Record*, 93rd Cong., 1st sess., October 3, 1973.

34. Ibid., 95th Cong., 2nd sess., March 7, 1978; see also 92nd Cong., 1st sess., October 12, 1971, 2nd sess., April 6, 1972, 93rd Cong., 1st sess., October 3, 1973, 94th Cong., 1st sess., May 1, 6, 1975. Brooke viewed the lack of representation by Washingtonians as a "glaring piece of unfinished business; see: *Congressional Digest*, October 1978. Brooke never officially joined the CBC but offered "frequent consultations" on all important legislation, but he did not join CBC members in boycotting Nixon's 1971 State of the Union address, see Walters, *Black Presidential Politics*, 45; Cutler, *Ed Brooke*, 336. As much as Brooke admired

Powell's activism on behalf of civil rights, an opinion emerged after the Republican's entry in the Senate that Harlem's representative would find himself overshadowed by an incoming African American official of "superior intelligence, probity and energy; see: Wendell More, "'Keep the Faith, Baby,'" *America*, January 21, 1967, 80; Brooke hinted at opposition to Powell's censure, stating "I don't rule out race" as the factor behind it. See Cutler, *Ed Brooke*, 233–4.

35. Ibid., 90th Cong., 2nd sess., June 13; see also May 7, 1968.

36. On encouraging entrepreneurship, ibid., 92nd Cong., 2nd sess., August 8, 1972, 94th Cong., 2nd sess., May 13, 1976, 95th Cong., 1st sess., February 3, 1977, 2nd sess., March 6, 1978; on housing issues, ibid., 90th Cong., 1st sess., August 7, 1967, 2nd sess., February 6–7, 14, March 5, 11, 1968, 91st Cong., 1st sess., August 4, 1969, 2nd sess., July 15, 1970, 92nd Cong., 2nd sess., February 1, June 14, 1972, 94th Cong., 1st sess., June 25, 1975, 95th Cong., 2nd sess., April 25, 1978. For failing to act on open-housing legislation, Brooke tried to block a major atomic-energy project from going to Illinois; he failed. See Cutler, *Ed Brooke*, 248–49.

37. Ibid., 91st Cong., 1st sess., June 19, 1969, 94th Cong., 1st sess., July 23, August 1, 1975, 2nd sess., May 4, 27, 1976, 95th Cong., 1st sess., January 10, November 4, 1977, 2nd sess., June 27, October 11, 1978. See "Up from Silence," *Time*, March 23, 1970, 14–15, for Brooke attacking the Southern Strategy.

38. *Congressional Record*, 90th Cong., 2nd sess., April 29, 1968.

39. Ibid., 90th Cong., 2nd sess., April 29, October 9, 1968, 91st Cong., 1st sess., December 12, 1969, 92nd Cong., 2nd sess., February 8, May 31, 1972, 93rd Cong., 1st sess., August 3, 1973, 95th Cong., 1st sess., March 15, October 31, 1977. Invited by Nixon to lead an American delegation to an African continent economic conference in 1969, Brooke concluded that he did not want to be "a nonfunctioning black 'front man'" for the administration; thus he spurned the president's invitation; see "Brooke Says 'No,'" *Senior Scholastic*, February 28, 1969, 23–24. To the Rubber Manufacturers Association, Brooke revealed what he calls the Business Corps; he thought experienced business leaders going on sabbaticals to advise Third World residents would do as much good as the Peace Corps; see "The 'Business' Corps," *Dun's Review*, March 1968, 19, 22.

40. *Congressional Record*, 92nd Cong., 2nd sess., May 16, 1972.

41. Ibid., 90th Cong., 2nd sess., February 15, April 8, 22, 1968, 91st Cong., 1st sess., January 15, 21, 1969, 2nd sess., March 9, 1970, 92nd Cong., 1st sess., September 16, 1971, 93rd Cong., 1st sess., March 6, 1973.

42. Ibid., 91st Cong., 2nd sess., May 26, 1970.

43. *Boston Globe*, November 3, 8, 1972.

44. Ibid., November 3–9, 1972. Mention of Brooke as a possible candidate for higher office first surfaced as early as 1968 and then continued to the 1976 GOP national convention; see Cutler, *Ed Brooke*, 299–300; "The Brooke Scenario," *Time*, December 13, 1971, 13; Walters, *Black Presidential Politics*, 160.

45. *Boston Globe*, November 3, 1978.

46. Ibid., November 4, 1978.

47. Ibid., November 8, 1978.

48. *Black Enterprise*, January 1979.

49. Chuck Stone, "Black Politics: Third Force, Third Party, or Third-Class Influence?," *Black Scholar* 1 (1969): 10.

50. More assessments on Brooke's career can be found in the following: *Boston Globe*, November 1–9, 1978; *Black Enterprise*, January 1979; Cutler, *Ed* Brooke, 392–93; early negativity about Brooke can be found in *Time*, February 17, 1967; Walters, *Black Presidential*

Politics, 145; Christopher, *America's Black Congressmen*, 231; further evidence of Brooke's 1978 reelection problems can be gleaned from Don Holt and Phyllis Malamud, "Can Brooke Survive?," *Newsweek*, September 11, 1978, 30; Ken Bode, "Party Games," *New Republic*, May 13, 1978, 14–17; "Cooking Brooke," *Time*, November 6, 1978, 29; "Family Feud," *Time*, June 26, 1978, 17; Susan Fraher and Phyllis Malamud, "Brooke: In Deep Water," *Newsweek*, June 19, 1978, 34, 37; David M. Alpern, Phyllis Malamud, and John J. Lindsay, "Costly Divorces," *Newsweek*, June 5, 1978, 29; James Barron and Marjorie Arons, "Massachusetts," *New Republic*, November 4, 1978, 20–21.

51. Edward W. Brooke, *Bridging the Divide: My Life* (New Brunswick, NJ: Rutgers University Press, 2002), 57–58, 107; for the senator's explanations for his personal positions on a range of topics including the Goldwater nomination, the Panama Canal treaty, people of African heritage and the Church of Latter Day Saints, abortion, Richard Nixon, his early political career, diplomatic relations with the People's Republic of China, etc., see pages 60–62, 64–67, 75, 78–79, 81, 91–93, 98, 102, 106–7, 136, 139–40, 143, 148–50, 153–55, 166–67, 171–73, 177–81, 183–85, 191–92, 194–206, 208–11, 213–16, 229–30, 232–34.

52. *Chicago Defender*, January 21, 1992; *Chicago Crusader*, February 15, 1992; Gill, *African American Women in Congress*, 148–51.

53. *Chicago Defender*, February 4, 1992.

54. Ibid., March 2, 16, 1992; Andrew Patner, "Facin' Dixon," *Nation*, March 23, 1992, 365, 381.

55. *Chicago Defender*, January 28, 1992.

56. Ibid., March 16, 1992; *Chicago Crusader*, February 15, March 14, 1992.

57. *Chicago Defender*, March 19, 1992.

58. Ibid.

59. Ibid.; Roger K. Oden, "The Election of Carol Moseley-Braun in the U.S. Senate Race in Illinois," in Perry, ed., *Race, Politics, and Governance*, 51–52.

60. *Chicago Crusader*, March 21, 1992.

61. Chicago *Defender*, March 23, 1992.

62. James N. Baker and Todd Barrett, "Voter Revolt: A Giant-Killer in Illinois," *Newsweek*, March 30, 1992, 38–39.

63. *Chicago Defender*, March 23, 1992.

64. *Chicago Defender*, October 1, 13, November 2, 1992; *Chicago Crusader*, October 17, 1992.

65. *Chicago Crusader*, June 13, July 4, 1992; *Chicago Defender*, October 15, 1992; John R. Coyne Jr., "Women of the Year?," *National Review*, September 14, 1992, 24, 26.

66. *Chicago Crusader*, September 5, 1992; *Chicago Defender*, October 15, November 3, 1992.

67. *Chicago Defender*, October 28, 1992.

68. Coyne, "Women of the Year?," 26.

69. *Chicago Defender*, November 2, 1992.

70. *Chicago Crusader*, October 31, November 7, 1992; Katherine Tate, "African American Female Senatorial Candidates: Twin Assets or Double Liabilities?," in Walton, ed., *African American Power and Politics*, 265–71.

71. *Chicago Defender*, November 4, 1992.

72. *Chicago Crusader*, November 7, 1992.

73. *Chicago Defender*, November 5, 1992.

74. Gill, *African American Women in Congress*, 160; Nancy Trevor, "This Is a Honeymoon?," *Time*, January 18, 1993, 28; Eloise Salholz and Todd Barrett, "A Senator's Uneasy Debut," *Newsweek*, January 18, 1993, 26.

75. *Congressional Record*, 103rd Cong., 1st sess., January 21, September 28, November 16, 1993, 104th Cong., 1st sess., January 18, August 5, December 7, 1995, 2nd sess., June 19, September 11, 1996.

76. Ibid., 103rd Cong., 1st sess., March 9, April 7, June 17, August 6, November 5, 19, 1993.

77. Ibid., January 21, February 3, March 17–18, June 24, September 15, 20, 1993, 2nd sess., July 28, 1994, 104th Cong., 2nd sess., September 26, 1996; Celia Moore, "Pensions Made Woman Friendly," *Ms.*, July/August 1997, 34–35.

78. *Congressional Record*, 103rd Cong., 1st sess., January 21, March 24, April 1, May 6–7, July 14, September 15, November 3, 5, 8, 1993.

79. Ibid., March 11, November 18, 1993, 104th Cong., 1st sess., January 27, March 15, 30, April 6, June 14, 1995.

80. Ibid., 103rd Cong., 1st sess., July 22, 1993; Canon, *Race, Redistricting, and Representation*, 37.

81. *Congressional Record*, 103rd Cong., 1st sess., April 29, May 5, 20, June 24, July 1, August 6, October 6, November 3, 1993, 104th Cong., 1st sess., September 27, 1995, 2nd sess., June 12–13, 1996, 105th Cong., 2nd sess., June 17, 1998.

82. Ibid., 103rd Cong., 1st sess., January 21, 26, February 2, April 3, July 30, November 19, 23, 1993, 2nd sess., May 23, July 25, August 25, 1994, 104th Cong., 2nd sess., February 29, 1996, 105th Cong., 1st sess., June 11, 1997, 2nd sess., February 25, June 19, 1998.

83. "Moseley-Braun, Carol," *Current Biography*, September 1994, 378.

84. "Carol Moseley-Braun," *New Republic*, November 15, 1993.

85. Ibid.; "Moseley-Braun, Carol," *Current Biography*, September 1994, 378–82; *New York Times*, October 11, 1972, July 24, 1993; *Chicago Tribune*, November 5, December 6, 31, 1992.

86. *Congressional Record*, 103rd Cong., 1st sess., October 14, 1993; see also the *Record* for same session: February 4, April 1, September 23, November 5, 18, 1993.

87. Ibid., January 21, February 4, March 4, June 9, July 29, November 9, 1993; 104th Cong., 2nd sess., June 6, 1996.

88. Ibid., 103rd Cong., 1st sess., February 4, 1993.

89. Ibid., 103rd Cong., 1st sess., November 5, 1993, 104th Cong., 2nd sess., September 10, 1996.

90. Ibid., 103rd Cong., 1st sess., June 17, 1993.

91. Ibid., 104th Cong., 1st sess., September 7, 12–13, 1995.

92. Carol Moseley-Braun, "Vouchers are the Wrong Way to Go," *Black Issues in Higher Education*, November 13, 1997, 108.

93. *Congressional Record*, 103rd Cong., 2nd sess., August 19, 1994.

94. Ibid., 1st sess., February 16, August 6, September 13, 104th Cong., 1st sess., June 14, October 26, 1995.

95. *Chicago Defender*, July–November 5, 1998; *St. Louis Post-Dispatch, Chicago Tribune, Chicago Sun-Times,* and *Arlington Heights* (IL) *Daily Herald*, October 15-November 4, 1998.

96. "Wilder, Lawrence Douglas," *Current Biography*, April 1990, 622.

97. Ibid., 622–26. For background into black legislative politics in Virginia and limited mention of Wilder's role, see Michael L. Clemons and Charles E. Jones, "African American Legislative Politics in Virginia," *Journal of Black Studies* 30 (2000): 744–64.

98. "Battling an Old Bugaboo," *Time*, April 17, 1989, 26.

99. Ibid., 26–27; *Black Enterprise*, January 1989.

100. *Black Enterprise*, January 1989.

101. Ibid.; Matthew Holden Jr., "The Rewards of Daring and the Ambiguity of Power: Perspectives on the Wilder Election of 1989," *The State of Black America* (National Urban

League), no volume (1990), 112–13; Ruth Ann Strickland and Marcia Lynn Whicker, "Comparing the Wilder and Gantt Campaigns: A Model for Black Candidate Success in Statewide Elections," *PS: Political Science & Politics* 25 (1992): 209.

102. "Breakthrough in Virginia," *Time*, November 20, 1989, 54.

103. Ibid., 54, 56; Holden, "The Rewards of Daring," 109–20; Fred Barnes, "Mild Wilder," *New Republic*, August 13, 1990), 27–29; Robert G. Holland, "The New Dominion," *National Review*, September 29, 1989, 25, 28; William Lowther, "A Shining Photo Finish," *Maclean's*, November 20, 1989, 41; Strickland and Whicker, "Comparing the Wilder and Gantt Campaigns," 204–11.

104. Alvin J. Schexnider, "The Politics of Pragmatism: An Analysis of the 1989 Gubernatorial Election in Virginia," *PS: Political Science & Politics* 23 (1990): 156.

105. Barnes, "Milder Wilder," 29; see also Schexnider, "The Politics of Pragmatism," 154–56; Jean Crichton, "Three Publishers Analyze Wilder and Virginia's Election," *Publishers Weekly*, March 23, 1990, 55–56; Barnes, "Mild Wilder," 27–29; Charles E. Jones and Michael L. Clemons, "A Model of Racial Crossover Voting: An Assessment of the Wilder Victory," in Persons, *Dilemmas of Black Politics*, 130–32, 136–40.

106. Fred Barnes, "Terminators 2," *New Republic*, July 8, 1991, 13.

107. "Virginia's Demolition Derby," *Time*, June 24, 1991, 23; see also Bill Turque and Eleanor Clift, "A 'Demolition Derby,'" *Newsweek*, June 24, 1991, 16–17; Barnes, "Terminators 2," 13; Christine Bridge, "Virginia is for Enemies," *Harper's*, August 1992, 20–22.

108. *National Review*, August 12, 1991.

109. Paula D. McClain and Steven C. Tauber, "An African American Presidential Candidate," in Walton, ed., *African American Power and Politics*, 297–303; *Chicago Defender*, January 20, 1992; Alvin J. Schexnider, "Analyzing the Wilder Administration through the Construct of Deracialization Politics," in Perry, ed., *Race, Politics, and Governance*, 17–18.

110. Schexnider, "Analyzing the Wilder Administration," 22.

111. *Roanoke Tribune*, June 18, 1992.

112. *Roanoke Tribune*, May 14, August 20, 1992; Schexnider, "Analyzing . . . ," 17–19; Ronald Roach, "Virginia's Experience," *Black Issues in Higher Education*, September 17, 1998, 22–23.

113. Andrew Bilski, "The Eccentric Democrats," *Maclean's*, September 23, 1991, 46.

114. Andrew Bilski, "And then There were Five," *Maclean's*, January 20, 1992, 29.

115. "The Underground Primary Begins," *Time*, April 8, 1991, 27. Finding frustration and bitterness at not being able to fulfill his goals as mayor, Wilder announced his intention to retire at the end of his term as mayor; see *Economist*, May 28, 2008.

116. Ifill, *The Breakthrough*, 189.

117. Ibid., 179–204. (Patrick was reelected to a second term on November 2, 2010.)

Chapter 5

1. Charles P. Henry, "Toward a Multiracial Democracy: The Jackson and Obama Contributions," in Charles P. Henry, Robert L. Allen, and Robert Chrisman, eds., *The Obama Phenomenon: Toward a Multiracial Democracy* (Urbana: University of Illinois Press, 2011), 16.

2. In describing Obama's announcement, the *New York Times* on February 11, 2007, noted the Illinois senator's race, a characteristic ignored in descriptions of his rivals for the nomination.

3. NPR, "Is Obama Black Enough?," February 2, 2007; NPR's *All Things Considered*, July 9, 2007; http://www.publicaffairstv.com/PublicAffairs/Podcasts/Podcasts.ht, June 11, 2007. For Obama and Patrick election victories in Illinois and Massachusetts, summary information gleaned from the *Chicago Tribune*, Autumn 2004, and the *Boston Globe*, Autumn 2006.

Regarding perceptions of Obama being "black enough," Senate majority leader Harry Reid privately expressed the belief that this was an asset; Reid "was wowed by Obama's oratorical gifts and believed that the country was ready to embrace a black presidential candidate, especially one such as Obama—a 'light-skinned' African American 'with no Negro dialect, unless he wanted to have one.'" John Heilemann and Mark Halperin, *Game Change: Obama and the Clintons, McCain, Palin, and the Race of a Lifetime* (New York: HarperCollins, 2010), 36.

4. For Jesse Jackson, see: George H. Hill, ed., "Jesse Jackson: A Perspective from the White Media," *Bulletin of Bibliography* 42 (1985): 80–88; Michael Parenti, *Inventing Reality: The Politics of the Mass Media* (New York: St. Martin's Press, 1986), 11; Adolph L. Reed Jr., *The Jesse Jackson Phenomenon: The Crisis of Purpose in Afro-American Politics* (New Haven, CT: Yale University Press, 1986), 1–65; Ronald W. Walters, *Black Presidential Politics in America* (Albany: State University of New York Press, 1988), 177; for Al Sharpton, see: Mark Bowden, Pompadour with a Monkey Wrench," *Atlantic*, July-August 2004, 88–106; Edward Ashbee, "Al Sharpton, the 2004 Presidential Election, and Black Politics," *American Studies in Scandinavia* 36 (2004): 35–48; Abigail Thernstrom, *Voting Rights—and Wrongs: The Elusive Quest for Racially Fair Elections* (Washington, DC: AEI Press, 2009), 300.

5. David Plouffe, *The Audacity to Win: The Inside Story and Lessons of Barack Obama's Historic Victory* (New York: Viking, 2009), 5–27. In his role as Obama's campaign manager, Plouffe used his insider's perch to describe candidly strategies and reactions to events; his study thus provides a basis for much that this study offers on the primaries and on the general election.

6. Good for background and personal perspectives, Barack Obama's two books were references but not a source for his thrust from anonymity to fame and the presidency. See *Dreams from My Father: A Story of Race and Inheritance* (New York: Three Rivers, 2004) and *The Audacity of Hope: Thoughts on Reclaiming the American Dream* (New York: Crown, 2006); except for specific citations, Obama's life and career prior to his announcement for president in 2007 came from David Mendell's *Obama: From Promise to Power* (New York: HarperCollins, 2008). In regard to how Obama viewed himself, he claimed, according to Heilemann and Halperin, that skin pigmentation never entered his mind "as a possible impediment to his running (or winning), [but] race was never really absent from his thinking." Moreover, he envisioned his success as a change for "millions of kids around this country who don't believe that it would ever be possible for them to be president of the United States." Heilemann and Halperin, *Game Change*, 71–72.

7. Mendell, *Obama*, 118.

8. Noam Scheiber. "Race Against History." *New Republic*, May 31, 2004, 22; Thernstrom, *Voting Rights—and Wrongs*, 19.

9. Scheiber, "Race Against History," 26.

10. *New York Times*, March 18, 2004; for details of Obama's win, see the *Times*, March 17, 2004.

11. Nicole Saunders interviewing Barack Obama, "The Next Black Senator?," *Essence*, March 2004, 32.

12. Alexandra Starr and Paul Magnuson, "After Sharpton: The Great Black Hopes." *Businessweek* (April 12, 2004), 47; it should be mentioned that both the *Chicago Tribune* and *Chicago Sun-Times* supported Obama in the Democratic primary, the former newspaper because of the African American's opposition to NAFTA and its rival because of Obama's anti-Iraq War position. See William Finnegan, "The Candidate: How the son of a Kenyan economist became an Illinois Everyman," *New Yorker*, May 31, 2004, 35; *Chicago Tribune*, November 3, 2004.

13. *New York Times*, June 23, 2004.

14. Ibid., July 29, 2004.

15. Ibid.

16. Ibid., August 1, 2004.

17. Ibid., August 5, 9, 2004.

18. Matthew Continetti, "The Anti-Obama; He no longer has an official opponent, but Justin Warfel is still on his case," *Weekly Standard*, August 2, 2004, 14–16.

19. *New York Times*, August 23, 29, October 25, 2004; *Chicago Tribune*, October 10, 2004.

20. "Interview (Barack Obama) by Barbara Ransby," *Progressive*, October 2004, 37.

21. *Chicago Tribune*, October 8, 2004.

22. Ibid., October 13, 2004; during the campaign, Obama confirmed his reasons for opposing the Iraq invasion; see the *Chicago Tribune*, October 26, 2004.

23. *New York Times*, October 27, 2004; see *Chicago Tribune*, October 15, 16, 24, 2004.

24. *Chicago Tribune*, October 27, 2004.

25. Ibid.

26. Ibid., October 30, 2004.

27. Ibid., October 31, 2004.

28. Ibid.

29. *Chicago Sun-Times*, October 15, 2004.

30. *Chicago Tribune*, October 24, 2004.

31. Ibid., November 4, 2004.

32. *New York Times*, November 7, 2004.

33. *Chicago Tribune*, November 4, 2004.

34. Ibid.

35. *Time*, November 15, 2004, 74–81.

36. Ibid.

37. Matthew Klam, "Barack Obama: Life of the Party," *Gentleman's Quarterly*, December, 2004, 320–21.

38. Mendell, *Obama*, 303; for more on the election, see *U.S. News & World Report*, November 15, 2004, 53; *Newsweek*, December 27, 2004, 74–87.

39. CNN's *Larry King Live*, September 30, 2006.

40. *Chicago Tribune*, October 1, 2006.

41. Mendell, *Obama*, 304.

42. Ibid., 305–17.

43. Ibid., 316.

44. Ibid., 316–17.

45. Ibid., 318–20.

46. Plouffe, *The Audacity to Win*, 17; http://blogs.abcnews.com/thenumbers/2008/02/the-role-of-rac.html.

47. http://www.desmoinesregister.com/article/20081109/NEWS09/S11090339/-1/caucus.

48. Dan Balz and Haynes Johnson, *The Battle for America 2008: The Story of an Extraordinary Election* (New York: Viking, 2009), 97.

49. Plouffe, *The Audacity to Win*, 124–25.

50. www.cnn.com/ELECTION/2008/primaries/results/state (cited hereafter as CNN.primaries).

51. Balz and Johnson, *The Battle for America 2008*, 135; for their complete analysis of the New Hampshire primary, see 129–45.

52. For an early discussion of the impact of the Hispanic vote, see *Economist*, January 26, 2008, 31–32.

53. Balz and Johnson, *The Battle for America 2008*, 155–6.

54. Ibid., 158.

55. Ibid., 159.

56. Ibid., 175.

57. Richard Wolffe, *Renegade: The Making of a President* (New York: Crown, 2009), 168.

58. *New York Times*, March 13, 2008.

59. Plouffe, *The Audacity to Win*, 196–97.

60. *New York Times*, March 13, 2008.

61. Plouffe, *The Audacity to Win*, 206–7, 209.

62. Balz and Johnson, *The Battle for American 2008*, 202; for two excellent articles discussing Wright and Obama, see: John L. Jackson, "Obama, Black Religion, and the Reverend Wright Controversy," 165–177, and Dwight N. Hopkins, "Race, Religion, and the Race for the White House," 181–99, both in Henry, Allen, and Chrisman, eds., *The Obama Phenomenon*.

63. Ibid.

64. Barack Obama, "A More Perfect Union," http://www.youtube.com/watch?v=zrp-v2tHaDo.

65. *New York Times*, April 23, 2008; *Economist*, March 22, 29, 2008; *Washington Post*, March 18–19, 2008.

66. Balz and Johnson, *The Battle for America 2008*, 206.

67. Ibid., 207.

68. Ibid.

69. Ibid., 208.

70. Ibid., 208–9.

71. *Economist*, April 26, 2008, 43–44.

72. Ifill, *The Breakthrough*, 165.

73. *New York Times*, April 24, 2008.

74. *Economist*, April 5, 2008, 39.

75. Except for specific citations, the information about primaries and the general election was pulled from: Ifill, *The Breakthrough*; Greg Mitchell, *Why Obama Won: The Making of a President 2008* (New York: Sinclair, 2008); Richard Wolffe, *Renegade: The Making of a President* (New York: Crown, 2009); Evan Thomas, *"A Long Time Coming": The Inspiring, Combative 2008 Campaign and the Historic Election of Barack Obama* (New York: Public Affairs, 2009); Balz and Johnson, *The Battle for America 2008*; Chuck Todd and Sheldon Gawiser, *How Barack Obama Won: A State-by-State Guide to the Historic 2008 Presidential Election* (New York: Vintage, 2009); Plouffe, *The Audacity to Win*. In *The Promise: President Obama, Year One* (New York: Simon and Schuster, 2010), Jonathan Alter captures in the first three chapters some key elements that account for Obama's victory and notes the Grant Park crowd's reaction to it.

76. Balz and Johnson, *The Battle for America 2008*, 211.

77. *Washington Post*, April 29, 2008.

78. Ibid., May 7, 2008.

79. *USA Today*, May 8, 2008.

80. http://www.firstread.msnbc.com/archive/2008/05/09/999566.aspx.

81. Ibid.

82. *Washington Post*, May 13, 2008.

83. www.newsweek.com/id/138456/output/print.

84. www.pbs.org/newshour/bb/media/jan-june08/race_05–07.html.

85. *Economist*, May 10, 2008, 37–38.

86. Balz and Johnson, *The Battle for America 2008*, 219.

87. Ibid., 220.

88. Ibid., 220–23; Plouffe, *The Audacity to Win*, 236–37.

89. Balz and Johnson. *The Battle for America*, 223.

90. Thierry Devos, "The Role of Race in American Politics: Lessons Learned from the 2008 Presidential Election," in Gregory S. Parks and Matthew W. Hughey, eds., *The Obamas and (Post) Racial America?* (New York: Oxford University Press, 2011), 231.

91. Ibid., 232.

92. *Washington Post*, June 22; for more evidence of race's potential effect on the presidential election, see *New York Times*, July 15, 2008; *Economist*, July 5, 2008, 37–38.

93. *Economist*, July 12, 2008.

94. www.vpr.net.npr/93235312.

95. *Economist*, July 12, 2008; PBS's *NewsHour*, August 1, 2008; NPR's *Weekend Edition*, August 3, 2008.

96. *New York Times Magazine*, August 17, 2008.

97. Ibid.

98. The trio of best-selling attacks on Obama: David Freddoso, *The Case Against Barack Obama: The Unlikely Rise and Unexamined Agenda of the Media's Favorite Candidate* (Washington, DC: Regnery, 2008); Jerome Corsi, *The Obama Nation: Leftist Politics and the Cult of Personality* (New York: Threshold, 2008); Dick Morris, *Fleeced: How Barack Obama, Media Mockery of Terrorist Threats, Liberals Who Want to Kill Talk Radio, the Do-Nothing Congress, Companies That Help Iran, and Washington Lobbyists for Foreign Governments Are Scamming Us . . . and What to Do About It* (New York: Harper, 2008). For a final word from McCain why race would not figure into the outcome of the election, see the *Washington Post*, October 29, 2008.

99. www.msnbc.com/id/26803840/ns/politics-decisions_08.

100. Ibid.

101. www.icrsurvey.com/.../ABC_Obamas_Rise_In_Spotlight_Gains_in_Race_Relations_9–23–08,htm. See also *USA Today*, September 23, 2008; *Washington Post*, October 12, 2008.

102. *Jackson Clarion-Ledger*, October 19, 2008.

103. *Washington Post*, October 30, 2008.

104. Balz and Johnson, *The Battle for America 2008*, 346–51.

105. *Economist*, November 1, 2008, 35. Note that checks were made of the following newspapers with editorial endorsements of Obama to ascertain their reasons: *Chicago Tribune*, October 17, 2008; *New York Times*, October 24, 2008; *Miami Herald*, October 19, 2008; *Atlanta Journal-Constitution*, October 19, November 3, 2008; *St. Louis Post-Dispatch*, October 12, 2008; *Pittsburgh Post-Gazette*, November 2, 2008; *Washington Post*, October 17, 26, 2008; opinions favorable to McCain were gleaned from the following publications: *Juneau Empire*, October 31, 2008; *Mobile Press-Register*, November 2; *Arizona Republic*, October 25, 2008; *Little Rock Arkansas Democrat-Gazette*, November 2, 2008; *San Diego Union-Tribune*, October 19, 2008; *Columbus Dispatch*, October 19, 2008. Moreover, on the eve of the election, the *Wall Street Journal* published many brief summaries of diverse newspaper editorials favorable to both candidates; see http://online.wsj.com/article/SB122485442010466443.html and http://online.wsj.com/article/SB122487558086867319.html.

106. *Jackson Clarion-Ledger*, November 5, 2008.

107. Ibid. For other insights about the election's meaning and the challenges ahead for Obama, see: *Economist*, November 8, December 6, 2008; *Washington Post*, November 5, 2008, *Starkville* (MS) *Daily News*, November 9; www.msnbc.msn.com/id/27531033/?GT1=43001&print=1&displaymode=1098.

108. Todd and Gawiser, *How Barack Obama Won*, 49–97.

109. www.msnbc.msn.com/id/27531033/?GT1=43001&print=1&displaymode=1098.

110. Balz and Johnson, *The Battle for America 2008*, 373. See also Vincent Alabiso et al., eds., *Obama: The Historic Journey* (New York: Callaway, 2009), 182–85; Scout Tufankjian, *Yes We Can: Barack Obama's History-Making Presidential Campaign* (New York: power-House Books, 2008), 184–85, 187.

111. www.theroot.com/id/48726/output/print.

112. *Economist*, August 23, 2008; *New York Times Magazine*, August 17, 2008.

113. Maulana Karenga, "The Ambivalent Embrace of Barack Obama: The Ethical Significance and Social Apprehension of Blackness," in Henry, Allen, and Chrisman, eds., *The Obama Phenomenon*, 152, 162.

114. David Axelrod had experience of running successful campaigns of African American candidates dependent in part upon substantial white support; since 2002 his consultancy firm had compiled a record of thirty-three victories in its forty-two primary or general-election campaigns involving African Americans seeking enough white votes to gain victories. As for knowledge and contributions from Obama, his post-election thrust showed a willingness to obtain valuable lessons from the histories of previous transitions. For evidence of Axelrod's experience and Obama's keen appreciation of history, see *Economist*, August 23, 28 and November 15, 2008, 35–36.

115. NBC's *Meet the Press*, January 11, 2009.

116. Balz and Johnson, *The Battle for America 2008*, 285. Without the context of earlier African American winners to elective offices of lesser importance than the presidency, Marc Ambinder of the *Atlantic* found the same strategy at work for Obama as Nordin has confirmed as successful in earlier political contests involving minority candidates. To Ambinder, "He [Obama] did not have to bring up race. And that was the key . . ." to his victory. Ambinder, *Atlantic*, January/February 2009, 65.

117. Plouffe, *The Audacity to Win*, 378–80.

118. Thernstrom, *Voting Rights—and Wrongs*, 201–2; for George Will's case against renewal, see http://www.realclearpolitics.com/printpage/?url=http://www.realclearpolitics.com/articles; http://electionlawblog.org/archives/2009_03.html.

119. Bullock and Gaddie, *The Triumph of Voting Rights*, 360–63; to this end, the authors cite as proof of change John Lewis's glowing assessments of change in the South and the many instances cited throughout the study of elections of blacks to offices which resulted from significant numbers of whites joining blacks to make these wins possible; see 97–98 for Lewis's remarks and for biracial voting, see 75, 94–95, 152, 163, 201–6, 212, 267, 293.

120. Thierry Devos, "The Role of Race in American Politics: Lessons Learned from the 2008 Presidential Election," in Parks and Hughey, eds., *The Obamas and a (Post) Racial America?*, 234–35.

121. Stephen Ansolabehere, Nathaniel Persily, and Charles Stewart III, "Race, Region, and Vote Choice in the 2008 Election: Implications for the Future of the Voting Rights Act," *Harvard Law Review* 123 (2010): 1435.

122. Kristen Clarke, "The Obama Factor: The Impact of the 2008 Presidential Election on Future Voting Rights Act Litigation," *Harvard Law & Policy Review* 3 (2009): 59, 84.

123. *New York Times*, January 10, 2010; *Columbus Dispatch*, May 23, 2011; David A. Bositis, "Blacks and the 2008 Elections: A Preliminary Analysis," Joint Center for Political and Economic Studies, 2008, 12–15; http://polysigh.blogspot.com/search?updated-max=2008-04-10; http://blogs.abcnews.com/thenumbers/2008/02/the-role-of-rac.htlm.

Bibliography

Newspapers and Newsmagazines

Atlanta Daily World
Atlanta Journal-Constitution
Atlanta Tribune
Boston Globe
Businessweek
Chicago Crusader
Chicago Defender
Chicago Sun-Times
Chicago Tribune
Columbus Dispatch
Dartmouth (Dartmouth, NH)
Economist
International Herald Tribune
Jackson Clarion-Ledger
Juneau Empire
Little Rock Arkansas Democrat-Gazette
Los Angeles Sentinel
Los Angeles Times
Miami Herald
Mobile Press-Register
New York Amsterdam News
New York Times
Newsweek
Oklahoma City Black Chronicle
Phoenix Arizona Republic
Pittsburgh Post-Gazette
Roanoke Tribune
San Diego Union-Tribune

Starkville (MS) *Daily News*
St. Louis American
St. Louis Post-Dispatch
Time
Tulsa Oklahoma Eagle
Tulsa World
Vital Speeches
USA Today
U.S. News & World Report
Wall Street Journal
Washington Post
Waterbury Republican-American

Books

Alabiso, Vincent, et al., eds. *The New York Times Obama: The Historic Journey.* New York: Callaway, 2009.

Alter, Jonathan. *The Promise: President Obama, Year One.* New York: Simon and Schuster, 2010.

Balz, Dan and Haynes Johnson. *The Battle for America 2008: The Story of an Extraordinary Election.* New York: Viking, 2009.

Barker, Lucius J., Mack H. Jones, and Katherine Tate. *African Americans and the American Political System.* Upper Saddle River, NJ: Prentice Hall, 1999.

Bositis, David A. *The Congressional Black Caucus in the 103rd Congress.* Washington, DC: Joint Center for Political and Economic Studies, 1994.

Brooke, Edward W. *Bridging the Divide: My Life.* New Brunswick, NJ: Rutgers University Press, 2007.

Browning, Rufus P., Dale R. Marshall, and David H. Tabb, eds. *Protest is not Enough: The Struggle of Blacks and Hispanics for Equality in Urban Politics.* Berkeley: University of California Press, 1984.

———. *Racial Politics in American Cities.* White Plains, NY: Longman, 1997.

Bryce, Herrington J., ed. *Urban Governance and Minorities.* New York: Praeger, 1976.

Bullock, Charles S. III and Ronald Keith Gaddie. *The Triumph of Voting Rights in the South.* Norman: University of Oklahoma Press, 2009.

Canon, David T. *Race, Redistricting, and Representation: The Unintended Consequences of Black Majority Districts.* Chicago: University of Chicago Press, 1999.

Carmines, Edward G. and James A. Stimson. *Issue Evolution: Race and the Transformation of American Politics.* Princeton: Princeton University Press, 1989.

Cavanaugh, Thomas E., ed. *Race and Political Strategy: A JCPS Roundtable.* Washington, DC: Joint Center for Political Studies, 1983.

Christopher, Maurine. *America's Black Congressmen*. New York: Thomas Y. Crowell, 1971.

Clavel, Pierre and Wim Wiewel, eds. *Harold Washington and the Neighborhoods: Progressive City Government in Chicago, 1983–1987*. New Brunswick, NJ: Rutgers University Press, 1991.

Clay, William L. *Just Permanent Interests: Black Americans in Congress, 1870–1991*. New York: Amistad Press, 1993.

Cole, Leonard A. *Blacks in Power: A Comparative Study of Black and White Elected Officials*. Princeton: Princeton University Press, 1976.

Corsi, Jerome. *The Obama Nation: Leftist Politics and the Cult of Personality*. New York: Threshold, 2008.

Cutler, John H. *Ed Brooke: Biography of a Senator*. Indianapolis: Bobbs-Merrill, 1972.

Davidson, Chandler, ed. *Minority Vote Dilution*. Washington, DC: Howard University Press, 1984.

—— and Bernard Grofman, eds. *Quiet Revolution in the South: The Impact of the Voting Rights Act, 1965–1990*. Princeton: Princeton University Press, 1994.

Dawson, Michael C. *Behind the Mule: Race and Class in African American Politics*. Princeton: Princeton University Press, 1994.

Eisinger, Peter K. *Politics and Displacement: Racial and Ethnic Transition in Three American Cities*. New York: Academic Press, 1980.

Freddoso, David. *The Case Against Barack Obama: The Unlikely Rise and Unexamined Agenda of the Media's Favorite Candidate*. Washington, DC: Regnery, 2008.

Foster, Ezola. *What's Right for All Americans: A Fearless Los Angeles Schoolteacher Challenges the Black Political Establishment*. Waco, TX: WRS Group, 1995.

Franklin, Jimmie L. *Back to Birmingham: Richard Arrington, Jr., and His Times*. Tuscaloosa: University of Alabama Press, 1989.

Franks, Gary. *Searching for the Promised Land: An African American's Optimistic Odyssey*. New York: HarperCollins, 1996.

Frymer, Paul. *Uneasy Alliances: Race and Party Competition in America*. Princeton: Princeton University Press, 1999.

Gidlow, Liette, ed. *Obama, Clinton, Palin: Making History in Election 2008*. Urbana: University of Illinois Press, 2011.

Gill, LaVern McCain. *African American Women in Congress: Forming and Transforming History*. New Brunswick, NJ: Rutgers University Press, 1997.

Goode, W. Wilson and Joann Stevens. *In Goode Faith*. Valley Forge, PA: Judson, 1992.

Grimshaw, William J. *Bitter Fruit: Black Politics and the Chicago Machine, 1931–1991*. Chicago: University of Chicago Press, 1992.

Grofman, Bernard and Chandler Davidson, eds. *Controversies in Minority Voting: The Voting Rights Act in Perspective*. Washington, DC: Brookings Institution, 1992.

Grofman, Bernard, Lisa Handley, and Richard G. Niemi. *Minority Representation and the Quest for Voting Equality*. New York: Cambridge University Press, 1992.

Gurin, Patricia, Shirley Hatchett, and James S. Jackson. *Hope and Independence: Blacks' Response to Electoral and Party Politics*. New York: Russell Sage Foundation, 1989.

Hacker, Andrew. *Two Nations: Black, White, Separate, Hostile, Unequal*. New York: Ballantine, 1995.

Hamilton, Charles V. *Adam Clayton Powell, Jr.: The Political Biography of an American Dilemma*. New York: Atheneum, 1991.

Hapgood, David. *The Purge that Failed: Tammany v. Powell*. New York: McGraw-Hill, 1960.

Haynie, Kerry Lee. *African American Legislators in the American States*. New York: Columbia University Press, 2001.

Heilemann, John and Mark Halperin. *Game Change: Obama and the Clintons, McCain and Palin, and the Race of a Lifetime*. New York: HarperCollins, 2010.

Henry, Charles P., Robert L. Allen, and Robert Chrisman, eds. *The Obama Phenomenon: Toward a Multiracial Democracy*. Urbana: University of Illinois Press, 2011.

Huckfeldt, Robert and Carol Weitzel Kohfeld. *Race and the Decline of Class in American Politics*. Urbana: University of Illinois Press, 1989.

Hurwitz, Jon and Mark Peffley. *Perception and Prejudice: Race and Politics in the United States*. New Haven: Yale University Press, 1998.

Ifill, Gwen. *The Breakthrough: Politics and Race in the Age of Obama*. New York: Doubleday, 2009.

Jackman, Mary R. *The Velvet Glove: Paternalism and Conflict in Gender, Class, and Race Relations*. Berkeley: University of California Press, 1994.

Jamieson, Kathleen Hall. *Dirty Politics: Deception, Distraction, and Democracy*. New York: Oxford University Press, 1992.

Karnig, Albert K. and Susan Welch. *Black Representation and Urban Policy*. Chicago: University of Chicago Press, 1980.

Kleppner, Paul. *Chicago Divided: The Making of a Black Mayor*. DeKalb: Northern Illinois University Press, 1985.

Lawson, Steven F. *Running for Freedom: Civil Rights and Black Politics in White America since 1941*. New York: McGraw-Hill, 1991.

Marable, Manning. *The Crisis of Color and Democracy*. Monroe, ME: Common Courage, 1992.

Mendell, David. *Obama: From Promise to Power*. New York: Harper, 2008.

Mfume, Kweisi. *No Free Ride: From the Mean Streets to the Mainstream*. New York: Ballantine, 1996.

Miller, Warren E. and National Election Studies. *American National Election Studies Cumulative Data File, 1952–1994*. Ann Arbor: University of Michigan Center for Political Studies, 1994.

Mitchell, Greg. *Why Obama Won: The Making of a President 2008*. New York: Sinclair, 2008.

Moore, Leonard N. *Carl B. Stokes and the Rise of Black Political Power*. Urbana: University of Illinois Press, 2002.

Morris, Dick. *Fleeced: How Barack Obama, Media Mockery of Terrorist Threats, Liberals who Want to Kill Talk Radio, the Do-Nothing Congress, Companies that Help Iran, and Washington Lobbyists for Foreign Governments are Scamming Us . . . and What to Do about It*. New York: Harper, 2008,

Nelson, William E. Jr. and Philip J. Meranto. *Electing Black Mayors: Political Action in the Black Community*. Columbus: Ohio State University Press, 1977.

Nordin, Dennis S. *The New Deal's Black Congressman: A Life of Arthur Wergs Mitchell*. Columbia: University of Missouri Press, 1997.

Obama, Barack H. *The Audacity of Hope: Thoughts on Reclaiming the American Dream*. New York: Crown, 2006.

———. *Dreams from My Father: A Story of Race and Inheritance*. New York: Three Rivers, 2004.

Parenti, Michael. *Inventing Reality: The Politics of the Mass Media*. New York: St. Martin's, 1986.

Parker, Frank R. *Black Votes Count: Political Empowerment in Mississippi after 1965*. Chapel Hill: University of North Carolina Press, 1990.

Parks, Gregory, Matthew Hughey, and John Jost, eds. *The Obamas and a (Post) Racial America?*. New York: Oxford University Press, 2011.

Perry, Huey L. *Political System*. Gainesville: University Press of Florida, 1995.

———. *Race, Politics and Governance in the United States*. Gainesville: University Press of Florida, 1996.

Persons, Georgia A., ed. *Dilemmas of Black Politics: Issues of Leadership and Strategy*. New York: Harper Collins, 1993.

Peterson, Paul E., ed. *Classifying by Race*. Princeton: Princeton University Press, 1995.

Plouffe, David. *The Audacity to Win: The Inside Story and Lessons of Barack Obama's Historic Victory*. New York: Viking, 2009.

Preston, Michael B., Lenneal J. Henderson Jr., and Paul Puryear, eds. *The New Black Politics: The Search for Political Power*. New York: Longman, 1987.

Reed, Adolph L. *The Jesse Jackson Phenomenon: The Crisis of Purpose in Afro-American Politics*. New Haven: Yale University Press, 1986.

Reeves, Keith. *Voting Hopes or Fears?: White Voters, Black Candidates and Racial Politics in America*. New York: Oxford University Press, 1998.

Rich, Wilbur C. *Black Mayors and School Politics: The Failure of Reform in Detroit, Gary, and Newark*. New York: Garland, 1996.

Riposa, Gerry and Carolyn Dersch, eds. *City of Angels*. Dubuque, IA: Kendall-Hunt, 1992.

Rivlin, Gary. *Fire on the Prairie: Chicago's Harold Washington and the Politics of Race*. New York: Holt, 1992.

Rush, M. E., ed. *Voting Rights and Redistricting in the United States*. Westport, Ct.: Greenwood Press, 1998.

—— and Richard L. Engstrom. *Fair and Effective Representation?: Debating Electoral Reform and Minority Rights*. Lanham, MD: Rowman & Littlefield, 2001.

Schuman, Howard and others. *Racial Attitudes in America: Trends and Interpretations*. Cambridge: Harvard University Press, 1997.

Singh, Robert. *The Congressional Black Caucus: Racial Politics in the U.S. Congress*. Thousand Oaks, CA: Sage, 1998.

Smith, Michael P., ed. *Power, Community and the City*. New Brunswick, NJ: Transaction, 1988.

—— and Joe R. Feagin, eds. *The Bubbling Cauldron: Race, Ethnicity, and the Urban Crisis*. Minneapolis: University of Minnesota Press, 1995.

Smith, Robert C. *We Have No Leaders: African Americans in the Post-Civil Rights Era*. Albany: State University of New York Press, 1996.

Sniderman, Paul M. and Edward G. Carmines. *Reaching Beyond Race*. Cambridge: Harvard University Press, 1997.

——, Philip E. Tetlock, and Edward G. Carmines, eds. *Prejudice, Politics, and the American Dilemma*. Stanford: Stanford University Press, 1993.

—— and Thomas Piazza. *The Scar of Race*. Cambridge: Harvard University Press, 1993.

Sonenshein, Raphael J. *Politics in Black and White: Race and Power in Los Angeles*. Princeton: Princeton University Press, 1993.

Stone, Clarence N. *Regime Politics: Governing Atlanta, 1946–1988*. Lawrence: University Press of Kansas, 1989.

Swain, Carol M. *Black Faces, Black Interests: The Representation of African Americans in Congress*. Cambridge: Harvard University Press, 1993.

Tate, Katherine. *Black Faces in the Mirror: African Americans and Their Representatives in the U.S. Congress*. Princeton: Princeton University Press, 2003.

——. *From Protest to Politics: The New Black Voters in American Elections*. Cambridge: Harvard University Press, 1993.

Thernstrom, Abigail. *Voting Rights—and Wrongs: The Elusive Quest for Racially Fair Elections*. Washington, DC: American Enterprise Institute for Public Policy Research, 2009.

——. *Whose Votes Count?: Affirmative Action and Minority Voting Rights*. Cambridge: Harvard University Press, 1987.

—— and Stephan Thernstrom. *America in Black and White: One Nation, Indivisible*. New York: Simon and Schuster, 1997.

——, eds. *Beyond the Color Line: New Perspectives on Race and Ethnicity in America*. Stanford: Hoover Institution Press, 2002.

Thomas, Evan. *"A Long Time Coming": The Inspiring, Combative 2008 Campaign and the Historic Election of Barack Obama*. New York: Public Affairs, 2009.

Todd, Chuck and Sheldon Gawiser. *How Barack Obama Won: A State-by-State Guide to the Historic 2008 Presidential Election*. New York: Vintage, 2009.

Tufankjian, Scout. *Yes We Can: Barack Obama's History-Making Presidential Campaign*. New York: powerHouse Books, 2008.

Walters, Ronald W. *Black Presidential Politics in America*. Albany: State University of New York Press, 1988.

Walton, Hanes Jr., ed. *African American Power and Politics: The Political Context Variable*. New York: Columbia University Press, 1997.

Watts, J. C. Jr. with Chriss Winston. *What Color is a Conservative?: My Life and My Politics*. New York: HarperCollins, 2002.

Whitby, Kenneth J. *The Color of Representation: Congressional Behavior and Black Interests*. Ann Arbor: University of Michigan Press, 1997.

Wilson, William J. *The Declining Significance of Race: Blacks and Changing American Institutions*. Chicago: University of Chicago Press, 1980.

Wolffe, Richard. *Renegade: The Making of a President*. New York: Crown, 2009.

Yancey, Dwayne. *When Hell Froze over: The Untold Story of Doug Wilder: A Black Politician's Rise to Power in the South*. Dallas: Taylor, 1988.

Yates, Douglas. *The Ungovernable City: The Politics of Urban Problems and Policy Making*. Cambridge: MIT Press, 1977.

Articles

Abney, F. Glenn and John D. Hutcheson Jr. "Race, Representation, and Trust: Changes in Attitudes after the Election of a Black Mayor." *Public Opinion Quarterly* 45 (1981): 91–101.

Alkalimat, Abdul. "Chicago: Black Power Politics and the Crisis of the Black Middle Class." *Black Scholar* 19 (1988): 45–54.

—— and Don Gills. "Black Political Protest and the Mayoral Victory of Harold Washington: Chicago Politics, 1983." *Radical America* 17–18 (1983–1984): 111–27.

Allswang, John M. "Tom Bradley of Los Angeles." *Southern California Quarterly* 74 (1992): 55–105.

Ambinder, Marc. "Race Over?." *Atlantic*, January/February 2009, 62–65.

Ansolabehere, Stephen, Nathaniel Persily, and Charles Stewart III. "Race, Region, and Vote Choice in the 2008 Election: Implications for the Future of the Voting Rights Act." *Harvard Law Review*, April 2010, 1385–1436.

Ardrey, Saundra C. and William E. Nelson. "The Maturation of Black Political Power: The Case of Cleveland." *PS: Political Science & Politics* 23 (1990): 148–51.

Arrington, Theodore S. and Gerald L. Ingalls. "Race and Campaign Finance in Charlotte, N.C." *Western Political Quarterly* 37 (1984): 578–83.

Ashbee, Edward. "Al Sharpton, the 2004 Presidential Election, and Black Politics." *American Studies in Scandinavia* 36 (2004): 35–48.

Barnett, Marguerite R. "The Congressional Black Caucus." *Proceedings of the Academy of Political Science* 32 (1975): 34–50.

Baron, Harold M. "Black Powerlessness in Chicago." *Trans-action* 6 (1968): 27–33.

Barrett, Edith J. "The Policy Priorities of African American Women in State Legislatures." *Legislative Studies Quarterly* 20 (1995): 223–47.

Bauman, John F. "W. Wilson Goode: The Black Mayor as Urban Entrepreneur." *Journal of Negro History* 77 (1992): 141–58.

Biles, Roger. "Black Mayors: A Historical Assessment." *Journal of Negro History* 77 (1992): 109–25.

Bobo, Lawrence and Franklin D. Gilliam Jr. "Race, Socioeconomic Status, and Black Empowerment." *American Political Science Review* 84 (1990): 377–394.

Bowden, Mark. "Pompadour with a Monkey Wrench." *Atlantic*, July-August, 2004, 88–106.

Bratton, Kathleen A. and Kerry L. Haynie. "Agenda Setting and Legislative Success in State Legislatures: The Effects of Gender and Race." *Journal of Politics* 61 (1999): 658–79.

Bullock, Charles S. III. "Racial Crossover Voting and the Election of Black Officials." *Journal of Politics* 46 (1984): 238–51.

Button, James and David Hedge. "Legislative Life in the 1990s: A Comparison of Black and White State Legislators." *Legislative Studies Quarterly* 21 (1997): 199–218.

Cameron, Charles, David Epstein, and Sharyn O'Halloran. "Do Majority-Minority Districts Maximize Substantive Black Representation in Congress?." *American Political Science Review* 90 (1996): 794–812.

Canon, David T. "Redistricting and the Congressional Black Caucus." *American Politics Quarterly* 23 (1995): 159–89.

Carton, Paul. "A Black Man Runs for Mayor: The Extraordinary Campaign of Arthur O. Eve." *Afro-Americans in New York Life and History* 4 (1980): 7–54.

Citrin, Jack, Donald P. Green, and David O. Sears. "White Reactions to Black Candidates: When Does Race Matter?." *Public Opinion Quarterly* 54 (1990): 74–96.

Clarke, Kristen. "The Obama Factor: The Impact of the 2008 Presidential Election on Future Voting Rights Act Litigation." *Harvard Law & Policy Review* 3 (2009): 59–85.

Clemons, Michael L. and Charles E. Jones. "African American Legislative Politics in Virginia." *Journal of Black Studies* 30 (2000): 744–67.

Conover, Pamela J. and Stanley Feldman. "Candidate Perception in an Ambiguous World: Campaigns, Cues, and Inference Processes." *American Journal of Political Science* 33 (1989): 912–40.

Continetti, Matthew. "The Anti-Obama: He no longer has an opponent, but Justin Warfel is still on his case." *Weekly Standard*, August 2, 2004, 14–16.

Cooper, James L. "South Side Boss." *Chicago History* 19 (1990–1991): 66–81.

Darcy, R. and Charles D. Hadley. "Black Women in Politics: The Puzzle of Success." *Social Science Quarterly* 69 (1988): 629–45.

DeGraaf, Lawrence B. "Worlds Apart: Two Views of Recent African-American Experiences in Los Angeles." *Pacific Historical Review* 66 (1997): 99–101.

Dowe, Kelly. "Richard Arrington: Birmingham." *Southern Exposure* 12 (1984): 76–78.

Eisinger, Peter K. "Black Employment in Municipal Jobs: The Impact of Black Political Power." *American Political Science Review* 76 (1982): 380–92.

Elliot, Jeffrey M. "The Congressional Black Caucus: An Interview with Yvonne Brathwaite Burke." *Negro History Bulletin* 40 (1977): 650–52.

Finnegan, William. "The Candidate: How the Son of a Kenyan Economist Became an Illinois Everyman." *New Yorker*, May 31, 2004, 32–38.

Fossett, Mark A. and K. Jill Kiecolt. "The Relative Size of Minority Populations and White Racial Attitudes." *Social Science Quarterly* 70 (1989): 820–35.

Gay, Claudine. "The Effect of Black Congressional Representation on Political Participation." *American Political Science Review* 95 (2001): 589–602.

Giles, Michael W. and Arthur Evans. "The Power Approach to Intergroup Hostility." *Journal of Conflict Resolution* 30 (1986): 469–86.

Glaser, James M. "Back to the Black Belt: Racial Environment and White Racial Attitudes in the South." *Journal of Politics* 56 (1994): 21–41.

Gove, Samuel K. and Michael B. Preston. "State-Local (Chicago) Relations in Illinois: The Harold Washington Era, 1984." *Publius* 15 (1985): 143–54.

Green, Donald P., Dara Z. Strolovitch, and Janelle S. Wong. "Defended Neighborhoods, Integration, and Racially Motivated Crime." *American Journal of Sociology* 104 (1998): 372–403.

Hahn, Harlan and Timothy Almy. "Ethnic Politics and Racial Issues: Voting in Los Angeles." *Western Political Quarterly* 24 (1971): 719–30.

Hahn, Harlan and David Klingman. "The First Bradley-Yorty Election: A Reanalysis of a Reconsideration." *Western Political Quarterly* 29 (1976): 645–46.

—— and Harry Pachon. "Cleavages, Coalitions, and the Black Candidate: The Los Angeles Mayoralty Elections of 1969 and 1973." *Western Political Quarterly* 29 (1976): 507–20.

Hajnal, Zoltan L. "White Residents, Black Incumbents, and a Declining Racial Divide." *American Political Science Review* 95 (2001): 603–17.

Halley, Robert M., Alan C. Acock, and Thomas H. Greene. "Ethnicity and Social Class: Voting in the 1973 Los Angeles Municipal Elections." *Western Political Quarterly* 29 (1976): 521–30.

Hartsock, Nancy. "Feminists, Black Candidates, and Local Politics: A Report from Baltimore." *Feminist Studies* 10 (1984): 339–52.

Hatcher, Richard G. "Black Politics in the 70's." *Black Scholar* 4 (1972): 17–22.

Hill, George H., ed. "Jesse Jackson: A Perspective from the White Media." *Bulletin of Bibliography* 42 (1985): 80–88.

Hirsch, Arnold R. "Race and Politics in Modern New Orleans: The Mayoralty of Dutch Morial." *Amerikastudien* 35 (1990): 461–84.

Holden, Matthew, Jr. "Black Politicians in the Time of the 'new' Urban Politics." *Review of Black Political Economy* 2 (1971): 56–71.

———. "The Rewards of Daring and the Ambiguity of Power: Perspectives on the Wilder Election of 1989." *State of Black America* 15 (1990): 109–20.

Holmes, Robert A. "The Georgia Legislative Black Caucus: An Analysis of a Racial Legislative Subgroup." *Journal of Black Studies* 30 (2000): 768–90.

Hornsby, Alton, Jr. "Andrew Jackson Young: Mayor of Atlanta, 1982–1990." *Journal of Negro History* 77 (1992): 159–82.

Jackman, Mary R. and Marie Crane. "'Some of My Best Friends Are Black . . .': Interracial Friendship and Whites' Racial Attitudes." *Public Opinion Quarterly* 50 (1986): 459–86.

Jackson, Bryan. "Black Political Power in the City of Angels: An Analysis of Mayor Tom Bradley's Electoral Success." *National Political Science Review* 2 (1990): 169–75.

Jamieson, Duncan R. "Maynard Jackson's 1973 Election as Mayor of Atlanta." *Midwest Quarterly* 18 (1976): 7–26.

Jeffries, Judson L. "The New York State Black and Puerto Rican Legislative Caucus, 1970–1988." *Afro-Americans in New York Life and History* 24 (2000): 7–40.

Joens, David. "John W. E. Thomas and the Election of the First African American to the Illinois General Assembly." *Journal of the Illinois State Historical Society* 94 (2001); 200–16.

Johnson, James B. and Philip E. Secret. "Focus and Style Representational Roles of Congressional Black and Hispanic Caucus Members." *Journal of Black Studies* 26 (1996): 245–73.

Jones, Joyce. "High Wattage." *Black Enterprise*, March 1999, 28.

———. "Racing toward the Finish Line." *Black Enterprise*, November 1996, 20.

———. "The Republican Way." *Black Enterprise*, June 1996, 38.

Jones, M. H. "Black Political Empowerment in Atlanta: Myth and Reality." *Annals of the American Academy of Political and Social Science* 439 (1978): 90–117.

Keller, Edmund J. "Electoral Politics in Gary: Mayoral Performance, Organization, and the Political Economy of the Black Vote." *Urban Affairs Quarterly* 15 (1979): 43–64.

Kinder, Donald R. and Tali Mendelberg. "Cracks in American Apartheid: The Political Impact of Prejudice among Desegregated Whites." *Journal of Politics* 57 (1995): 402–24.

—— and David O. Sears. "Prejudice and Politics: Symbolic Racism Versus Racial Threats to the Good Life." *Journal of Personality and Social Psychology* 40 (1981): 414–31.

Kleppner, Paul. "Mayoral Politics Chicago Style: The Rise and Fall of a Multiethnic Coalition, 1983–1989." *National Political Science Review* 5 (1994): 152–80.

Lewis, Claude. "The Black Caucus in Congress." *Black Politician* 3 (1971): 13–17.

Lewis, Denise J. "Victory and Defeat for Black Candidates." *Black Politician* 2 (1971): 66–73.

Lieske, Joel and Jan William Hillard. "The Racial Factor in Urban Elections." *Western Political Quarterly* 37 (1984): 545–63.

Lusane, Clarence. "Unity and Struggle: The Political Behavior of African American Members of Congress." *Black Scholar* 24 (1994): 16–29.

Mansbridge, Jane J. "Should Blacks Represent Blacks and Women Represent Women?: A Contingent 'Yes.'" *Journal of Politics* 61 (1999): 628–57.

—— and Katherine Tate. "Race Trumps Gender: Black Opinion on the Thomas Nomination." *PS: Political Science & Politics* 25 (1992): 488–92.

Marable, Manning. "Black Power in Chicago: An Historical Overview of Class Stratification and Electoral Politics in a Black Urban Community." *Review of Radical Political Economics* 17 (1985): 157–82.

——. "Harold Washington and the Politics of Race in Chicago." *Black Scholar* 17 (1986): 14–23.

——. "Reaganism, Racism, and Reaction: Black Political Realignment in the 1980's." *Black Scholar* 13 (1982): 2–15.

Massey, Douglas and Zoltan Hajnal. "The Changing Geographic Structure of Black-White Segregation in the United States." *Social Science Quarterly* 76 (1995): 527–42.

Maulin, Richard L. "Los Angeles Liberalism." *Trans-Action* 8 (1971): 40–51.

Mayfield, Loomis. "Chicago Wasn't Ready for Reform." *Journal of Urban History* 20 (1994): 564–76.

McCoy, Frank. "Black GOPers on the Rise?." *Black Enterprise*, March 1995, 24.

McCrary, Peyton. "Racially Polarized Voting in the South: Quantitative Evidence from the Courtroom." *Social Science History* 14 (1990): 507–31.

Metcalfe, Ralph H., Jr. "Chicago Model Cities and Neocolonialization." *Black Scholar* 1 (1970): 23–30.

Mitchell, Parren. Interview by David Hatchett. *Crisis* 93 no. 2 (1986): 34–40.

Mladenka, Kenneth R. "Blacks and Hispanics in Urban Politics." *American Political Science Review* 83 (1989): 165–91.

Moeser, John V. and Christopher Silver. "Race, Social Stratification, and Politics: The Case of Atlanta, Memphis, and Richmond." *Virginia Magazine of History and Biography* 102 (1994): 519–50.

Mollenkopf, John. "New York: The Great Anomaly." *PS: Political Science & Politics* 19 (1986): 591–97.

Morris, Carolyn M. "Black Elected Officials in Ohio, 1978: Characteristics and Perceptions." *Ohio History* 88 (1979): 291–310.

Munoz, Carlos Jr. and Charles Henry. "Rainbow Coalitions in Four Big Cities: San Antonio, Denver, Chicago and Philadelphia." *PS: Political Science & Politics* 19 (1986): 598–609.

Murray, Richard and Arnold Vedlitz. "Racial Voting Patterns in the South: An Analysis of Major Elections from 1960 to 1977 in Five Cities." *Annals of the American Academy of Political and Social Science* 439 (1978): 29–39.

Nelson, William E. Jr. "Black Mayoral Leadership: A Twenty-Year Perspective." *National Political Science Review* 2 (1990): 188–95.

———. "Black Mayors as Urban Managers." *Annals of the American Academy of Political and Social Science* 439 (1978): 53–67.

Obama, Barack H. Interview by Matthew Klam. "Barack Obama: Life of the Party." *Gentlemen's Quarterly*, December 2004, 320–21.

———. Interview by Barbara Ransby. *Progressive*, October 2004, 35–38.

———. Interview by Nicole Saunders. "The Next Black Senator?." *Essence*, March 2004, 32.

O'Beirne, Kate. "Bread and Circuses." *National Review*, April 21, 1997, 21.

O'Brien, Darcy. "The Great Black Hope." *New Yorker*, February 10, 1997, 29–30.

Perkins, Jerry. "Political Ambition among Black and White Women: An Intragender Test of the Socialization Model." *Women & Politics* 6 (1986): 27–40.

Perry, Huey L. "Black Political and Mayoral Leadership in Birmingham and New Orleans." *National Political Science Review* 2 (1990): 154–60.

———. "The Political Reincorporation of Southern Blacks: The Case of Birmingham." *National Political Science Review* 3 (1992): 230–37.

———. "The Reelection of Sidney Barthelemy as Mayor of New Orleans," *PS: Political Science & Politics* 23 (1990): 156–57.

Petropoulos, Constantina. "J. C. Watts, Jr." *Current Biography Yearbook* (1999): 29–30.

Pierannuzi, Carol A. and John D. Hutcheson Jr. "Deracialization in the Deep South: Mayoral Politics in Atlanta." *Urban Affairs Quarterly* 27 (1991): 192–201.

———. "Electoral Change and Regime Maintenance: Maynard Jackson's Second Time Around." *PS: Political Science & Politics* 23 (1990): 151–53.

Randolph, Lewis A. "A Historical Analysis and Critique of Contemporary Black Conservatism." *Western Journal of Black Studies* 19 (1995): 149–63.

Reed, Adolph Jr. "Narcissistic Politics in Atlanta," *Telos* 48 (1981): 98–105.

Regalado, James A. "Organized Labor and Los Angeles City Politics: An Assessment in the Bradley Years, 1973–1989." *Urban Affairs Quarterly* 27 (1991): 87–108.

Roggemann, Peter J. "When Blacks Win Municipal Elections," *Social Policy* 11 (1981): 46–53.

Ruffins, Paul. "Interracial Coalitions." *Atlantic*, June 1990, 28–34.

Santoro, Wayne A. "Black Politics and Employment Policies: The Determinants of Local Government Affirmative Action." *Social Science Quarterly* 76 (1995): 794–806.

Sawyer, Mary R. "A Moral Minority: Religion and Congressional Black Politics." *Journal of Religious Thought* 41 (1983–1984): 55–66.

Scheiber, Noam. "Race Against History." *New Republic*, May 31, 2004, 21–22, 24–26.

Schexnider, Alvin J. "The Politics of Pragmatism: An Analysis of the 1989 Gubernatorial Election in Virginia." *PS: Political Science & Politics* 23 (1990): 154–56.

Sigelman, Carol K. and others. "Black Candidates, White Voters: Understanding Racial Bias in Political Perceptions." *American Journal of Political Science* 39 (1995): 243–65.

Sleeper, Jim. "The End of the Rainbow?: The Changing Politics of America's Cities." *New Republic*, November 1, 1993, 20–25.

Smith, Robert C. "The Black Congressional Delegation." *Western Political Quarterly* 34 (1981): 203–21.

———. "Black Power and the Transformation from Protest to Politics." *Political Science Quarterly* 96 (1981): 431–43.

———. "The Changing Shape of Urban Black Politics: 1960–1970." *Annals of the American Academy of Political and Social Science* 439 (1978): 16–28.

———. "Financing Black Politics: A Study of Congressional Elections." *Review of Black Political Economy* 17 (1988): 5–30.

Sonenheim, Raphael J. "Biracial Coalition Politics in Los Angeles." *PS: Political Science & Politics* 19 (1986): 582–90.

———. "The Dynamics of Biracial Coalitions: Crossover Politics in Los Angeles." *Western Political Quarterly* 42 (1989): 333–53.

South, Scott J. and Glenn D. Deane. "Race and Residential Mobility: Individual Determinants and Structural Constraints." *Social Forces* 72 (1993): 147–67.

Stone, Chuck. "Black Politics: Third Force, Third Party, or Third-Class Influence?." *Black Scholar* (1969): 8–13.

Stone, Clarence N. "Atlanta: Protest and Elections are not enough." *PS: Political Science & Politics* 19 (1986): 618–25.

Summers, Mary and Philip Klinkner. "The Election of John Daniels as Mayor of New Haven." *PS: Political Science & Politics* 23 (1990): 142–45.

Taylor, Quintard. "The Chicago Political Machine and Black-Ethnic Conflict and Accommodation." *Polish American Studies* 29 (1972): 40–66.

Teaford, Jon C. "'King Richard' Hatcher: Mayor of Gary." *Journal of Negro History* 77 (1992): 126–40.

Terkildsen, Nayda. "When White Voters Evaluate Black Candidates: The Processing Implications of Candidate Skin Color, Prejudice, and Self-Monitoring." *American Journal of Political Science* 37 (1993): 1032–1053.

Thernstrom, Abigail. "Black Republicans?." *Public Interest* 120 (1995): 106–10.

Thompson, Heather A. "Rethinking the Politics of White Flight in the Postwar City: Detroit, 1945–1980." *Journal of Urban History* 25 (1999): 163–98.

Thompson, J. Phillip. "David Dinkins' Victory in New York City: The Decline of the Democratic Party Organization and the Strengthening of Black Politics." *PS: Political Science & Politics* 23 (1990): 145–48.

Travis, Toni-Michelle C. "Boston: The Unfinished Agenda." *PS: Political Science & Politics* 19 (1986): 610–17.

Tryman, Mfanya D. "Black Mayoralty Campaigns: Running the 'Race.'" *Phylon* 35 (1974): 346–58.

Vanderleeuw, James M. "A City in Transition: The Impact of Changing Racial Composition on Voting Behavior." *Social Science Quarterly* 71 (1990): 326–38.

Waldman, Amy. "The GOP's Great Black Hope." *Washington Monthly*, October 1996, 34–40.

Walters, Ronald N. "The Black Politician: Fulfilling the Legacy of Black Power." *Current History* 67 (1974): 200–5, 233.

———. "The Imperative of Popular Black Struggle: Three Examples from Miami, Los Angeles and Chicago." *Black Scholar* 24 (1994): 32–38.

———. "Two Political Traditions: Black Politics in the 1990s." *National Political Science Review* 3 (1992): 198–208.

Walton, Hanes Jr. and Lester Spence. "African-American Presidential Convention and Nomination Politics: Alan Keyes in the 1996 Republican Presidential Primaries and Convention." *National Political Science Review* 7 (1999): 188–209.

Warren, Christopher L., John F. Stack Jr., and John G. Corbett. "Minority Mobilization in an International City: Rivalry and Conflict in Miami." *PS: Political Science & Politics* 19 (1986): 626–34.

Watson, Elwood. "Guess What Came to American Politics?: Contemporary Black Conservatism." *Journal of Black Studies* 29 (1998): 73–92.

Watson, S. M. "The Second Time Around: A Profile of Black Mayoral Election Campaigns." *Phylon* 45 (1984): 165–75.

Watts, Eugene J. "Black and Blue: Afro-American Police Officers in Twentieth-Century St. Louis." *Journal of Urban History* 7 (1981): 131–68.

Williams, Linda F. "Beyond the Race Issue in American Politics?." *Congress & the Presidency* 21 (1994): 137–45.

——. "White/Black Perceptions of the Electability of Black Political Candidate." *National Political Science Review* 2 (1990): 45–64.

Williams, Patricia J. "Home on the Range." *Nation,* November 4, 2002, 10.

Winn, Mylon. "The Election of Norman Rice as Mayor of Seattle." *PS: Political Science & Politics* 23 (1990): 158–59.

Wright, Sharon D. "Electoral and Biracial Coalition: Possible Election Strategy for African American Candidates in Louisville, Kentucky." *Journal of Black Studies* 25 (1995): 749–58.

——. "The Impact of Harold E. Ford, Sr.'s Endorsement on Memphis Mayoral Elections, 1975–1991." *National Political Science Review* 7 (1999): 210–20.

Young, Carlito H. "Constant Struggle: Coleman Young's Perspective on American Society and Detroit Politics." *Black Scholar* 27 (1997): 31–41.

Unpublished Sources

Bushell, Gerrard P. "The Politics of Fiscal Scarcity and the Mobilization of Political Power in New York City: The Electrical [*sic*] and Governing Strategies of New York City's First Black Mayor." PhD diss., Columbia University, 2004.

Gay, Claudine. "Taking Charge: Black Electoral Success and the Redefinition of American Politics." PhD diss., Harvard University, 1997.

Gray, Pamela Lee. "Yvonne Braithwaite Burke: The Congressional Career of California's First Black Congresswoman, 1972–1978." PhD diss., University of Southern California, 1987.

Guerra, Fernando J. "Ethnic Politics in Los Angeles: The Emergence of Black, Jewish, Latino, and Asian Officeholders, 1960–1989." PhD diss., University of Michigan, 1990.

http://blogs.abcnews.com/thenumbers/2008/02/the-role-of-rac.htlm (February 15, 2008)

http://cnn/ELECTION/2008/primaries/results/state

http://columbia.edu/cu/alumni/Magazine/Spring2004/hamilton.html

http://desmoinesregister.com/article/20081109/NEWS09/811090339/-1/caucus

http://electionlawblog.org/archives/2009_03.html

http://elections.gmu.edu/voter_turnout.htm. 2008 General and Primary.

http://firstread.msnbc.com/archive/2008/05/09/999566.aspx

http://msnbc.com/id/26803840/print/1/displaymode/1098

http://msnbc.com/id/27531033/?GT1=43001&print=1&displaymode=1098

http://newsweek.com/id/138456/output/print

http://online.wsj.com/article/SB122485442010466443.html

http://online.wsj.com/article/SB122487558086867319.html

http://ourgeorgiahistory.com?chronpop/1000028

http://pbs.org/newshour/bb/media/jan-june08/race_05-07.html

http://polysigh.blogspot.com/search?q=klinkner
http://socialhistory.org/Biographies/bradley.html
http://theroot.com/id/48726/output/print
http://time.com/time/printout/0.8816.995609.00.html
http://uselectionatlas.org/RESULTS/index.html.

Index